Lifeline Sampler

CELEBRATING

1960 **25** 1985

OA's 25th YEAR

Other Overeaters Anonymous Books

Overeaters Anonymous
For Today

Lifeline Sampler

Overeaters Anonymous, Inc.
TORRANCE, CALIFORNIA

ISBN: 0–9609898–2–X
Library of Congress Catalog Card No.: 85-60461
Overeaters Anonymous
2190 W. 190 Street
Torrance, California 90504
© 1985 by Overeaters Anonymous, Inc.
Printed in the United States of America

Contents

Steps and Traditions

Spiritual Insights

OA Experience

Relationships

Food and Weight

Slips and Relapse

Humor

Service and OA History

Preface

THE STORIES AND ARTICLES that fill these pages first appeared in Lifeline, the monthly magazine of Overeaters Anonymous. They are the work of people who write, not as professional authors, but as compulsive overeaters who are recovering through practice of the twelve-step program.

Like all the presentations in Lifeline, these pieces reflect individual members' experiences and viewpoints, not necessarily those of OA as a whole.

Selections were made by members representing a broad cross-section of the Fellowship. They hope the reader will share their enjoyment of this sampler from the treasure-trove of recovery that is Lifeline.

Slogans for All Seasons

TO PARAPHRASE Will Rogers, I've never heard an OA or AA slogan I didn't like. There are three, however, that have special significance for abstinent compulsive overeaters trying to cope with seasonal fun, festivities and food.

Abstinence is the most important thing in my life without exception.

Not a few OAs balk at this. How can it be true? Doesn't a family or loved ones come first? Isn't it a selfish statement?

Not at all. By believing unequivocally in this precept, and practicing it with a sense of total commitment, we benefit both ourselves and everyone with whom we come in contact. Many astounding things happen when we put abstinence first in our lives. From the moment we give up the delusion that we can control our eating at will, hope appears. Everything becomes possible, yet at the same time we experience a deep contentment with what *is,* a fuller appreciation of today than we have ever known. Gone is the despair which at times plunged us into sullen silence and at others erupted in angry outbursts against those closest to us. "Fat" thoughts and actions do not make us lovable or easy to live with, nor do they enable us to be of real service to others.

With abstinence, a new person emerges. We come to love ourselves and the world around us. As butterflies shed their cocoons, we reappear with a new outlook on life and a wonderful feeling of accomplishment and worth. The past is over.

Abstinence is essential for compulsive overeaters. Once broken, even for a short period, the old person we left behind comes back. It is actually an act of love toward ourselves and others, rather than selfishness, to make abstinence the most important thing in our lives without exception.

Try it!

Easy does it.

"The sky is falling," said Chicken Little in the children's story. This seems to apply to some of us when suddenly, in spite of our brand new

3

self-worth, serenity and OA support, we happen to deviate ever so slightly from the OA program.

So what? Easy does it.

Our train of thought runs along a familiar track: "I've failed, so why not give up and start binging? Later, I'll start the program again."

But "later" may not come; we may get sidetracked or derailed, and we may panic — unless *easy does it* sticks in our minds. OK, we've strayed — perhaps because we were too rigid in the first place. But we don't have to let ourselves get rattled. All we have to remember is, easy does it. It really does!

One day at a time.

"There's no way I can start abstinence now; there are parties coming up, holiday meals and so on. I'll wait until I can see my way clear so I won't fail."

This is "bait" few of us have been able to resist over the years. It is an easy rationalization. But in OA we do not project future acts. We live today. By being abstinent just for today — no matter what the season or the circumstances — perspective is automatically restored to us. To eat or not to eat is not only no longer a problem; it is not even a question. Unless we make an issue of it, no one really cares what we eat or drink at parties, and as for holiday meals, only martyrs insist on setting themselves apart from everyone else. Thousands of OAs know they can enjoy good food and remain abstinent.

When compulsion to overeat sets in, try to get by for fifteen minutes. It helps to call another OA member. Usually, after a short while the obsession is gone. There is a realization that what you can do for fifteen minutes can be done for several hours, for a whole day. That's all we need.

With small accomplishments, a little at a time, and not worrying in advance about breaking abstinence, it becomes progressively easier.

One day at a time takes the worry out of worrying.

During the holidays I am surer than ever that abstinence is the most important thing in my life without exception; that I can hold on to it if I approach each day's trials and joys in the spirit of easy does it; and that it will not be too much to ask of myself if I remember that I only need to do these things one day at a time.

Happy holidays!

December 1978

Visit to a Small Meeting

I HAVE RECENTLY returned from a six-week tour of the country, visiting friends and family. It is good to be back "in the groove." (It's no longer a rut.) It is good to see my dear friends and go to "my" meetings. It is even better to be grateful for all that we in the Fellowship have in this area. Meetings daily, many understanding friends, the visible assurance that we are not alone.

While at my mom's home, surrounded with temptations, I often read the *Lifeline*. That helped. But her holiday confections, just waiting there on a plate to be eaten, telling me the time will come when Mom isn't around anymore and I won't have the chance to eat them ever again; the smells coming out of the oven . . . well, even *Lifeline* has its limitations.

So I bundled up my temptations and trudged the happy road to destiny — or is it the road to happy destiny? — to the one weekly meeting listed in the newspaper in the little Montana town. Driving Geraldine, my elderly Toyota, down the road with the towering Rocky Mountains seemingly almost a stone's throw away, I basked in the glory of God's creations as I went the three miles to the meeting.

(Do cars need to remain anonymous at the public level? Geraldine certainly goes to a lot of meetings, but at thirty-five miles per gallon, I'd hardly consider her an overeater. Even under the stress of a broken valve spring, she performed with serenity.)

When I arrived at the meeting place, one member was already there, setting up coffee and a few chairs, and preparing a tape recorder with tape. As we sipped our coffee and waited, she looked at her watch and announced, "It's time to start the meeting."

She read the portion of Chapter Five, then turned on the tape and sat down to listen. It was a good tape, full of meaning and inspiration.

Then, when the tape was finished, we had discussion. Just the two of us. It was at this time that she explained that she is the only member. She attends weekly, plans the meeting as if there were others, listens to the tape and then meditates. She is abstaining. No complaints, no self-pity. She is grateful she found OA.

And I am grateful I found her. Because she has made me aware of all the blessings I have.

March 1979

"The Best Is Yet To Be"

NOW THAT I HAVE passed my fifteenth year with Overeaters Anonymous, I pause to reflect on the many benefits I have derived from our program and those that continue to unfold.

When I took the first step, these many years ago, I admitted my powerlessness over food, my emotions and my disease. Today, I still have to confront this powerlessness, accept it and go on from there.

I have learned that no matter how discouraging it may seem, no life situation is permanent and inevitable. Through OA, the door to change is always open.

I, a woman who never in the world would have let you know how I felt, can now express my feelings. Secrecy was the chief symptom of my disease: I had a secret world in which I did my secret eating. The day this world began to disintegrate was the day I started opening up to people.

Where once I ran to escape myself, needing to be surrounded constantly with noise and excitement, I now meditate and find strength in silence.

Gradually I have assimilated the words of the Serenity Prayer. I find myself bending more readily to what I must accept. And when I need courage to face the hard challenges, it is usually there. Often, it turns out that what I need is the courage to fail. The lessons I have learned from failure have, in the long run, brought me rewards surpassing those of easy successes. To know this is to realize that I have not really failed.

I have learned that it is easier to dwell on what is right than what is wrong, and that positive thoughts establish a pattern for positive action.

I have learned to be flexible in all things, including abstinence. It has been said that when a person falls, it is less likely that any bones will break if one is relaxed. If, on the other hand, one is tense and rigid, a fall may well fracture an arm or a leg. So it is with abstinence. If I am flexible, I know that I can begin again; that a break in abstinence is not unforgiveable; that I always have a chance. It is my spiritual condition that is important, not what I eat.

I have learned that OA is not a diet program, a reducing program, a twenty-one day program or any other kind of program except a one-day-at-a-time program. I refuse to project my abstinence beyond this twenty-four hours.

I have learned that if I cannot accept myself fat, there is no way that I will accept myself thin. I accept myself exactly as I am, *where* I am, knowing that with all my imperfections, I am the best me I'm capable of being today.

Because I can now "go with love," I tell everyone I sponsor to do so. There isn't a human alive who can resist a positive affirmation of love. I can only give love when I see you through the eyes of love. It doesn't matter if you are unable to respond. Sending is my business; receiving is yours.

I have learned the art of listening. I can now hear you. Listening is a way of loving.

I have learned, after years of yearning to be a part of someone or something, that I belong to a community. Although I was married for forty years to a man I loved, I still felt I did not belong. I found that it is impossible to have a sense of belonging when one is alienated from one's real self. With acceptance of myself and this Fellowship of loving men and women, I find a common belonging and a common goal with them and with all of life.

I have learned that there are no coincidences in my life. I am put in the right place at the right time by my Higher Power. I no longer have to live this program by myself. The guidance and direction I once longed for and despaired of attaining are mine for the asking.

I have learned that I am worth saving. Once, when I heard an AA speaker say that, I couldn't understand it. Today, worth and dignity are elements in my life that I cherish.

Today, I can give to others what the program has given to me. I must give service to my group, to the intergroup, to my region and to World Service. It is only by giving that I can hope to keep the gift of this blessed program.

These fifteen years have been the happiest, most fulfilling, most "learning" years of my life. Above all, I have learned gratitude.

Only in Overeaters Anonymous is it possible for me to believe, with Robert Browning, that as I grow in the program, "the best is yet to be."

July 1979

Blooming Conditions

I T'S SO EASY to get muddled. I have a threefold illness. I need to go all the way. I cannot recover from one-third of it and ignore the remainder.

It is physical, emotional and spiritual. No one part is any more or less important than the other parts. None of it is of much use to me unless I have all three parts fastened together, securely. I must go for the full treatment. That is so simple. Yet it is hard. But compromise — half measures — is harder. In fact, it is impossible.

It may be hard for a seed to turn into a flower. The seed may seem to be destroying itself when it is rent apart. Yet it would be impossible for it to bloom while remaining a seed.

When I came into the Fellowship, I was like a planted seed: I could stay intact and rot, or sprout and grow. Nothing else will do. That's all of it.

December 1979

Abstinence: A Personal Definition

SOME TIME AGO a neighboring OA group asked me to speak on the topic of abstinence. I accepted and found myself frowning mentally. I would rather share my feelings, my understanding of the steps, my awareness of character defects, my search for progress, my newfound self-esteem. I was not happy to be tied into abstinence.

How lucky for me that I didn't say No to that request! I am grateful that my eyes and ears have opened and allowed my attitude to change.

Our area recently abolished abstinence requirements for speaking at special events. Somehow, this group conscience decision brought to mind my previous reluctance to discuss abstinence. I realized I felt guilty about sidestepping this issue. I don't like making anyone uncomfortable, especially those I love in this Fellowship. Sharing my views on some subjects may make some still suffering overeater even more uncomfortable, and then I may not get the love and approval I want so much.

Once I recognized this, I realized that I was willing to take the risk because I can't afford confusion about the role abstinence has in my recovery program. It is essential for my continued progress to remember the road I followed to get where I am today.

I have been listening to OA members explain what abstinence means to them. A number of those who are struggling with abstinence express the hope that concentration on the steps and working toward emotional and spiritual growth will give them the gift of abstinence.

I hope it happens on their terms.

I also hear recovering members with stable, contented abstinence speak of the gift of abstinence they receive as a result of working OA's twelve steps. When they talk about the gift of abstinence, I understand them to mean they have received freedom from their obsession with food.

We need to hear more about this treasured gift: freedom from obsession with food. It gives me faith and hope to hear that this program works.

I believe that abstinence from compulsive overeating and freedom from the obsession with food are two different experiences which are not necessarily simultaneous, though we can eventually enjoy both.

The dictionary defines abstinence as "staying away from something." My experience has been to follow OA's suggestion and use abstinence as a tool for my recovery. Abstinence for me, especially in the beginning, was not free of fear, hunger, craving and obsession. Abstinence is a conscious, daily action I take in order to recover from the physical part of my threefold illness. Following a food plan for physical recovery will not make me content unless I apply the rest of the OA program.

Practicing my program in one or two areas did not bring me freedom from my obsession. AA tells the alcoholic to stay dry (stop drinking) and practice the twelve steps. OA tells the overeater to abstain (stop overeating) and practice the twelve steps.

When we become willing to follow a threefold program, then we will receive the gifts that AA's Big Book promises. Sobriety — contented abstinence — and freedom from obsession can and will become a reality.

I will not argue that this freedom does not come at the outset for some; God works in many ways. But there are countless members, like myself, who first had to practice physical abstinence (staying away from excess food).

I was three years practicing recovery on an emotional and spiritual level through the Al-Anon twelve-step program when I attended my first OA meeting. My twofold program did *not* relieve my obsession with food. My weight continued to increase during these program years. I did not realize that healthy emotions and spiritual depth were impossible for me while still physically self-destructing.

That was six years ago. I came to OA at 220 pounds and was given the suggestion that I abstain from excess food through an eating plan of my choice to be followed one day at a time. I "white-knuckled" it for six weeks on this plan, experiencing fear, hunger, cravings and obsession with food; but I did not overeat.

My powerlessness became clearer. But I was promised that God could and would remove the obsession if God were sought. Food was no longer controlling me; I was ready to seek a closer, conscious contact with a God of my understanding.

As I stopped using excess food as a crutch, I confronted many hidden emotions. OA suggested the twelve steps as the way to face my feelings without overeating. The steps took on new meaning for me now. As I continued to abstain, my obsession became less acute. Abstinence was not always difficult; sometimes it was easy. I came to have faith that this program works.

I am now at goal weight, but I know that maintenance is not insurance against my disease. My path to recovery is through OA's twelve steps. I cannot practice the steps with honesty while acting out my compulsion. It is only through a willingness to abstain that I can apply the twelve steps effectively to those problems I once escaped by eating.

The Big Book promises that God will do for us what we could not do for ourselves. To me that means there are some things I must do for myself, beginning with abstaining from excess food. The obsession with food can be removed. It does happen.

I pray to remember the essential part abstinence has in my recovery. Sharing these thoughts helps me understand that "Abstinence is the most important thing in my life without exception."

March 1980

Mornings Are Miracles

I AM TAKING a "mental health" day to just sit back and rest, feel my life and God's presence in it.

I have been in the program more than eleven years and have never sent anything in to Lifeline except subscription forms from our meeting's raffle. Why? I was waiting until I worked a perfect program.

Today I have a quality sponsor who tells me to stop holding my breath until that day. My program is good today; not perfect, but fine.

Life is good today. Things around me aren't perfect, and certainly people don't always do what I wish they would. But that's nothing new; what's new is me, by the grace of God.

Today is a warm, sunny New England morning. I woke up to the phone calls of the people I sponsor, and then got down on my knees to give thanks for God's loving care. I pulled on my blue jeans, ate an abstinence breakfast and sat down to share this, my gratitude. The day is fine, and it will be fine, whatever happens, because the calm is within me.

It hasn't always been this way. I used to wake up daily filled with self-hatred, anger and terrible fear. The only thing I got on my knees for was food — to clean up my mess from the night before or to search for my hidden fix. And blue jeans are a gift of the program: I had only a polyester pantsuit, eternally a size 14.

The only thing I knew in those days was my addiction — I *had* to have that food; I had no other way to face life. Every night before I went to bed I got rid of whatever was left, vowing a new start in the morning. And every morning I ravaged, half-crazed, for something to quiet the panic.

These days my mornings are miracles. I am free of the panic, free of the self-loathing and free of the groundless fears. I don't eat compulsively today, but that is the means, not the end of my program. It starts with "Don't overeat, no matter what" and ends with "Use me as your instrument."

My days are not always wonderful. I feel feelings and many of them hurt. But I'm free in a way I never imagined possible: God is doing for me what I cannot do for myself. And life is good. It's better than ever.

October 1980

In Grateful Acceptance

I. WANTED TO QUIT OA but I didn't know where to go to pass on the news . . . who to call (Rozanne? God?) . . . what membership card to tear up (I had none — only a few Serenity Prayer cards and some One Day at a Time leaflets) . . . or how to erase from my mind the many principles of a far better way of living.

I couldn't shake from almost instant recall the many positive experiences: growth-inspiring meetings, loving phone calls, even an OA wedding.

I could not let die the many life-giving friendships with which five and a half years in the Fellowship had blessed me.

How could I gaze upon the Prayer of St. Francis engraved on a plaque which hangs on my wall, gently reminding me to be an instrument, a channel of peace — and not miss OA?

Was I no longer to sing the many songs we OAs have adopted, songs that are so much a part of me?

Would the Lord's Prayer be uttered without tears flooding my eyes if it were never again to be said with hands linked to the hands of men and women who suffer from a disease like my own?

Where could I go on a Saturday morning to be fed the nourishment that the Morning Awakening meeting freely gave me? No restaurant in the world could feed me so well.

I wanted to quit OA, but the emptiness would be so great, no mountain of candy, no pile of money, no wonderful person, no special thing could ever begin to fill it.

If I quit OA, a gift freely given would be lost. A treasure too precious to describe would be thrown away. The best part of me would be left to stagnate, perhaps even wither and die.

No, I can't quit OA. I am too special. I love what OA has made of me too much.

The beautiful gift of Overeaters Anonymous is freely given and I, of my own choice, gratefully accept. I accept the other gifts of OA, too: the wealth of rich friendships, the faith, hope, love and peace.

I accept OA and its many blessings, always remembering that OA accepted me first.

Thank you, O loving Gift Giver, for all these gifts.

November 1980

A Morning Meeting

I HAVE JUST COME from an OA meeting. It starts at ten o'clock in the morning. By 9:45 I was there and had the clubhouse door open to the sunshine and clean, cool air. I put water in the coffeepot to heat, set out the literature attractively and arranged the chairs. By ten I had done all the usual secretarial chores and had my cup of coffee beside me.

Having been away on vacation I didn't know which of our few OA members would lead the meeting, but if it were my turn I would choose gratitude as my subject.

I opened the meeting by saying the Serenity Prayer aloud and with deep feeling. Then I read Chapter Five aloud to the empty chairs. I reviewed the tools, considering whether I was slacking up on any of them. Next it was time for the leader to qualify, telling what I used to be like, what happened and what I am like now.

I thought of vacation trips in the past, filled mostly with thoughts of where I'd get the next binge food and where I would eat my next full meal although I was uncomfortably full already. That's how it used to be. That's what vacations were for. On this vacation, I had eaten sensibly and stayed on my food plan the entire time. Frankly, I am amazed at the length of my abstinence, my weight loss and my intuitively knowing how to handle situations that used to baffle me.

With another cup of coffee, I meditated on my chosen topic: gratitude. So much to be thankful for, none of which I would be aware of had I not reaped the benefits of several years in this program. I would be bemoaning the fact that there is no OA for fifty miles and that my efforts to start a group locally are meeting with little interest. It is difficult and disappointing, but overeating will only make it worse. During my less sane years I would not have realized that.

Then I read a story from the OA book, *Overeaters Anonymous*. It reminded me of my sponsor who is 1500 miles away now that I've moved to Little Town, Mid-USA. I miss her dreadfully, as I miss the big open meetings I once attended. There are no sponsors here, and certainly no large meetings.

I read Chapter Five once again, making the appropriate changes. I also read the chapter titled, "A Vision for You" with considerable thought.

I clasped my own hand as I said the Lord's Prayer to close the meeting.

Before leaving, I emptied the remaining hot water, cleaned up the room, put the chairs back in rows, and loaded the OA material back in the car. As I locked the door behind me, I took off the sign that reads "OA Meeting in Progress. Come On In."

It had been a good meeting.

February 1981

Maintenance

IN THE FIFTEENTH year of the most exciting journey of my life I am still learning amazing things about myself.

First, let me share that I have been maintaining a 75–80 pound weight loss for fourteen years through the miraculous recovery program of Overeaters Anonymous.

When I came into the Fellowship in September 1966 I was sure that if I could take the weight off once and for all, my troubles would be over. OA taught me, as I became willing to listen, that the weight was only the tip of the iceberg.

It was not easy for me to admit that food had me licked and that I needed help. It was painful to recognize that I was filled with false pride, fears, burning resentments and guilt. These were the human frailties that were submerged under the tip of that iceberg.

My thinking had to change if I were not to return to compulsive overeating. The world could no longer revolve around me. God would do for me what I could not do for myself. I had to let God into my life and get out of the way. I had to give up the controls.

For me this was a very difficult process because it took me so long to see how self-will was operating within my life. Step meetings slowly helped to reveal this defect to me. I was willing.

The healing process takes place through spiritual recovery. This means that to the extent I can continue to seek direction from a Power outside myself I will continue to recover.

I have come to accept that I am not perfect, nor will I ever be perfect. God loves me just the way I am.

The compulsion is still there, like a sleeping lion. A day at a time, it will continue to sleep as I continue my spiritual growth. That is what maintenance is all about: maintaining a normal, healthy body and developing a sound mind.

I am grateful to Overeaters Anonymous for giving me this opportunity.

May 1981

Staying Power

THIS MONTH I am celebrating my fifth year of abstinence. I weep as I tell you, for these five years have been a miracle. Never in my life have I consistently done anything that was good for me for so long a period of time.

Throughout my first year of freedom from compulsive overeating I was filled with cravings which gave me joy because they reminded me of two things: (1) I had a disease that almost destroyed my sanity and (2) with God's help, one day at a time, I did not have to be at its mercy any longer. Every time I set eyes on once-loved binge foods a sign that flashed "poison" went on in my head.

In my second year of abstinence I had to deal with the defect of pride. My former depression and self-hatred were almost nonexistent and I was no longer doing the crazy things I had done under the influence of junk food. I jumped to the conclusion that there was nothing wrong with me. And since the people in OA listened to me eagerly and loved me unconditionally, I figured I must be great.

My fall was emotionally quite painful but, thank God, my abstinence was preserved. Fortunately, I came to understand that I am just another abstinent compulsive overeater — and happy to be so.

My third year I married. My husband, a member of Alcoholics Anonymous, spotted my hangups and played on them to satisfy his own. I returned the favor. But out of love and devotion to our programs and to one another we put our childishness aside and began to build a good marriage.

My fourth year I gave birth to a son, graduated from college at age twenty-nine and took an extended trip to the east coast — all in the same month. If you don't think that puts some pressure on abstinence, try it. Still, God preserved my abstinence. (The only time my cravings were completely gone was during my pregnancy; God has quite a sense of humor!)

In my fifth year of abstinence my husband died, just two and a half months after we learned he had cancer. In those ten weeks, during which my husband was bedfast, God gave me the strength to care for him and our two babies (we had custody of a child only two months older than our son) — and to remain abstinent.

My gratitude goes out to all those from our program who helped me care for my children and clean my home during that difficult period.

I grieved for a long time after my husband's death, but I was abstinent. I took responsibility for the care of my son, managed to stay out of the mental hospital and remained abstinent. I did not always remember to brush my teeth or wash my face, and I had to learn again how to overcome depression — but I abstained.

With much love, gratitude and joy, I can truthfully say that abstinence *is* the most important thing in my life without exception.

June 1981

Is There Life after Recovery?

I T WAS A QUESTION I put to myself several years ago when the highs of the program began to wear off, leaving me to face the everydayness of life at last: Is there life after recovery?

Abstaining and losing weight are exhilarating. People exclaim over us. We sometimes get to tell them who we are because we've changed so drastically we aren't recognizable. Buying a whole new wardrobe is an adventure; the awakening sexuality that often comes with weight loss is a constant for many months. In short, the rapid-fire changes make for daily excitement. Even the first year or two of maintenance can produce continual overstimulation. Many of us found that going to OA events or giving service to the Fellowship produced that sought-after "high" quite effectively.

And isn't that really the same old way we've lived all our lives? I couldn't stand a moderate emotional level. I was always looking for the "up" and was even willing to deal with the resultant "down" in order to have the lift at least some of the time. Any kind of excitement would do. If there was no upcoming party or project, I'd pick a fight with my husband. Midnight was best, just as he was drifting off to sleep. It was even better if he had an early morning meeting; that made him really snappish. After an hour or so of arguing, the conversation would grind to an angry halt, and I'd fall asleep with what felt like a self-satisfied smirk on my face.

Early in my post-weight-loss OA life, I began to seek a more regulated inner state. My writings during that period speak of trying to find balance, of hating the rollercoaster ride I was on and longing for the peace that had been promised me.

What a surprise I had coming! When some of that serenity actually appeared, I found it deadly boring. I discovered I didn't know how to use leisure time at all. Even magazines, let alone books, presented a serious challenge. For the next two years I read nothing but OA and AA literature, and much of that only with a struggle. Even television failed to shelter

me as before. Serenity quickly turned either to a lethargy I found frighteningly familiar, or to a restlessness that completely dissolved tranquility.

It has taken years, but gradually I learned to consider my alternatives
amiably rather than to grab frenziedly at an activity out of fear. I am
no more the restless, driving worker, constantly in motion. With the faith
in life the program gave me, little things began to be genuinely rewarding
and I no longer sought the highs I once needed. It's such a pleasure to
find that I enjoy playing checkers with my son or listening to an animated
account of his latest adventure. I know many OAs share with me the
intense joy of watching a newcomer catch the program and bloom. And,
yes, it is even nice to complete peacefully some of the tedious tasks of
job and home, rather than mutter angrily to myself while doing them.

Now, statements such as these always make the writer sound just wonderful. Although I am happy to be steady much of the time, I must report
that I lose it often enough to be reminded that I'm still human. I have
a few things to work out before I sprout a halo and wings and rise straight
upward. I still get "zippy" and it never fails to do me in. An overinflated
sense of self tells me I'm so busy, so rushed . . . (translation: so important).
If I fall into perpetual motion, I lose my ability to enjoy the passing
hours and days.

It *is* possible to live without making a big deal out of it. I know, because
I've managed it more than once. The deep contentment of a job quietly
well-done is more than a match for the exaltation of the frenzied accomplishments of the past.

OA tore jagged holes in the material of which my life was made. It
took everything: the fat, the complacency, the pride and, finally, the highs.
It removed much more than I bargained for in the beginning, and thank
goodness for that!

Is there life after recovery? There certainly is, but it has taken me a
long time to grow into an appreciation of it.

January 1982

When a Sponsor Is Away

BY THE TIME I finished doing my laundry early Sunday morning, I found I was too late for the early meeting. I had looked through the area directory to find a participation meeting. I needed to talk about what had happened during the past week.

My sponsor had left for his two-week vacation and I was afraid. Who would I talk to? He was the only one who understood me. I was worried that I would eat if I was alone and I couldn't call him.

Before he left, my sponsor assured me that I would not have any trouble. "You have friends now," he said. Besides, he is a compulsive overeater just like me and I had to be careful not to make him my higher power.

The night before my sponsor left I went to a meeting where I met a man who was also a member of AA, sober twelve years. I told him my problem, and I'll never forget what he said. He had been in the same boat one time, he told me. His sponsor had gone out of town and he was afraid he wouldn't make it alone. But when his sponsor had been away only a few hours, my AA friend realized that his sponsor was not really gone. All he had to do was think about him and all the things he had said to him, and his sponsor was there. He knew then that his sponsor would always be with him.

For the first week of my sponsor's vacation, I did OK. I felt really close to my Higher Power and I wanted to share that at a meeting. But, as I said, it was too late for the morning meeting. The only other meeting was at the Gay Community Center, which I certainly did not want to go to.

Then I thought about my sponsor, and I knew what he would say: "Keep an open mind."

I went to the meeting and I loved it. I felt so comfortable and at home there. And to think, all I had to do was keep an open mind. Simple — but for me the simple answers are the hardest to find.

I'm discovering that, even though life has a lot of ups and downs, there are two things I have now. One is my Higher Power, whom I call

"Father." I'm not always close to him, but when I am, it's beautiful. I'm learning to depend on him, one day at a time.

Second, I have all of you in OA. You are my family — my brothers and sisters. You love me no matter what mood I'm in when I walk into a meeting. I'm starting to love you back, little by little. It was hard at first, but it's getting better.

May your Higher Power take care of you.

March 1982

The Bargain of a Lifetime

DO YOU EVER FEEL deprived at a social gathering because you are abstaining while all those around you are gorging themselves? I recently experienced such feelings at an elegant affair, and my sponsor encouraged me to write about it. My reflection took the form of a dialog.

In this scenario, it is the morning after the big event. I am feeling deprived, self-pitying and on shaky ground. Suddenly, a mysterious stranger appears.

Stranger: I've got a terrific deal for you! How would you like to have people who love and accept you; closeness to a Higher Power; freedom from compulsive overeating; serenity; improved relationships; greater self-awareness, self-acceptance and self-confidence; a slim, healthy body; purpose, hope and direction; and progress in every area of your life.

Me: That sounds too good to be true, and way beyond my reach. What will it cost me?

Stranger: The price is that you must go to any lengths to maintain and safeguard your abstinence. This will seem difficult at times, especially when you feel lonely, bored, frustrated or deprived. And that's bound to happen, sometimes because you are alone, sometimes because you are in a social situation.

Me: Wait a minute! If I merely endure some fleeting discomfort now and then I will get everything you mentioned?

Stranger: Yes, and more. In fact, as you continue to live the twelve steps you will experience less and less discomfort; your food obsession will eventually be lifted and you will experience peace.

Me: An offer like that I can't refuse. It's the bargain of a lifetime! I accept. Thank you, God.

April 1982

Abstinence Is Easier

IT IS GENERALLY accepted that most compulsive overeaters go through a period of looking for "an easier, softer way." Does this mean that abstinence is harder? Not at all. What it means is that before we can accept our illness we try to prove that, like "normal" eaters, we can occasionally eat for purely social reasons, for pleasure, for a "pick-me-up" or to pass the time. For compulsive overeaters, such a feat is neither easy nor hard; it is impossible.

In Overeaters Anonymous we find, to our everlasting relief, that abstinence is easier. Here's why.

When I'm abstinent, I get to eat satisfying and nourishing food at mealtimes, one day at a time. (When not abstinent, I eat all kinds of junk I don't really want — and I can't stop.)

When I'm abstinent, I get to be hungry at mealtime and I enjoy my food. When I've finished my meal, I know I'm through eating. (When not abstinent, I wolf down everything in sight, with nothing to put a stop to my eating until I become full to the point of feeling sick, or fall into a stupor.)

When I'm abstinent, I get to feel good regardless of my size or weight. I wake up with a light, thankful feeling and look forward to a new day, free from the bondage of the scale. (When not abstinent, I wake up feeling fat and dreading the day ahead. I punish myself further with the scale, which determines how I will feel about myself that day.)

When I'm abstinent, I get to choose clothes that look and feel good.

(When not abstinent, only my biggest, most hated clothes fit, and they bind and feel uncomfortable.)

When I'm abstinent, I get to go to bed feeling thankful that I abstained, "just for today." (When not abstinent, I go to bed feeling stuffed, hating myself and resolving to do something on that day that never comes: tomorrow.)

When I'm abstinent, I get to live life, enjoy my children, make rational decisions, do what I need to do. (When not abstinent, I isolate from family, friends and other people, and I go around in circles. Fat, misery and despair stick to me like glue.)

When I'm abstinent, I get to feel positive emotions and I have the desire to make contact with a Power greater than myself. (When not abstinent, I have only negative emotions; and I feel that nothing, not even a Higher Power, can get in.)

Abstinence is easier because all I have to do is accept my disease and surrender — and, just for today, not take that first compulsive bite. (When not abstinent, I am insanely willful, feeling deprived, envious and resentful. I am insatiable, even though I know food cannot give me what I'm looking for.)

Abstinence is easier because it breaks open my cocoon, releases me from the bondage of food and sets me free to live. (When not abstinent, I am locked in the prison of my food obsession, wanting freedom but looking only for more food.)

God, please let me accept abstinence, just for today. And thank you for this easier way.

May 1982

Two Mugs and a Twelve and Twelve

I HAD IT ALL PLANNED. I would slip one of those cute plastic expresso mugs into my purse before the flight was over. I wanted just one.

When dinner was served, there was the coveted mug, perched prettily on my tray. I sneaked it into my handbag, right next to the Twelve and Twelve I'd brought along to read on the return flight.

Oh boy! Red lights flashed in my head. Somehow that mug and that book could not live in my purse together. The words, "practice these principles in all our affairs" popped into my mind. I certainly didn't feel I was doing *that* very well.

Maybe I'll ask the stewardess if I can buy one, I thought. But what if she says No? Better not to ask.

Then a little voice whispered a disquieting thought into my ear: "You don't feel good about this. You'll end up writing about it in your next inventory and making amends to the airline company. Or worse, what if you eat over it, or quit OA so you won't have to deal with it?"

Slowly, I got out of my seat. My knees were jelly and my ears rang. I made my way to the flight attendants' galley, took a deep breath and asked the stewardess, "May I purchase one of those expresso mugs?"

"I'm not allowed to sell them," came the disappointing reply. I was so annoyed I almost missed her next sentence: "But I'll see if I can let you have a couple."

I stared at her blankly and mumbled, "One will be fine."

"No, no," she insisted, "I'll get you two."

She disappeared for a few minutes and came back with two brand-new mugs, which she handed me with a pleasant smile. I thanked her and returned to my seat. I pulled the stolen cup out of my bag and replaced it with the gift mugs.

They looked great next to my Twelve and Twelve. And needless to say, I *felt* great. I knew those mugs and that book belonged together.

June 1982

Vacation Sponsor

BEFORE LEAVING for my vacation, I called the OA office in the place where I would be staying. The answering service gave me three names and telephone numbers.

When I got there, I was thrilled that the first person I called was home. My vacation was on the right track. I asked her whether she would be my vacation sponsor, explaining that I wanted to call in my food plan each day, something I hadn't done in a long time, and to be guided with the steps. To my delight, she said she'd love to be my sponsor away from home.

I told her I felt tempted to indulge in extra food while away, but I wanted neither to gain weight nor to lose my vacation to food.

"What do you usually eat at home?" my new sponsor inquired. I told her, and she said, "Why don't you eat that today?"

I did just that. It was fine, and it freed me to play instead of concentrating on meals.

I went to two meetings and discovered that only the faces were different from my meeting at home. I felt wanted, and I knew I needed what they had to give me.

It was a special treat to meet my vacation sponsor in person. I'll always be grateful to her for letting me call her every day. She helped me truly enjoy my vacation, from start to finish.

June 1982

Nothing Is Going *My* Way, Thank God

THIS MORNING I realized that nothing can shake the joy of living that fills my being. I see with clear eyes, think with a keen mind, smell, touch, taste and hear with alertness. I marvel at the sound of my own laughter. In four years I have undergone a metamorphosis deep within. It did not happen in a moment (I am slow to learn) but steadily, day by day.

I became aware of the indestructibility of my joy when my oldest offspring called this morning to tell me unwelcome news.

"Mom," she said, "I don't know how to break this gently."

"What's wrong? Can we help?"

"I don't think you can." She paused, but only for a second. "I'm pregnant."

I was stunned into speechlessness. My daughter is divorced and supporting herself and her young child, our only grandson. Fear filled my heart and questions crowded my mind: How will she manage? What will happen to them? How could she . . . ?

I deliberately stopped that line of thinking. "Please, God," I prayed, "take charge of their lives. Guide them. Hold them in your perfect love and supply all their needs." I felt a calm come over me.

Looking back, I see how miserable I was four short years ago. My whole world was out of kilter. I never laughed, nor even smiled. I hated life. Each day was torture, somehow to be muddled through. Our young son suffered from a combination of physical and psychological problems and the neighborhood children reacted with ridicule. My husband was cranky and irritable, and we were not getting along. I found fault with everything he said or did and he, in turn, was hypercritical of our son, often sending him off in tears instead of building up his confidence.

The situation went downhill. At the age of ten, our boy withdrew, stopped trying and became suicidal. At that point I felt everything was hopeless. I wished I could commit the act our son talked about; but then who would fight for him? If only I could change my husband; if only I could change our son; if only I could change the neighbors. But I could

26

not change anyone. I dealt with my feelings of helplessness and despair by gorging myself with food. In six months I gained 60 pounds.

One day I wandered into a church hall and sat in the back of a room where an OA meeting was in progress. I thought what I heard was a bit far-out but I recognized, through my fog, that the people there had a quality that appealed to me. I realized later that it was their spiritual strength that attracted me: their happiness despite adversity, their lack of fear in the midst of troubles, their ability to cope with problems, their serenity.

I was particularly impressed by one small incident. When the scheduled speaker failed to show up, the program chairperson casually approached someone just entering the room and asked her to speak. I would have been frantic in either of their positions, but the woman said an immediate Yes even though she wasn't prepared.

I returned for more meetings and learned about the steps. The third stirred up a slim ray of hope. I began by turning over my son's life to God each morning, and when I saw him getting better, I turned over my own life and will.

Slowly, this program taught me a new way of living. I learned that I was the only person I could change, that I would simply be frustrated if I tried to control others. And *I* could change just by getting in tune with God, whose power, like the electricity in my house, is always available if I just plug into it.

I also learned that taking good care of my body helps nurture my spiritual growth. In the process, I went from size 22 to size 10, my mind became lucid again and my senses alert.

Today I see with new eyes. After thirty-four years of marriage, I love and accept my husband as he is and I've discovered that he loves me. Our son is confident, loving and outgoing; the neighbors are friendly and caring. Can it be that my negative attitudes stood in the way all that time?

It has been four years since I found OA and I am still learning, growing, changing. My joy radiates outward to everyone around me like ripples on a pond. At the age of fifty-seven, I am excited, knowing that growth can continue day by day for as long as I live and keep God in my life. There is no graduation, just new goals to reach for. What a wonderful prospect.

It's true: nothing is going *my* way today — and everything's great!

September 1982

Words to the Willing

OA IS NEW TO ME but already I feel myself growing as I learn how to deal with my compulsion. I hope the following suggestions, heard at my first meetings, will be as helpful to other willing newcomers as they are to me.

Listen and learn. During my first two weeks in OA, I just listened — and boy did I learn! I learned that I am not alone in this compulsion, that my weird eating habits weren't unique after all and that there is a way to arrest my disease. I learned that if I overeat again I do not have to give up on myself. If I stub my toe, I can still get up and walk.

You are not alone. We have our Higher Power with us all the time. Therefore, we are never alone. And we have our telephones. Just a few words with another OA can take our minds off the food and get our thinking onto something more constructive.

We don't need to punish ourselves. We stuff in "a little snack" in an attempt to stuff down feelings of guilt, anger, disappointment, self-pity or whatever. We "reward" ourselves with special treats to celebrate birthdays, weight loss, moon landings and you-name-it. But the truth is, we are punishing ourselves with self-destructive thinking and unnecessary food, which benefits nothing except that roll of fat around our middle. But OA offers us ways to treat ourselves well, which in the long run means to free ourselves from the obsession with food.

We can do this by working on our inventory, making a phone call, reading program literature or having a delicious abstinence meal. We can endorse ourselves for our accomplishments.

Be patient longer. As a newcomer, I have a long way to go. How long have I had this problem? Do I expect instant changes? Crash diets are useless to the compulsive overeater. As I learn to be patient longer, I am discovering that time and faith will do what I cannot. I have God's patience to guide me when my own is weak. I learn slowly and I am changing slowly; but I was happily surprised with a weight loss and the ability to breathe better. Slowly and steadily, I keep on keeping on —

and I keep improving.

If you fail to plan, you plan to fail. Being home from work is difficult for me, so I plan each day off so it does not become a disaster. Likewise, I plan my food ahead to avoid meals with low nutrition and high calories. I find that by having both a work plan and a food plan I avoid worry, hurry and indecision. In this way I steer clear of excess food, and of emotional excesses that entice me to overeat.

One day at a time. Just for today I will be abstinent. For this one twenty-four-hour period I can get through life with all its joys and problems and resist the urge to overeat. One day at a time, with the help of my Higher Power, I can improve my outlook on life and keep my outlook on food in its proper perspective.

Let go and let God. Strange how I turned so many difficult tasks over to God but never once thought of turning over my eating problem. I thought of it as just a simple matter, not significant enough to bother God with it. But this is a very real problem for me, and all my problems are important. My abstinence is essential to my physical health, my emotional health and my spiritual health. Now I turn all of it over to my Higher Power and I am having success. I can't; God can.

October 1982

Abstinence: A Decision

EVERYTHING I HAVE today begins with abstinence, which is a decision to ask God for help, to plan my day and to work at my recovery.

Recovery is a process for me. It has taken work and planning to maintain a weight loss of more than 200 pounds for five years.

Even overweight, I was never able to maintain. My weight never stabilized; it was either on the way up or down. Most of the time it was going up — higher and higher, continually, unrelentingly tormenting me. My emotional and spiritual condition waxed and waned with the rise and fall of my weight. I felt as if I lived in a blender: churning, which was most of the time, or subdued, which was only while in the process of compulsively overeating. I was never at peace, never free of the guilt of having given in again, breaking the earnest promises made on a full stomach.

How often had I assured myself, "I won't do it tomorrow, but tonight I'll just finish this up." When my tomorrows became today and my won'ts became "I will," then "I can't" changed to *God and OA can*. We — God, OA and I — are doing together what I cannot do alone. When I started to pray only with, "Oh, God, I don't want to eat; please help me," it began to work. Everything fell into the place I live in today. How? I don't have an answer, any more than I know why I am a compulsive overeater.

In the beginning my tough, "weighed and measured" abstinence was a bondage for me. But it laid a strong foundation that replaced old habits. Through a long, slow process, I learned that I have trigger foods as well as trigger emotions; that I must heed the warnings as a driver heeds road signs. In a very relaxed and God-trusting way, I yield when necessary, stop before crossing, do not speed into anything and never cross certain solid lines.

Although it's rare, I still experience white knuckle abstinence at times. Today, I have the freedom to share that fact at a meeting, to allow myself to be human. I also allow myself the individuality God gives me. Trying to fit the mold, even in the Fellowship, doesn't work for me. Someone else's way never worked while I was actively into my compulsion and it doesn't work in recovery.

Spiritual fitness is not a fair-weather thing; I feel its solidness when the only insight I have is that life can sometimes be unbearable — and that this fact no longer has the power to make me eat compulsively. That is real, almost physically touchable answered prayer. I asked for, worked hard at and received my abstinence.

From deep within me comes God's power, showing me who I am every abstinent day of my life.

November 1982

A Time To Rejoice

HANUKAH will soon be celebrated by Jews and, shortly after, Christians will celebrate Christmas. At no other time are the similarities of our religions more evident than during this holiday season.

Sharing ideas and feelings with OAs of different beliefs and lifestyles has heightened my awareness of other people and added depth to my program. Before, all my friends were of my faith. Then, in OA, I shared my most personal thoughts for more than a year with a sponsor of another religion. Since then, I have chosen sponsors and friends without regard to their religious background. My life has been enriched.

Whether we're celebrating Chanukah or Christmas or both, the true spirit of these holidays is often lost in the barrage of food and food preparations. How can we, as compulsive overeaters, find joy in festivities that place so much emphasis on eating?

For myself, I can only do it with the help of my Higher Power, the twelve steps, the tools of recovery and myself — the person I have become by developing strength, confidence and self-awareness during my years in OA.

The Twelve and Twelve, the Big Book and our OA literature are filled with phrases appropriate to this time of year. When faced with the food obsession, that "rapacious creditor" of my insane past, I will find solace in such suggestions as, "Entrust yourself and your abstinence to your Higher Power every day, all day long." ("A Commitment to Abstinence," p. 3) I will remind myself that I have made my peace with God and that, just for today, my days of gorging are over. I will recall slogans such as "Keep it simple," "One day at a time" and "First things first"; and I will treat myself to extra meetings and calls.

During the holidays many of us will visit friends and family. Whether we look forward to enjoying the beauty of a Christmas tree, the fun of playing spin-the-dreidel or the pleasure of sharing a holiday meal with loved ones, we will undoubtedly be confronted with mounds of tantalizing food — far more than we choose to eat. But unwanted food can be declined graciously. I have learned to say No in a manner that commands respect, always assuring my hosts that I am there for the pleasure of their company and that I feel well satisfied with that. Often, I simply say, "I've had enough, thank you."

Sometimes the holidays are clouded by sad memories, unresolved conflicts and disappointed expectations. When unhappy thoughts pass through my mind, I try to focus on things that make me feel good: the beauty of our Fellowship, the example of oldtimers, the freshness of newcomers, the serenity that comes with accepting God's will.

This holiday season is a special one for me. With all its possible pitfalls, it is a time I approach with a spirit not only of joy, but also of gratitude. I am grateful for my unparalleled growth as I reach for my full potential. I am particularly thankful to those who have encouraged me through the year; and I am grateful that, buoyed by my Higher Power and my abstinence, I am free to fully enjoy the festivities.

Finally, I am grateful for the constant awareness of what is perhaps the truest and most appropriate OA saying of all: NOTHING tastes as good as abstinence feels.

Like legions of sober alcoholics, I gladly accept the limitations my illness imposes, as I greet my seventh holiday season of program and abstinence.

December 1982

B's Are Beautiful

FOUR YEARS AGO I dropped out of college with a nervous breakdown brought on by abuse of food, alcohol, diet pills, caffeine and incessant power driving.

Today, I am a full-time student working toward my bachelor's degree. And, to show you how incredible this program is, here I am writing about my appreciation for Overeaters Anonymous when I have a mathematics exam in the morning. Three years ago I ate over a math test.

What has me so thankful tonight is the two and a half years of abstinence that led me to where I am today. Abstinence has released me from binging and vomiting, guilt feelings and self-hate. For two years, I was able to work as a computer programmer so I could save enough to go back to school. I wouldn't have been able to keep the job without abstinence and OA.

This program has given me a sense of balance and a clear enough head to know I am not perfect and I don't have to be. I am learning to be more considerate of myself in that I set my priorities with myself first, school second. I am having a lot of fun this quarter. And my grades? I get an A for not overdoing. My motto is "B's are beautiful." My self-worth is no longer based on how I do on exams or what teachers think of me.

I know there are plenty of perfectionistic, power-driving overachievers out there binging their guts out because they can't live up to an impossible standard. Let them know it's OK to be less than perfect. B's are still better than average, and they're far less painful than the compulsion to make straight A's.

March 1983

Accepting Childlessness

WHEN MY HUSBAND and I decided to begin our family, a year passed with no results. We sought the help of a fertility specialist and went through test after test. Finally, I was diagnosed as having endometriosis, a condition that often prevents pregnancy. Following corrective surgery, I was told, "The next eighteen months will be the best time for you to get pregnant." It was also suggested that we consider adoption.

These simple facts don't relay the emotional and spiritual pain I endured. Anyone who has looked forward month after month to conceiving knows the grief and disappointment of yet another failure. Sometimes I was sure "This is it!" and I'd dream up color schemes for the nursery, agonize over names and eye baby clothes in the stores. My hopes were always dashed a few days later.

When friends announced their pregnancies, sometimes not so happily, I was crushed. "Why not *me?*" I thought, "I want a baby with all my heart." I built up a heavy resentment against God. I was at normal weight, maintaining a 70-pound weight loss, healthy, had a good marriage, and we were financially secure. We had everything to give a baby, including an abundance of love in a "program" home. It just wasn't fair!

Fortunately, I have loving friends in the program who listened and were supportive. One friend came back with some tough questions as I cried on the phone. "Why do you want a baby so badly? Don't you feel you two are a complete family? Maybe your Higher Power has some other plan for you."

Her comments stopped me cold. I had to do some deep thinking about my motives. I had been baby-oriented all my life. I had always planned on becoming a wife and mother. I majored in early childhood education primarily because I thought it would help me be a better parent.

Not long after that conversation, the thought struck me that I'd even gotten married mainly to fulfill my goal of motherhood. Oh, I loved my husband deeply, but until now I had never acknowledged my real reason for marrying him, even to myself. I had an amends to make.

I gulped and told him. His surprising reply was, "I know that. It's always been obvious that you want kids. It's OK. I know you love me for other reasons, and I love you."

After a lot of thought and prayer, I came to realize that I do really want children, for good reasons. We have an unending supply of love in our home and we both want to share it. It's true that we *are* a family, with our dog, three cats and assorted outdoor birds and tame squirrels; but we both have the desire to be parents, to raise a child.

I'm still not pregnant. Although we have not given up hope, we are in the process of applying for adoption. Our child will be a gift from God, for us to love and cherish. How it comes to us really doesn't matter. A little one who needs us and whom we need will be given to us at the right time.

Acceptance and willingness to let go and let God have come slowly for me. It was very hard to give up trying to force an outcome I wanted so badly, and to trust that whatever happens will be right for us.

Finally, my experience has given me an advantage I hadn't anticipated. I have been able to help another woman in the program who is going through the same thing. It's nice to be able to give comfort and understanding to someone whose pain I know so well. It makes both of us aware that we're not alone, that it happens to others and that our feelings are normal.

April 1983

Lucky Me

ONE OF MY WORST character defects has been the tendency to think, "I'm the only one," which leads to self-pity and negative thinking.

To my unending surprise and delight, in OA I often find myself thinking, "I'm like that," and I get such a warm feeling when I can identify.

I believe I have undergone a complete personality change during the five years I've been in OA. When I look back and remember what I was like and how ineffectually I coped with minor frustrations, I see that I was like a child.

Although I am aware that I will never stop growing, today I feel comfortable. My weight is acceptable to me, and so am I as a person. I like myself. (I've come a long way to be able to say that!)

I can be aware of character defects I have yet to eliminate without feeling I must do it right now. I am learning to give and receive love, and I am able to retain friendships. I can cope with pain and embrace life without escaping into food. Oh, the freedom that brings, and the self-respect!

I am making progress, not only emotionally, but spiritually too. My spiritual growth seems to be slower, but I can feel the strength it brings to my life. Just not having to run the whole show is a great relief — to say, "God, it's in your hands," and to feel the peace and serenity.

My abstinence is mostly good. When it's a little shaky, I have many sources of strength to turn to: meetings, OA friends, telephone calls and program literature.

Each day, I try to remember to be grateful, which I truly am. I am grateful for my life and my health, for being who I am and for the wisdom I have gained. I feel comfortable and life is an exciting adventure.

I remember well the "poor me" syndrome brought on by thoughts of being "the only one." These days, having people to whom I can relate in so many ways invariably makes me think of myself as "lucky me"!

June 1983

Courage, Wisdom — and Trust

BEFORE I CAME to Overeaters Anonymous six years ago, courage was a foreign word to me. Grasping its full meaning and implementing it in my life has been a slow process.

For twelve years I have held the same job. For at least eight of those years I have wanted to resign, pack up my kids and move to a smaller, cleaner environment where the pace is slower. During the past few months I have felt guided to move to a particular city in another state — a place I've never seen and where I know no one. At first I totally rejected the idea, but the thought persisted.

As my defenses began to weaken, I found myself asking questions such as, "How do I know whether this is my idea or God's guidance?" Hadn't one of my old character defects been to resort to geographic fixes whenever life got unbearable? I had humbly asked God to remove the defect and it was lifted; but how could I be sure I wasn't taking it back?

I am not one to let go a secure position without a definite replacement, especially as I am the sole support of three children. But my Higher Power gently and assertively encouraged me to have faith.

God's steadfast love has been shown to me in the most difficult circumstances, from financial catastrophe to the incestuous rape of my two daughters, to my horrible, debilitating bouts of binging and vomiting. My Higher Power has led me through the good times too: a 125-pound weight loss, economic stability and tremendous emotional and spiritual growth.

Despite all these assurances of God's care, however, I still held onto my job — until one day I felt as if I were strangling in my own noose. Finally, I made the decision to trust God with complete abandon. An inexplicable serenity enveloped me, and I breathed freely again. This total acceptance and the firm conviction that I would be taken care of gave me the courage to quit my job. My boss was so overwhelmed she was speechless, a condition alien to her.

For three nights straight after I gave notice, I experienced anxiety attacks and I was obsessed with food. I prayed continually, read program literature, attended meetings and used the telephone. I was thereby able to express my intense fear. I knew God had to be taking care of me. Wasn't I walking through this experience without binging and vomiting?

I got mixed responses from people. They were either wholeheartedly for or adamantly against my decision. My conservative parents and my longtime sponsor, surprisingly, assured me that my plan was not irrational, and they gave me their complete support. I was flabbergasted and relieved.

But now I had to do the footwork and follow through. More fear crept in. My doctor advised against the move, believing the stress of such a drastic change might reactivate the binging and vomiting. Before coming to OA, I would have considered the mere fact that he was a doctor sufficient reason to follow his advice. But today my trust is in God alone.

During the intense week after I announced my decision, my boss tried hard to influence me to stay. I am a good employee — as a direct result of working the steps — and she did not want to lose me. I began to waver. Here was my chance to tie the security knot again, to stay in my safe cocoon. I told her I would give her my answer on Monday.

When I awoke Saturday morning I realized I had been thrashing out the decision in my sleep. Before getting up, I said a silent prayer: "God, what *should* I do?"

"Go," a serene, resonant voice answered gently. In the background, a chorus of cacophonous voices screamed shrilly, "Stay!"

I knew the answer then and there. "God grant me the courage to change the things I can."

Since then, there have been no more anxiety attacks, no more doubt, no more fear. I completely trust that my life is in the best of care and that the promises of this beautiful program are coming to fruition one day at a time.

Boise, Idaho, here we come!

August 1983

I Can Smell the Roses

HERE I AM, in a hospital bed. It's not all that unusual for me, nor is it all that bad. I have a chronic disease that requires periodic hospitalization but, thanks to this loving twelve-step program, I've learned to do so much living on my non-hospital days that I don't mind.

As I lie here, I am reminded of earlier years: the kidney biopsy that left a twelve-inch scar because all they could get from a needle biopsy was fat tissue; the high blood pressure pills I took three times a day because I was so obese; and, worst of all, the hatred I felt toward myself for being the person I was.

Life is different today. I am 70 pounds lighter and I've been maintaining my weight loss for three years. Last year they did a needle biopsy and it was easy. I no longer take blood pressure medication, and I giggle like a child when my doctor takes my pressure, shakes his head in disbelief and smiles with satisfaction. But my greatest joy is feeling the Promises being fulfilled in my life every day.

For today, my food plan is, essentially, "salt-free medical maintenance." I get scared when I go into uncharted territory with this precisely defined plan but, with the help of God, my sponsor and OA friends, I'm able to handle it with serenity.

I admit I sometimes get panicky feelings that make me think, "What an order! I can't go through with it." I had those sensations just before I entered the hospital. I projected that my blessed abstinence would slip away. Perhaps that is why I feel motivated to reflect on how God and OA work in my life *everywhere*. If I let God in, ask for help and talk about my fears, I can stay abstinent in the hospital, in my kitchen, in a restaurant or at a friend's home. I just have to be honest, do some planning and tell myself, "You are worth the effort."

Let me share some of what helps me survive. First, I take steps one, two and three each morning, accepting that I am a compulsive overeater and surrendering myself to the care of my Higher Power. Then I take whatever actions are necessary to care for myself.

When I come to the hospital, I remind my doctor that I am a compulsive overeater, and I ask him to write on my chart both the dietary requirements he has imposed and those essential to my personal abstinence. I request a consultation with the hospital dietician, and we discuss my food plan. Hospital personnel, to my amazement, neither resent me nor think me a nuisance; they respect me for being alert to my needs.

When I travel, I carry with me foods important to my medical maintenance; and, as soon as I arrive, I look for OA in the phone book, and I make calls and go to meetings — just as I would at home — so I can feel the love and support of friends.

When I am invited to friends' homes, I discuss my food needs with my hosts, keeping in mind that I love the people I'm visiting and they love me, so I need not feel embarrassed. I refrain from calling myself a freak (sometimes that's hard!) and I repeat to myself that, just as some handicapped people need a ramp to enter a building, I need a special food plan to maintain my health. I am grateful that I love myself enough to do that.

I am making new discoveries every day. Each positive experience shows me that I can live free of my compulsion and enjoy my food and be myself. I can smell the roses. I can love people. And I can delight in the program that teaches me life is good, and rich with joys.

September 1983

Living in the Solution

YESTERDAY I got into a real funk. As I compared my state with past depressions, however, I noted two major differences.

First, I was feeling down because of other people's problems rather than my own. I visit my elderly neighbors and they pour out their woes. I go to church and I learn that thousands are homeless right in my area, apartheid still reigns in South Africa, government spending has increased for nuclear weapons but decreased for children's needs. I see a film about Central America and am assaulted by atrocities I couldn't have imagined. I read a book and discover that millions are hungry, malnourished and dying, not because of scarcity but because of unjust social and economic conditions.

Eeeek! When it all gets too overwhelming for me, I close down, feeling absolutely helpless.

While I don't appreciate my paralysis at these times, I am astonished that I can get all wrapped up in issues outside myself. For someone who wallowed in her own pain for nearly two decades, and for much of that time consciously chose to bury her head in the sand, this is quite a change.

Until a few months ago, I did not visit my neighbors, go to church, see films about human rights violations or read books on the plight of our planet. After almost nine years of devoting myself to recovery in OA and hardly seeing past the program, I at long last identify with an excerpt from one of Bill W.'s letters: "I just know that you are expected, at some point, to do more than carry the message of AA to other alcoholics. In AA we aim not only for sobriety — we try again to become citizens of the world that we rejected. . . ." (*As Bill Sees It,* AA World Services, Inc.)

The other big difference between the blues, past and present, is that my recent lows aren't nearly as severe as the depressions of yesteryear. For a long time suicide seemed enticing and I feared I would succumb. Now, in my bleakest moods, that is not even a consideration. I want to live; and no longer do I want to live just for myself.

The principles of OA have been seeping into me for a long time, and I think they're starting to show. I still catch myself playing God (no wonder I feel overwhelmed!) but my dependence on God is growing. I feel as if I'm living less and less in the problem and more and more in the solution — with respect to all the ills of the world, as well as my own.

September 1983

Declaration of Recovery

IT'S HARD for me to know what I'm feeling, at times. I learned well to hide my emotions, even from myself. But when I allow myself to feel, I realize that I am a member of the human race, the same as everyone else.

Thanks to the program and people of Overeaters Anonymous, I am living more in the now. I find myself giving away more and more of myself — more love, more caring. A wonderful thing happens: I get everything back a hundredfold.

I have so much for which to be grateful, including my very life. I was at the gates of suicide a couple of times during the past few months. I still have days when I shut down my feelings; but even then I have hope, knowing deep down that I only need to start giving again to receive.

Being in the doldrums tells me it's time to review my Declaration of Recovery:

"I declare myself free to feel my feelings, free to be part of the human race, free to be me. I will do my utmost to stay free of negativism and self-loathing. I commit my life to OA, and when I feel myself slipping back into my disease, I will treat myself with massive doses of program.

"I will no longer let the fear of people intimidate me into keeping my feelings secret. I will keep striving for progress, always recognizing that part of me will continue in the old habits. For today, I will accept myself as I am."

I am a baby in this program, even though I've been in it almost three years. I've lost 80 pounds and have about 50 to go. I like the beautiful person I see coming out — and not just because of the weight loss. That's a bonus.

September 1983

Think Flowers

W HAT DO YOU DO when there are no problems in your life? What do you do when you are thin and love life? What do you do when you realize life is a game and you're learning to play? What do you do when you have an irresistible urge to dance a hula with your mother and your brother's kids — and follow through? What do you do when you take a deep breath and savor your aliveness and know there's a purpose for your being?

I'll tell you what I do: I send a special delivery thank-you letter to God and, in this case, Lifeline as well.

Before I came to Overeaters Anonymous, there was a thick, heavy portable prison I took with me everywhere. I was sure disaster was around the corner, and I ran the show with retakes of failure, frustration and gloom.

Today I know what the weather feels like. I know what flowers smell like. I know what it is to laugh until my sides hurt. I know what it's like to feel pain and keep going. I know the special connectedness of watching people grow. I have my own theory of living today. I believe I'm not too different from a budding rose. I'm perfect in all stages of growth, and I make no judgment as to when the rose will be "more perfect." I'm growing. I'm learning. I'm loving.

I am provided for in all areas of my life. I have a job where I touch people and can create beauty. I have friends who laugh and cry with me. I have a body that dances many a tune and manifests what this program promises: health. I have a sponsor who continues to find ways to open my eyes to the wonder of life and the comfort of a loving God.

Somehow, somewhere in my life, I learned to zero in on the negative. My computer is being reprogrammed and, thank God and Overeaters Anonymous, I'm learning to think flowers, not weeds.

September 1983

How I Stopped Chasing Happiness and Chose To Be Happy

Y LIFE is very much the same today as it was when I walked into my first OA meeting more than eight years ago. What has changed is my attitude.

When I came to OA I knew exactly what I wanted out of life. I would be happy if I had certain things, or so I thought. I lost weight, then proceeded to make the other changes that would make me happy.

A housewife and the mother of two small children, I thought happiness would be found by getting a job. So I called my former company and was hired. Now I was doing something I called important and fulfilling.

Ever since I failed a driving test when I was eighteen, I was convinced I could never drive. Encouraged to try again, I succeeded and have been driving for more than seven years.

Next on my list was college. I took the entrance test, was accepted and have earned forty credits so far. I found out that I am intelligent — not stupid and incapable, as I mistakenly believed.

There was only one problem now. I was doing all these wonderful things for myself, but I was feeling very pressured. I had gotten as compulsive with positive achievements as I had been with overeating.

In early December, caught up in the rush of Christmas (in addition to my fulltime job, exams and term papers, OA service and my family), I ran for a bus, tripped and fell flat on my face. I got a black eye and other bruises — and realized that my life was still unmanageable. Forced to take a few days off from work, I had a chance to observe that I needed to slow down.

I decided to stop school for one semester to see whether that would help, but my life was still so hectic that I had little time for my family and my responsibilities at home. I began to question the wisdom of continuing at my job, and I turned it over. Two months later a merger moved my boss to another part of the country, and that settled that.

After the initial shock, I realized I needed time off to look at my life and determine what was really important. All the extra money I was earning and all that activity did not bring me the happiness I sought. Happiness, I learned, comes from within.

I don't know where my life is going, but for today I don't have to know. I totally trust the promise that God will do for me what I could never do for myself.

What have I learned in my eight years of program? That money, education and worldly accomplishments will not make me happy if I am not in good shape spiritually. My emphasis has changed. I get up each morning and ask to be shown exactly what I should do for this day only. Then I put all my energy into doing the most important thing, and then the next. My simple days of housework, laundry and cooking are bringing me more joy than the days when I lived life *my* way. I am trying not to play God anymore. Humility was not my favorite word, and it still isn't, but I am learning that being humble does not mean being subservient.

Today I can see that my life, imperfect as it still is, is OK. Trying to be perfect kept me unhappy. Now I accept my imperfections and I appreciate the progress I am making. I'm not recovering as fast as I think I should, but I'm recovering as well as I can.

My attitude has changed. I've discovered that happiness is something I can choose, and I choose to be happy.

October 1983

Laughing Matters

ONE OF MY FAVORITE Big Book quotes is from "Bill's Story":

"There is, however, a vast amount of fun about it all. I suppose some would be shocked at our seeming worldliness and levity. But just underneath there is deadly earnestness. Faith has to work twenty-four hours a day in and through us, or we perish."

The truth of Bill's observation was brought home to me a few weekends ago at a regional assembly. As I was getting ready to leave, a woman I see only at assemblies said to me, "You really don't take it too seriously, do you?"

Thinking back to that wonderful line in Chapter Four of the Twelve and Twelve that says, "Don't take yourself too damn seriously," and knowing she wasn't implying that I consider OA a social or diet club, I felt I had been complimented.

No, I don't take it too seriously. I have a life-affecting, life-threatening disease, but I also have the option of recovery and that knowledge makes me ecstatic. A fit of the giggles only shows what I am today — a happy person.

I've always had a sense of humor, but in my pre-OA days it was usually expressed in sarcasm at the shortcomings of others. Now, I have a more spirited sense of humor, and I see the amusing side of a great many things. These days, no innuendo is too subtle, no buffoonery too obvious to draw a hearty guffaw from me. So what if my asthmatic laugh sometimes erupts at less-than-appropriate times? Seeing the insanity in the world makes me fit in a bit easier.

There's another reason I feel no compunction about expressing my joy-in-living: this is a program of attraction. I don't know what would have happened had my initial exposure to OA been a meeting of the pain gang. It wasn't, and I'm grateful for that. I'd spent so many years analyzing myself and agonizing over my lot that when I walked into that room full of smiling, happy, glowing, thin people, I wanted what they had. In the months after I began attending meetings and before I started working the program, I would compare the misery I was feeling to the joy I knew was possible, and maybe that helped in finally making me willing to surrender.

Like most people, I feel "down" sometimes, but I talk things over with my sponsor or a friend, and when I've resolved the matter or simply lived through it, I share the experience with my group if I feel there's something interesting or worthwhile in it. I don't enjoy going to meetings that are only gripe sessions. Problems are a part of life, but so are solutions. For this twenty-four hour period, I choose to work the program from the positive end: to be happily abstaining and staying in constant conscious contact with my Higher Power.

I think a lot about "our personal adventures before and after." Life *is* an adventure, and I want to enjoy it to the fullest — now.

October 1983

Good for Something

PAIN. The word sounds like it feels: unpleasant, unwelcome, doomy and gloomy. I react by wanting to hide, run, eat — anything but feel it.

In following the steps of this program, however, I have come to see that many of my most valuable insights are born from the feelings I am having at the moment, if I am willing to be with them fully. When I meet pain head-on, I am often led to a light-filled experience that at times borders on joy.

This week (today, especially) has been like that for me. I knew it was useless to run, so I continually asked God to give me the courage to face the pain, to show me the lessons to be learned, to open my heart more. It wasn't until a couple of hours ago that I detached from the pain and it spoke to me.

"Slow down!" it said. "Feel me completely."

I began to see things I usually miss in my hurried, busy, though generally happy life. I listened more intently to people at work. In touch with my own vulnerable feelings, I was more compassionate and patient with my co-workers. I returned kindness for the abruptness of a customer; then he, with a sheepish grin, returned kindness to me. It was as if each of us knew it was more important to treat one another with care than to get the sale over with quickly because his parking meter was running out or because I wanted to beat the rush-hour traffic.

These responses were born out of pain. I did not try to be different; I did not think about what would be the best way to act.

What I have learned through twelve-step recovery is that there are few experiences and feelings, honestly faced, that are not good for *something.* May I remember the next time pain touches my life that it always leaves me richer than I was.

December 1983

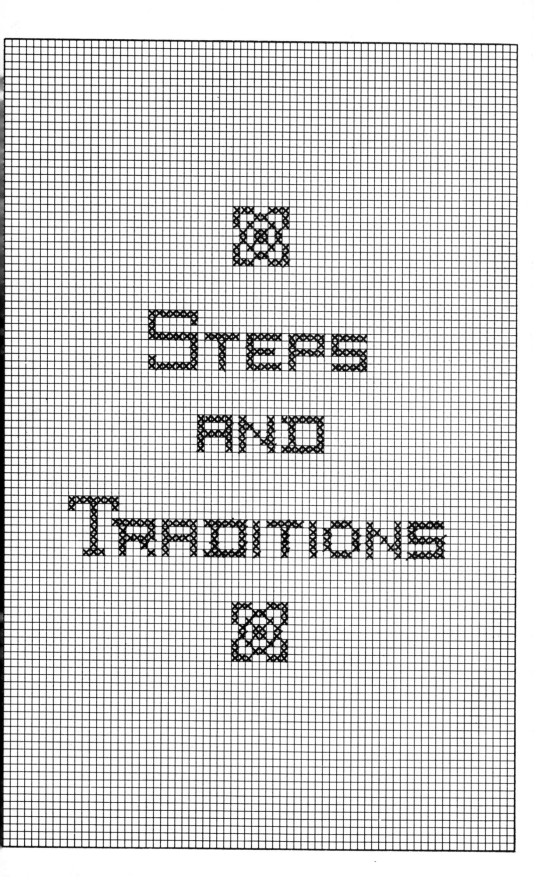

Steps
and
Traditions

Compassionate and Kindly Forbearance

"THE QUALITY OF MERCY is not strained . . . it is twice blest . . . it blesseth him that gives and him that takes . . . it is an attribute to God Himself."

Beautiful words, aren't they? These are the thoughts incorporated in the "We Care" signs at many of our meetings. Yet, do we really understand the meaning of "mercy"? Do we make the spiritual sacrifice necessary to practice this attribute toward each other?

The dictionary defines mercy as "compassionate and kindly forbearance." It isn't easy. It requires the very best we have to offer. It means letting go of resentment, anger, fear and the like. It means reaching out and saying, "I accept you and care about you, no matter what you look like *now* or how you are acting *now.*"

It's not always difficult to forgive past actions on the part of others (or ourselves, too), but forgiving and caring while we and other OAs continue to be human . . . well, that's the real test of progress with our program.

What about the member who maintains normal weight but continues to have severe emotional slips? Do we not frequently pull away in fear or impatience? How do we treat the member who comes to OA and is unable to lose any weight? How do we treat the member who has been at normal weight and then returns to overeating? Do our phone calls slacken off as these hapless members break abstinence over and over? Do we smile with our mouths and avert our eyes when we see them at meetings? Do we say to ourselves, "What's the matter with them? If they really wanted to abstain, they would."

Furthermore, what happens to those whose illness has returned, the ones who are regaining weight (or who have never lost any)? Are we full of guilt and shame? Do we lack a sense of self-worth? Do we expect no mercy and acceptance at the hands of our fellow members?

It's easy to accept a member who is abstaining and losing weight and staying on a fairly even emotional keel. But this is no test of our program; it requires no struggle and sacrifice on our part, no practice of compassion and patience.

The real test comes when, despite our best efforts, a baby or friend continues to react violently or to break abstinence repeatedly or to gain some weight.

We need to remember that we're all here because OA is our haven, a place of last resort. We have nobody but each other and no place else to go. Therefore, for one overeater to make another overeater feel guilty or ashamed is the greatest tragedy of all. If we judge one another or make each other feel, in any way, the way we felt in the outside world, we have destroyed what we believe in and defeated our own purpose.

Let us reexamine what Shakespeare meant when he said, "The quality of mercy is not strained." It's rather like elastic — expanding with the giving and taking, contracting with being withheld. Mercy is an expenditure of attitude, not of time or money. "It is twice blest . . . it blesseth him that gives and him that takes." Isn't that remarkable? In this hectic and unsure world, the givers and receivers of mercy will feel only joy and serenity, resulting in a sense of self-worth beyond imagining. Incidentally, for those still struggling with weight loss, the willingness to accept mercy offered is a sure step toward peace of mind.

In the natural scheme of things, some of those now maintaining will regain their weight and some of those now trying and retrying will abstain and maintain their normal weight. Those emotionally upset will even out and some fairly stable will have emotional slips. But none of this is as important as the spiritual growth we attain by being merciful with one another, no matter what our physical or emotional state of being may be.

"Mercy is an attribute to God Himself."

July/August 1973

The Desire To Be Thin: A Leaky Dike

THE THIRD TRADITION states that "The only requirement for OA membership is a desire to stop eating compulsively." When I came into Overeaters Anonymous four and a half years ago at 255 pounds, I thought this meant that I had to want to be thin. It has taken me four years of maintaining a weight of 155 pounds to discover that there is a great difference between wanting to be thin and wanting to abstain from compulsive overeating.

The dream of the alcoholic is to learn to drink socially. The dream of the compulsive overeater is to learn to "eat socially" — that is, to indulge in the kind of socially accepted overeating represented by snacking and eating for reasons other than sustenance at parties, picnics, outings and social occasions of every description. The alcoholic prays, "Lord, let me drink and not get drunk"; the overeater says, "Lord, let me eat and not get fat." What the compulsive overeater really means, however, is "Lord, let me eat the way others eat *in addition to the way I want to eat* and not get fat."

Those of us who are fortunate enough to reach the Anonymous programs discover that not only is it not enough to want to be a sober social drinker or a thin social eater, but that the stubborn desire to be "normal" drinkers and "normal" eaters is both root and branch of our self-destructiveness. If I, as a compulsive overeater, want to be "sober," it means I must give up the dream of the smorgasbord — all I can eat at no extra cost. I need to be unreservedly willing to have the compulsion to overeat removed. Merely wanting to lose weight indicates nothing more than a willingness to submit to yet another diet or, to put it differently, to go on an "empty" binge.

Wanting to be thin is like trying to plug up a dike that has thousands of leaks — the flood will eventually burst in upon me. It is only when I truly want to abstain from the insanity of compulsive overeating that I am able to take step one.

The conditions of having true abstinence and being on a diet, or an empty binge, are worlds apart. An alcoholic who is not drinking but who continues to indulge in offshoots of the same behavior patterns is said to be on a "dry drunk." Similarly, many of us OAs walk around saying we have been abstinent for so many days, months or years when we really mean we have been dieting, or "empty binging."

To want abstinence from compulsive overeating is truly not the same as wanting to be thin. It is only when one quits worrying about the symptom — excess weight — and attacks the disease itself — compulsive overeating — that sanity begins to return, the promises begin to come true and abstinence is finally a joy instead of a struggle.

The question, then, is not whether I am willing to be thin but whether, once I accept the fact that I am a victim of the disease of compulsive overeating, I am truly willing to be free of it. It is this initial confrontation of my motivation that first, and in my opinion most importantly, demands rigorous honesty; and it is *this* and no other willingness that leads me freely and joyfully to begin to practice the twelve steps of recovery.

November/December 1977

You Don't Look Like a Sister

WEEK AFTER Labor Day, 1976, just four blocks from the religious community in which I live, the weekly OA meeting — my first — began.

I sat, listened and attended the newcomers meeting. Then I went home, relieved that no one had discovered I was a nun. To preserve my anonymity I did not take a sponsor, but tried to abstain alone. The program does not work that way, I found; eventually, I had a slip.

Week after week, some OA members spoke of how their Higher Power, God, had restored them to sanity. But I, a thirty-six year old woman who had experienced a call to religious life six years earlier and now was in the beginning stages of religious formation for one year, seemed uncomfortable at the thought of professing God as my Higher Power. This, I rationalized, would be imposing God on others. I took literally the suggestion that each individual is to determine the nature of his or her Higher Power.

After the one break in abstinence, I took a food sponsor at the beginning of Thanksgiving week, 1976, calling in my food through Christmas. I continued to go to weekly meetings, maintaining my abstinence — and my misused anonymity. But a noticeable change was beginning to take place within and without.

One winter day, a Sister commented on my weight loss. My response was, "Yes, and my whole self-concept is changing." Then I realized what I had said. I had joined OA just to lose weight, and without my being aware of it, changes were occurring in areas of my life that I did not even know needed changing.

After many years of being self-supporting, I had only partly adapted myself to living in a religious community. The many changes this kind of life requires did not come easily, and I fought many of them. But OA has helped me to transform my thinking. In the middle of a cold winter night, as I struggled to overcome a tendency to self pity, I felt defeated. How vividly I recall that night — lying in bed, tearful, filled with self-doubt — when those words of step three flashed through my mind: *Made a decision to turn our will and our lives over to the care of God as we understood Him.*

I was startled to find that although I had repeatedly heard the twelve steps read during six months of weekly meetings, I had not assimilated their meaning. Now, suddenly, I realized that they were more than just words. "Those steps are *real,*" I said to myself.

I belong to a religious congregation whose spirituality is one of self-surrender, and I began to see a close relationship between both programs of living. Through my practice of abstinence from compulsive overeating, I soon found that abstinence is also an attitudinal disposition and a way of living my religious vocation.

Feeling a need to share my story with other OA members, I gradually "broke my anonymity" within my group to reveal my identity as a Sister. But I was afraid: what if the word got around? Responses from fellow members ranged from, "I knew it all along," to "But you don't look like a Sister!" Some were surprised, others seemed to feel deceived and many were delighted.

A number of people told me, "I never thought Sisters had any character defects," or "I thought Sisters had their faith all together." This honest sharing served to remind all of us that I am first a human being, and that my religious vocation in essence challenges me to dare to live my life more fully and with more "humanness," as does the OA program.

As people noticed the changes and growth in me, I began to grasp the significance of the second aspect of anonymity: to avoid self-glorification. For a while I was the only OA member in our area from a religious community, and I was aware of occasional subtle feelings of superiority. But, to "thoroughly follow our path" is to learn that I am not entitled to any special status, nor do I have a corner on God. Though I sit week after week among people from all walks of life, I am just one of them, no better or worse; we have a common disease. More than that, I began to discover how much lay people have to teach me about faith in a Higher Power. I became more aware of the fact that this Sister and her God did *not* have it all together. At the same time, I was able to contribute, when asked, to others in their journeying search for God, especially since my formation studies were in providing spiritual direction.

As months passed, I experienced a deeper, more authentic transformation through the OA program. Steps four and five became an essential bridge to this plateau. I realized that while the sacrament of reconciliation (confession) had an indispensable value in my life, I could use it as an excuse for not taking these two steps. It was essential for me to take a searching and fearless moral inventory, and to give it to someone outside the confession framework. The immediate rewards of steps four and five lay in leading me to accept my own humanity, while not justifying my character defects; and in recognizing, once more, that because I am a Sister, I am not automatically exempt from an array of personal shortcomings. The OA program has highlighted this!

Through the sixth and seventh steps, God is gradually removing and transforming some of my character defects, enabling me to see where I have misused some gifts and showing me how these mistakes can be turned around. Amends to persons in my life are coming one at a time.

As I change, I also struggle with the expectations of others. God can and does remove some of my shortcomings, but I am constantly reminded that our program is ongoing, that I am always in the *process* of recovering, so that neither my own nor others' expectations become unrealistic. There are moments of rude awakening when I realize that though I have the program, I am not living, working and manifesting it in my life as fully as I would hope. In such moments I am reminded that I am still powerless, unable to manage, and only God can continue to restore me.

In meal planning I had to consider that I live as a member of a community. I was able to commit a food plan which would permit me to choose to eat from whatever was served each day, and not ask to have special food prepared for me. My experience has been that there is always sufficient food from which to select — take what you want, and leave the rest.

A more delicate and complex matter was learning to achieve a balance between responsibility to the work of my community and service in OA. I am sure that the degree to which OA is effective in my life can only be measured by the quality of my relationships in my daily community life with my Sisters. What this means is that recovery in OA is not attained at the expense of the primary commitment in my life. On the contrary, I have found that each greatly enhances the other, so interrelated are they. There is room — and need — in my life for both.

Overeaters Anonymous has helped me far beyond my expectations of recovery on the physical, emotional and spiritual levels. I have shared my experience in the hope that other men and women in religious callings who are struggling with compulsive overeating will consider OA. A religious vocation does not make me spiritually above any person or program. Indeed, the full development of my vocation depends on the extent to which I am able to integrate my daily actions into my work.

Overeating, along with isolation, anger, resentment, jealousy, boredom, self-pity and so on, is only a symptom of a deeper longing to be filled instead with the goodness of God. A constant reminder that I am powerless over compulsive overeating keeps me mindful that only a Power greater than myself can continue to restore me. Scripture often tells us that God, not compulsive overeating, has filled the hungry with good things. Prayer has a value and importance in my life. OA has made me even more aware of the fact that I must always seek knowledge of God's will for me.

I am a compulsive overeater, a human being and a Sister who is recovering thanks to Overeaters Anonymous and the help of my Higher Power whom I choose to call God. Come, let us step along together — neither behind nor ahead of each other, but side by side.

November 1978

"Clothe Me in Your Beauty"

SEVEN YEARS AGO I felt a need to learn to work the eleventh step. I had just been taken off the critical list and I was willing to take drastic measures to avoid a recurrence.

Being an agnostic added to the problem, but I was reassured by the Big Book: "Our own conception, however inadequate, was sufficient to make the approach . . ." and "Do not let any prejudice you may have against spiritual terms deter you from honestly asking yourself what they mean to you."

I began with the prayer of St. Francis — "Where there is hate, give love" — and suddenly I was angry. I had given love in the absence of love for so many years that I was being destroyed by it. I did not know then that psychologists label this condition neurotic dependency.

And I thought I was so strong! Fortunately, the strong one was the hospital priest on whom I vented my anger. He said I seemed to be trying to force myself to accept a higher power. He suggested that I work on "easy does it" and begin by loving *myself*. He was confident that I would find an acceptable way of improving my conscious contact with my higher power.

Because church and religion make me feel defiant and hypocritical, I was forced to find my own way. Fortunately, I now have the wisdom and the humility to be grateful that it works, no matter how inadequate it appears to others.

The place in which I meditate is, for now, the bubble bath where every morning I'm alone and apart from the rest of the world and yet I feel secure and warm. My higher power is still without definition; it is no more than an internally felt "force for good." Meditation has come to be tied to getting "clean," which is a normal part of the day's beginning. (Is this where "cleanliness is next to Godliness" comes from?)

This "easy does it" way of meditating began to make subtle changes in me over a period of years. The prayer I chose to recite was more like a poem. Without realizing it, I gradually memorized it and it is now part of me. Recently, I learned that it is from something called a "Prayer for Virtue." If I had known that seven years ago, I would have rejected it, as I already felt virtuous and a fourth-step inventory had revealed no defects!

I am aware that if I had a choice I would abandon the practice even though I know that the joy of living I now experience is a direct result of working the steps. But I also know that I would be a fool to let it slip away because of a natural inclination to spend my time on something more exciting.

There is a tiny new fear replacing my once unlimited arrogance, which tells me that if I abandon step eleven I'd soon be my former self again saying "Why me?" as I lay in the intensive care unit. So, for today, I'm willing to surround myself with bubbles and improve my conscious contact by reciting:

"In the quiet of the morning hour I come to you for peace. Give me the power to view the world today through love-filled eyes. Help me be patient, gentle, wise; to see beyond what seems to be; . . . O clothe me in your beauty, this I pray — give me the grace to do your will today."

June 1979

Old Me, I Love You

THE ELEVENTH STEP talks about seeking God through prayer and meditation. I am a meditator; at least, on my "smart" days I meditate. On my not-so-smart days, I skip that discipline.

I believe in universal law, and that law is made simple for me by knowing that if I start my day off on a firm spiritual foundation, I am able to deal effectively with whatever life sends my way. By the same token, if I don't care enough about myself to take time to establish my daily foundation, my day usually falls apart and I fall apart with it. That is my daily universal law.

In meditating, I always used a mantra that I paid big money to get, thus assuring myself that it must be a dynamite mantra. It is the focal point, the vehicle which is supposed to take me to those deep, dark recesses of my mind where all will be disclosed to me. So far, I've never reached there.

Today, I used a new technique. I benched my $125 mantra and, for free, said, "Here I am, God, reporting for duty. I ask only to see what You would have me see." What I saw is the basis for this sharing-article.

I am the sum total of every experience and thought I have ever had and if, by the grace of God, I am learning to love this person God created, I have to value every experience I have ever had. I have to learn to be gentle and respectful of that growing, learning person I was, as much as the person I am becoming today and the person I will become tomorrow.

In writing a fourth step inventory, I saw some painful character defects. I saw a lot about me that I didn't like, and I've let that hurt me. My simple meditation today has disclosed to me that this is not what inventories are about. The past is not my nemesis; it is the healthy foundation on which today is built. The past is my heritage — my experience, my growth, my awareness of what works in my life and what doesn't. What other personal measure can I use to mold and shape today?

My experience is who I *am*. How have I been hurt in the past? Have I hurt others? Have I loved and been loved? Have I felt alone? Have I felt full and overflowing? Have I binged on food and emotions? Have I been abstinent from eating and feeling compulsively?

These are the precious foundations that have brought me today's growth and decisions. Do I want abstinence today? Do I want peace and serenity? Do I want to be happy and content with what I have and who I am this very minute? Do I understand the price? Am I willing to pay it?

All these questions, and more, find their answers in my life experience. What has my life taught me so far? How can I hate my experience and hate the person I was, if it took all of that to give me today?

Suddenly, I had such a feeling of warmth and compassion for my past and the learning-growing old me, that I said out loud, "Old me, I love you. I don't like everything you did, but I like what you are trying to become and what you are this very day."

I meant it. It was a special gift from my Higher Power, one I'll have to care for on a daily basis, for it must be nurtured.

I am a questioning person, but I am beginning to find out that my answers are all here within me, just waiting patiently to be tapped. I feel like a walking gold mine. That is a beautiful revelation for someone who used to think all the answers were anywhere but within me — or that there were no answers at all.

I can see today that even overeating provided me with an answer, and that answer is, "It doesn't work anymore; it is no longer your solution." How would I have found that answer if I hadn't gone through my learning process of melting, molding and refining?

Not long ago, a person in the program said to me, "I love this program, but the people are impossible to deal with."

I understand what she meant. I have days when my behavior makes me really hard to love, let alone like. Maybe you're like that, too; I don't know. But I do know the steps of this program are beautiful; yet without people working them, frail and imperfect though we may be — even obnoxious on occasion — the program is just a beautiful philosophy. That philosophy comes alive through you and me. It stops being a philosophy and becomes a way of life when we work it.

If my Higher Power calls upon me to love you and to love myself, in compassion, God is also giving me the power and ability to do it. I have never been called to action and then been deserted at the front lines of life.

Expensive mantras are fine; I've enjoyed mine. Tricks and gimmicks that work are OK too, if I seem to need them. But I am finding that the longer I live, the simpler life is becoming — when I allow it to be. And with all the mantras, tricks, gimmicks, dogmas, tools and steps, for me, it always comes back to: "What do You want for me today and, please, give me the faith and willingness to carry it out."

Hey, isn't that step eleven again? "Sought through prayer and meditation to improve our conscious contact with God *as we understood Him,* praying only for knowledge of His will for us and the power to carry that out."

What a step! What a program!

Old me, I love you. New me, I love you, too. And God, thank You for giving me the generosity of spirit to be tender in giving and receiving that love. May I spend my lifetime sharing it in this beautiful program and in all my daily affairs.

July 1979

A Surpassing Nonsense

THE OA PROGRAM makes absolutely no sense at all.

Look at it: "You can only keep what you give away." That defies every scientific principle. "Pray and meditate." For heaven's sake, you can't burn up any calories that way! "Admit your powerlessness." Are these people really off the deep end? How can a person develop enough willpower to stay on a diet while claiming to be powerless over the situation?

These were some of my arguments. Although I could never have won any prizes for logic as it was — my behavior while intermittently eating compulsively and dieting was far from rational — I wanted the program to conform to every notion of pragmatism that I could bring to mind. Parts of it did, but they were mostly the auxiliary parts, the tools and those suggestions that support the program but that are not the program.

It made sense, for example, to go to meetings for moral support and make phone calls for an instant fix of fellowship. I understood the reasoning behind H-A-L-T and why we would be wise to avoid getting overly hungry, angry, lonely or tired. The admonition not to scale-hop was a practical one. But the steps — those twelve wordy wonders written in the past tense: where did they fit in?

My answer today is that they don't "fit in" my program anywhere: they *are* my program. They are the materials with which I'm building my life. The tools are great as tools; they're useful and necessary. It would be hard to build a house without tools, but one wouldn't get much of a structure if all one had were hammers and saws but no building materials.

This new life of mine has twelve steps as its stone and brick and wood and mortar. It's a strong house because it has a firm foundation.

The steps as they relate to compulsive overeating still make no sense at all to my intellect. There is no earthly reason why taking a moral inventory or making amends to people I have harmed should keep the refrigerator from crooning its siren song. The fact remains that those steps and the other ten have kept the fridge silent for me for a year and seven months. That is a gift from my Higher Power. There's also no earthly reason why God as I understand God should give me such a gift. The fact again: God has done it and continues to do it as I work — feebly sometimes, sloppily often, even stubbornly on occasion — the program of recovery.

My conclusion has to be that this program really makes perfect sense, but its rationale is on a subtler level than the one on which I think. I call it spiritual sense. The steps are no less nebulous than the teachings of any inspired religion or philosophy as I see it. The concept of tithing that one might prosper in the old testament is clearly ridiculous to human sense; everyone knows you should keep every penny you can get! Jesus' "turning the other cheek" is clearly absurd — and a fine way to get beaten up. The yoga principle of non-attachment to the fruits of our labors is a solid blow at free enterprise; and the nonviolent resistance of Gandhi and Martin Luther King is, when intellectually dissected, an exercise in futility.

Amazingly, though, all these work for those who incorporate the principles into their lives. The same is true with us as the threads of the program are woven into our lives on a daily basis. We're told to "resign from the debating society," to stop trying to figure it out, just to work it and let it work. Curiously, since I've stopped trying to analyze and why-i-cize the program, it makes more sense all the time.

November 1979

How I Rewrote the First Step

THIS IS NOT the happiest of stories, but it isn't a tale of failure. It is one of success because in this program we generally learn something of value, particularly when we're in the pits.

I am not a person who normally copes well with the daily ups and downs of life, but over a four-month period recently I sanely handled major surgery, my grandfather's critical illness, a surprise three-week visit from my mother (with whom I've had a turbulent relationship), a disastrous haircut that left me looking like a porcupine, a large medical bill that was rejected by our insurance company, a new job doing something I'd never tried before, a visit from my father and sister over the holidays that included their getting snowed in and out of the airport for days, a major misunderstanding with a much-loved OA sister, an unexplained weight gain of eight pounds in one week and some minor items I've forgotten. I met every problem head-on, said the Serenity Prayer, stayed abstinent and survived.

What went wrong? I began thinking. I had some good ideas and this tremendous "recovery" of mine was proof that I could now manage things.

Knowing that one of the reasons I overeat is to blot out my feelings, I decided that every morning, after I had done my meditations, I would write down whatever it was that I was feeling. This accomplished two things: It put me in touch with what I really was feeling (which I often mistook for hunger), and it gave me the opportunity to try to figure out what if anything I could do about those feelings. (Accept the ones I couldn't change, change the ones I could, and so on.)

This worked out so well that I changed the first step to read: "I admitted I am powerless over my feelings, and that they cause my food consumption to become unmanageable." As the days of abstinence increased and I passed those "magic" landmarks — twenty-one days, sixty, ninety — I grew more and more casual about food itself.

I no longer found it necessary to ignore graphic "goodie" commercials on television; they couldn't get to me anymore! I no longer avoided certain magazines that I know contain more full color ads for food than good reading. Instead, I started to look at the pictures and actually told myself I was admiring them for their "artistic" quality. I even began to read recipes of things I knew I'd never eat again — just out of curiosity, or in case I needed something special for company. I allowed the family to start bringing my binge foods back in the house (all terrible for them, as well as me), because the *food* just didn't bother me anymore. It was those blankety-blank feelings I had to worry about.

Gosh, it felt so much better to know that I was just overemotional, too sensitive, had a short temper, was even a little neurotic — rather than powerless over a stupid thing like food. That had always been so humiliating. Those poor *other* people in OA!

I could probably stop right here and you could fill in the rest of the story. But I'll go on because I'm working on not leaving things undone.

One day I realized that circumstances were such that I was going to have to quit the new job I had come to like. I was overwhelmed with self-pity, depression, anger and frustration. I was going to have to start gearing up to handle these feelings. But what I did was walk straight into the kitchen to a certain food — just to look at it. I surely didn't want to eat it; I just had to handle the feelings. I went on cleaning the house, but before long I was back in the kitchen, *smelling.* Of course, I wasn't thinking of eating . . . what was wrong with me?

I didn't call for help. I didn't pray, I didn't read any literature; I still thought I didn't need to. So the food I had scoffed at, laughed at and flirted with for four months became all powerful, and I chose to go back into the squirrel cage that is the life of the practicing compulsive overeater. If I thought I had been having unhealthy feelings while abstaining, I'd forgotten what sick feelings could really be like with self-respect gone and self-hate rampant.

It took me a long time to get back on anything I dared call good abstinence again. But that was all right, because I learned something I don't think I'll ever forget. The program is just fine the way it is. No one has ever been able to come up with anything better. You can bet on one thing: *I'll* never try again.

January 1980

Steps to Serenity

IN THE BOOK, *Alcoholics Anonymous,* we are promised certain results if we are painstaking about working the first nine steps. Among these idyllic sounding prospects is the assurance that we will comprehend the word *serenity* and know peace.

To be serene, one must learn how to be quiet, to be alone with oneself, to enjoy sitting for a few minutes without jumping up to take care of some forgotten detail. Comprehending the word serenity is for me equivalent to being comfortable enough with myself not to have to create problems or confusion in order to keep from being bored.

The word *peace* suggests to me the Hebrew word *shalom*. Shalom actually means "to be complete." It implies an appreciation of the people and things around us that arises from having paid one's debts, discharged one's duties and made restitution where needed. When we know peace, we are complete. We can accept ourselves as we are, being fully aware of our positive and negative traits.

My pre-OA experience was just the opposite. I did not think much of myself, and I was sure that everyone agreed with me. I had concluded that only when a long list of conditions was met could I be happy. I needed money, power, prestige.

My last few days prior to being led to the twelve steps were agonizing. The hours were filled with longing for tomorrow, planning for next week, plotting out next month, scheduling next year. Life was a series of meaningless question marks and misunderstandings. I was told that I had potential, but I could not see what good it would do me. I felt too much pain to enjoy my sour existence. I identified with Walter Mitty and cried because of lack of opportunity.

Now, many twenty-four hours later, having worked each of the steps numerous times, I look back with amazement. I can at last comprehend the word serenity and I have come to know peace. All the things I said I needed to make me happy have come, but they are not the source of my joy. I knew happiness before any of my material goals was reached.

Today, my physical surroundings are less than perfect, but my spiritual inner self is improving daily. Instead of bemoaning what is wrong externally, I try to develop internally. It is more important for me today to want what I have than to have what I want. I know that most things in life are possible, if we are willing to pay the price.

Overabundance of possessions can create worry. Too much acclaim can lead to discomfort. Excessive power distracts us from the real values of life. In moderate proportions, such external achievements may enhance our lives; yet, we must not expect the world to be perfect in order for us to be serene. We must continue to keep our own house in order — working to complete our inner selves, growing emotionally and spiritually.

By myself, I am not sufficiently intelligent to know how to live at ease. Prior to OA, I read psychology books, attended self-help groups and deluded myself into thinking that I was a "together" person. The closest I came to feeling secure was when I was so stuffed with food I could hardly feel; yet, even then, the dull ache was still there.

Presently, because of OA, my Higher Power, the steps and the tools — and most important, my willingness to use all of these resources, I am living in today.

I am not one who gets up on a cloudy day and says, "It's a beautiful day." But upon arising on a dreary morning, I am able to think about the positive aspects of the rain. I spent far too many years ignoring and denying reality. The truth may be painful or it may make me uncomfortable. When I take an honest look at the facts, accept what I cannot change and do the best with what I am given, the hurt is soon replaced with gratitude and satisfaction.

I am, for today, a complete person. I am experiencing a feeling that everything is OK. I can sit still for a while and enjoy being alone. This is not a permanent condition. As my disease is arrested for only one day at a time, so my serenity is dependent on my spiritual and emotional effort and growth *this* twenty-four hours.

For those who are just beginning this path, take heart. In the words of the Big Book, "We shall be with you in the Fellowship of the spirit and you will surely meet some of us as you trudge the Road of Happy Destiny."

February 1980

I Believe!

BELIEVE in the program.

I believe in a Higher Power.

I believe in the AA Big Book, which tells me I have a threefold illness: physical, emotional, spiritual.

I believe that "when the spiritual malady is overcome we straighten out mentally and physically."

I believe the shortest route to recovery is by going directly to the twelve-step recovery program outlined for us in the Big Book.

I believe compulsive overeaters can be spared years of struggle, years of fighting for self-discipline, years of rigid dieting followed by equally abandoned eating.

I believe my recovery began when I stopped trying to figure out what OA is all about and started concentrating on the instructions of the recovery program as they are given to us in the Big Book.

That's how I found abstinence: by going to the basic program, working it to the best of my ability and helping others, as the alcoholic pioneers did.

I was given this program three years ago. I had tried desperately to lose weight every day for seven months, but after years of dieting, losing weight and regaining it — plus more — I found I was totally unable to diet. My doctor suggested I join a weight-losing group. He told me Overeaters Anonymous is the best of them all.

I believed him. I lived the program for six and a half months. I was relieved of 95 pounds. My character defects diminished. I was a far more accepting, loving, giving person.

Why, then, was I again compulsively overeating? Why couldn't I stop? Why couldn't I stick with the food I needed to maintain my weight? Why were they trying to convince me that "calling in" my food would do it when it didn't?

The Big Book says don't be concerned with the whys. I may never know the answers. I now believe that the answers come, through my

Higher Power, when I need to know them in order to help others. My probing only perpetuates the self, and the Big Book tells me I must be rid of self and strive to do God's will.

That is what these steps are giving me: a deep, trusting relationship with God based on the unshakable conviction that God always gives me what I need.

Before turning to the steps, abstinence for me meant dropping the 10 pounds or so I had regained and then promptly returning to the nibbling that always turned into binging. Today I am experiencing a contented abstinence unlike any I have ever known. It feels real and comfortable, not at all like the artificial "high" of all those false starts.

I believe my recovery is contingent on admitting and really believing that I am powerless over food, powerless to control my life, powerless over people, places and things. I am powerless to do anything about any of my character defects. As I admit and keep mindful of my powerlessness, God can and does help me through the process of the steps. The lifting of countless burdens makes me ever more willing to turn my will and my life over with no reservations.

Each morning brings a new surrender, a new admission of my powerlessness and a new commitment to abstinence through steps one, two and three. It is a quiet time, a new beginning, a new day.

I believe studying the Big Book and following its directions is giving me contented abstinence, automatically, just as promised.

I am powerless to give advice as a sponsor. When I start giving advice, I am abusing this beautiful program and putting my own recovery in jeopardy. All I can do as a sponsor is listen with patience and then offer the one suggestion that works every time: Keep it simple. Try the basic, unadorned program. It works.

To those who want to know how, exactly, to proceed, I say: Read the Big Book, follow the instructions given there and let's get together and start the journey through the steps. By the time we have worked thoroughly and honestly through the first nine steps we indeed begin to know a new freedom, as stated in the promises.

A Higher Power — God — led me to OA and into recovery. God is leading me in effective sponsorship, following the procedure that worked for Bill W. I am grateful to all who helped me along the way, whom God used as channels.

I am grateful for the freedom from obsession, the tremendous peace, joy and serenity that have been granted me. The journey goes on — and what a journey it is! — but the search is ended. The insatiable yearning is being satisfied. The emptiness within is being filled. And it is all coming about through these twelve simple steps.

My greatest joy is the growth I have experienced through the privilege of working with compulsive overeaters who want recovery.

I am grateful to OA. I am grateful to AA for the use of their *infallible* program. I am grateful to the OA person who brings Big Book recovery

·to our area every year via an annual retreat — a great factor in my finding my own way in the Big Book.

My wish for every compulsive overeater who wants recovery is that you, too, find your way to this simple program. Put your total faith and trust in these steps. They show the way to "let go and let God." This is the way to contented abstinence and a peaceful, satisfying life.

Whether any of this is helpful to others I do not know. The only thing I feel certain of is that this program works if we let go all the embellishments so many of us try to bring into it.

Through honest, total abandonment of self in the process of working these twelve steps, we will begin to experience the freedom and contentment for which we yearn.

June 1980

How I Fell in Love with the Traditions

"OA IS NOT an excuse for craziness," I complained. "Can't they get their act together and be logical? Can't they see how it should be done?"

Organization is my middle name. I was looking for firm lines of authority and for rigid standardization of policies and procedures. The way things were run — or not run — in OA was extremely frustrating, to say the least.

I thought the traditions, with their weak-kneed lack of control, were a bore. What a waste of time to read them at every meeting! I refused to listen. And in step study, when they got to the traditions, I refused to go.

Since then I have done a complete turnabout. I feel blessed when I'm asked to read the traditions at a meeting, and I always listen intently when they are read by others.

What happened?

It started several months ago when I was questioning my membership in OA. How could I belong here when few of the personal stories I heard matched my own? My experience was different from that of most of my fellow members. I felt like a misfit.

But I do compulsively overeat. I could not deny that.

One day I voiced my dilemma to a fellow member. His immediate response was, "The only requirement for OA membership is a desire to stop eating compulsively."

During the following weeks I kept hearing that. Finally, it took hold. It was a handle I could grasp while participating in the Fellowship to the extent that I was able.

Not long afterward, I realized that this sole membership requirement was given in tradition three. Thus began my real introduction to the twelve traditions.

I observed that OAs with long-term abstinence seemed to revere the traditions, so I began listening to what they had to say. Their love of the traditions was tied in with a deep love of the Fellowship — a nurturing love of immense proportions.

When I expressed my desire to better understand the traditions and the ways of the Fellowship, someone suggested that I read *Alcoholics Anonymous Comes of Age.* This book gave me a thorough understanding of the experiences that led to the steps and traditions of Alcoholics Anonymous.

OA hasn't been the same for me ever since. Learning about the first twenty years of AA was like viewing OA by stepping back and seeing the wider context — the ebb and flow of significant events over the years.

Thanks to the perspective the AA history gave me, my reactions to what a speaker says, what a meeting decides, what a piece of literature states or what another member believes are always tempered by a profound sense of the flow of Providence-guided history. If I disagree or think a grave mistake is being made, it's not that big a deal in the greater scheme of things. A loving God guides us. We have no way of knowing at any particular moment whether the step we are taking is a step forward or backward, to the right or to the left. Over a twenty-year span we might see the pattern more clearly.

And what of my penchant for organization? I have had to surrender the conventional sense of it because I see a paradoxical wisdom in the twelve traditions. I am called to trust in the ultimate authority of a loving God. I am called to trust in the autonomous group. I am called to trust that the Conference delegates and board of trustees are responsible to the rest of us in the Fellowship — that is, to you and to me.

It's crazy, I tell you. The lines of authority are all mixed up. In fact, there is no authority except each one of us trying to get in touch with our loving God and striving to love our fellow sufferers without condemnation and without conditions. Simply to love.

Out of our love, our Fellowship evolves.

December 1980

The Only Requirement

EVERY OA MEETING I attend begins with readings of "How It Works" and the twelve traditions. That means I've heard the words of tradition three hundreds of times:

"The only requirement for OA membership is a desire to stop eating compulsively."

I thought I understood that. There is certainly nothing complex about the desire to stop eating compulsively.

There were times when I clung to the solace of that single qualification for belonging here. When I felt like a failure at everything in my life, including the program, the only hope I had was to keep coming back. To know there was a place for me no matter how badly I messed up was small consolation at times, but I was desperate. Overeaters Anonymous was the only place where I truly felt I belonged. I couldn't lose that.

Sitting in a meeting recently I suddenly realized that I have not really been hearing tradition three. What I heard this time was: ". . . *the desire to stop eating compulsively.*" It brought me up short.

I made a quick mental list of my "desires" in this program. What I have wanted out of OA included: to lose weight, to be pretty, liked, accepted, sexy, needed, successful, in control of my eating, to feel good, to eliminate an addiction to sugars and starches, to improve my health and to have friends. Tradition three doesn't talk about any of those goals.

It talks about my disease. About recovery. About doing what is necessary to let go what is wrong. I tend to concentrate on the symptom: weight. The issue of facing the fact that I am not like normal people is an uncomfortable one.

Tradition three, however, asks me to put aside the frills and side benefits of the program and stay with the basics, the root of my problem. Whether I am pretty, slim, well liked, or ever do anything on my list of "wants" is beside the point. First I have to want to do something about the compulsion. I have to want to get better. I have to want to work the program for that reason. The rest is gravy.

The real motivation for this "wanting" is very simple: I don't like being crazy. No, I don't care at all for the pain and humiliation and all the nasties that go along with compulsive overeating. And because of that dislike, and the desire to get help, I am guaranteed a home for life. I do belong and will always belong because I am and always will be a compulsive overeater.

I thank you, OA, for showing me that I am not a failure in my life or in my program just because I haven't fulfilled all my desires. I am a success because I am getting better.

June 1981

Sexuality and the Steps

FOR MY FIRST TWO and a half years in the program I skimmed over the final section of step four in the Big Book, which is about sex, leaving it to the alcoholic — who is obviously more lustful.

Or so I thought. But during most of the past year I have been dealing with my sexuality in much the same way I have learned to deal with compulsive overeating: by working the steps.

My alcoholic father committed suicide when I was fifteen. The effects of his disease on me during my childhood, combined with the rejection I felt at his death, warped my ability to have normal relationships with the opposite sex.

My father treated me like a princess when he was drunk. Consequently, I felt superior to men. I was OK when I had the upper hand, but if men treated me as an average human being I took it as rejection.

When I was still quite young I set high ideals for myself and the boys with whom I related. At age eleven I concluded that no one could meet my expectations, so I created my own fantasy world of romance. Whenever I had a crush on someone, I dreamed that one day he would fall in love with me, invite me to the dance, we would be married and life would be fine ever after. Not surprisingly, my favorite fairy tale was Cinderella.

This pattern, with some variations, continued for ten years. When I discovered sex, I expected it to fulfill me and I sought its comfort. No one wanted my chubby body and resentful eyes, however, so I got what I thought I wanted only from an occasional brief and sadly superficial escapade.

Finding my Higher Power with the help of the church and OA three years ago did not change my behavior overnight. I still lived in a fantasy world, either denying my sexuality under the guise of spirituality or living out a crush solely in my imagination, thinking it was "feminine" to be unassertive.

Last winter I reached rock bottom. I admitted my powerlessness over my feelings about men and I declared that my sexuality was unmanageable. Every day I made an effort to believe that God would restore me to sanity in this area. I turned my will and my life over to the loving care of my Higher Power and I reached out to others for help.

Talking with other women showed me that my problem was not unique. I found someone to be my sex sponsor and I agreed to go to a competent professional for counseling.

The next few months were turbulent and painful. An inventory on my sexuality disclosed many fragmented pieces of the jigsaw puzzle. As each new awareness came, I diligently gave it away. In return I received support from others and freedom within.

I became willing to have God remove all my defects in this area: my fear of men, the waiting for Prince Charming, my tendency to put one man on a pedestal while stomping on the rest, my sexual fantasies and the denial of my body.

Coming to step eight, I knew that the person I had harmed most was myself — with pride, self-pity, lust, greed and harsh condemnation. So with step nine I forgave myself for the past. Today I am free to be the beautiful, whole woman I was meant to be, enjoying for the first time such sensual pleasures as long walks, hot bubble baths, nice clothes and jewelry. I read the women's magazines and self-help books, and each day I look in the mirror and affirm that I am lovable.

Steps ten and eleven sustain me in this new adventure of true sexuality. Every day I surrender to God my attitudes and actions regarding men and I take a careful inventory of myself. I meditate on how whole I am, on how relaxed I can be in the presence of men and on my femininity. The twelfth step comes easily because so many people need guidance in this area.

The results of working the twelve steps on my sexuality have been wonderful, but they are totally different from what I expected. I am experiencing an inner peace and regard for myself that surpass the best romantic relationship I could have imagined. Free of the obsessive fantasy crushes of the past, I am thoroughly enjoying my work, hobbies, women friends and nature. And, yes, I am dating. I am reaching out to men I find attractive and I even encounter reciprocal feelings. Facing reality means acknowledging that there will always be some people who don't care to be close to me; but it also means knowing that others will want to pursue the challenges of intimacy.

I am new to all this and it's wonderfully exciting. I am learning to communicate my feelings, to risk saying No, to be discriminating about my sharing and to reach out for what I want.

January 1982

Past Perfect

WHEN I WOBBLED through the doors of Overeaters Anonymous five years ago I thought that, except for "a little weight problem," my life was perfect. I had a perfect marriage, a perfect child, perfect grades and a father who was beyond perfection — he was God.

I remember going to OA meetings and feeling sorry for the people there who had so many problems: compulsive overeating, marriage difficulties, trouble with their children. *Me* a compulsive overeater? *My* life unmanageable? Never!

Of course, if my life was perfect, how could I have character defects? And how could I see them, much less work on them, if I didn't believe I had them? I could only see black or white, right or wrong, good or bad. There was no in-between, no moderation. Everything I did had to be perfect. I got straight A's in school. When, after much procrastination, I finally cleaned house, it had to pass the white-glove test. At work, where I was a manager, I drove people crazy demanding that they do everything perfectly — which meant my way.

I remember telling myself that I could not work steps six and seven perfectly until I knew the difference between "character defects" and "shortcomings." If I had taken the cotton out of my ears I would have learned that there is no difference; that Bill W., an English major, changed the wording to avoid repetition, not to alter the meaning.

I had a rude awakening one day when I looked at the index of *As Bill Sees It* and saw entries such as guilt, envy, procrastination, rationalization and perfectionism. I was all too familiar with every one of them! God lowered a ton of awareness on me that day. I realized then that I shared the very same character defects I'd heard other OAs talking about at meetings.

Now that I have this awareness I am confronted with a choice: I can work the sixth and seventh steps on my defects or I can be miserable. Not always willing to practice the steps, I sometimes wallow in my defects until I get so miserable that I finally surrender and beg, "Please, God, I'll do anything." God smiles, pats me on the head and says, "Go back to step one."

Many of my shortcomings have been removed, including my perfectionism. My perfect marriage? Well, now I am divorced, and that is OK. My perfect child? He is sixteen years old and not so perfect, which makes for a good relationship. My perfect father? I know now that he is not God. I love him, but this program has taught me that I do not have to like his character defects, and that is OK too. My perfect grades? I still do well in school but I am no longer compulsive about it.

I don't have to be an extremist anymore. Through the twelve steps I am finding moderation in every area of my life: housecleaning, job, school, personal relationships. I don't have to have a perfect food plan or a perfect program, and that feels good. All I have to have is my Higher Power and the twelve-step program.

God has turned my character defects into character assets. From guilt has come serenity; from envy, self-acceptance; from procrastination, willingness; from rationalization, honesty; and from perfectionism, moderation.

Through practicing the steps of OA I have been shown that all I am is an imperfect compulsive overeater. Thank God for the awareness!

February 1982

Step Eleven Is the Key

WHY WAS I even mildly surprised that the compulsion had hold of me again? I had walked away from the light, stepping back into the darkness, letting it engulf me. I had stopped praying for only two days and there I was, unable to fill the hole in my stomach.

At times, after a quick prayer, there would be a glimmer of hope and then the feeling that it was slipping through my fingers. Why couldn't I catch it, hug it to me? I did want it again, didn't I?

"Let go and let God," I remembered hearing in OA.

Let go of what?

"Let go of self-will."

Then who will hold me up? Not my husband; he has to work. Not the group; they have their own lives. Who will hold me up?

"Let go and let God."

That's what I thought I was doing, and look where I was yesterday — back in that cave I used to live in. But I had forgotten the key; the key is prayer. I unplugged the phone, shut my bedroom door, got down on my knees and opened my heart to God. I talked to my Higher Power as to my mother or father. I prayed to be able to pray. "How can I best serve you, not me?" Asking for freedom from that forceful self-will, I prayed for the courage and grace to deal with my fears and for the strength to abstain.

I am no authority on what others need, and I have no answers for anyone else. I can only share what I have learned. In giving God a small part of the twenty-four hours a day I am so graciously given, I keep the channel clear and allow God's will to be active in my life.

I can't make it in this program without daily practice of step eleven. If I want to get well, I pray — each day, on my knees, in a quiet space cleared for that purpose. Only then am I able to let go.

Today I am living in the light again. Today all is well.

March 1982

In Defense of Mom

WHEN I WAS NEW in the program, my group was also new. Consequently, my first attempt at a fourth-step inventory was made without an experienced sponsor to guide me. Guess whose inventory I took. Not mine, but my family's — mostly my mother's. It was a tale of self-pity and woe, lamenting how they had all hurt me, griping especially about the many times my mother had let me down.

A sponsor well-versed in the program would have told me to get off the pity pot and take my own inventory. Instead, people in my fledgling group said, "If your first inventory is causing you too much pain, put it away; you aren't ready yet." This gave me the perfect excuse to back off on step four for another year.

Before I put my inventory away, however, I did accomplish one noteworthy feat. I went home for a weekend and told my mother how much she had hurt me and let me down while I was growing up.

A strange thing happened during the year between my first and second inventories: I started to grow up. I made mistakes, but I learned that it was OK to make them and even better to admit them. I abstained that year, so I was able to look at my relationships sanely; and, not feeling miserable, I had no need for self-pity.

Another interesting thing happened that year. My two children, aged one and three, became a year older, and I learned that mothers get tired, restless, lonely and bored at times. A mother can spend her whole day caring, helping, holding and loving, but she cannot always be there to prevent all hurts. I learned that sometimes a mother has to allow her children to feel pain, that growing pains are part of life.

I was then able to look more clearly at what my mother really did and did not do. She had six children and a husband who was seldom home (and not very helpful when he was). There was never enough money, so she had to sew and garden, as well as manage our home and look after her own mother, who needed help.

I asked myself, "Can I go on resenting this woman for not always meeting my emotional needs? Is it really a mother's job to keep her children perfectly happy for eighteen years?" I decided my thinking had been a little offbeam.

When I took my second inventory I came face to face with my distorted notions. I put my mother at the top of my amends list. Could I ever apologize enough for the biting remarks I made after writing my first inventory? I knew I would have to take steps eight and nine.

Of course, my mother accepted my amends. She had forgiven me the day I said those things, and she responded to my amends with the love only a mother can give.

It occurred to me recently that many of my fellow OAs also give their mothers a bad rap. If I had a nickel for every time we compulsive overeaters blame our mothers for everything from our eating binges to our unhappy love lives, I could retire at the age of thirty-one.

True, we are creatures of habit and we carry on many of our parents' patterns. But as adults we can change.

As a child I was not allowed to play on Saturday mornings until the house was clean from top to bottom. As an adult, if I want to attend our Saturday morning OA meeting I just go, no matter how messy the house is.

As a child, I was permitted a bath only once a week, and that in shallow water. A long hot bath, with the tub filled to the brim, has been a daily ritual since the first day I lived on my own.

I am an adult now. Just as I changed those childhood patterns, so can I choose to change my eating patterns. I am responsible for my food plan and for doing whatever is necessary to live abstinently today.

I cannot honestly say my mother made me overeat. She did her best for me, but I somehow needed more and got it through food. Now, it's up to me to turn that around.

Happy Mother's Day, Mom!

May 1982

The Great American Inventory

THERE SEEMS TO BE an overwhelming desire on the part of many OAs to avoid an inventory, lest we see in black and white what we already know: that we are human beings with human reactions to events, mishaps and situations that shape our lives.

Once the truth is faced — that there will be no lasting recovery without a housecleaning — there sometimes occurs a desire to write the Great American Novel. A novel is a piece of fiction, designed to entertain. The effort the writer must put forth to make an inventory good reading diminishes the energy necessary for self-honesty.

After the inventory is completed, quite a few of us get hung up on the search for the "right" person to hear it. If we start out with the belief that the inventory is for our personal benefit, what happens next can be put into better perspective. It is important to remember that in sharing our innermost selves we are taking step five; no other human being can take us through any of the steps, especially the fifth. This is a passage that must be walked by the individual. A sponsor or other person, no matter how qualified to give advice, serves as ears alone.

Personally, I have a difficult time dealing with ceremony in program. It seems to me the very antithesis of keeping things simple. Setting ablaze the sins of one's past may be symbolic, dramatizing that what's done is done, but it certainly makes it hard to proceed with steps six, seven, eight and nine unless the inventory — which is now ashes — has been photocopied.

Like everything shared in OA, these are my own opinions, arrived at through eight years of experience as both writer and hearer of inventories. I believe that the inventory is the beginning of a new belief system. In putting together that sheet of credits and debits, we experience the joy of seeing where we were, where we are now and where, by the grace of God, we can be.

May 1982

A Second Look at Tradition Three

I T IS SAID that you can leave OA, but OA will never leave you.

I learned how true that is one night while doing the dishes. I hadn't been to a meeting for several months after attending regularly for a year and a half.

Somehow, I got to thinking about tradition three: "The only requirement for OA membership is a desire to stop eating compulsively." I realized that during the time I had been a member, I misinterpreted that statement. I had always thought of it as the desire to lose weight, to be thin.

Now, suddenly, it was obvious to me that tradition three says absolutely nothing about weight. I knew at that moment that I had never really wanted to have the excess food removed. I just wanted to be thin. The whole time I was attending meetings, I only looked forward to the end result and blinded myself to anything that did not provide specific tips on how to lose weight.

Sure, I had lost 60 pounds. But I put most of it back on because I never really met the simple requirement set forth in tradition three: I did not have a desire to stop eating compulsively.

I realize now that sanity can only come from first humbling myself to the fact that I am powerless, and then being willing to turn my life over to a Higher Power.

What a relief to know that I can't even fool myself anymore!

August 1982

How I Quit Stonewalling Step Four

GOD MUST LOVE the challenge of working with hardheads because, so far, H.P. hasn't given up on me.

I spent my first year in Overeaters Anonymous and, before that, three years in Al-Anon stonewalling the suggestion that a written inventory would aid my recovery. During this rebellious period I took mental inventories in all kinds of places — for example, standing over the kitchen sink washing dishes. Then I conveyed them to my sponsor on a share-as-you-go basis. It seemed a fine system. I kept hearing "written" is best, but I clung to my own ideas.

Then I heard a gifted speaker sum up the underlying attitude of people who procrastinate in taking a written inventory: "Fear says I dare not; pride says I need not."

Wrong, my head screamed. Sure, I had defects; but fear wasn't a biggie for me. Maybe a little pride, but certainly not the inventory-blocking kind. I laugh now at the con job involved in this thinking. The deception, of course, affected no one but me.

The "fear and pride" quote haunted me until I finally decided to write a fourth-step inventory and be done with it. Still, excuse after excuse delayed my acting on this half-hearted decision. I thought, "I'll never finish . . . Who'll have time to listen? . . . It'll be too long . . . Where should I start? . . . What's the right way so I don't have to do it twice? . . . Where shall I keep it? . . . What if someone reads it?"

A small, quiet voice inside said, "It doesn't matter how. Just do it."

I took out my notebook and wrote, even though it wasn't what I thought I should write: no past history or list of defects, simply what was causing me anxiety at the moment. The next day I reread what I'd written and began again, this time putting down similar feelings and behaviors from the past. I learned a little about myself that day. I was encouraged and enthused as I glimpsed the benefits of inventory writing.

Quick thinking may be great in its place, but it is a handicap when it comes to in-depth inventory taking. Writing slows down my thought processes and enables me to backtrack over the thoughts I have expressed on paper. This increases my self-awareness far beyond what was possible over the kitchen sink. As I wrote, I could see threads weaving through my life, all connected to certain key defects. These defects were causing me a great deal of pain.

I learned the importance of taking a positive attitude when writing an inventory. It fosters humility to gain an honest understanding of myself — to see both my positive and negative sides and put the whole in perspective with God and the world around me.

Since that first experience, much of my inventory writing has been a God-given accident. Often a letter to an OA friend turns into an inventory. I haven't lost a friend yet. On the contrary, it is through my friends' love and acceptance of me in spite of my "craziness" that I am able to love myself even when I'm feeling squirrelly.

Amazement, gratitude and love overwhelm me when I think about what OA has done for me over the past eight years. Where it all began for me was with the decision to do without the excess food for just one day. It was the best decision I ever made. It wasn't easy at first, but looking and feeling as I did at 220 pounds wasn't easy either.

Today I see so many blessings in my life. I maintain a 90-pound weight loss. Food is no longer an obsession. My relationships with family, friends and co-workers keep improving.

I am so glad I didn't settle for half-measures and become a one- or two-stepper. Instead, I use everything OA offers me to make my life better both inside and out.

September 1982

Confidentiality

IN MY TWO YEARS in Overeaters Anonymous, I have come to believe that one of the least understood — and practiced — aspects of anonymity is that of confidentiality at the interpersonal level. This is quite understandable: anonymity does not come naturally to most humans; it has to be worked at.

The town I live in is rural and underpopulated, and our OA group is small. I frequently run into my fellow OAs "in public" — in the drugstore, at PTA functions, at civic events and social gatherings. Often, the person I encounter is someone I sponsor or with whom I have recently discussed the program. In the presence of other people, I have to control my urge to ask, "How is such and such a problem coming along?" I talk instead about something of interest to everyone.

When I first came to OA there was only one meeting in our town, but later a second group was started. Some people stayed with the original meeting, some attend only the new one, and some of us go to both. From time to time, members who switched to the new meeting ask quite personal questions about those who remained at the old meeting — people who often have entrusted me with their confidences. I am convinced these queries are prompted by loving interest rather than a desire to gossip, but I believe anonymity precludes repeating any personal sharing heard at a meeting or in private conversation. So, though I fully understand the impulse to ask after one another, I explain how I feel and say, "So-and-so would like it if you called and talked to her yourself."

The same principle applies when someone who usually attends our meeting is absent. We are such a small group that every person is vital to the meeting, and you are missed when you're not there. It is natural to ask, "Where is Jane?" but I feel uneasy when someone volunteers an answer. I remember the time I missed a meeting because I was in an embarrassing jam. I had discussed my dilemma with a few people from the meeting, but I certainly would not have wanted the reason for my absence disclosed to the group. However, if members have established the practice of explaining why people are absent, it's hard to avoid doing so when a situation such as mine comes up.

In our little group, a special effort is made to introduce newcomers to everyone. But I'm afraid some members go overboard when, in their eagerness to demonstrate the group's professional and social diversity, they disclose personal information about absent members, forgetting that the only person we are free to divulge anything about is ourselves.

When someone I sponsor has a problem which another member has experienced, I try to get the two of them together. It would be natural to say, "Why don't you call Janet; she had the same problem." But I say, "I know someone more familiar with that than I am. Would you like me to ask her to call you?" Then I call Janet and, if she is willing to share her experience, I give her the other member's name and number. This takes a little extra time, but each person's anonymity remains intact and they are both free to share only as much as they wish.

Anonymity means I don't tell my friends or family if someone they know comes to a meeting; if I call an OA who is not home and someone offers to take a message, I leave my name and number but I don't say I'm from OA; if a member who has moved to another city writes me a letter, I don't share it with the group unless the writer tells me to do so.

Anonymity means all this and more, but between group members and their circle of friends and family, it is very simple: I am free to share only my own experience with you. I am not free to share your experience with anyone, or to share anyone else's experience with you. That is confidentiality, one of anonymity's many treasures.

January 1983

Giving It Away

AFTER THIRTY-TWO years of trying unsuccessfully to curtail my overeating, I had reached that point of "pitiful and incomprehensible demoralization." At my very first OA meeting in May 1969, I saw a glimmer of hope. I asked someone to be my sponsor, and that daily link with an abstaining member provided me with the key to recovery. I learned that abstinence is the most important thing in my life without exception and, with the loving guidance of an abstaining sponsor, I was taught how to abstain. I learned that the power to abstain comes to a powerless overeater through the persistent practice of the twelve steps of recovery. I have been blessed with nearly fourteen years of continuous abstinence and have been maintaining a 115-pound weight loss.

Sponsorship has played a large part in my own recovery. I learned to be a sponsor first by having a sponsor and then by study and discussion of the *Twelve Steps and Twelve Traditions* and "Working with Others" (chapter 7 in the Big Book). The writings of Dr. Bob, co-founder of Alcoholics Anonymous, have also impressed me with the necessity of working with others as an aid to my own recovery. I believe that sponsoring others into this lifesaving way of life is the most satisfying and important work that any of us can do.

When newcomers ask me to sponsor them, I first arrange a definite time for the daily call. I work full time and am away from home most evenings, so I limit my sponsorship to just three people. To begin the discipline of abstinence, I encourage the establishment of — and commitment to — a sound food plan. Usually the menu falls into a comfortable pattern after the first two or three days so that the daily phone calls can deal with the program of recovery.

To prepare for program work, I often ask the newcomer to pick one item from "Just for Today" and focus on it each day. I also suggest that the person call one or two other OAs each day to practice the tool of telephoning. Soon, the sponsoree is ready to start a program of daily reading from the Big Book or the Twelve and Twelve. We talk about

86

what they have read, and I find that these discussions not only clarify the subject matter but motivate newcomers to establish the habit of daily reading on their own.

After the person has three weeks or more of continuous abstinence, we discuss the steps in depth, following the guidelines in the OA pamphlet "A Guide to the 12 Steps for You and Your Sponsor." As we turn to the Third Step Prayer on page 63 of the Big Book, I share that this prayer is a very important part of my life and that it is a great privilege to give it to another. To help sponsorees write a personal inventory, we read and discuss pages 64–71 in the Big Book. I suggest they follow these directions as well as those given in steps four and eight in the Twelve and Twelve.

After our discussion of the first four steps, I encourage sponsorees to take step eleven. I share my own difficulties as well as my successes in the spiritual life, and suggest daily meditation and receptivity to God's will. To help them work through any resistance or difficulty while writing the inventory, I invite them to call me every day.

To me, listening to an inventory is a sacred trust and a privilege. I prefer a face-to-face meeting for hearing a fifth step. It enables me to help the person go on to complete steps six, seven and eight immediately afterward.

The satisfaction of playing a part in the transformation of a person's life through sponsorship in OA is a joy that the rest of the world cannot even imagine. We are especially fitted to be receptacles and channels of God's grace.

March 1983

The Archeologist

I ALWAYS WANTED to be an archeologist. I used to daydream about finding something wonderful, like the seven cities of Troy or King Tut's tomb.

In God's usual, offbeat way, God has fulfilled that dream. I am in the fifth year of my "dig," working in the second level of step four.

The work here is not easy. Something in me insists it doesn't have to be done, that I've found all there is, and isn't three years' work enough?

No, it's not enough. The first level was as far as I was capable of going during that time, which is fine. There were many discoveries to assimilate and learn to use in my life, all of which takes time.

Just as an archeologist returns to the dig when new funds are available, I go back and dig deeper as my inner resources grow and awareness of still unmet needs increases. Archeological digs take years, and so does fourth-step inventory if I want to unearth all the wreckage of my past.

I may shake in fear and my stomach may knot as I write, but it shows I'm hitting paydirt, uncovering shards of resentment, pain, anger, vengefulness and pride buried long ago in my soul. I hold them up to the light, then ask God to help me let them go. As they pass out of my life, I feel at peace with myself, better able to abstain under all circumstances, to serve, sponsor, encourage and reach out. I see a greater capacity for patience, humility, kindness and love. My value to OA and to the people around me increases as I continue to probe the deeper levels of my past.

Underneath it all is something more wonderful, more alive and more priceless than anything I could ever have dug up as an archeologist. It is a temple of God: the unique human being that is me.

July 1983

Big Book Refresher

AFTER MORE THAN nine years in Overeaters Anonymous, I am still amazed at how simple the principles of the program are.

Lately, as a kind of refresher course in recovery, I have been rereading the stories in the Big Book. While there are many similarities as well as differences, a major element of all the stories is the recovering alcoholics' commitment to the twelve-step program as a way of life, not just an interesting topic of discussion.

From the shared experiences of the Big Book, I have gleaned the following pointers:

1. I need to get honest with myself. Do I want to stop overeating? Do I think I can quit on my own? Am I willing to believe in a Higher Power — and to ask this Higher Power for help? I don't need to be one hundred percent willing. If all I can muster is the willingness to be willing, that's a good start.

2. I must make this program my number one priority; without it, I can't maintain abstinence and, if that goes, so do all the other good things in my life. To make program a way of life, it is vital to continue thinking, learning and living recovery. That means going to meetings, reading the literature and working with others.

3. Ours is a twenty-four hour program. Nearly every story stresses the importance of living one day at a time. I spent so much time stuck in the past or dreaming about the future that the now got lost. I need to focus on today — do the best I can, and move on.

4. Inventory is essential. For a long time I looked at the fourth step with fear. It seemed an overwhelming task. But inventory has become vital to me, for it clears up my past and is a springboard to growth and change. Writing inventory is simpler than it appears. I don't have to produce the great American novel, nor do I have to enumerate every wrong I committed from age one. I usually do a daily tenth step and a yearly "housecleaning" in addition to my original fourth step.

5. Giving service helps *me*. Every story stresses service, at whatever

level. Many times I think, "I don't have anything to give"; but the great paradox of service is that, if I reach out to help another, I get back what I thought I didn't have!

If you want to enrich your recovery, pick up the Big Book and read the stories. You may be delightfully surprised.

August 1983

Time To Meditate

MEDITATION has been progressive for me. I started with prayers I had memorized as a child, adding the Serenity Prayer as a protective touchstone against eating compulsively.

After I learned the Third Step Prayer, I began to be more formal. I got up earlier and, closing my eyes, I said the Serenity Prayer, followed by the Third Step Prayer, then just talked to God as I'd talk to another person.

I learned that I could do this at other times, too, such as when I needed to slow myself down, quiet my thoughts or take action when I'm frozen in indecision. Consequently, much of my meditation has taken place at work: at my desk, in the lounge, between filing cabinets — anywhere I could have a little quiet and not be observed. Sometimes I get caught. Most people assume I'm resting my eyes or thinking. One man said, "Now I know what you do under stress. You meditate."

My formal meditation is still in the early morning, after my bath. I read the page for the day from *For Today,* then a passage from the Bible, using a Bible study magazine to which I've recently subscribed. Then I close my eyes and follow my basic routine, described above. Always, I thank God in meditation.

Not long ago, a change at work, totally unexpected, removed a major obstacle to my remaining with the company. After the meeting, I went into the lounge and sent a string of thank-you's off to God. I could feel the words going into the air. That, too, is meditation, as is the tenth step I take each night. Again, I end by thanking God for the day.

If all this sounds as though meditation takes a long time, it doesn't really. It takes me from ten to thirty minutes in the morning, depending on when it feels right to stop. I set no limits. Considering how I act when I don't meditate — angry, confused and obsessed — it's a small price to pay.

There are many ways to meditate, varying considerably in length and formality. But meditation doesn't have to be long or formal. One can begin with a simple prayer or a favorite inspirational quotation. I'm glad I started somewhere and allowed meditation to progress as it did. I'm confident it will continue to grow as I do.

November 1983

The Crossing

I WOKE UP ONE MORNING with the conviction that I, alone among toilers in the twelve-step vineyard, had experienced a reneging on the promises by my Higher Power.

Not all the promises, mind you. Certain freedoms and insights had begun to manifest themselves in my life. One particular promise, however, was beginning to look more and more like a decidedly mixed blessing. It was all wrong, somehow: inside out, upside down, all askew — not at all the way it should be.

I called my sponsor. I would confront him with my discovery and challenge him to deny that I was right.

"Tell me I'm wrong if you can," I said. "Go ahead, tell me I'm *not* unique."

"What are you talking about?" he asked, with a nice tolerance.

"What am I talking about? What am I talking about? Pull out that Big Book of yours. Look at page 83. Look at the last paragraph. Look at what it says."

My sponsor gave a kind of sigh. "I am fully aware of the promises, son, but what are you getting at?"

"You know where it says, 'We will intuitively know how to handle situations which used to baffle us'? Well, quite frankly, I'm being baffled by situations I used to intuitively know how to handle!"

"Give me a for-instance."

"OK. Someone called me the other day and started talking about another OA member. I didn't know what to say, how to handle it. All I could think of was those signs at railroad crossings that say STOP, LOOK and LISTEN.

"I was embarrassed as hell, but I *stopped* the guy from talking. I *looked* at what was happening. I felt rotten about it, but I said, *listen,* I don't feel I have the right to be having this conversation."

"So what's the problem?" my sponsor asked.

"Don't you see? Where before I would have been civil and sociable, I

95

was boorish and hostile. I'm sure that guy hates me now. And I don't blame him. Is that what you call 'intuitively knowing how to handle' things?"

I heard my sponsor chuckle on the other end of the line. "If you read just a little bit further you might find the next sentence will have an answer for your problem," he said. "Goodbye." He hung up.

As I stared at the receiver in my hand, I tried to remember what the next line of the promises was. I couldn't. Hanging up the phone, I walked over to where my copy of the Big Book lay. I opened it, and as my eyes focused on the line I was searching for, I read:

"We will suddenly realize that God is doing for us what we could not do for ourselves."

April 1978

The Feast

THE FIRST BIG feasting holiday of the year arrived just three weeks after I began abstinence. It was Thanksgiving, 1971.

Abstinence had come to me one bright Saturday morning after I had attended my third OA meeting the previous evening. I had gone reluctantly and returned exhausted; certainly, I had no reason to suspect what was about to happen.

On arising, I sat quietly in the sunshine, not wanting breakfast yet. I picked up the OA literature I had brought home three weeks earlier and began to reread it. It sounded good, the tone soothingly low, almost a whisper. Strange, how there was no stridency, no sternness, no moralizing, lecturing, haranguing, coaxing or appealing to my better — or worse — nature to lose weight. In fact, the word "weight" did not appear at all.

I found myself drawn repeatedly to a tiny folder entitled, "Just for Today." It measured, and still does, 2¼ × 4¼ inches. Somehow, the size itself was reassuring.

Inside the folder, several passages kept pulling at me. I read them over and over. Impossible to think that these amiable ruminations had anything to do with weight loss.

"Just for today I will try to live through this day only, and not tackle my whole life problem at once.

"Just for today I will be happy. This assumes to be true what Abraham Lincoln said, that 'Most folks are as happy as they make up their minds to be.'

"Just for today I will be agreeable . . . talk low, act courteously . . . criticize not one bit . . . .

"Just for today I will have a program. I may not follow it exactly, but I will have it. I will save myself from two pests: hurry and indecision.

"Just for today I will be unafraid. Especially I will not be afraid to enjoy what is beautiful and to believe that as I give to the world, so the world will give to me."

I studied the food plan. It, too, looked good: simple, low-key and sweetly reasonable.

At length, I got up from the chair, showered, dressed and drove to the market. I was a stranger in the produce department. Had fruits and vegetables always looked this good? Large bunch of this, the choicest that; I was liberalizing the food list — not to any remembered specifications, but according to some inconceivable plan of idyllic moderation. (Who did you say *could* and *would* if he were sought? The question is asked at this point because I weighed more than 350 pounds and moderation had eluded me through a lifetime of physical selves that ranged from doll-like petite to sideshow fat, and because each step I took up and down the supermarket aisles proclaimed that sometime during the past ten or twelve hours my adversary of twenty-seven years had been struck down.)

It was true. The war was over. Just like that. Suddenly all the rose gardens of the world bloomed. Tobacco smoke drifting through the market became at once and for all time the perfume of freedom. A singing began somewhere deep in my being, and I recognized it as the pure sound of joy.

I walked, talked, ate, slept, worked, rested and went to meetings suffused with this music.

Will it ever leave me?

No, never.

Thanksgiving Day approached. I had been talking almost daily with my sponsor, now friend, discussing Vietnam, the weather, politics, movies, love, friendship, miracles. Yes, mostly we talked about miracles, trying to fathom this magnificence, this abstinence, this cosmic gift.

The subject of my food plan seldom arose; there was no need to discuss it or to call in my food. Since that early November day, abstinence for me is all the goodness and beauty of creation, plus amazing quantities of delicious food. You'd have to be crazy to think of rearranging all that. Happiness — the real thing — is its own discipline.

The day before the holiday, however, I confided to my sponsor a mild

apprehension about allowing this precious — and who knew how fragile —
possession to fly into the teeth of a family feast. I come from a family
of "normals" who, like all good Americans, hold sacred the Thanksgiving
tradition of gratitude through gluttony. And why not? Gluttony is for
those who can handle it.

My sponsor is an exceptional human whose economy with words can
be pure genius. At the OA meeting the evening before I got sober, she
listened quietly as I spewed out my rage on the subject of "Why Can't
I Eat What I Want When I Want It without Paying Such a Price?"
Only slightly abashed, I wound down with, "What is this abstinence,
anyway? I can't figure it out."

My sponsor's two-word answer was spoken so casually she might have
been joking, but there was no trace of humor in her voice. What she
said was,

"Be dumb."

Now, she listened as I expressed concern about Thanksgiving dinner.

"What are you going to eat?"

"Turkey, green beans with mushrooms in butter sauce, salad and fruit."

"OK."

That was it. As routine as,

"Hello, how are you?"

"Fine, and you?"

"Fine, thanks."

And it *was* fine. The finest Thanksgiving I ever had, with music and
dancing and feasting fit for the gods and the fragrance of all the roses
of the universe filling the air.

November 1978

The Hoop Is Wider than It Looks

PROBABLY THE HARDEST THING a fat, bitter, sarcastic, angry and superior newcomer has to put up with in OA is people who talk about God a lot. Every time they pitched, led or spoke at a meeting, this fat, bitter, sarcastic, angry and superior compulsive overeater would turn her head in disgust.

That was three years ago. I had arrived fresh from a breakdown, feeling that my problems were much too severe to be helped by a bunch of amateurs. The only reason I went to meetings at all was because I had no car and my friends promised me a night out. I didn't have to "join," they told me, just sit through the meeting and go out for coffee afterward. It wasn't until much later that I realized they had been twelfth-stepping me.

I sat, bored and hostile, through three weeks of meetings. Then one night a woman spoke on defiance and suddenly I saw that there might be something here for me. The next week I took a sponsor and plunged into abstinence and the steps. By the grace of God, I am still on that first abstinence.

By the grace of God. That is not a phrase I could have written three years ago. I knew, once I started the program, that I had to live the steps if I didn't want to spend the rest of my life in and out of mental hospitals. But *God* — that was a concept I wasn't ready to swallow.

As I did the reflections that took me through the first three steps I came to see, with the help of my sponsor, just how defiant I had been. We still joke about my refusal to say the word, "God," referring to my Higher Power as Sidney. I knew that for me HP had to be more than the group, but I could not bring myself to say the word.

I took the third step backward — but I took it. "The hoop you have to jump through is wider than you think," is the way one old adage puts it. I knew I had no choice but to go on through the rest of the steps. I turned my will and my life over to the care of God as I understood God, by default — because I knew beyond a shadow of a doubt that my way had not worked.

As I grew in the program I found that I needed to worship; that steps three and eleven were an important part of my life, and that I could live them more fully through worshipping within the religion I had been born into and had walked away from. I was already attending services "for my son's sake." Now I began to go for me. I began to really listen to and understand prayers I had memorized years ago. To my delight, I found they were all "program."

I completed my fourth step inventory at the same time that my coreligionists atone for the sins of the past year. Never had that holiday meant so much to me; never before had it been a "holy day."

Through living my OA program and my religion together, I found so much. I decided I needed to observe my Sabbath. It is a day of prayer, meditation, reading of religious and program books. I am working on my sixth step now and leading a fourth step group. But if I don't live my religion and my program with those I love most, then my life is a fraud. So the Sabbath is also a day to play games with and read books to my children; a day to write letters to loved ones who are far away; a day to attend to small amenities for myself; and with regard to my husband, a day for me to remember to live and let live. He didn't marry a religious woman and I have to respect his right to travel his own road.

Living the steps and the slogans frees me from so much that used to tie me down. Weights have been lifted from my shoulders that were never really mine to bear in the first place. But I in my grandiosity had taken them on. In trying to live steps three and twelve, my life has become more active and fulfilling than ever before.

I love the weekdays — they're full and busy, though not hectic. But I need my Sabbath to renew and refresh me. It is the one day when the ties of the material world are loosened; when, in living more spiritually I appreciate more fully the glory of my humanness. The Sabbath is a haven to which I can return each week without feeling I'm copping out. It is a day that makes my life complete: a gift from God I have only learned to accept by first accepting the gift of program.

December 1978

Do You Really Want To Stop?

The time has come, the walrus said, to talk of many things, of shoes and ships —
and sealing wax — of cabbages and kings, and why the sea is boiling hot — and
whether pigs have wings. But wait a bit, the oysters cried, before we have our
chat, for some of us are out of breath and all of us are fat.

Lewis Carroll

IN THE COURSE of several retreats and meetings I attended recently, I
was prompted to reflect on some of the things I've learned during my
eight years in Overeaters Anonymous.

I came here with a self-image I called "being fat." Being, in addition,
self-willed and egotistical, I didn't want to stop overeating; I just wanted
to be thin and I wanted some magic to be sprinkled upon me.

I didn't hear the words from the Big Book of Alcoholics Anonymous.
I thought I was working the program. It's true that I had lost nearly all
my excess weight, but I kept my fat person's attitude toward life. The
feelings I had previously covered up with fat were unchanged.

Instead of looking to the Big Book and to the simplicity of our program,
I searched for answers in various formulas, systems and diets advanced
by people who were themselves groping for a way to live. Like many
OAs before me and a lot who came after, I took the suggestion to "keep
it simple" as an invitation to louse it up.

But the time came when I had to go beyond the diversions and the
diets. I had to get to what the program is about. I had to be *willing* to
recover, and recovery for me means more than just losing my weight.

I remember when I first heard the statement, "Abstinence is the most
important thing in my life without exception." I didn't want to believe
it and I was told that that's the way it is and I better believe it if I was
to abstain from compulsive overeating. There were many definitions of
abstaining from compulsive overeating and the one you adopted depended
on which meeting you attended.

My first problem was I didn't want to stop overeating. I was directed to a story entitled, "Anonymous Number Three," in which Bill W. and Dr. Bob, the co-founders of Alcoholics Anonymous, went to see the man who subsequently founded the first AA meeting. They approached this man in the hospital where he lay dying of alcoholism and asked, "Do you really want to stop drinking?"

That would seem a ludicrous question to ask anybody who was dying of alcoholism, and yet that's the question we have to ask ourselves. Do we really want to stop overeating?

Unlike alcoholics, we cannot abstain totally from food as they can from alcohol. Therefore, I firmly believe that there is no such thing as perfect abstinence. It's been eight years since I have indulged in refined sugars and carbohydrates, and I have not binged. But there were times when I ate too much. I know that my compulsion is there, except when I allow God to remove it.

In one of the stories in the Big Book, a woman says, "The AA members who sponsored me told me in the beginning that I would not only find a way to live without having a drink, but that I would find a way to live without *wanting* a drink."

Well, that is what I want. I not only want to live without compulsively overeating, I want to find a way to live without wanting to overeat. I want my appetite for too much food taken away; and the promise is there — that if I am to be restored to sanity, it will happen.

In another story in the Big Book it says, "God will keep a man sober if he will let Him." Abstinence is God's gift to me, contingent upon my working this daily program of recovery. I have found this to be a spiritual program, not a food or diet program.

Yes, the time has come for us in Overeaters Anonymous to talk of many things: of ordering our priorities; of putting in perspective diets, food sponsors and requirements. It is, above all, time to stress the importance of the statement in Chapter Five of the Big Book: "When the spiritual malady is overcome, we straighten out mentally and physically."

The time has come, my fellow sufferers, to stop suffering and accept the joys of this program and the promises so freely given to us.

December 1978

A Spiritual Life

IN DECEMBER of 1972, when I came into Overeaters Anonymous, I was studying to become a rabbi. Because of my theological training, I believed that I was capable of describing God and God's relationship to us more eloquently than anyone, except for one priest in the area. Luckily, he lived in the next county and I didn't have to compete with him!

While it may be true that I was gifted in my verbal ability to discuss how one may find God, I had no idea how to follow my own directions. I was stuck in quicksand and sinking fast.

In the Book of Exodus, when the children of Israel accepted the law, they said, "We will do and we will hear!" When I came to OA, I was told to utilize, not analyze and to take the cotton out of my ears and put it in my mouth. I was to take one step at a time.

Because those who undertook to guide me were thin and I was fat, and because my misery was so all-encompassing, I recognized my human stupidity and stopped questioning. I accepted and did whatever I was told. "We will do and we will hear" applied to many OA newcomers, myself among them.

I was told that not only would I lose my weight but that there were many fringe benefits to the program. From all the happy abstainers I heard the same thing: there would be great miracles in my life. What I heard at my first few meetings led me to understand that there was unlimited potential for growth and development in the program.

Today, some six years later, I am even more in awe of the program. The twelve steps are not only a blueprint for living life, but by repeated daily practice they enable one to attain a state described by Martin Buber as having one's "feet planted firmly upon the ground, yet his head reaches up to heaven."

During the last few years, I have done some reading on the subject of mysticism, the essence of which is the same in all the great religions. Jewish, Christian, Moslem, Hindu and Buddhist mysticism offer the same basic description of a mystical experience. Usually it takes some major crisis in life to spur us into readiness for such an occurrence.

First, one must be willing to have something spiritual happen to one. Then, one must be willing to turn one's ego over to a Higher Power; to let an influence stronger than one's own guide one's will and life. Next, one must start looking deep within to find one's faults and character defects and be willing to remove or reduce these obstacles which stand in the way of a fulfilling, or spiritual, life. Lastly, one must continue by means of ego surrender and character improvement to search for God and God's will in all areas of one's life.

If this sounds like the twelve steps to you, then you have come to the same conclusion I have: the twelve steps of OA are a plan for a mystical experience, or in less frightening language, a spiritual awakening. I searched all my life, until I came to OA, for an exciting existence, for some way of living that would have meaning. I took unnecessary risks and pursued unsound goals. Had it not been for OA, I might have wound up in a cult that demanded suicide, instead of a program that offers me life.

Today, I am a practicing rabbi, thanks to OA. My theology has been greatly simplified. My Higher Power has knowledge of the right way for me to live. I try each day to align my thinking with this beautiful flow of the universe. That is, I make a decision to turn my will and my life over to the care of God as I understand God. I try to pray only for this knowledge that God wants me to have and the power I am to use.

I was living in hell when I rolled into OA. One step at a time — sometimes missing the step and falling on my face — I "reach toward heaven." I have met many of you, also trudging this road to happy destiny. To any of you who are afraid to begin this program because it seems different from your religion, I can relate both from my experience and from that of priests and ministers who are working the program: The twelve steps will only illuminate the best in your beliefs. We all come to OA with prejudices. Some of these may kill us. Let go! Let God!

To those who have no religion, you don't need one. For you, OA will supply directions for a spiritual life. The promises can — and do — come true for you, too.

When I came in, they told me to be honest, open-minded and willing. If you are having trouble catching on to the program, resign from the debating society. Be willing to stop worshipping and paying homage to food.

Because of all of you in the Fellowship and the twelve steps, I am living the exciting and meaningful existence I dreamed of for so long. It is a journey that can last a lifetime. Granted, it is more difficult to go forward than to fall back, but all the energy is worth it. For with each step, the view is better and the air is fresher, and the brightness that illuminates the path reaches straight into the soul with warmth and sustenance no food could ever give.

April 1979

The Second Miracle

REDISCOVERY of a Higher Power is not an exceptional experience for the wanderer from faith who joins OA.

When my husband decided, much against my will, to move to another state, I was faced with the loss of my friends, my home and a teaching career which had given me the secure feeling that I was doing something with my life both fulfilling and significant. I buried my growing resentment under a ton of food and my concern over my eating under the next ton.

My pleas to a Higher Power to give me control over my eating went unheeded, which only confirmed my suspicion that God had remained behind when we moved. What was left when even faith had gone? More food. That was where I found God again: at the bottom of the barrel.

I can only describe my complete acceptance of OA suggestions — and the accompanying loss of 48 pounds in six months — as a miracle. It is a miracle that I respect and treat every day of my life as a gift which, taken for granted, can be lost at any moment.

Another year and a half of maintenance saw me well along in all the things an OA is expected to do: working the steps, sponsoring, attending several meetings a week and giving service in various capacities. I was a model of dedication to the program. I wrote my fourth-step inventory, gave it away and was satisfactorily making amends.

Yet, a barrier seemed to remain. It was the eleventh step. I *could not,* through prayer and meditation, seek knowledge of God's will. Something had happened to my ability to pray.

As they say, it's the small things that undo us. Whereas back home I had used the simple chore of dishwashing as a period of meditation, an automatic dishwasher now eliminated this task. Absurd as it sounds, I couldn't seem to find a replacement.

I felt I was a paradox, alienated from God and yet a model of OA success. I knew that my abstinence was God's miracle, yet acknowledging my gratitude was as close as I could get to "conscious contact."

Eventually, the barrier I had raised against step eleven began to show.

I started complaining bitterly to my sponsor that I was surrounded by one-steppers who could talk about no part of the program except their slips and struggles with food.

Patiently, my sponsor pointed out that one-steppers were attracted to me because of my success, and this attraction gave me an opportunity to lead them to the rest of the steps.

There it was: the rest of the steps. That was why I saw only one-steppers around me; it was *I* who was one-stepping.

Always, in the past, I had asked God to change me. In fact, I asked God to change everything. But asking seldom resulted in change, so I lost faith that God was even listening. What could I ask for and really count on getting? A thought crossed my mind: Don't ask for changes, ask for answers.

My first prayer, then, was, "How can I pray?"

The answer was immediate and overwhelming. "Pray thanking, not asking."

I wasn't sure I completely understood the answer, only that the answer had come from a source outside my own thinking. I immediately prayed, thanking God for everything I could remember. It was a prayer completely composed of thanks. I remembered my concern for several people I knew who were having problems. Was it all right to pray asking if you were asking for someone else?

Again the answer came back, "Pray thanking, not asking."

I worked the prayer around, trying to find a way to be thankful instead of demanding anything, even for someone else's welfare.

"Thank you, God, for caring about So-and-So. Thank you for letting me see that You are responsible for helping him solve his problems, not I. That his life and his problems are in Your hands is a great relief, for which I am thankful. I know that when he is ready, You will be there."

It is so good just to give back to God what was never mine in the first place! Now, I pray for myself in this fashion. The only thing I ask for is the answer to questions.

I have told OAs who are struggling with abstinence that I never plead for abstinence. It is a gift which has already been freely given to us; to plead for it implies that it is God who is withholding it, when actually, it is only the barrier in ourselves that puts abstinence out of reach. I suggest to those who still struggle against those inner barriers to begin thanking God for the gift of abstinence, even though they may be unable at that moment to accept the gift; it is still there. Many people have told me they were helped by this change in their approach to prayer.

In continuing to pray thanking rather than asking, it was not long before I became so genuinely grateful in my general outlook and attitude that the desire to do God's will was a natural outgrowth of my new prayer life. Step eleven has brought me the second miracle!

June 1979

Staying Spiritually Fit

STAYING SPIRITUALLY FIT is vital to abstinence because without this fitness there is only willpower to rely on. Willpower has failed me again and again, although I have sincerely and earnestly tried. Willpower is not only inadequate, it is counterproductive. It makes me cranky, mean, miserable and bingeful. It has never allowed me to live simply and serenely. Instead, it has kept me on guard duty, policing a violent battle zone.

Today, breaking abstinence and getting it back are no longer issues because my abstinence depends not on willpower but on spiritual fitness.

Weight loss has to take second place in OA because we are not a diet club but a Fellowship bound by certain spiritual principles. Paraphrased from the chapter titled "Working with Others" in the Big Book, the following statement leaves no doubt as to the spiritual aspect of the program: "We simply do not stop eating compulsively so long as we place dependence upon other people ahead of dependence on God." As often as not, "other people" have been ourselves.

For me, spiritual fitness is a condition that allows me to remain abstinent by means of the following actions:

1. Living one day at a time; remaining dependent on a loving, caring, nurturing God; focusing on this dependence and not allowing myself to think ahead. Staying spiritually fit means I cannot concern myself with bills due twelve months from now, or Johnny's ability to meet graduation requirements in the spring. Instead, I must place dependence on God.

2. Reaching out in a responsible manner. "Always to extend the hand and heart of OA to all who share my compulsion; for this, I am responsible." This means sharing the program with someone in need, not worrying about having friends but rather *being* a friend.

3. Keeping a vigil on my emotional life. That is, talking with people who are trying to live the program, becoming more and more honest with them, reporting feelings so that I stay aware of just where I am emotionally. Anger or resentment can creep in quite unobtrusively. Contact with people who are practicing the twelve steps is vital.

The writer of one of the stories in the Big Book notes, "For the only problems I have now are those I create when I reach out in a rash of self-will." To remain abstinent — that is, to give up self-will — I must stay spiritually fit.

December 1979

Higher Power: An Atheist's Concept

I NEARLY RAN from my first OA meeting when God was mentioned. But I was impressed with the things people were saying about themselves.

"I'd better try it," I thought. "Nothing else has worked. Last year I was twenty-five pounds overweight. This year, thirty-five."

My first problem came with step two. I couldn't believe, as others seem to, that God is a kind of super-being who lives in the sky and orchestrates everything on earth.

On the other hand, I had to recognize that I do have a kind of faith in what I think of as the "righting mechanism" in human beings. I believe that people seek health. They may deny it. They may behave like the devil incarnate. But if they can be reached — if someone they can trust is able to drive home a message of love — they would confess their misery and open themselves to change.

I have no scientific support for this belief. It may or may not be true. But I believe it. If this righting mechanism does exist, and if it can be considered a higher power, then I too am God's child.

And that's how I, an atheist, found myself talking about God. I feel I can trust this quality in the same way people talk of trusting God. It makes me feel less insignificant and alone.

I still hesitate when others talk of God. I can't agree with their interpretation. But I certainly plan to hold onto the good feelings that accompany my evolving thoughts.

December 1979

Losing the Need

WHEN I CAME INTO the program and learned that I had to abstain one day at a time, I believed it meant nothing more than short-term willpower. By that I mean having to use my desire to lose weight as a prod to keep from eating *this* minute, *this* meal, *this* day.

I found myself asking, "What is the difference between OA and all the diets I've been on? Didn't they, too, depend on willpower?"

For me, what made dieting so difficult was that I could never look forward to a time when willpower was not going to be needed. I knew that year after year I was going to have to fight to control my eating or lose everything I had worked so hard to accomplish. I lived every day with the fear that I would put all my weight back on plus a few pounds more. This had happened dozens of times.

But I found a big difference in OA, something wonderful and new! I did exactly as I was told. And I got exactly what I expected: clenched-fist abstinence one day at a time. As I absorbed the program and worked the steps, twenty-four hours at a time, I don't know when it happened, but my compulsion to overeat was lifted automatically. It was just as the Big Book had promised, and as of today I know that as long as I keep spiritually fit, I have lost my need for willpower to control my compulsive overeating. What a great feeling! Freedom at last.

I believe this can happen to anyone who will work the full OA program and abstain one day at a time. The fact that the Big Book says it will happen automatically also tells me that I am not able to predict when it will happen for anyone. We can't rush it. We must have faith and believe it will happen in its own time. In other words, we must pay our spiritual dues. Only then are we assured it will come to us.

February 1980

109

A Question of Quality

IF YOU HAVE EVER watched people at a buffet, you have noticed that some put just a little food on their plates, while others pile theirs high. One might label those who put less on their plates the "less-ons" and those who keep adding more, the "more-ons."

It is surprising to realize that this play on words holds great wisdom for us compulsive overeaters. For when we ignore the lessons (less-ons) of life, we often become spiritual and emotional morons (more-ons). Though not deficient in IQ, we cannot figure out how to live.

Severely handicapped in the process of living, many of us find it difficult to admit that we have a disability. Thus the lack of recognition and acceptance of our condition continues to create more problems for us.

As my days of abstinence and working the program accumulate, I am becoming increasingly aware of how low my efficiency level has been all my life. Only now do I realize that I may have spent twenty hours on a project which only required four, and that I rarely got much satisfaction out of what I did, however long it took.

Thus, with comparatively little quality in my life, my only remaining choice seemed to be to try for quantity. You might say that I suffered from the "more syndrome." As my soul seemed to shrink, my body made up for it, and I physically became larger and larger.

The twelve steps offer each of us directions for adding quality to our lives. We may at last begin to learn from the lessons of life, and step out of the constricted world of "more-ons." We must constantly remember, however, that our achievements are but for this twenty-four hours.

There is a great temptation, when we have achieved some good in our lives, to begin to think that we can coast. In learning to be moderate, we often also moderate those areas of our lives in which we should constantly strive to achieve more, such as more spiritual progress and a life that is continually improving in quality.

Being human, we have various ways of categorizing people in OA: how much weight they have lost; how long they have been around; how well they speak; how long they have been abstaining or maintaining. Yet, for me, it is a question today of quality: Do I have what others want?

The best way I know to help fellow members in OA and others who have yet to join us is to live the steps to the best of my ability. How am I living today? Am I a lesson for others or am I a spiritual and emotional moron? Am I willing to change? Do I want quantity or quality?

If I am looking for quality, then I am ready to take those steps. If I am ready to fulfill my potential, then OA is the right place for me. If I want the best that is available for me, I need to look no further than this program of recovery because it contains the specific set of directions for which I have searched all my life.

The decision is up to me — and you.

March 1980

The Changes You Can't See

MY DESIRE to see concrete results, and to see them now, fosters in me a certain resistance to working the program on all three levels. My weight loss was visible to me and others, so I abstained; but many of the program's benefits are not that obvious. These include serenity, self-worth, love, humility, spirituality and countless others.

No one gives us a special pin when we begin to work the steps. No one publishes a notice in the newspaper when we refrain from having a temper tantrum. No one congratulates us when we stave off an emotional binge.

We *feel* the changes in ourselves and know they are far more valuable than the drop in weight measured by the scale or reflected in the mirror. Sometimes we wish they were more apparent to people outside the program who judge our progress by our physical appearance.

But there's so much more!

I work the steps and live this program because I know what my life is like without it. I want it more than anything else. I work for it because

I know at gut level that returning to my old way of life would be slow death.

Emotions and spirituality are not tangible. I must be willing to simply feel the countless benefits I've reaped from OA in addition to my weight loss — qualities that are perhaps not even communicable to others, much less visible.

But *I* know they're there.

Isn't that enough?

May 1980

Who's Weak Willed?

NORMAL PEOPLE think we overeaters are weak willed.

We know better. I, for one, am very strong willed. As a matter of fact, that is my real problem, not the food. It's what I, with my unyielding determination, choose to do with the food that kills me. That's why the program does not work for me until I choose (i.e., am *willing*) to work the program.

Some OAs take the first step and use it as an excuse for continuing to practice their compulsion. But it is not enough to admit that I am driven to compulsive overeating and that it is destroying me physically, mentally and spiritually. That is the necessary first step, of course, but there are eleven more steps after that.

When the fog begins to lift and I see that my path is leading me to the cliff's edge, it's time to change course. But which path to follow? I know all the diets and all about proper nutrition, so why can't I just do it?

Fact number one is that I do not behave rationally around food. I have to admit that I don't know all the answers and that I can't change myself without help. The answers and strength must come from outside myself.

That is step two.

What a blow to the ego that admission can be for some of us! But it is this leveling process that gives me success. I stop playing God.

If I know of a path that can lead me to the good things in life such as physical health, positive thinking and true spiritual serenity and I wisely decide to follow that path, then I have taken step three. This is giving up my old self-destructive "I'll do it my way" attitude and accepting a new and beautiful way of life.

The only spiritual belief I need at this point is that the OA program is an infinitely better one than my own. It is my will again that makes this decision.

My will is at work throughout all of the following steps and my sustained abstinence. I alone choose to either put the food into my body or use the tools and the program. Every day I make these choices. At every meal, through every between-meal temptation, I choose: Revive the old self-destructive ego or follow the OA program.

Weak-willed compulsive overeaters? No way.

July 1980

Perspective on Spiritual Fitness

O H BOY, HAVE I done a number on myself with that phrase, "a fit spiritual condition"! It is intended to be a reassurance, but it can also be used as a bludgeon. I see so many people beating themselves for their lack of serenity, their mishandling of situations or their recurring food obsession.

"I spent the whole afternoon thinking about peanut butter," or "I yelled at my son, putting him down just like in the old days." *Bad person!*

There was a time when I believed that if I had emotional relapses or occasional thoughts about (whisper) food, it meant I wasn't working a good program, I wasn't recovered and I was still a sick individual.

Lately, all this talk about "freedom from food obsession" seems to me to have led to paranoia on the part of some. No one seems to want to admit that compulsive ideas about food cross his or her mind from time to time. Everyone wants to have an "easy" abstinence, a "gift from God." The current line appears to be: If it's hard, I must be doing something wrong; I'm not in spiritually fit condition.

I say Nuts to that. A fit spiritual condition does not mean absolute freedom from stress. Working a good program does not preclude times in which one is not particularly serene. Just because we don't trip through life with balloons tied to our toes every single day of the year doesn't indicate that we are sick.

I have not found total freedom from food obsession. After five years in the program and more than three and a half years of continuous abstinence, there are still difficult days. They are fewer and farther in between, however, and I am confident that I am on the right path.

Am I recovered? I believe I practice and live in the recovery, not the illness. Do I "work a good program"? I think that my willingness to deal with situations as well as I can indicates that I do. Am I a sick person? Not on your life! The disease I have is one that can be — and is — arrested one day at a time. I am physically, emotionally and spiritually healthy, and this includes a human lack of perfection in all three areas.

114

I don't consistently take care of my body the way I'd like to: I don't jog as regularly as I think I should and I don't always eat as carefully as I might. Emotionally, I have occasional self-pity trips — not to mention my perverse grandiosity, which often gets away from me and goes on a rampage. I have far too little spiritual discipline in my life, though I plug away at cultivating it, and it improves steadily.

So what do I do with these imperfections? Use them. It's possible to see food obsession as an effective means of getting my attention — a catalyst that can get me off a plateau — rather than a state to be feared or ashamed of. "Aha, I'm food obsessed; what's going on, what can I look at, what am I covering up that I don't want to face?"

I don't always recoil from compulsive thoughts, but I certainly recoil "as if from a hot flame" from the idea of returning to the illness. This reaction varies. Some days such mental leanings are almost laughable, some days they're repugnant and at times I have no sense of humor about them at all and am overly impressed with both myself and the illness.

Oh, sacrilege! It's not possible to be overimpressed with the illness, is it? Yup, it sure is. It is, after all, just an illness. It has its ways, but the program has its own ways, and in comparing the power of the program with the power of the illness, it becomes obvious that there is no contest. Put an honest, willing person up against the compulsion, turn on the valve which lets that higher power flow through, and the ability to live in the recovery will appear every time. Those who know the program know there is nothing to fear. Proof of the strength available to us is evident at every turn, if we look for it.

Guilt and overanalyzing my own spiritual condition have at times turned off that flow of power. It made me freeze, or panic and run. Yet it wasn't what I did or didn't do that made the difference. A Big Book or meditation schedule perfectly adhered to did not assure me recovery; neither did a faultless food plan. Reading in one of the daily thought books, or writing for ten minutes every morning without fail couldn't promise me anything.

I ran all around the country, from speaker to retreat leader, from sponsor to guru, looking for a way to feel safe. Finally, I had to face reality. Dorothy in *The Wizard of Oz* clicked her heels together three times and went home to her own backyard. I sighed, conceded defeat in my quest and the resultant relaxation let that power move right through me. Thus, I discovered that it had been there all the time.

To me, a fit spiritual condition means being an open channel: "Thy will, not mine, be done, in me and through me." A healthy spirituality is as close as the heartbeat in my throat, or as far away as a guilt trip. Moment to moment, the distance is my personal choice. I measure my progress by my ability to make better and better choices as the years go by.

October 1980

When All Else Fails

FOUR YEARS AGO, when I came into Overeaters Anonymous, I felt as if I were in the middle of an incredibly confusing maze. A number of inviting passageways beckoned, all promising to lead me to the serenity I sought.

I began running down the corridors that looked the most cheerful, opening doors that seemed friendliest. I went from one sunny path to the next, but all I found at the end of each was emptiness, frustration and guilt.

First I tried the door marked "Fat Serenity." I concentrated exclusively on my emotional recovery and completely ignored my need to change physically. Why, I wondered, did the compulsion still haunt me?

Approaching the door labeled "Spiritual Recovery," I opened it a crack and peeked in. Frightened by the silent darkness, overwhelmed with fear of the unknown, I slammed it shut and fled in search of another avenue.

Next I entered the "Rigid Discipline" door. Here all that mattered was the physical. Weight loss was promised and delivered, along with an attractive body and stylish clothes, all enticing me to continue to take this easier, softer way. It worked for a while — as such things do — but I soon began to experience more guilt, more fear, more resentment. The awful compulsion kept growing, gnawing at me, killing me, even though I was thin.

"Is this all there is?" I cried.

Only one door remained — the one opening into darkness, fear, the unknown. I had no choice now. No easier, softer ways were left. I had tried them all.

Afraid, alone, sobbing, I groped my way down that passage, inching ahead on faithless faith.

"God would be here to help me if there were a God," I challenged.

Suddenly the darkness lifted. The sun shone beautifully and peace surrounded me.

"Where have you been?" I asked.

"I've been here all along," came the reply. "You were afraid to look."

The Big Book promises, "When the spiritual malady is overcome, we straighten out mentally and physically." I had finally surrendered, opened the door to spiritual recovery and found peace.

Why did I leave that door until last? Why didn't I believe the Big Book sooner? Why did I try all those easier, softer ways first?

Because I just wasn't desperate enough, I guess. Only when I ventured into the doorway I had most resisted did I find what I had been so frantically seeking everywhere else.

November 1980

Doing God's Will

CAME INTO the program six years ago, an atheist of long standing. This represented no rebellion, no falling away. The values of my family were non-spiritual and all my friends and co-workers were atheists. In our circles, religion and spirituality were considered the property of the ignorant and the mentally unbalanced.

If I was short on spiritual understanding I was long on secular knowledge. Having had extensive training in psychology, group process and the different schools of therapy, I surveyed the OA meetings and decided they were really a form of group therapy. What made them work, I concluded, was the acceptance, the unloading, the chance to practice at relationships in a non-threatening social situation. Told that I could take what I liked and leave the rest, I took the human part of the program and ignored the spiritual — easy enough to do in my group, where there was much emphasis on counting days and calling in food, little emphasis on working the steps.

While I was outwardly a success, I knew that I was a crying mess inside. I was deeply depressed, had many psychosomatic symptoms and could never seem to get anything in my personal life to turn out the way I told it to.

Since I was always longing for someone to listen to my troubles, I loved the part of the program which encouraged me to telephone. I picked a sponsor who was willing for me to call her many times a day, any time of the day or night. ("Insatiability" is still on my inventory!) I leaned on her for everything, and she taught me my first priceless lessons in letting go. For the first time in my life I knew I was not supposed to try to make everything come out my way, to win.

But without realizing it I was using the same tactics in OA which had failed me in every group or relationship in my life: I was trying to get along by appointing someone my protector and becoming absolutely dependent.

After I had been in OA about a year, my sponsor began overeating again and dropped out of the program. I was terrified at losing her because, actually, this woman had been my program.

I took care to select for my next sponsor someone with more time in the program. I was disappointed in her, however, because she was not strict enough. I was still looking for a human being greater than myself who could control my eating. For, while I was continuing to lose weight, my food obsession was still active and I constantly felt shaky. So I got a new sponsor — an oldtimer who was thin, strict and did not know me personally. (I thought this would make me more honest.)

I also began to attend step meetings, simply because they met at a time of the week convenient for me. I bought the book *Twelve Steps and Twelve Traditions* and instantly loved it. I felt it was describing me: "We have not once sought to be one in a family, to be a friend among friends, to be a worker among workers, to be a useful member of society. Always we tried to struggle to the top of the heap, or to hide underneath it."

At my step meeting there were many members who were recent, enthusiastic converts to a particular religion. They talked about it a good deal (I suppose in the honest belief that their religion was synonymous with spirituality) and I felt out of place and discouraged. One day I astonished myself — and them — by bursting into tears and exclaiming, "If this program works only for members of your religion, I'm lost. I need this program but I'll never get your religion!"

My new sponsor, I soon learned, was a member of the same denomination as the folks at the step meeting. However, a wonderful thing happened. When I told her of my desire to work the steps and of my anxiety that I could not otherwise maintain my weight loss, she did not try to sell me her religion. Instead, she sent me a copy of the AA book, *Came To Believe.*

Reading it, I learned the difference between religion and spirituality. I felt a new hope for myself. My mind was closed, however, to all the stories in which God was in any way represented as anthropomorphic, or like a human being. I could only accept God as a life force, a first cause, the great *tao* (or Way) of the universe. I went through *Came To Believe* marking the dozen or so sections which were acceptable to me because they mentioned no concept of God with which I could quibble.

Although I understood the psychology behind a fourth-step inventory and had written one and given it away, I now realized that I had done step four without giving more than lip service to step three: turning over my will. True, I had made considerable progress in letting go certain problems and my life had become simpler and more satisfying in the process. But I was giving up control, in order to become personally and professionally more successful. Now I learned that letting go meant something else entirely. It meant, mysteriously, doing God's will.

A period of heightened confusion and desperate seeking followed. I now accepted the reality of a Higher Power, but I could not make out how this "God of the atom" could manifest its will to me, one human individual with a very rusty receiver. I was willing to do God's will, if only I knew what it was. No angel, however, was whispering good advice in my inner ear.

One Saturday things came to a head. I got myself all worked up about the necessity of knowing God's will for my day. The choice was between staying home and waxing the floor or going down to the farmers' market. Floor or market? Market or floor? What was the right answer? I tortured myself about this till it was almost too late to do either.

Then from someplace came the grace to understand that I was manufacturing my own dilemma. Like the insecure child I had always been, I was seeking reassurance — this time from God — that I was doing "the right thing." No reassurance, and I'd show God. I'd withdraw and do nothing.

That day I learned that my Higher Power lets me decide things like whether to scrub the floor or go to the market. My Higher Power wants me to get on with life, to do *something* — but without banging my head against anything that's already going on in God's world. If I feel frustrated, if I am fighting to make something happen or battling against something that is already in progress, that sense of bucking things — of going against the current — shows me that I have ceased doing God's will. This is so even when the force I am exerting is internal — when I am flogging myself with willpower or self-control.

To cease fighting is to accept what is happening. I do what I see needs doing in my life, starting with the most ordinary things. I put one foot in front of another, take care of business and try to avoid destructive choices. When I stumble, I go on.

Now I have two slogans to help me do God's will: "If you are frustrated, give up" and "If you are exerting self-control, stop." It might seem impossible to get anything done this way. On the contrary, by not wasting energy fighting circumstances or battling with myself I accomplish far more than I ever did.

When I am befuddled by choices or victimized by my own emotions, prayer offers me another way to know God's will. Sometimes when I center down in prayer, God's will actually happens to me. I become more patient, more loving, more calm, more just — or whatever it may be I need. The very act of addressing God reminds me that I am not in charge around here, and this reminder has a way of putting all sorts of problems into their proper perspective.

For a long time I could not pray. Since it seemed clear to me that God was not like a person, it felt dishonest to address God in a personal way. Finally, it came to me that, while God is not like a person, I am a person and I have no way to communicate except as a person. Rocks talk to God in rock-talk, trees in tree-talk. I am a person and I talk in person-talk. Of course, God knows my thoughts all along. My suddenly opening up to God doesn't enhance God's knowledge of me. It enhances my knowledge of God.

I have been maintaining my 25 to 30 pound weight loss for four years. My relatively small weight problem was by no means an accurate indicator of my extreme and crippling compulsivity. Only a slow but total personality change, only a reorganization of my whole personality around spiritual concerns has allowed the degree of healing I have experienced in OA.

My spiritual beliefs have not changed: I have joined no one's church, I have not decided that God is like a person after all.

What has changed is that I have become able to practice my beliefs — to do God's will as I understand it.

January 1981

The Recovery Is Spiritual

HEN I BEGAN attending Overeaters Anonymous meetings almost ten years ago I really didn't want to *do* anything. I wanted to eat as I always ate and still lose weight.

I was told that it wouldn't work that way, however, and what I really had to strive for was a "spiritual recovery."

Being an atheist I found those words abhorrent. I heard them as an injunction to become religious in some way.

As was my usual pattern, I ignored such suggestions and joined what I call the OA "diet clubbers." I lost 75 pounds and kept it off by sheer ego, willpower and self-centeredness. I attended many meetings, spoke at marathons and retreats and thought I was practicing the program.

In reality, however, I was as obsessed with food and keeping my weight down as I ever was, perhaps even more. Food was my God and seemed to doom me to a life of white-knuckled abstinence.

Finally, I couldn't stand it any longer. I had heard about hitting bottom in terms of both overeating and weight gain, but here I was, abstaining and thin and feeling no better and perhaps even worse.

I had run out of excuses for my misery. I could not blame my unhappiness on my fatness anymore. Life was not worth living, and if this was what Overeaters Anonymous offered me, then what was the use?

I kept hearing those words, "spiritual experience." Yet I saw no burning bush, heard no words from anything I could construe as God. I knew only that I was more unhappy than I had ever been. I had come to OA because I thought being thin would make me happy. OA had failed.

When I spoke to my sponsor, he said that OA does not fail if we are *in the program* rather than just talking about how to lose weight. Being in the program, he told me, meant living within the principles of the twelve steps and I could learn how to do that by reading the textbook called *Alcoholics Anonymous.*

For once, I followed directions and eventually came to the chapter titled, "There Is a Solution." What solution were they talking about, I wondered. I thought being fat was my problem, and hadn't that been solved? Then, in the same chapter, I read about "a certain American businessman" who had consulted the great psychiatrist, Carl Jung, for his alcoholism. After a period of treatment, the man believed he had learned so much about the way his mind worked that he was cured. But he was soon drunk again and returned to the doctor, who now told him that he had "the mind of a chronic alcoholic."

For the first time, I began to understand my problem. I realized that the doctor's next words to the alcoholic applied to me: "I have never seen one single case recover, where that state of mind existed to the extent that it does in you."

Dr. Jung had not told the man there was anything wrong with his body. It was his mind, he said, which was that of a chronic alcoholic. I had the answer now to the question of why I was still unhappy though thin, and barely hanging on to abstinence. I was no longer fat, but I had the mind of a chronic compulsive overeater.

Was there, then, a solution?

There was — and is — even for the alcoholic given up as hopeless by Dr. Jung. "This man still lives, and is a free man" says the Big Book. "He can go anywhere on this earth where other free men may go without disaster, provided he remains willing to maintain a certain simple attitude."

What is this simple attitude and how is it attained?

Questioned by his alcoholic patient, Dr. Jung replied that, from time to time, there were occasional recoveries from alcoholism. These were a result of "vital spiritual experiences" which he termed "phenomena." What seemed to take place, according to the pioneering psychotherapist, were "huge emotional displacements and rearrangements. Ideas, emotions and attitudes . . . are suddenly cast to one side and a completely new set of conceptions and motives begin to dominate them."

The alcoholics who banded together to form Alcoholics Anonymous did not wait for such phenomena to occur by accident. They created a twelve-step program containing a set of principles which, when followed, bring about the spiritual experience described by Dr. Jung.

So my salvation would not happen on a physical level, I now realized. What had to change was my state of mind. That had been my problem all along: my thinking — the ideas and feelings that defined my personality.

I did not have to figure out how to go about changing my state of mind, nor did I have to leave it to chance. I had before me a specific program of recovery, and all I needed to do was to begin living it.

What joy it has been to know finally what a spiritual experience is and "how it works"! And it does work for me. Slowly, step by step, God is taking over my life, and my state of mind changes.

The symptom was physical, the illness was emotional, the recovery is spiritual.

February 1981

Slow Growth

"WHY DO I HAVE to go through this again?"

I had been in Overeaters Anonymous for two years and I was sharing my feelings with an OA friend.

"Why does it hurt so much? Why is it taking so long?"

Her response, one I was to hear often, was simple: "Slow growth is good growth."

I did not like to hear that, not then nor in the years to come. I was angry, impatient and questioning. Today, seven years later, I am grateful that I learned the truth of that philosophy. For me, slow growth *is* good growth.

Another statement — "It's time" — also keeps flowing through my new life. Before coming into the program I lived in total dependence on food and on other people. I was desperately unhappy but I didn't know what was wrong. As I sat watching a TV interview of OA members one evening (and eating, of course) I realized that I didn't think of those OAs as weirdos because I knew I had the same disease. And I knew without a doubt that OA was where I belonged.

I came to the Fellowship seeking approval and acceptance. I attended meetings, read, shared and did everything that was suggested except to be totally honest and to abstain. It still wasn't time. First I had to learn to accept myself.

I kept coming back and finally, two years later, I became abstinent. But something was missing. I began losing weight in my body but not in my head. I looked good and my ego knew it. I talked the talk about the steps and my Higher Power to anyone who would listen but deep down I still didn't believe. But it was OK. Slow growth is good growth. At times I compared myself with others and wondered why they were progressing so much faster and why they seemed to have it all together. I was not yet willing to see that I had to accept myself first, to find my own program — what worked for me — and to be honest. It wasn't time. So I kept going to meetings, listening and sharing.

As a newcomer to OA I kept hearing that abstinence comes first. But I no longer believe that I have to wait until I am abstinent before I can work the steps. The steps are my way of life. Without them, all I do is exist. If I hadn't started working the steps I would not have received the gift of abstinence. By the grace of my Higher Power it has been more than four years, one day at a time, since I put the hell of compulsive overeating behind me.

My abstinence today is different, too. Abstinence for me is simply not overeating compulsively and being thankful to my Higher Power for the food I choose to eat. When the obsession returns, as it sometimes does, I know I must turn to my Higher Power for it to be removed. If I allow it, my Higher Power will guide me and will reveal things to me when it is time for me to see them.

Recently my dog died. This much-loved pet was thirteen or fourteen years old so it was time, but the loss still made me sad and I cried and cried. Sharing my feelings with a close OA friend on the telephone, I suddenly remembered that when my grandmother died many years ago I never cried. After coming into the program I had questioned my Higher Power about this. I loved my grandmother dearly. Why hadn't I been able to cry? At the time people said, "Go ahead and cry. It will make you feel better." So I tried to cry. It didn't work. Then they said, "Well, sometimes there is a delayed reaction. Once you come out of shock and feel the loss you will cry." It never happened, and the question remained unanswered for seven years. It wasn't time for me to know.

Then my dog died and I cried — and the answer was revealed to me. It was so simple and so clear: At the time of my grandmother's death I had been shoving my feelings down with food, not allowing myself to feel anything, good or bad.

Whenever I become discouraged with my slow growth I stop and think how grateful I am that I discovered this twelve-step program and that I am growing in my Higher Power's time, not mine. Slow growth is good growth.

March 1981

The Power To Carry It Out

GOING THROUGH my collection of literature recently I came across a pamphlet put out by a local intergroup: "A Food Plan for Recovery." I smiled, remembering what it was like when I came to Overeaters Anonymous in June of 1975.

I accepted that food plan then because I was desperate and it was my last hope. I was told that unless I listened to what my sponsor said and followed that food plan to the letter I would die. I listened and I followed. I "took" the first three steps, was "stepped up" and "graduated" to sponsorhood after only one month in OA. I lost more than 110 pounds in ten months.

The years passed, attitudes changed, meetings came and went, I "took" more steps and was working them. So I thought. Then the boom fell, the roof caved in, my life passed before my eyes. Also, the sugar, the starches and the garbage passed between my lips. On came the pounds: 10, 20, 40, 60. How fast could I gain? I was insane, I was powerless and my life was again unmanageable. It was worse than before. I couldn't stop. I woke up saying "Today is the first day of the rest of my life," got into my car and drove to a stop 'n' shop store where I stocked up for the drive to work. I was powerless and I admitted it as I stuffed my puffy cheeks.

I fought the obsession. I couldn't go on a diet because that was not recovery; it was only a diet. I talked at length with friends and with God. Finally, through prayer and meditation, I knew that only God could make me whole. God told me what to do: Go on a diet and turn your will over. So very simple. I needed to lose weight and I needed to lose my obsession with food.

I had to trust again. I had to give my life over to a Higher Power without reservation. I had to understand that being powerless over my food obsession meant that the power to deal with it had to come from outside myself. That power came from God. God not only gives me the power to diet the weight off, but restores me to sanity.

The key word here is *give*. God *gives* me the power. God won't do it for me; others in the program won't do it for me. Only I can do it for me, with God's help. God does not live my life; I do. From God I receive the strength, the serenity and the way to live it. I have the choice to follow that way or to live my own way.

The OA program is founded upon solid ground. The principles set before us are hard to live by, but if I follow them to the best of my ability they will give me a life of beauty and serenity.

I must be honest with myself, with God and with others, for a lie will surely trip me up and cause me to fall. I must be unselfish, for by giving my gift to others I keep it for myself. I must use the steps to clear my path of emotional impediments (hate, anger, resentment, jealousy, greed), for that is the only way I can continue my progress on "the road to happy destiny."

God has given me another chance: a life of peace and harmony wherein I may eventually recover from my obsession with food.

I do not need a food plan for recovery. I need a food plan to lose weight. For recovery, I need God, the twelve steps and the fellowship of Overeaters Anonymous.

April 1981

What To Do about Powerlessness

WHEN I CAME INTO Overeaters Anonymous I wanted abstinence more than anything, and of course I wanted it right now. I went to meetings those first few months and complained: Why couldn't I achieve abstinence? I must be no good to anyone at all if I couldn't even quit eating compulsively. Why did it work for others and not me? Wasn't I good enough?

An OA friend explained that we are in the process of growing, of finding abstinence, of learning about ourselves. It is unrealistic to expect instant success. Recovery is many-faceted and takes time, lots of time.

I learned that I had to be willing to be willing: willing to be abstinent, willing to admit my powerlessness, willing to hand my compulsions over to my Higher Power. I prayed, "Lord, give me a willing spirit." After doing this daily for a week, I woke up one morning and it was like a light clicking on in my head. I knew that today was the day. Since that day, through the grace of God, I have been abstinent. It was a gift. All I had to do was receive it. God actually took the cravings, the uncontrolled compulsions away.

The next step for me was to realize that the first three steps of the twelve steps are actually tools for me. They are like a technical manual or a how-to instruction guide.

Each day I admit I am powerless over food, my husband, my kids, the past, other people, my feelings, plus anything that is bothering me on any given day. I was even "addicted" to diet soda. One day I realized that I was powerless over it. When I admitted that to God, the compulsion was removed.

I was also compulsive about getting on the scale. When I admitted my powerlessness over that, God took it away.

What an adventure step three is — giving it all to God!

I am so thankful for the things I'm learning because Overeaters Anonymous exists.

August 1981

Two-Thirds of the Mountain

IT'S THE END OF SUMMER vacation and the beginning of what is usually a rewarding time for me, time to explore my needs and avenues of growth. It lasts only about six weeks. Then I become involved in family responsibilities.

I can't let this time pass without sharing something that had profound meaning for me.

My family and I took a much needed vacation at Crater Lake. This is the kind of vacation my husband and I choose to renew ourselves and escape from telephones, doorbells and obligations.

When we arrived, the park was gorgeous — clear, cool and peaceful. We hiked many of the quiet, neatly laid out trails, marveling at the wonder of nature and how each intricate fragment of life is tied to every other in a balance so delicate it convinces us that there is a pattern and plan to all life and that we are a part of that pattern.

After hiking a few of the easier trails, my husband and son wanted to try a challenging mountain trail which offers a panoramic view of the whole park. My husband takes scenic pictures to show his classes, so he was eager to tackle the mountain. My son is eager to try anything, and my daughter was heavily into a romantic novel. So that left Mom, available and with no excuse to stay behind.

My husband assured me that the trail was wide and gradual, so I decided, "Why not?" Just as we started to climb, two beaming faces appeared around the first bend, assuring us that the climb was easy and well worth the effort. Then they added, "We're both asthmatic and we found it easier than we thought!" My husband and son smiled at me hopefully.

After climbing awhile we met another party coming down. This one included an elderly gentleman who told us that the wind eased up farther on and the climb was easy. Another triumphant conqueror of the mountain! My two companions cast encouraging looks in my direction. So on we huffed and puffed.

The trail wound upward, getting steeper and rougher as we climbed.

The altitude made breathing difficult for me, but the scenery was glorious and I became more determined to keep on. It was easy, wasn't it? Hadn't the asthmatic couple and the elderly gentleman guaranteed it? I kept climbing.

Soon it became evident that it was too much for me. The altitude made me feel ill and my lungs ached from the thin, cold air. I went a little farther and then told my husband and son I'd have to wait for them while they finished the climb.

I could feel their disappointment. I had failed them and I had failed myself. They reluctantly found me a comfortable, flat rock and went on.

As I sat there by myself I began to cry. "Why is it that I never seem to make it?" I thought. "I try so hard but I always fall short of my goal."

Maybe that was it: *my goal.* The words rattled around in my mind for a bit, then the utter peace and tranquility of my perch began to penetrate my weariness. The clouds floated effortlessly across a clear blue sky. The rolling hills lay in gray-green velvet mounds for miles and miles. Aside from the slight whisper of a breeze in the pine trees, there was absolute silence. I might as well have been totally alone in the whole world.

As I gazed at the wispy clouds I became transfixed by their frail beauty and movement. Unexpectedly, the words "my goal" popped into my mind again. I envisioned a glass two-thirds full. Suddenly I realized that I fail because I think I fail. I want my glass completely full, no matter how big it is. Instead of being aware of my accomplishments I always focus on the empty third of the glass. I was almost at the top of the mountain, not at the bottom stubbornly refusing to try. I had done my best, given it all the energy and determination I had, and I could be pleased with myself and thankful for what I had achieved.

My sadness faded quickly. By the time my husband and son returned, smiling with satisfaction at their accomplishment, I was smiling too. I had done far more than climb two-thirds of a mountain.

October 1981

Old Patterns

COMMITTING MYSELF to a specific food plan has always been one of the most difficult aspects of the program for me. I am just beginning to see how self-willed I am about food, and how hard it is for me to be honest with myself about what I eat.

To help me give up my will about food an OA friend suggested that I commit myself to a food plan every day. Sticking to my commitment has been quite a challenge because I always seem to end up making substitutions at the last minute. I tell myself it is just a matter of taste or preference. Recently, however, I was struck with the awareness that it is really a matter of self-will. By making last-minute substitutions, I was repeating the same pattern I had followed throughout my lifetime of dieting: I would promise myself a low-calorie meal, then at the last minute I binged instead.

This morning I asked my Higher Power to help me commit myself to a simple plan for lunch. It was quite acceptable to me then, but about an hour before lunch I began to feel dissatisfied with it. To distract myself, I got involved in my work and the time quickly passed.

But as I got up from my desk at lunchtime, the dissatisfaction about my meal plan returned and all the old, familiar feelings about food — anxiety, resentment, deprivation — swarmed in on me. I really wanted to stick to my food plan so I again decided to distract myself, this time by keeping my mind on my work while walking to the cafeteria.

Suddenly an important insight hit me. Trying to use distractions to control my illness was just another of the old patterns I was holding on to. I probably would have "distracted" myself all the way to the cafeteria, then promptly ordered something not on my plan and wondered why it had all gone wrong again.

I immediately directed my thoughts to the Serenity Prayer, and the lessons of the program came flooding back: "We are without defense against the first bite." "Turn it over." "Let go and let God."

I walked up to the counter and ordered the food to which I had committed myself. I knew it would be all right.

And it was.

This simple program has helped me so much and my God has been so gentle and patient with me. I really do have a place to go with my illness — with all my pain and fears and character defects.

October 1981

I Was an Unfat Sugar Freak

NEVER HAD a severe weight problem. Newcomers who ask how much weight I lost seem to lose interest when I reply, "Not much — 10 or 15 pounds at most." I know they relate easily to OAs with big weight losses. All I can do is tell them what my life was like before abstinence became a rule for living.

There were the days when I drove my car to a junk food place, loaded up, then drove around, eating and crying. With one hand on the steering wheel and the other fishing something out of a bag, I was lucky I never had an accident. If driving while intoxicated with food were an offense, I would have been fined countless times.

"I'll never eat that stuff again," I repeatedly promised; but those promises were soon broken.

I had been in and around Overeaters Anonymous for four and a half years and I had left three times. I considered myself a hopeless case. Angry at those who could abstain, I often left meetings and ate myself sick. I'd show them!

Shortly after I dropped out for the third time, I celebrated my birthday. I abstained that day but I was filled with anger and self-pity because I could not eat cake — sanely, that is. The next day I went on a four-day spree of non-stop eating. A sugar freak and junk food addict, I passed up any and all real food. It was tears and Twinkies, sobs and sweets all the way.

After four days I was sick of eating. I also knew I was sick, period. I had neglected my husband, my home and everyone I cared about during that bender. I could not cope with life. With or without food, living was hell.

"I can't go on like this," I admitted in my helplessness. "Life like this isn't worth living."

But I wasn't ready to die. I cried to God to help me stop the insanity. That day my Higher Power used a non-OA friend to help me. We were in a restaurant and I was eating pastry, crying and telling her I couldn't stop eating. She spoke to me and I began to hear and understand, although I can't explain why. I knew then that sugar and God could not both be my Higher Power. Either God was first or God wasn't. There wasn't room at the top for two Gods. To this day I cannot recall my friend's exact words. All I know is I left that restaurant knowing sugar and I had parted company.

Two months later, still sugar-free, I returned to OA. I knew the twelve steps were a design for living I could not afford to pass up. Also, I felt I had to tell my story and give others hope that they too can make it.

How beautiful these past two years have been! Oh, I've had my problems — who doesn't? And some days are crummy. But I have never had the slightest urge to eat sugar. That is a miracle. If someone offered me a truckload of candy bars it wouldn't interest me. I have something that feels much better than any junk food tastes.

December 1981

The Paradox of Powerlessness

I FELT I DIDN'T HAVE any power over life. I couldn't make things happen and I couldn't get people to do what I wanted them to do.

But food I could get right away. I had supreme power over it. I could buy as much as I could carry and eat as much as my stomach could hold. Food was the symbol of all the things I couldn't get. I used it for power and pleasure and it made me fat and ugly and sick.

Now the paradox: the first step. I admit I'm powerless over food.

Yes, I can see that. It has become a compulsion, a physical addiction and a mental game I can't stop. From the beginning I knew I had no power over circumstances, so I set up my food game.

So now what have I got left? I'm powerless. I'm beaten. I surrender.

When I look in the mirror can I honestly say that's all there is?

No. There is a Power greater than myself. It's absolutely available to me. It's mine, it's there — it's God.

If I can accept that Power now and let God love me and give me things and care for me, then . . .

I can accept myself and love me and give me things and care for me and . . .

I can accept you and love you and give you things and care for you.

When I allow this surrender, miraculously I cease starving and start living.

So, operating the old way I was powerless. But in using the Power greater than myself, I'm not.

It is my wonderful secret! I'm loved and loving and free.

February 1982

133

A Love Like No Other

NO AFRICAN SAFARI, no Polar expedition, no flight to outer space is more filled with mystery and wonder than the journey each of us must make in search of our own Higher Power.

I was raised in a devout fundamentalist home. Religious training began before memory. I heard people speak of "our Father in heaven," and I saw the deity to which they referred as a being like my father: mighty, righteous, demanding — and indifferent to me. I was never good enough, bright enough, pretty enough to win my father's notice, so how could I be worthy of God's?

No doubt I was told about God's love, but I never really grasped that picture. Too often I heard of God's wrath and punishment, and when I was told that I should love God, I wondered why.

My feelings toward God didn't change much as I grew older. I joined a church that was more acceptable to me and I made earnest efforts to be "good" so as to escape God's judgment.

When tragedy struck my life, taking from me first a beloved husband and then a child, I was not to be comforted. I felt great anger along with my grief. Existence became so painful I turned to food for relief. It was my drug, my tranquilizer. I was thought to be placid and calm; indeed, I even fooled myself. Truth is, I was sedated with excess food. The result, naturally, was obesity.

Today I am grateful that my illness took this highly visible form because it led me to recovery in Overeaters Anonymous. I found abstinence and weight loss without difficulty, but the steps appalled me. I would have evaded them if I could. Turn my life over to the God I knew? Impossible.

One morning, as I reluctantly did the reading my sponsor recommended, I was startled by a sudden full-blown sentence in my mind: "God loves you." That was the beginning of my recovery.

It was not an easy path. Over the years I had to admit and finally release the old anger at God. I have said that I "fired" God. What I meant was that I could no longer accept a life of fear, not even fear of

God. I had to let go old ideas.

When I was a child I heard a young minister tell of making pastoral calls. At one home, he was talking with a woman when her little boy came in from play, ragged, filthy and runny-nosed. She called him to her and tenderly kissed him. My own children have often come in from their play like that. I hugged them and steered them to soap and water, but I never considered putting them out with the trash. Yet it has taken me all these years to grasp the minister's point: the love of God is like that. God does not wait for me to be perfect or worthy to love me. God loves me *now,* just as I am.

That I might return God's love more fully, I put away the thought of God as "Father." I brought to mind the other parent in my life, the one whose love never failed me from the first moment of my life to the last of hers. Recalling my mother's constant, tender, nurturing love, I realized that God's love has always been there and will always be there — just like hers.

March 1982

An Unknowable God

I WOKE UP ONE MORNING after attending an OA meeting the previous evening and found I had been delivered from twenty-seven years of bondage to my overeating compulsion.

What does an atheist make of such an experience? I don't know about others, but I immediately refrained from looking a gift horse in the mouth. The word "miracle" came unbidden to my mind, but I quickly shut the door on its implications.

For some months, at the same time that I spoke of my freedom from obsession as the greatest — and most inexplicable — gift I had ever received, I took pains to inform my fellow OAs that I was not a believer.

Then, driven by an overpowering gratitude, I tentatively adopted a concept of God as a non-hostile force existing simultaneously in the universe and somewhere deep inside my psyche. I now began referring occasionally to something I called God, but I continued to call myself an atheist, pointing out that the God of my understanding was not like most people's.

As the years passed and I remained thinner, saner and happier than I'd ever been in my pre-OA life, I began to feel uncomfortable with the atheist label. An ever-present awareness of unearned grace had created attitude shifts that would not be denied. I had fallen into the habit of saying "I don't know" and "I'm not sure" about all sorts of cosmic issues without feeling at all threatened.

A little humility is a dangerous thing. One day, speaking at an OA meeting, I was startled by a feeling of embarrassment at the thought of saying I was an atheist. I didn't say it.

That began a noncommittal phase that lasted quite a while. As in "The Lady and the Tiger," I told my story and let people draw their own conclusions. It wasn't that I had come to believe; it was that I no longer had an opinion.

About two years ago I began to feel completely comfortable praying to a God about whom I had no information. The process has not changed. Day in and day out, I thank this God of mine, just as I've done for years. What is different is that I no longer feel strange about not visualizing God. I have no need to know in order to communicate. I accept, without reservation and without wishing it were otherwise, the magnificent reality of an unknowable God.

March 1982

Conscious Contact

ALTHOUGH I HAVE BEEN in OA for sixteen months, maintaining an 85-pound weight loss, I am still a food-obsessed newcomer. So I have begun to seek greater intimacy with my Higher Power.

I first turned my will and my life over to God two years ago, but recently I felt a strong desire to get to know this Higher Power better. I reflected on how I learned in OA to be closer to people: spend time with them, talk with them, listen to them. I decided to do that with God.

I began by consciously placing myself in God's presence for about thirty minutes of "anchor praying" each morning. After my husband leaves for work and before my children awaken, I find a quiet spot where I can see the trees and there I relax, close my eyes, tip my head back and say, "Hi, God; thank you for my life, for my abstinence and for all the gifts you have given me."

Then I repeat the third-step prayer from page 63 of the Big Book of Alcoholics Anonymous, offering myself to God and asking for freedom from self. I ask to be filled with love, praying for serenity, courage and wisdom, and asking God to bless me and the people in my life.

An OA friend passed on a thought the truth of which is apparent to those of us who share at meetings and on a one-to-one basis: "Talking is receiving and listening is giving." As I talk to God I receive attention, love, understanding, strength and peace.

During this prayer and meditation time I also do a tenth step, searching my conscience. "Did I step on anyone's toes yesterday?" If I did, I ask how to make amends. "Did anyone step on mine?" If so, I ask for help to forgive. Last, I pray for knowledge of God's will for me and the ability and willingness to follow it.

Throughout the day I use "arrow prayers," short emergency prayers I direct to my Higher Power whenever I need help.

"OK, God," I say, "this one is all yours." Turning problems over in this way strengthens my confidence in myself as well as my trust in God.

Listening to God, for me, means being quiet and openminded. I have made the mistake of straining to hear God but I found that the effort must be relaxed. God's voice is all around me, all the time. If I listen, I will make the right choices — and those choices will keep me on the path of abstinent living.

It is true, of course, that my Higher Power is always with me. I feel God's presence whether I am jogging, attending meetings, playing with my family, reading or worshipping. But the really intimate times are when all other activities cease. When I am afraid or anxious I find it especially helpful to go off by myself.

Before I came into this program I had only minimal awareness of God. Through OA I have established conscious contact. I believe that, as I continue to pray and meditate, my relationship with God will grow and I will experience the joy and contentment of an even deeper faith.

March 1982

Unconditional Abstinence

JUST AS I DIDN'T NEED a reason to compulsively overeat, I find I don't need a reason to be abstinent. If I am abstinent in order to lose weight, feel good, be healthy or even to attain serenity, the expected results may not come immediately or they may fade from time to time; I become discouraged. For me, conditional abstinence — abstaining for a specific reason or reasons — is at best a short term attempt at control, a half measure.

When I was able to see clearly the unmanageability of my life and the futility of believing I was in control, steps two and three came as blessed relief. At that time I was given the willingness to accept whatever the day brought, to accept any pain or joy my recovery took me through.

When I focused on doing, to the best of my ability, what I saw as God's will for me, and took the focus off whether I felt bad or good, my abstinence was no longer at the mercy of my emotions.

What freedom it is not to feel I have to hold onto those good feelings! I am prepared to let them go at any time. Letting go everything — the desirable along with the undesirable — paradoxically brings a deep inner security that goes beyond my emotional or physical state. It is a "peace the world can neither give nor take away."

April 1982

The Criminal and the Princess

S I GREW in the program I discovered I was wrong about not having any character defects. In fact, they far outnumbered the physical defect of 65 excess pounds I carried when I arrived. So I wrote the inventory I didn't think I needed to write and shared it with another person.

That brought me to step six: "Were entirely ready to have God remove all these defects of character." How do I know when I'm ready, I wondered, and what do I do to get ready? I found two answers: "act as if" and "practice makes perfect." The ancient Chinese tale of the criminal and the princess applies here.

Once upon a time there was a princess in search of a husband. She wished to marry the man with the most beautiful face, one that radiated honesty, generosity, kindness, patience and gentleness.

Hearing of the royal quest, a criminal with an ugly face that reflected cruelty, dishonesty and hatred schemed to deceive the princess into marrying him. He commissioned an artist to make him a most wonderful mask and, wearing it, he appeared before the princess. Putting on an amazing performance, he managed to fool her completely. She made up her mind to marry him. The engagement was announced and the wedding date set for one year hence.

For a whole year the criminal had to wear his mask and play the part of the princess' betrothed. At first it was most uncomfortable for him to act kind and generous, and to be honest, patient and gentle. But little by little he began to behave in this manner out of habit.

As the wedding date drew near, the criminal realized his deceit would soon be discovered. He decided to be honest with the princess and told her the whole story. Angry, she banished him from the palace.

"But first," she said, "remove your mask so I can see your face."

He knelt humbly before her and removed the beautiful mask. The princess was astonished.

"Why did you go to all that trouble to have a mask made exactly like your own face?" she asked. The criminal had become the kindly man he had practiced being.

In the same manner, my character defects are slowly being removed. I was dishonest, so I practiced telling the truth and I became an honest person. I was fearful, so I practiced putting my trust and faith in God, and my fear was removed. I was gluttonous, so I practiced putting down the food, and abstinence became a way of life.

The more I "act as if," the more I am changing from within to truly become the kind of person I'm practicing being.

July 1982

On Giving Thanks

"I N EVERYTHING give thanks," my father was fond of quoting, but I considered that absurd, impractical and impossible. How could I give thanks for everything when there was so much for which I was not thankful?

Then I came to OA, and here too I kept hearing about the benefits of an attitude of gratitude. I scoffed and went on grumbling. I even coined the decidedly un-OA slogan, "Bitch when you pitch."

One time I followed my sponsor's suggestion that I make a gratitude list. I was amazed at how much better I felt; then I promptly forgot about it. Wallowing is so much easier.

Over the years, bits and pieces of evidence pointing to the therapeutic effect of gratitude filtered through my thick screen of nonthankfulness. Sometimes I was so filled with awe at the changes in my life that I wanted to do cartwheels to express my thanks. I became more receptive to being grateful.

At a meeting one Thanksgiving, a problem-ridden woman gave thanks for the bare basics: her ten toes, her arms and legs, stuff like that. Hmmm, if I looked at it that way, there was plenty for which I was thankful.

When I recounted my sorrows at another meeting, the leader suggested I make a list of difficulties I'm grateful I *don't* have. I did, and that too changed my perspective dramatically.

Then I heard a story that hit home. Two sisters in a concentration camp kept their spirits up by following the suggestion, "In everything give thanks." That became extremely hard to do at times. Once, a swarm of insects invaded their living quarters and remained there for weeks. It was all they could do to mumble, "Thank you for these insects." Later they learned that a guard who harrassed other prisoners left them alone because he didn't want to contend with the bugs.

Diehard ingrate that I am, I often forget to be thankful for the things I'm glad are in my life, much less for those I resent. Far too often I weep and wail about a problem, and when it gets beautifully resolved, I start beating my breast about the next dilemma without muttering so much as a quick thanks.

When I do remember to give thanks for everything, the transformation is amazing. Saying thank you for gifts I truly appreciate keeps me conscious of all the joy and loveliness with which I've been blessed, and which I frequently take for granted. Saying thank you, however reluctantly, for things I consider a nuisance helps me to see them differently. When I'm lonely, making myself say "Thank you that I am alone" reminds me of the pleasures of solitude. When my car broke down and my trip got canceled, saying thank you gave me the feeling that I was being protected from a greater danger.

When I can't get any purpose out of seeming negatives, it is still possible to find something for which to give thanks. I can't be grateful that my car broke down? Thank you that it happened near a service station, that they can get the parts and that I have a credit card. Impossible to say thank you that a romance ended? Thank you that I loved, and that I had so many good feelings and experiences.

If there's anything for which I can shout a one-hundred percent honest thank you, it's looking back at what I was like before I came to OA eight years ago. The changes brought about by all these years of abstaining and working the program as well as I can are so astonishing that it's sometimes hard for me to believe I am the same person.

Thank you that I am a compulsive overeater. All the creativity and blessings in my life come from that.

November 1982

The Gift of Life

LAST YEAR I celebrated my first OA Christmas, the best one of my entire life. For the first time I actually forgot that I would be getting presents, so engrossed was I in preparing for the holiday.

My childhood Christmases were filled with painful experiences that I relived year after year. Last Christmas was the first one I have ever experienced without getting depressed. It was truly a joyous holiday, and an abstinent one.

The Christmas before last had seen me do my usual holiday "thing," gaining yet another ten pounds. I felt more miserable than ever. Each year brought larger belts, larger pants, larger neck sizes — and less self-confidence, less self-respect, less hope for the future, less joy in living.

My doctor had told me I was a borderline diabetic and had heart trouble, a revelation that sent me home awash in self-pity. "It's not fair!" I raged. "I'm only thirty-one years old!"

Ordered to follow a new diet, I tried, failed, tried again, failed again — and on went the cycle, always ending with failure. That year I hit an alltime high of self-contempt. As I lost the weight battle, I noticed I was getting along with fewer and fewer people. I turned everyone away, even severing relations with my parents. I hated them for being themselves and I hated myself for being myself. I couldn't lose weight to save my health, much less my life.

January arrived and my wife, who is also a compulsive overeater, discovered Overeaters Anonymous and began attending a local meeting. I was an agnostic and a skeptic who greeted anything new or offbeat with sarcasm. When my wife came home and shared her OA experiences, however, I listened with uncharacteristic openmindedness. I don't know why or how, but I sensed something different here, something spiritual being shot to me like a bolt of lightning.

In February I reached a turning point. After binging one day, I woke up the next morning with severe heartburn, a terrible headache and an

143

uncomfortably full stomach. As I lay in bed, my thoughts turned to OA and I felt a warm presence, a sense of something serene.

For the first time since I was a child, I prayed. I asked God to please help me live, to help me find the strength to try an OA meeting.

"I've sunk to the bottom," I admitted. "I'd like to give life another try. Please help me."

I had been sure I was rapidly approaching a premature death, but at that moment something changed — and nothing has been the same since then. I felt a warm rush of confidence, courage and serenity which has never left me.

The next day I began following a food plan and three days later I attended my first OA meeting. To my wife's great surprise, I was neither disgusted nor turned off. I so wanted what those OAs had that I was willing to keep coming back. I have been going back ever since. By Christmas I had lost 92 pounds and had been maintaining my goal weight for five months.

My doctor is amazed at my success. I, too, appreciate the weight loss; but I love the emotional and spiritual life OA has given me. I am a free man today. I love life and all its opportunities. I not only love myself now, I even like myself. I am not afraid to fail today and therefore I am able to risk.

I look forward to another wonderful Christmas of abstinence and sobriety. As I celebrate the gift of OA life, I pray that God will grant that gift to compulsive overeaters everywhere.

December 1982

Benevolent Omnipotence

NTIL I WAS ALMOST in my teens, I was not absolutely sure Santa Claus wasn't real. You might say I believed in the *possibility* of Santa Claus. Then, at twelve, I made up for my gullibility: I cut both Santa and God out of my life forever.

Through all those years of childhood storms, I had been greatly comforted to think there was benevolent omnipotence in the world. I loved the story of my grandmother's actually seeing and talking with Santa Claus one Christmas Eve when he came to our house to deliver presents. She told me that story when I was four or five, after I'd heard some older kids say there was no Santa Claus.

As for God, Grandmother's God was a kind and loving deity who answered prayers if you asked for nothing but good things to happen to everybody. Every night for five years I prayed for my parents to be happy. It never happened. So, rather than believe there was a God who refused to do good works, I became an atheist.

It was both scary and exciting, but by then I was well into using food to cushion my feelings. Like my younger sisters, I had been a thin child. Then, when I was around nine, the skinny arms and bony knees began to be submerged in dimpled "baby fat." Soon, big sister was nearly as wide as the other two combined.

My sisters remained thin. I got fatter — and fatter. By the time Overeaters Anonymous found me, many years later, I weighed more than 350 pounds. I'd had a long career as a dieter. It was all in a year's work for me to lose 100 pounds or more, reach goal, then turn right around and put it back on.

One time I went to a famous diet doctor who weighed me and took an EKG. I weighed 220 pounds (at 5'2") and had an enlarged heart. When he told me about my heart, the doctor looked at me accusingly and said, "An enlarged heart *never* goes back to normal."

If my heart was overworked then, imagine what it must have been five years later, with well over 100 additional pounds to sustain. That was the gutter OA plucked me out of. No longer able even to think about dieting, I had at last given in to my disease, fully expecting it to kill me. And it almost did. I had two terrifying bouts of bronchitis that final year of three chins and several layers of chest blubber.

Then, a few short weeks before Christmas, I became abstinent, sober and free in OA. I lost weight so fast (on well-balanced moderate meals) that by the following December I was within sight of goal weight.

At that point, I learned of the sudden death by heart attack of an acquaintance exactly my age. I had never felt better in my life, but I kept thinking of that EKG and what torture I'd put my heart through since then. I went in for a checkup, complete with a battery of lab tests. When I saw the doctor for a final report, she handed me a sheaf of papers with the test results.

I was stunned. "These can't be mine," I said. The doctor assured me they were.

Everything was perfect. Blood pressure, cholesterol, sugar — everything — was in the "low normal" range. From sky-high five years before.

I looked at the EKG report. Below the peaks and valleys of the graph were the words: Heart, normal. That, I could not believe. The doctor had to show me. "Look. Here's what normal is. It's normal. *Your heart is normal.*"

It really was. And is.

This will be my twelfth Christmas in Overeaters Anonymous. Whatever has been taking care of me all these years — call it benevolent omnipotence, Higher Power, God or Santa Claus — is still here for me today, as real and dependable as the day it came back to me.

December 1982

Survivor

IT SURPRISED ME, this instinct for survival. I surrendered. I gave up. Complete abandon took hold of me.

God help me, I said to myself, I'm going to do this thing. I'll do anything to get out of this hell. Give me those twelve steps. I'll swallow my pride: I *am* powerless over food. I don't like people; I resent my parents; I feel sorry for myself; I hate life, work and society; I hate God; I hate myself; I am afraid of everything; I am dominating and controlling. I accept all this about myself without judgment, even though I don't like it.

I was willing to own up to every one of these truths because I knew in my bones that not to admit them would lead me back to food, and to eat was to die. Better to accept. Better to work with other compulsive overeaters. Better to come to terms with whatever God there might be.

I came back to OA. I crawled in out of defeat; I walked the walk out of desperation.

I was given a choice: check in or check out. I took the first step and discovered, in the words of St. Francis of Assisi, that only in dying are we born.

January 1983

Atheists in OA

WE OFTEN READ that many who come into Overeaters Anonymous are atheists or agnostics. A question these newcomers ask is: Are there any recovering members who have remained nonbelievers or whose Higher Power is not God?

The answer is Yes; there are many atheists and agnostics who are recovering in OA. I am one of them, and I find others at meetings.

Overeaters Anonymous has helped change my life. I no longer eat from morning to evening and cry continually. While it has been grand to lose more than 100 pounds, I awake most days glad I am alive, and that is the program's main benefit. This is in marked contrast to my life as a person who felt unable to cope with life and stuffed garbage in her mouth rather than talk about what was eating her.

I was sent to OA by a psychiatrist. I was depressed, having been told that the severe uterine precancer I had developed was caused by morbid obesity. I felt at home in OA immediately. Here were people who openly discussed the pain of being fat. I had been obese for twenty-seven of my thirty-three years, and all that time I felt alone because I never heard anyone express anything like what I was feeling and thinking. At OA meetings I hear someone do this each week.

When I complained to the psychiatrist about the "religious" nature of the program he said, "I don't want to hear what you didn't like; what did you gain from attending the meeting?" I named many things, and still can. Thus, I have come back week after week for three and a half years because I always learn something that helps me deal with my psychogenic obesity and with my life.

Spirituality, as a concept, troubles me less when I am working on myself and not others. I try not to be confused when people mistake it for Western religion, which I sometimes see as a negative force. Having been required to study the Old and New Testaments at a religious college, I am well aware that the Bible can be seen from a historical and political perspective. I study it because I was raised and programmed on its patriarchal approach and because it affects us in even the most secular aspects of society. It also has some useful ideas. Again, the object, for me, is to "take what I need and leave the rest."

The concept of acceptance is useful to me. I can accept the idea that I cannot control many aspects of my life and that I will live in great stress if I do not determine what I can do and learn not to worry about uncertainty. On a good day, I find it exciting to live in a world of probability and chance; it makes life interesting. I seem better able to deal with life when I am working the steps because they lead me in a positive direction. They are, after all, for everyone who wants them, and I want them.

If I am being honest, I cannot pretend to believe — and rigorous honesty is needed to confront compulsivity. The program requires only a belief that something exists outside oneself which can restore one to sanity, and I have decided to let several outside forces help me find a healthier way to live. I realize I am not the most important thing in the universe, and I believe that if I want to have my rights respected, I must respect those of others.

OA can help because the program contains important countermeasures for dealing with compulsion. It espouses a nourishing, balanced, thoughtful lifestyle.

If you want what OA has for you, keep coming back. Many atheists and agnostics are working the program and seeking the answers within themselves. If you voice your beliefs, you may find others who need to hear what you have to say. I did.

April 1983

Lost in the Woods

IF YOU WANT TO FEEL humble and realize what a small dot you are in the universe, do what I did: get lost in the woods at night.

At first I was mad at myself as well as at my son and husband. I just knew they were in the house all cozy watching television. They were supposed to be worried about me; hadn't they noticed it was dark and I was still out? They should have known that I was dumb enough to go off the road and into the woods on my way home, at dusk.

During the next few hours I felt foolish, anxious, resigned, grateful and relieved.

I was elated when I finally worked my way out of the forest into an open field which I thought I recognized as one near my house. Silly me, I thought, I've been walking in circles for hours. Imagine my dismay when I realized I had never seen that field before in my life. I stood there looking up at the stars, thinking, "Nobody knows where I am. *I* don't even know where I am. But God does."

I tried to find a way out of the field; there were signs that a tractor had been there to cut hay. But I couldn't find a path. And I certainly did not want to go back into the forest again.

I heard a dog bark in the distance and I thought if I could hear that, maybe somebody would hear me if I yelled. The fact that I was wearing shorts and it was about 55 degrees helped me decide to yell. So I gave in and called for somebody — anybody — to help me. I yelled "Help" for about fifteen minutes until people came looking for me with a search-light.

There are some obvious but nonetheless impressive parallels between the experience of being found after getting lost in the woods and deliverance in Overeaters Anonymous. I don't ever want to go back into the dark forest of compulsive overeating. But I can't stay in the open field of abstinence alone. I need to give in and yell for help.

June 1983

A Secret Place

I'D LIKE TO TELL YOU about a secret place where I go every morning, and sometimes in the evening.

It is beautiful in my secret place. Birds twitter in the trees, and everything is shady and cool. A small river runs clear in the bright sunshine. The weather is always perfect, and an atmosphere of calm prevails.

What do I do here? I sit and listen to God and concentrate on knowing God better. I ask about situations in my life and how to handle them. Though the answers often come later — through literature, sponsors and other channels — this quiet time opens me up so I will hear the answer when the time is right. Sometimes God and I sit under a tree, and sometimes we float lazily down the river; but always, God is there.

Sometimes it is difficult to sit still and empty my mind of all thoughts, but I know if I just make the effort, I will be rewarded. I am trying to know God better — what God wants of me, what God is like.

Then I leave and venture out into the world. Because I had that time with my Higher Power, I am able to cope with life much better. I am less inclined to anger or emotional upset and I tend to stay in an attitude of gratitude and acceptance. I am also able to listen to others better and to say constructive things to them.

One of the greatest rewards of my meditation time is awareness of my craziness before it gets too crazy. With ten minutes in my secret place, I can be restored to the peace and quiet of sanity.

Won't you find a secret place to be with your Higher Power? Though it takes a few minutes more than merely saying, "Help me not to eat compulsively today," it is worth it. The other hours in the day are more productive and serene. I find myself as I get to know God.

Best of all, by going to my quiet place every morning I achieve comfortable abstinence, for God's spirit fills that void in me that I used to try to fill with food.

July 1983

Unlocking the Manacles

WHEN I SAID the third-step prayer this morning, the words, "Take away my difficulties," made me realize that one of my greatest difficulties has indeed been taken away.

I have had a long-standing resentment toward an aunt of mine. The bad feelings went back twenty years, and I tried a variety of therapies in an effort to get at them. Some attacked the problem directly, others obliquely. Among the suggestions I tried was to imagine putting my aunt in a chair and having a conversation with her. Nothing helped; the resentment persisted.

It was so intense that when my uncle died a year and a half ago, I didn't attend the funeral. Living only twenty miles apart, my aunt and I saw each other from time to time at family gatherings; but I always avoided her, and I never spoke.

Last November, just three months old in Overeaters Anonymous, I learned I would be seeing my aunt at a holiday dinner. I asked my sponsor for help. She suggested I read the Big Book story, "Freedom from Bondage," and do what that AA did. I wanted desperately to be free of my resentment because it kept me in emotional turmoil and was driving me toward relapse. So I did what was suggested: I prayed for the person I resented, asking God to give her health, prosperity, happiness and all the other good things I want for myself.

At the dinner gathering, I was able to sit across from my aunt and be civil — but just barely.

Three months ago, when it was time to take the eighth step, I listed my aunt as someone I had harmed and to whom I was willing to make amends. I knew in my gut I had to do this if I wanted to recover.

I wrote to my aunt, apologizing for any pain I had caused her. A couple of days later, she called and asked me to have lunch with her. We set a date, but on the appointed day I woke up with laryngitis and couldn't talk. I cancelled our date and made a new one three weeks hence. That day I had such a sore throat I could swallow only with great pain.

What resistance! But I went anyway. Though I felt nervous and awkward, I accepted these feelings, reminding myself that, under the circumstances, they were natural.

That was two weeks ago. Yesterday, I attended a golden anniversary party, and my aunt was there. I walked into the hotel reception room and gave her a big hug, then hugged all my other aunts and uncles and cousins. I felt fine, and I continued to feel relaxed and happy all during the dinner party and the festivities that followed.

The resentment has been taken away. Through the twelve-step program and the many good companions who walk this spiritual path, my Higher Power has given me freedom from bondage and a new peace of mind. I am truly experiencing victory over a difficulty.

August 1983

Higher Power vs. Food Power

NEXT TIME you feel tempted to take that first compulsive bite, remember: food power lasts only briefly, but Higher Power endures.

If you feel the urge to eat because you're tired or bored or in need of comfort, turning to food instead of to your Higher Power is like lighting a match in a dark room instead of putting on an electric light, which has power continually flowing into it. If you turn to food, you will have to keep going back, just as you would need to light one match after another. But if you turn to your Higher Power, your heart will be continually comforted with God's peace, and the empty feeling will be filled.

When your troubles are burning out your spirit, turning to food instead of to your Higher Power is like trying to put out a fire with a small pail of water instead of using a hose with a constant flow. If you ask and are willing to accept God's will instead of your own, you will be given peace. We have only a limited concept of what we need; God is not limited. So give yourself over, commit yourself to your Higher Power's loving care.

Compulsive overeating will keep you in a cocoon. If you want to feel as free as a beautiful butterfly, turn your life over to God, and your spirit will fly.

September 1983

A Fishing Companion

AS A COLLEGE graduate who majored in the sciences, raised by parents with a similar background, I did not believe in any sort of God. The only thing resembling a higher power in my life was food.

One time, a group of college friends, impressed by a popular book which had been made into an even more popular movie, tried to exorcise my compulsion to overeat. They were convinced I was possessed by a demon, they told me — a demon of gluttony. Small wonder: I was approaching my top weight of 400 pounds.

My friends' efforts to cast out my insatiable demon didn't work, of course; but they were partly right, for I did have a spiritual malady.

At a recent retreat I attended, it was pointed out that step eleven says we seek to *improve,* rather than establish, conscious contact with God. We had contact all along; we just need to cultivate it.

A great enlightenment for me was the awareness that true recovery is spiritual recovery — and the twelve-step program is a spiritual program. A religious program would tell me what to believe, how to act, maybe even how to dress, eat and spend money. The steps do none of this.

Step eleven says that we try to improve our conscious contact with God *as we understand God* — that I can hire my own God. So I did. I hired a God I could relate to — a friendly old fellow who likes to go fishing with me, enjoys my simple life, is a good listener and gives good, orderly directions.

The program tells me that God will do for me what I can't do for myself; and, conversely, if I *can* do it, God won't. Recently, I had an opportunity to test this principle. Due to circumstances not of my own making, I wound up in a gourmet food store after hours with no one there except me — and, of course, God. It was not I who was able to leave without taking any food or drink.

That night, my trusty old fishing companion carried me.

October 1983

The Most Important Thing

HEN I CAME to Overeaters Anonymous thirteen years ago, I thought the reason I was there was that I was fat and didn't want to be fat. OA is like AA, I was told, but that didn't enlighten me much. I was not an alcoholic and all I knew about AA was what I had once seen in a movie. I thought if you felt like eating you called someone up and that person talked you out of it.

The saying most often heard in OA at that time was, "Abstinence is the most important thing in my life without exception." As I lost weight, I repeated it every time I shared. I never asked what people meant by it, though most OAs used the term "abstinence" interchangeably with "food plan."

As the years passed, I began to look at this statement through the eyes of experience. Was abstinence — call it a food plan, a diet or a disciplined way of eating — more important than my children, my relationships, my God? (I found God eventually.) I heard people say, "Without abstinence, I am nothing." Was I nothing without abstinence? Was my value as a human being determined by whether I ate in a certain way?

Eventually, I began to change my thinking. I heard a speaker from AA say that if you come to AA to stop drinking you're better off going to an alcohol rehab center, but if you come to learn how to live without alcohol, you're in the right place. I had come here to learn to live without eating compulsively, not to learn how to eat a certain way.

After much prayer, meditation and confidence in my relationship with God, I concluded that abstinence is important, if abstinence is a sane way of eating; but it must be kept in perspective. It is not the most important thing in my life without exception. My relationship with God is. I do not equate abstinence with sobriety. Sobriety for the alcoholic is more than just not drinking; it is a state of mind brought about by communication with God. I did not need to achieve abstinence before I could have a relationship with God, because the relationship was always there. God had not abandoned me because I didn't eat a certain way; I had abandoned

156

God.

I have different priorities now. My continuing growth through the twelve steps is of primary importance. Through those steps I "react sanely and normally," and sane and normal people are not obsessive about how they handle problems. My life is more important than what I eat. My wellbeing is dependent on how I relate to God and those about me. Growth takes time. I have come to see that the pursuit of abstinence is a way to set myself up for failure, and I have done that all my life. I don't believe perfect "back-to-back" abstinence is ever going to be permanently attainable. Nor should it be pursued as *the* goal of OAs.

The twelfth step promises us only that we will have a spiritual awakening as a result of the steps. A spiritual awakening is just that — an awakening — not instant maturity or instant wisdom.

Of course, I want to eat sanely. If that means not eating certain foods, then, with God's help, I won't eat them. But not eating them is not the most important thing in my life, nor should it be. To live a sane and normal life means to live with some successes and sometimes with failure. But success or failure at eating a certain way is not a criterion for sanity. On the contrary, it seems to me that obsessiveness with abstinence is as far removed from sanity as obsessiveness with overeating.

God is, and always has been, the most important thing in my life without exception. I didn't know that before.

November 1983

The Healing Process

'VE BEEN AROUND OA for more than three years, abstaining for about fifteen months. During the past few weeks I've been having trouble with a particular food I normally eat. I tried ruling it out, then reintroduced it, only to find myself reacting as compulsively as ever. The things I've done to hold onto my abstinence! Justifying a meal two hours long; eating "breakfast" a few hours after my evening meal. Crazy? You betcha!

But what would happen if I were to say, "You've blown it. Start from scratch"? I suspect I would get myself into my old sugar and flour fixes, constant eating and an even crazier mind and fatter body than before.

When I became abstinent, my food plan was just three meals a day with nothing in between and no refined sugar and flour. My meals weren't even necessarily moderate. As often as five times a week I felt a need to pig out at a salad bar.

But that was better than the alternative, and it gave me enough sanity to begin looking at my emotional life. Eventually, my need to pig out at salad bars lessened. I still do it sometimes, and I tend to be compulsive about diet pop and sugarless mints, but I have to accept that that is the stage of development I'm in right now. It certainly is better than the alternative.

How easy it is to be blinded by perfectionism and to forget how far I've come! How easy to forget that my life before OA was without a glimmer of hope, that I never prayed or talked out my feelings or realized there was more to life than eating. If I have abstinence — any kind of abstinence — it's far better than none at all. At least I have something I can improve on.

That's why meetings and the telephone are so important. I cannot always see the progress I am making. I have to be with people who can remind me where I've come from to counteract the part of me that's into whipping myself. When I look at the positive, I move out into life. When I dwell on my imperfections, I tend to say, "I might make a mistake. I'll wait until I'm perfect before I do that."

As scary as it is, going out and risking the errors has proved to be far better than waiting to be perfect. I'm finding out there are other people in the world (surprise!) who make mistakes and are scared, just like me. And that's when I start to heal.

Ironic, isn't it? Like step one. Once I accept my humanness and let you in on it, you can help me. Of course, it would be wonderful if I could say, "I *used to* have a problem with this food." But waiting until I can tell you how perfect I am is not how the healing process works. By sharing now, I may hear the positive side of myself. Maybe someone will identify and reach out to me. Maybe by admitting my frailties I'll become more accepting of myself and find new strength.

I've come a long way, thanks to this program and the friends who tell me they've noticed changes in me. I intend to keep on being honest with them — and with you — and continue to be healed.

November 1983

It's Up to Me

I KNEW I NEEDED Overeaters Anonymous long before I learned of its existence. I used the term "food-aholic" and often thought, "I feel as if I'm strung out on drugs. I wish I *were* strung out on drugs so I could quit taking them. But I'm not on drugs, so what can I do?"

I had my stomach stapled and found that it simply turned me into a vomiter because after the surgery, even when I thought I ate correctly, excess acid would cause unbelievable pain and I vomited because that was the only relief I could find. I lost 60 of my 300 pounds and started right back up. Within a few months of surgery, it seemed the only things I could keep down were soda-pop and salty snacks, which I consumed by the gallon and by the pound bag.

A few years later, my husband found Alcoholics Anonymous and I was jealous because I saw him getting well and I was stuck in my illness. (Even before AA, we spent more on junk food than on beer.) I even tried going to open AA meetings in the hope of hearing "food" instead of "alcohol." Often I was so inspired, I found myself telling someone about it — with a half-eaten donut in my hand.

Finally, at a Narcotics Anonymous meeting, I heard the leader say she had started gaining weight after becoming sober from alcohol and drugs, and she was now in Overeaters Anonymous. (NA was very understanding about my problem; speakers talked of "your drug of choice, be it alcohol, drugs or food.") I spoke to the woman after the meeting and arranged to accompany her to an OA meeting near my home town.

She never made it, but somehow I found the courage to go alone to that strange town, to a building whose exact address I didn't know. And I found home!

Those first few weeks were discouraging. I sat reading my OA literature and binging. Then one night, something I was reading hit the little switch in my head and a lightbulb popped on. I said, "God, please take away this compulsion to overeat." And it worked.

The next day, a man called and said my husband had won a new home computer at a drawing and could he come and deliver it. The day after that, our former landlord returned our deposit, which I had thought lost forever, and an extra fifty dollars for improving the property. Friday, someone called from a place where I'd had a job interview months before and said I was hired if I was still available.

Well, I thought, this OA program is magic. Here was my Higher Power doing for me all the things I could never have done in three lifetimes.

The next day, my dog bit the delivery man and I had to deal with the Health Department. The day after that, my husband slipped and came home drunk. The day after that, my prospective employer called and said the funding was mixed up and they couldn't hire me after all. And you know what? That is when I *knew* the OA program is magic, because I still didn't want to overeat.

Today I know I just have to keep working the steps, that the "softer, easier way" is to work all twelve just as fast as I honestly can. Through OA I know that my serenity doesn't depend on other people. When my best friend is working her OA program and my husband is working his AA program, things are heavenly. But when I am the only one working a program, I find that things can still be heavenly. It is up to me.

I used to be the sort of person who could win a million dollars and gripe about the income tax. Now I am the kind of person who is grateful to be a compulsive overeater because it brought me to my Higher Power and a life that is joyous and free, no matter what's going on anywhere.

December 1983

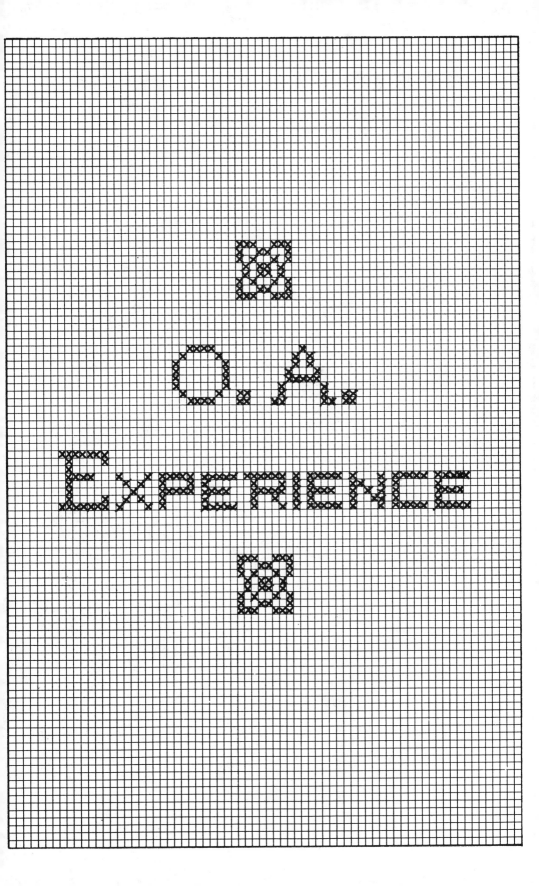

Q.A.

EXPERIENCE

What Abstinence Means to Me

IMMEDIATELY two words come to mind: sanity and self-worth. I can't separate the two words to give one more importance over the other.

Newcomers may be puzzled by the implications of sanity. "But I'm not crazy, I'm just overweight," they might say. That was my reaction in the beginning when I heard talk of restoring one's sanity. Perhaps some of you can identify with this: never overeating in front of normal eaters, then going home and devouring everything in sight that was over 200% carbohydrate in content; sneak eating at home, in the dark, carefully and stealthily, so as not to rattle paper wrappings or cupboards.

How about the ingenious methods used all hours of the day and night in search of the overpowering and all-consuming food? For example, finding different stores to go to so as not to be recognized; then concocting fantasies at the checkout counter to explain the phenomenal quantities of junk food at such strange hours!

I'm sure we all have our little games that we can add to those above. None are rational or sane; they are insanity. I will be eternally grateful for no longer having to live with such torment as I experienced at the thought of being found out. With sanity I can, with a clear mind, make the choice to overeat or not to overeat.

The insanity of the sneak eating — the guilts, anxieties and fears — destroyed my self-worth. I felt I was worse than anyone who ever lived; my habits were the worst, I was the most obese and if it happened that someone larger than myself was present, either my fat was uglier than hers or she was far superior to me mentally and emotionally. It was a subtle form of egotism; everything was self, only it was diverted and limited solely to the negative aspects.

Even though I have always been strong-willed and outgoing and functionally happy (laughter and comedy are cunning methods of self-defense), in the end I always came out with the short end. My opinions seemed valid, but they were different than "theirs," so naturally I was wrong and not just wrong, but strange. This was carried over into the minutest detail: "She cleans house differently and more often than I do! She must be doing it right and I must be doing it wrong!"

I agonized over these differences, hiding my pain from others and most especially from myself, not only by consuming junk almost continuously, but also by looking for and finding, with amazing skill, the flaws and foibles of those around me. I could then say, "Well, see there, at least *I* don't do that."

So abstinence means that I have been given sanity and self-worth. I say "given" carefully; the abstinence simply presents the opportunity to find and work for both sanity and, especially, self-worth, for the old habits are hard to break.

While abstinence has given me new life — that "something" that was always just out of my reach and that I went clear across the country searching for — it is not a "they-lived-happily-ever-after pill" served on a silver platter. It is the key, however. Without abstinence, I cannot even begin to claw my way out of the darkness of a lifetime career of the progressive and destructive disease of compulsive overeating.

I am free at last to continue the path which I left many years ago — the path to a full life of learning, growing and changing. I am free to choose abstinence or death. It has come to that for me. Abstinence is the softer, easier way.

November/December 1974

Abstaining through the Holiday Season

N MY FAMILY, holidays were eating days. The morning was spent preparing a feast. Afterwards I was in a stupor and would watch TV, sleep and think about the evening meal while I nibbled and "snuck" food. I was full of self-pity because I felt that everyone else was out there living — going to football games and so on, while I was being a good girl and staying at home with my parents as if I were responsible for their happiness and I could prevent the loneliness they felt in not having taken the action to invite friends to share with us, for whatever reason they thought was logical.

Last Thanksgiving I had no plans for dinner. I went to an AA meeting with a friend who called and needed a ride.

I knew that I did not want to be alone. I shared my feelings at that meeting, not really understanding them all. Later I went to a dinner, prepared and served by volunteers, program people like myself who needed desperately to get out of fear, self-pity and melancholy, all of which were strangely comfortable old attitudes of self-centeredness. I saw love in action and realized that my relations in the past were misdirected. I was seeking love, yes, but I was waiting for it to come to me. I didn't know that love comes to me in double measure to that which I initiate.

My mother showed her love by cooking and creating a home. My problem was expecting more from her than she could give, rather than accepting her. My inability to be satisfied with what I had, and a combination of fear and resentment forced me to look elsewhere for my needs, which were very real. I had learned, by sharing at meetings and through twelve-step work, to give away what I had. I made a mental gratitude list: abstinence, health, five senses, the freedom to choose, laughter, friendship, serenity, sunshine, a home. The list grew and grew. Soon I was dancing to the band and enjoying the people I was with.

I didn't have to live in the fear of food and myself, a fear that would endanger my abstinence! I turned my life over to a Higher Power, the source of all my strength, and I was restored to sanity. By sharing with others, I tested reality. I asked God to remove my fears and other shortcomings and made amends to myself and others by seeking opportunities to give of myself.

Upon meditation at the end of the day, I realized I had called upon God and been given everything I needed that day, especially the gift of abstinence and the desire and willingness to accept it.

The steps tell me that I alone can make a change in attitude and apply my new knowledge in other areas of my life. I feel whole and comfortable, knowing that God is preparing me and shaping me, like clay.

November/December 1974

An Open Letter to You from Someone Who Cares

MY HEART GOES OUT to you when I catch a glimpse of you at the store, on the bus, on the street, in a home. Sometimes your weight problem is obvious and sometimes it is not. I sometimes detect that you may be a compulsive overeater and sometimes I'm not sure. The only person who can answer that question is you. Because I am a compulsive overeater, I care about you and want you to know that there are others like me who care about the way you feel. We know the loneliness, pain, despair and shame that go with struggling unsuccessfully with an obsession to overeat.

Completely defeated and ashamed of my lack of willpower, I came to my first meeting 30 pounds overweight but feeling as if I was eligible for the fat lady's job at the circus.

I can still remember the sensation of being in a dream. As I listened, I heard OA members share familiar feelings and experiences. My heart skipped a beat as I realized that I was among my own kind. I knew I had come home and that someday I would be all right. I discovered that

I was a compulsive overeater who needed to learn to stop using food to face life.

Since OA offers us a new way of life as well as the help and support we need in order to lose our excess weight, it is impossible for me to do more than to plead with you to reach out to Overeaters Anonymous for help if you even suspect that you are a compulsive overeater. You will then find what you need to know about our lifetime program.

I understand only too well how difficult it is to take that first step and admit that you may need help. But if you can find the courage to bury your pride for one hour and come to an OA meeting, you may see the beginning of a whole new life. The acceptance, love and understanding waiting for you here are far too deep and wonderful to describe. The only requirement on your part is a desire to stop eating compulsively.

At a glance, you would be unable to identify with me because I am 5'2" and maintaining my weight at 104–107 pounds. But I can assure you that my physical appearance has nothing to do with the fact that I am a compulsive overeater who has known all the unhappiness and anxiety that you are suffering.

One day at a time, I am learning to deal with my emotions without using food as a crutch. I have also come to accept emotional pain as a necessary part of my growth. As I dare to become better acquainted with myself, I have discovered assets that I can develop and liabilities that I can let go, a little at a time. Negative emotions are being replaced by feelings of love and acceptance for myself and others.

As a result, I am a happier person than I ever dreamed possible, and the beauty of it all is that the people around me seem to be happier too. Yet, I fully accept what OA said to me at that very first meeting: "The only person I can change is myself. I do not try to change anyone else."

As OA continues to grow in all directions and areas, our attention is often focused on you — the person who hasn't yet discovered Overeaters Anonymous. Please come and let us help you, because when you allow us to help you, we are able to continue in our own personal growth.

January/February 1976

Compulsive Overeating: A Disease of Isolation

ALWAYS FELT so alone." "I was sure no one else thought or acted like me." "How could anyone like me? I'm so different, so worthless."

Don't these phrases sound familiar? I know that I thought and felt this way for years, even long after I had been in OA.

Then recently, a small miracle occurred. I had been fighting the idea of calling in my food for many years. "Just another gimmick," I said. "It's not necessary as long as I commit my abstinence to God each day. This isn't a diet club, and calling in puts too much emphasis on food."

But what was wrong? Why couldn't I abstain for very long? Why did I feel so terribly alone, left out in the cold? I felt shut out of OA activities, cut off from the mainstream of life. I suffered alone and said nothing. Until one day. . . .

At a beautiful morning meeting, my need for help broke through my wall of fear. "Somebody help me," I said. "I'm dying in front of you and don't know what to do." God worked another miracle. Three wonderful OA members answered my plea. Now they call me when I am unable to reach out for help (one of my major problems). They are patient whether or not I abstain. I am allowing myself to believe they really care. Most important, one of them said something to me during that first call that really changed my direction.

"Compulsive overeating," she said, "is a disease of isolation. And calling in your food plan means contact with another human being once a day."

That did it! All my years of resistance melted away like ice on a sunny winter morning. "Contact with another human being once a day." Those magic words and the precious promise they held have given me hope at last. "Okay," I said. "I'll do it."

Now I don't feel so terribly alone. I have a growing awareness that my worth is not based on my abstinence and weight loss, but just on my value as a human being. What a relief!

The word "sponsor" isn't used, but the word "friend" is mentioned frequently. I am accepted just for myself, not for what I eat or don't eat, not for what I look like, not for how I behave. I believe these people to be channels of God's love, showing me how things can be at their very best.

And guess what? I don't need to run to excess food the way I did. Strength comes when I least expect it. For reasons unknown to me, I was paralyzed by my illness and unable to reach out for help. That still happens. But as a result of my one plea, born of desperation, help is being given to me without asking.

That's the real miracle of Overeaters Anonymous, you know. As we work through our growing pains as a Fellowship, we will no longer sigh and say, "What's the matter with *her*? Why can't she quit overeating the way I did?" We will no longer turn our backs on those who "can't seem to make it." We will stop saying, "If she wanted help, she'd call. I'm not going to call and make it easy. You have to want this badly enough to go to any lengths."

We will have patience and more patience. We will be loving instead of cruel. A friendly smile and a phone call can go a long way in letting other overeaters know they're not alone.

Sure, abstinence is an inside job. Of course, willingness and discipline must begin with us. But what if you can't do it? (No, I didn't say "won't." That used to be my pat answer in my thinner days. "It isn't that she can't; it's that she won't.")

How much do we really know about our illness? What do we understand about the terrible sense of isolation that is not a symptom but an integral part of the disease? What can we do about it for ourselves and for each other?

Well, we can recognize that it exists. Not being a brand-new newcomer doesn't mean that the feeling of aloneness has gone away. Many people who have been coming around for years still suffer from it. Sometimes they abstain, sometimes they don't.

At this point, we all need a friend. Sponsors are terrific, but there are no qualifications for being a friend. You don't need twenty-one days, you don't need a fourth step, you don't need any weight loss or gain. All you need to do is smile, put out your hand and say "Hi." And you need to do it over and over for those who can't reach out themselves, who feel alone, yet who want more than anything what this program has to offer. If they didn't, why would they keep coming around? Think about that a little.

Let's give to each other what we never felt we had before: friendship. Let's really care, no matter what. Is there someone in your group who comes week after week, sits there and doesn't lose weight, but keeps coming back? Please call her or him. Let that member know she (or he) is not alone. And do it more than once or twice. How can God speak through us if we don't open up our mouths to talk to someone else?

Those of you who are abstaining and losing weight (or maintaining), don't be impatient with the rest of us. You have been given a gift. Cherish it. Respect it. Strengthen it by giving it away to others.

The worst thing we can do to one another is what society does to us on the outside: treat an overeater with impatience, hostility, cruelty.

Each day, I remember my OA friend's statement: "Compulsive overeating is a disease of isolation. And calling in your food plan means contact with another human being once a day."

March/April 1976

The Disease, the Progression, the Recovery

COMPULSIVE OVEREATING is progressive. When I was a child, I ate not only out of hunger, but to earn my parents' approval and love for being a "good eater" and obediently cleaning my plate. But in a few years the amount of food that was enough for others was not enough for me. I wanted more, even when I felt full, and I can remember eating until my stomach was painfully distended, but still regretting that I could not fit in more food!

For some years, I had the choice of whether or not to overeat, and I dieted many times for many reasons. But it got harder to stick to a diet; each time I regained the weight faster, and I got fatter than before. As my craving for food got worse, I realized I could not do it alone and began joining weight control programs. At first they worked, and I lived from weigh-in to weigh-in. But I never reached goal, and my craving to eat, first piles of "legal" food and then anything I could get, got worse, and I dropped out of those programs one by one, ashamed to go back.

The emotional imbalance of compulsive overeating is also progressive. As a child I was a "people pleaser" and a "praise earner." I would do anything anyone asked me, and the attention I got was enough. But like my food craving, my need for attention grew. Along the way I learned how to get attention for failure. No wonder I overate: I had two unhappy marriages, I was tired all the time, and wouldn't anyone do the same?

Spiritually, I grew sicker as the illness worsened. Raised in an open-minded family, comfortably involved with church activities, I became an angry agnostic, ridden with guilt, and blaming God for not preventing me from doing the things that made me feel guilty. I turned my moral sense around until I believed whatever I did was automatically right, and I stuffed down the growing sense of guilt and frustration with tons of food.

Then, OA came to Smalltown, Nowhere, where I live, and I am, by the grace of my Higher Power, an arrested compulsive overeater, overwhelmed with gratitude for the whole new life I have. I have been given once more the power of choice over the first bite, blessed with a serenity that had escaped me all my life. The slender, healthy body, 75 pounds lighter, is only one of the benefits of living the program. I was spiritually bankrupt, and now I have at least a small "savings account" to carry me over some bad days.

I was obsessed with food and the great *I am,* and the Fellowship of OA has saved me from that terrible isolation and given me the ability to love and be loved and to forget myself through caring about other people. I was helpless and angry in the hands of fate, and I have been given the beautiful sense of peace that can come only from faith that a Power greater than myself is running things, and that the final outcome of it all will be good, because that Power is a loving teacher.

Finally, the bottomless well of need has been filled with joy and transformed into a pipeline through which that lifesaving message flows into other empty people. I used to feel that I had to grab for every good thing I wanted, and it would probably be snatched away from me. Now it seems that the more I give, the more I am given, and my world is filled with beautiful people. I hope, by the grace of God, I never let myself get stupid enough, or sick enough, to trade all that for the false promise of compulsive overeating!

March/April 1976

Tunnel Vision

TIRED, heavy, dejected, isolated, I stand at the far end of a long tunnel that stretches before me. A pinpoint of light at the other end of the tunnel is barely visible, somehow shining through heaps of junk.

Someone has handed me a small shovel and I begin to dig. At first the thought of the work almost overwhelms me, but I am encouraged by the realization that for once I am not alone. I am in a network of tunnels and other people shout encouragement from up ahead. They tell of seeing more light as they dig and finding less junk as they progress.

Already, more light is shining in the tunnel. I dig, then rest, reflect and replenish my body. Inside me is a warmth that is growing. My way appears clearer. Newcomers far behind me now stand where I once stood and I take up the shout of encouragement.

"Pick up a tool. We'll share what we have. There is hope if you are willing. You will see only a glimmer at first, but the light is there for you and you will be changed by it. Work toward that light."

Sometimes a person drops a tool and leaves the tunnel, backing into total darkness. Others inside call, "Keep coming back." They know that in time a deserted tunnel will fill up again with junk and the light will fade.

The light is there. Pick up your tool and dig. It becomes easier as you become more willing to work. Rest, reflect, replenish and rejoice.

The tunnels join in the network and there is fellowship with others. No longer alone, and with a common goal, we share the light in humble gratitude, knowing the promise that is ours.

July/August 1976

Welcome Home!

HAVE YOU EVER WISHED you could lose ten pounds, twenty, forty, or a hundred or more? Have you ever wished that once you got it off you could keep it off? Welcome to OA; welcome home!

Have you sometimes felt out of step with the world, like a homeless orphan without a place where you really belong? Welcome to OA; welcome home!

Have you ever wished your family would get to work or school so that you could get busy eating? Welcome to OA; welcome home!

Have you ever awakened first thing in the morning and felt happy because you remembered that your favorite goodie was waiting for you in the fridge or in the cupboard? Welcome to OA; welcome home!

Have you ever looked up at the stars and wondered what an insignificant person like you was doing in the world anyway? Welcome to OA; welcome home!

Have you ever cooked, bought or baked for your family and then eaten everything yourself so that you wouldn't have to share? We know you in OA because we *are* you. Welcome to OA; welcome home!

Have you ever wanted to hide in the house, without going to work, without getting cleaned up or even getting dressed, without seeing anyone or letting anyone see you? Welcome to OA; welcome home!

Have you ever hidden food under the bed, under the pillow, in the drawer, in the bathroom, in the wastebasket, the cupboard, the clothes hamper, the closet or the car so that you could eat without anyone seeing you? Welcome to OA; welcome home!

Have you ever been angry, resentful, defiant — against God, your mate, your doctor, your mother, your father, your friends, your children, the salesperson in the store whose look spoke a thousand words as you tried on clothes — because *they* were thin, because they wanted *you* to be thin, and because you were forced to diet to please them or shut them up or make them eat their words and their looks? We welcome you to OA; welcome home!

Have you ever sobbed out your misery in the dark night because no one loved or understood you? Welcome to OA; welcome home!

Have you ever felt that God (if God existed at all) made the biggest mistake when God created you? Can you see that this is where such feelings get turned around? Welcome to OA; welcome home!

Have you ever wanted to get on a bus and just keep going, without ever once looking back? Did you *do* it? Welcome to OA; welcome home!

Have you ever thought the whole world was a mess and if they would just think and act like you, the world would be a lot better off? Welcome to OA; welcome home!

Have you ever thought that OA people must be a bit nuts? That *they* might be compulsive overeaters, but *you* just have a weight problem which you can take care of beginning tomorrow; they might be one bite from insane eating, but you are just a little or a lot overweight? Welcome to OA; welcome home!

Have you ever told anyone who would listen how great you are, how talented, how intelligent, how powerful — all the time knowing they would never believe it, because *you* didn't believe it? Welcome to OA; welcome home!

Have you ever lost all your weight and found that you were thin-unhappy instead of fat-unhappy? Welcome to OA; welcome home!

Have you ever worn a mask or hundreds of masks because you were sure that if you shared the person you really were no one could ever love or accept you? We accept you in OA. May we offer you a home?

Overeaters Anonymous extends to all of you the gift of acceptance. No matter who you are, where you come from or where you are heading, you are welcome here! No matter what you have done or failed to do, what you have felt or haven't felt, where you have slept, or with whom, who you have loved or hated — you may be sure of our acceptance. We accept you as you are, not as you would be if you could melt yourself and mold yourself and shape yourself into what other people think you should be. Only you can decide what you want to be.

But we will help you work for the goals you set, and when you are successful we will rejoice with you; and when you slip, we will tell you that we are not failures just because we sometimes fail, and we'll hold out our arms, in love, and stand beside you as you pull yourself back up and walk on again to where you are heading! You'll never have to cry alone again, unless you choose to.

Sometimes *we* fail to be all that we should be, and sometimes we aren't there to give you all you need from us. Accept our imperfection, too. Love us in return and help us in our sometimes-falling failing. That's what we are in OA — imperfect, but trying. Let's rejoice together in our effort and in the assurance that we can have a home, if we want one.

Welcome to OA; welcome home!

September/October 1977

A Diminishing Bag of Tricks

ECENTLY I watched as another prop in the saga of my life was loaded onto a truck. This trip, the cargo was valuable to the recipient — a well-known charitable institution — but to me it was one more service performed (at my request) by the "Wreckage of the Past Clearing and Hauling Company, Inc."

If you happened to be a bystander at the time, you would have sworn that what the truck picked up was fourteen boxes of used books. But you would have been misled. Those were not really books but another of my disguises.

I had always believed that when visitors came to my house they would look at my overcrowded bookshelves and think, "Obviously, this person is an intellectual; therefore quite superior." It meant nothing to me that I had read very few of the books. Appearances were what mattered; they deceive, and I needed that.

Other items of trick gear have been discarded. Gone are the long vests that covered fifty extra pounds and made me think that *you* thought I was thin. My double-duty oven, which served as a depository for dirty dishes because hiding them was easier than washing them is back to being just an oven again. And the household furniture has been relieved of its role of accomplice in my sleight-of-hand housekeeping. My motto when cleaning house was "When there is too much to sweep under the rug, shove it under the couch."

Not even my son escaped being used. He was a particularly versatile bit player, one day a sickly little fellow languishing in bed (a perfect excuse for not fulfilling commitments I preferred to shirk), and the next day a remarkably agile errand boy who fetched and carried because I was too busy and important to be bothered with such things as getting my own shoes out from under the bed. The kid could also vanish if I needed to pass as a virgin.

Along with stage props, of course, there was the standard dialog. My favorite lines were, "Of course, I don't mind." (This made you think I was wonderful.) "I just *love* to babysit." (Ditto preceding audience reaction.) "No thank you, I'm not hungry." (This convinced you I was thin, or, if you didn't fall for that, you might figure I had gland trouble or a water retention problem.)

Absent from my script were the lines, "I don't know," "I disagree" and "I'm to blame."

I used to be very powerful. I knew I could trick you into thinking whatever I wanted you to think of me. I was positive that you spent at least seventy-five percent of your time thinking about me, because I spent about ninety-five percent of mine thinking about me.

Well the unread books are gone now. My bookshelves hold only books I have read and value and those I am currently reading. My dishes are clean. There's nothing under my bed except carpeting. And the kitchen floor isn't sticky when you walk on it. My bag of tricks is gradually emptying and my toolbox is filling up.

For today, I am a retired prima donna who sometimes remembers to think about others. And as for all that power I thought was mine, today I know I can tap into power far greater than my own, which gives me abstinence one day at a time, normal weight for more than two years, a gradual emotional recovery and moments of purposefulness.

October 1978

Qualifying

PLEASE DON'T TELL ME I'm not a compulsive overeater.

I know you love and care for me. But, please, don't offer me just one bite, one sip or one lick. When you do this, I realize that you don't understand my illness. For, if you did, you wouldn't offer me any food or drink between meals.

But, offer it though you may, I will always say, "No, thanks." I don't need that one bite, one sip, one lick — that poten'al first step into the land of madness.

Yes, madness. I have a compulsion which can multiply a moderate lunch by seven between lunch and dinner. This compulsion has led me to eat the contents of a large economy size snack package and lick my fingers, my hands and the bag.

I always had trouble waiting for hot foods to cool, and for cold foods to be warmed. I have eaten in the car, the bed, the bathroom and even in places where no food is allowed.

I ate when I was glad, mad, happy or sad; when I was broke, when I was flush, in sickness and in health. I can, with cool impartiality, eat the foods I hate as well as those I love. I have eaten food from my own and anyone else's plate. I have eaten fast and I have eaten slowly. I have dined on the premises, and then ordered some more to go.

Oh, and I have lied blandly to waitresses about why I was taking out food after I'd eaten. I took food home to my family which they rarely saw, and surely didn't eat.

I planned my whole life around food. And I saw to it that food was always around me.

Yes, I am a compulsive overeater. Please don't tell me I have a mild case. Compulsive overeating is an incurable disease which I must live with all the days of my life. There's nothing mild about that.

There's nothing mild about an unmanageable life, either. Mine was, in fact, so unmanageable, I was bankrupt in the business of living.

I have since found a new business manager: God. We are working together to restore my sanity.

Would you still offer me one bite, one sip, one lick? Would you offer a recovering alcoholic just one teensie weensie drink?

Don't tell me I'm stronger than the alcoholic. Our compulsions, our lack of control and our unmanageable lives are the same.

I pray that the recovering alcoholic does not become a compulsive over-eater. I pray that I do not become an alcoholic. But, thank God for OA and AA; we can both find help there.

May God help me never to look down on an alcoholic or anyone else with a living problem.

Yes, I am a compulsive overeater. Please don't tell me I'm not. And there's no need to feel sorry for me, either. Why feel sorry for a person who can:

Eat three balanced meals every day.

Lose weight and gain sanity.

Keep what I have by giving it away, and enjoy a new way of life by living one day at a time.

I am a very grateful abstaining compulsive overeater.

Thank God.

Thank OA.

Thank you.

February 1979

Food, Fat and the Facts of Life

YEARS AGO, I heard a statement that apparently rated a slot in my mind's information bank: "Compulsion binds fear."

I filed and forgot it, until I began abstaining and losing weight in OA. Suddenly, there it was, demanding to be examined.

If compulsion binds fear — that is, if compulsive behavior arises out of a need to confine, or neutralize fear, what was I so afraid of that caused me to become a compulsive overeater?

That question was answered during the ensuing months as my weight melted away and my sleeping sexuality slowly awakened. One hundred pounds of fat had bound my libido pretty effectively: no one wants a fat woman. For the previous ten years I had made my asexuality readily apparent to every male who crossed my path. If my intellectually overbearing manner of dealing with men didn't keep them away, that blubber certainly would!

Four months into the program and with not yet half the weight lost, I suddenly realized one evening that a friend thought I was hustling him! After stewing about it a while, I finally spoke to him.

"You know," I told him in my most businesslike manner, "as I lose weight, I'm going to become a more sexual person. But that doesn't mean I'm after your body."

He nodded seriously and graciously accepted my "revelation." How kind he was! Looking back on that conversation, I'm sure that it had never occurred to him that I might be coming on to him. The sexuality was all in my head, not his.

A few months later, my abstinence was gone. I simply couldn't, or wouldn't, deal with that rising level of awareness of myself as a sexual being. It took a year of the pain of on-and-off abstinence to make me willing to work at it in order to lose the rest of the weight and be able to abstain continuously.

Now, with two years of abstinence, I have become aware that my femaleness is something I had never dealt with; that it was one of the main

179

causes of my overeating in the first place, and that it was one of the primary reasons I was not willing to part with the fat, even though it was causing increasingly serious problems in my life. The hassle of dealing with a husband who was dissatisfied with our barely active sex life was definitely preferable to dealing with what I apparently saw as my rampant passionate nature.

How did I learn to handle this? By talking with other women, experimenting, making some rather painful mistakes and finally, accepting myself for what I am.

A while back, I heard a wonderful panel of three women — a former prostitute, a lesbian and a nun. All were extremely generous in sharing their feelings about their sexuality and the choices they had made. Although my own decisions about how I would handle my physical nature had been entirely different from theirs, I was deeply moved by my sudden awareness of the bond between us. I realized that all human beings are sexual, whether extremely active sexually, celibate or somewhere in between.

At the beginning of the panel, before the women spoke, the audience was asked to write down a one or two-word gut-feeling description about each of the three labels — "whore," "lesbian," and "nun."

I scribbled "gutsy" for the first, a question mark for the second and "dignified" for the third. At the end of the session, we were again asked to write a brief description for each woman. This time my paper contained the words, "warm," "warm," and "warm." I think it was at that point that the last vestiges of my non-acceptance of myself vanished.

It is frightening to stand up at meetings and mention to motherly older women that sexuality has much to do with overeating. But I try to do it occasionally because of the benefits dealing with it has brought me. It used to be very threatening to me to be turned on by someone who would not be an appropriate bed partner, because I didn't know how I would handle it.

Enough time to work things out and a continuing effort to face each situation as it arises have given me such a marvelous peace about it all! I am content with myself now; content with the talents, the loving, the dignity, the passion, the humor I possess. And I am also content with the progress I am making on the bossiness, the grandiosity, the irritability and the bouts of poor judgment and downright cruelty which are also sometimes mine.

I love all the good things, including the passion. And I am working on what I don't like — what holds me back, what gives me, and others, pain. My life today is interesting, challenging, *thin*, fun, and getting better every day!

March 1979

The Situational Cure

URING MY NEARLY eight years in Overeaters Anonymous, I have often patted myself on the back for not trying the "geographic cure" for my problems. Until recently, I've been proud that I always sit still and face my problems head on, without running away or returning to compulsive overeating.

The truth is, I've been using a variation of the geographic cure known as the "situational cure." When I first joined OA, I was in my sophomore year of college, majoring in something that sounded good. After some abstinence, I naturally felt pretty awful — all those feelings creeping up all the time. I knew I'd feel better when I was through with that year of school.

I met a man, fell in love, wanted to be with him all the time. I knew I'd feel better when I lived with him. I felt very guilty living with a man and so I returned to compulsive overeating for a couple of months.

Then I knew I would feel better if we got married. I had quit college by this time because I thought I would feel better if I was making some money. I worked for three years in well paid secretarial positions and was bored, so I thought I'd feel better if I returned to school to prepare for a more meaningful career.

After one and a half years of college, majoring in something I liked, my husband got a job offer in a city halfway across the country. I thought it would be nice to get a bigger house, make new friends, start over in a strange town. So we went. I couldn't start school again for almost a year, so I worked as a secretary. I knew I would feel better once I adjusted to the new city, lack of family and the different kind of OA here.

When I began my year of internship, I knew I would feel better, finally getting a chance to use all the book learning I'd acquired. It was a physically and emotionally draining year and I knew I would feel better when it was over.

In the middle of the year, I got pregnant. I couldn't wait until I could stay home, feel the baby move, not have to study (or feel guilty because

I wasn't studying) and finally get the windows washed.

I've been home now about a month. It feels great not to have to study. I have only five more windows left to wash. I often lie down and "listen" to our child explore his-or-her world. But I'm thinking I will feel better when the baby comes. And I'll feel better when the weather is cooler; when we start our childbirth classes; when all the windows are washed.

Yesterday, I was driving by myself, feeling a little down, when the baby moved. That usually makes me feel better, but it didn't. That was when I realized that the baby moving doesn't make me feel better, that I won't feel better when the baby comes, that anticipated happenings, situations and feelings won't make me feel better.

What I do feel in a new situation is different. Not better. I am who I am in every situation; who I am doesn't change with the scenery. So, for today, I am a college-educated housewife, very pregnant, with five windows to wash, a loving husband and a God who gives me realizations while I'm driving a car and the gift of abstinence.

That makes me feel better!

December 1979

I Am a Vomiter

IT ISN'T a pretty term. Nor does it leave anything to the imagination, as "compulsive overeater" might. But it is what I am, and it feels wonderful to face up to it and to be able to talk about it. Someone asked me the other day why I still call myself a vomiter if I have been abstaining for three months. I replied that it was for the same reason I still call myself a compulsive overeater. For me, the two are inseparable: I cannot overeat without making myself throw up.

When did my career as a compulsive overeater begin? I remember distinctly. One evening when I was about fifteen, I was feeling emotionally overwrought. I don't remember what caused it, but I had stayed up very late watching television. It was then that I went on my first binge. I wanted to throw up, but I couldn't. It wasn't long, however, before I learned to stick my finger down my throat to force vomiting.

My binges have been too numerous to recall. The past seems to fade away into one long struggle with food. Some days stand out, as do some daylong meals and places where I have bought binge food. But mostly I choose to keep my memories hidden from consciousness. I know there is no way I can change my past. All I can do is accept it.

This year was the worst ever. I worked as a cook in a small restaurant for a time. I used to close up alone late at night. Imagine — all the free food I could eat and nobody around to stop me or to watch me throw it up. I always knew God was watching but I shut God out, told God to go away and was resentful because God seemed to frown upon what I was doing.

I ate until guilt over what I was doing (stealing) overwhelmed me, or until the dent in the restaurant's supplies began to be noticeable. I paid for some of what I ate, but for the rest I am still paying with guilt.

Even with the stealing, I spent a great deal of money on food. I tried to hide my eating from my mother with whom I live. But she knew. She heard me going to the bathroom and she knew when I came out at eleven o'clock at night to replenish my supplies. Still, I kept up the deception, hiding junk food under my bed and even a bucket to throw up in.

All the time I was eating, I knew of OA. I was too afraid to reach out and ask for help. Finally, I met an overeater who was a member and she took me to a meeting. I felt so good after that meeting. It was as though a great burden had been lifted from me. I knew my problem was shared by others and that I didn't have to be alone with it again. Here were people who could help me. Here, I could help myself.

I have been abstaining from compulsive overeating, and vomiting, for three months. It has been wonderful, easy, hard and almost impossible all at the same time. OA has pulled me through the hardest times. As long as I was willing to use some of the tools of the program when I felt like eating, I made it through. I knew that I could willfully ignore OA at those times and eat anyway. So far, I have chosen not to.

I found serenity, security, happiness and friends where I was only seeking abstinence. Most importantly, I now have a weapon, an effective one, to fight against despair. I only have to use it. It works.

January 1980

Gratitude Behind Bars

M Y NAME is Sherman. I am — and always will be — a compulsive overeater.

I remember my childhood: going to the bakery for the hot pastries I loved so much.

Going to religious school after regular school, feeling ashamed.

Realizing I had stopped growing at five foot, six and a half and being terrified I would be less than a man.

I remember my father dying when I was ten; hating him, only to learn later that I loved him and he loved me.

I remember after Dad died not being able to get any help or answers from my mother. I hit the streets. I loved street life — always new things and people to experience.

The streets were my classroom after I quit school at fifteen. I owned a car when I was fourteen, and I stole a car for parts at fourteen and a half. I learned how to be undisciplined and dishonest. I learned about drugs, sex, money, people and food. Somehow, I knew I was looking for something. I didn't find it until I found OA.

My drug career escalated into hard drugs and big money, sex and power until I was thirty-two years old, with a thirty-nine inch waist and weighing just over 200 pounds. I was out of control.

Then I was arrested. My bail was one hundred thousand dollars. Almost everything I owned was confiscated. I thought my life was over. I couldn't figure out why it was happening to me, especially on the twelfth of the month — my lucky number.

That was the bottom I had to hit. A few months later, I met a psychiatrist whom I intended to con for my upcoming trial. He eventually became my sponsor because I couldn't be honest with anyone else at the time.

I learned about OA from a brother who was trying to kick drugs in AA. After my first meeting, I knew I was home. I didn't get immediate or perfect abstinence, but my weight went down to 150 pounds and my waist to thirty-two inches. Little by little, I learned honesty and self-discipline.

That first year was very painful. Getting honest was new to me and much of the time I felt as though I was in a fog, an often painful and uncomfortable one. But I continued to go to meetings, sometimes ten a week.

Finally, I think I may be starting to "get" it. Along the way, someone said, "If you don't like the word 'God,' add an 'o' and call it 'Good.'" My search for a Higher Power started there.

It is now almost a year since I was arrested. I am in the first two months of a four-year prison sentence. You may not believe how happy I am to have found all this freedom. Thank God for compulsive overeaters and OA.

March 1980

Hippie Housewife

I CAME INTO OA after my annual Christmas binge, wearing my traditional wreath of added holiday fat.

My life was in a state of collapse. I was overeating, drinking too much and using drugs every day. I was close to a divorce. My young children were obviously troubled. And I was in the midst of declaring bankruptcy. Most devastating, I was unable to stop eating. I had quit weighing myself at 180 pounds and now, ashamed and terrified, wore a size 24.

I began overeating early in life. I also sniffed cleaning fluids and gasoline, and sipped liquor whenever I could find it.

My parents wanted me to be a "good girl." Good girls don't swear, talk back to adults, fail in school or have sex. But it's OK to eat. Eating is the compulsion of a good girl afraid to be real.

I managed to maintain my good girl front throughout most of high school. After I graduated, I moved to Berkeley, a garden of delights for an addictive personality, where I was admitted into the university. My addictions burgeoned. I ate exotic foods and tried every drug that hit the streets, seeking the high that would obliterate all pain.

I went barefoot, stopped bathing, refused to wear makeup and joined the radical groups that flourished in Berkeley during the early Sixties. I seemed to have found my identity at last. I was a free spirit, a child of God, undominated by the traditions of a decadent, violent society.

When I met a fellow student who shared my addictions — overeating, alcohol and drugs — I married him. We became a fat couple. We blew a small fortune on our habits, always baffled as to where our money was disappearing. When we could no longer afford education for two, I quit school to work as a typist while my husband finished college.

By age twenty-three I was fat — size 18½. As I went from one job to another, I ate more and more. I felt trapped by my marriage, my endless typing jobs and my compulsions.

Finally, I got my husband to go to work while I finished my education. With teaching credential in hand, I got a job teaching educationally handicapped children. I worked compulsively. It seemed I had found the right solution.

Then I became pregnant. I ate constantly, hiding behind maternity smocks and tossing out alibis of eating for two. When my daughter was born, I was 40 pounds overweight.

Motherhood did not agree with my free spirit. I felt that my daughter had ruined everything. I rejected her, leaving her with a babysitter while I "did my thing" at work.

But teaching was no longer doing it for me. I began to smoke marijuana at work. I went to work with terrible hangovers, taking pills to feel better; I continued to binge and diet.

My husband and I participated in a personal growth seminar that turned out to be a spiritual experience for both of us. I realized that I had to change my life. "My career is my problem," I announced. "If I stay home as a mother, I will be whole."

For five years I was a middle class housewife married to a prestigious scientist. We had a second daughter. We bought a house. I thought I had found peace at last.

But my resentment toward my husband was growing. We were fighting bitterly. I was afraid I couldn't support myself, however, so I had to be a "good wife" — which meant letting him dominate me, then hating him for it.

We were heading toward bankruptcy. I had to do something. But work? Me? Fat me, who was too fat to venture out of the house, and who had failed at every job? No!

I stole clothes and food for a year. After all, I had to take care of my family; my husband was out of love with me and no one understood me. Besides, I was fat.

I gave up on myself. Every afternoon I took the phone off the hook, then got stoned and binged. My children grew like untended weeds, running through the house as I sat stoned in my chair.

Soon I was bursting out of a size 24. I decided I would live with conflicts and be a fat housewife all my life.

One day I visited a fat friend whom I hadn't seen in over a year. She had always been a great binge buddy and her hostility toward the world was marvelous to behold.

A thin body — hers — greeted me, and her hostility seemed to have disappeared. No fair! My spirits hit bottom.

It was several hours before I could bring myself to ask how she had done it.

"I go to Overeaters Anonymous twice a week," came the reply.

"I tried that once," I retorted. "Too religious. What kind of diet are you on?"

She had stopped dieting, she claimed, and had learned how to live.

She looked good to me, and I was impressed with an inner glow that had always eluded me. Surely she had discovered something besides the right diet!

I entered OA and surrendered to my inability to diet. I looked to my body for answers instead of to a diet, and I lost 30 pounds.

Five months later, at an AA dance, I noticed that people were neither drinking nor stoned, but they were having a ball. If they could quit, I realized, so could I. Since that night I have not taken a drink or a drug.

Three months later, I stopped stealing.

Life in OA has been marvelous — exciting, successful, unusual. I am finally receiving the love, acceptance and understanding I have always needed. One day at a time, I am happy.

April 1980

One of the "Weirdos"

"NO SWEETS or junk foods."

"Sugar rots your teeth."

"Eat lots of vegetables."

As a pudgy ten-year-old girl, I resented these admonitions from my nutrition-conscious parents. I sneaked sweets, overate at meals and envied my friends whose mothers gave them sugary snacks.

Some of the kids teased me about being chubby. My clothes were always too tight and I split a lot of seams, especially when I bent over.

Suddenly I was thirteen and *fat*. Boys and their opinion of me became all-important; my parents were beginning to have marriage problems; and I was given certain responsibilities, including babysitting for my younger sister and brother.

But I didn't want to grow up and face things the way they were. So I overate, still sneaking sugar foods.

My father tried to help me diet his way: fast for five days, splurge for two. But it didn't work for me.

My mother gave me diet pills. They worked for 10 or 15 pounds, but then I stopped taking them because I wanted to overeat.

My parents got divorced and I lived with my mother. I tried many diets, but I never wanted to stop eating the junk. My weight went up and down, though never below 155 pounds — a cute "plump." I was a fat hippy, and my life was a mess.

By the age of seventeen I weighed almost 210 pounds. I tried to commit suicide. Shortly after, I dropped out of high school.

One night I couldn't even turn to food anymore. I called my father and he took me to live with him. Dad knew that my main problems were my weight and low self-esteem, so we went on a diet together. He kept everything tempting out of the apartment, and I trusted him, so it worked. My weight shot down to 145 pounds. I finally felt like a human being.

I graduated. I got a job. I met my future husband. Things looked the best they had since the beginning of my teen years.

But I was growing away from Dad and slipping back into the world of food and temptation. I moved into my own apartment and started overeating again. I got engaged and was married eight months later weighing 190 pounds — and not even pregnant!

My husband must really love me to have endured the hell I put him through. I was a fat, mixed-up wife, happy one day, depressed the next, constantly overeating except for a few attempts at crash dieting.

One year I strained our budget by going to a diet doctor. I quit taking the pills just in time to avoid a nervous breakdown; but then I didn't have enough energy to work, so I had to quit my job.

We went to live with my grandmother. I joined a diet club and lost 25 pounds, then began to fall back into my old pit.

"It's because we live with Grandma," I complained to my husband. "She cooks all that good stuff and makes me eat it."

We got our own apartment and I continued with the diet club. That worked for about two months, but I again began to overeat and gain weight. This time it was my husband's fault: if only he earned more, I would go on an all-protein diet; if only we were rich, a nurse could plan and prepare all my meals.

"How are you doing with your diet club?" my father's well-meaning new wife questioned one day.

"I've stayed the same," I lied.

A friend of hers had lost 60 pounds through Overeaters Anonymous, she told me. She explained that OA was like AA and that it was somewhat spiritual.

I felt hurt and angry that my stepmother thought I might be one of those weirdo compulsive overeaters (even though I didn't really know what that meant); but now I know that she loved me enough to risk jeopardizing our close relationship.

Three days of crash dieting ensued.

Then I needed my fix. I hit the sugar bowl.

My husband walked in as I was shoveling tablespoons of sugar into my mouth. I was so startled I toppled the sugar bowl.

"Maybe I am one of those compulsive overeaters." The thought flashed through my mind at that instant.

"Maybe!" What further proof did I need?

I called my stepmother for her OA friend's telephone number, which I dialed immediately. Susie took me to my first OA meeting and she became my sponsor. She cared.

I loved the meeting — except for the spiritual stuff, which scared me at the time. I liked the anonymity.

The people in OA all knew how I felt. Some of them had come out of the same maze I was in. They really did love and care for me. I felt hopeful.

My life has changed so much since then. During the first eight months

I lost about 60 pounds, and I have kept it off for five years — with God's help, one day at a time.

About a year and a half ago I had a beautiful baby boy. My abstinence got rocky during my pregnancy, but it has been getting better.

I trust that my higher power, God, is everlasting. I believe that if our higher power — whatever each of us chooses to call it — is everlasting, so are our chances for abstinence.

Many wonderful things have happened to me since I joined OA. I use the tools; I ask questions of longtime abstainers; I read and absorb the literature. Most of all, I keep coming to meetings. They are lifesavers.

There is hope and love here.

May 1980

Who, Me?

THE WEIGHT WAS piling on and I didn't like it. I wanted a slim wife. She really should do something about that fat, I fumed to myself. Why didn't she just stop eating so much?

I loved her, even though she was much too heavy, and even though she kept stuffing all that food into her mouth. I knew she was suffering and I wished I could help her.

So intent was I on resolving my wife's problem that I hardly recognized my own. I was on the big side myself but, worse than that, I suffered from terrible sugar hangovers. The headaches that came upon me after a bout of compulsive overeating were intolerable.

I weighed 140 pounds for a long time — until I stopped smoking in my mid-twenties. After that I gradually put on weight. It didn't bother me until one day I found I had gone all the way up to 180 pounds. I ate normally for a while and went down to 165, but later on I gained it all back and the yoyo never stopped. Up and down. Gain and lose. Binge and diet.

Whenever a woman I was dating broke off with me, I got upset and devoured mounds of food.

"I'll eat this stuff just this time," I consoled myself. "I won't get too overweight. Besides, who really cares?"

Little did I realize what compulsive overeating was doing to me. I spent money recklessly on junk food or alcohol. When I was overloaded with sugar, I withdrew from everyone around me. Even after I was married, I would get depressed after overeating and feel as if I could never be close to anyone. Yet, I couldn't seem to stop having second, third and even- fourth helpings of my favorite foods. My weight climbed to 190 pounds.

Still, in my mixed-up mind my wife was the one who needed to lose weight. After all, I wanted a helpmate I could be proud of.

When my sister-in-law told us about Overeaters Anonymous, I thought it sounded great — for my wife. Off she went to an OA meeting. The following week, I went with her — not for myself, but because I was worried about her and cared for her so deeply.

I happened to have a sugar hangover and couldn't mix with the OA people. But I didn't let this change my mind. Assessing the meeting, I thought, "This is really good for my wife, but it's not for me." When it was my turn to introduce myself, I said I didn't consider myself a compulsive overeater.

Even after I began attending meetings regularly and sharing, I refused to say I was a compulsive overeater. Naturally, I felt left out. I wouldn't talk to anyone unless someone talked to me first — and hardly anyone ever did.

My weight kept rising; I was afraid of going over the 200 mark. By that time I was familiar enough with OA to know that I was in fact a compulsive overeater and that I was overeating out of anger and resentment. Finally, I decided to become a member.

Four years ago, although I still was not ready to surrender my will, I admitted that I, too, am a compulsive overeater. I took a sponsor — only because I wanted to feel accepted by the group — and I went through the first three steps. I lost 30 pounds, the most I have ever lost, during the first month. My headaches left me, and in place of pounds and pain, I gained serenity and peace of mind.

Then I had some breaks in abstinence. Lo and behold, the headaches came back each time — and so did the weight. Gradually, I came to know that abstinence feels better than compulsive overeating, and that it also looks a hell of a lot better on me. It even tastes better. So I have been maintaining my weight between 160 and 165 for a year now.

Because Overeaters Anonymous has given me so much, I now have a lot to give back. With my weight stabilized, I'm able to turn my attention to others. I can reach out to OAs who are suffering and tell them, "I care about you."

I have come a long way in this program. Giving service — first as a group representative, later as a public information chairperson and a World

Service Conference alternate delegate — has given me opportunities and experiences I never dreamed possible.

I thank all my OA friends who have helped me along the way, and I am looking forward to celebrating my OA birthday with them at an upcoming retreat.

In my experience, the handicap of compulsive overeating can be overcome through the willingness to change. I had to reach that place of surrender before I was ready to let God do for me what I could not do for myself.

The only suggestions I can give to anyone who wants to try it are: quit fighting, ask for help and reach out for a hand. It will be there.

Oh yes, I almost forgot to tell you about my wife. She is working the program just as enthusiastically, and our mutual caring has been a great help to both of us. We are very fortunate to be in this program together.

We invite compulsive overeaters everywhere to join us.

October 1980

Which One Is Me?

I HAVE A TRUNK full of masks ready for any and every occasion. How easy it is to lift the lid and select the appropriate disguise! Whenever I don't want to deal honestly with my life, I simply don a mask and hide behind it.

Did you say you wanted a perfect daughter? That mask is right over here. Would you like an accommodating woman for the night? Or perhaps a gracious hostess? These masks, too, are readily available.

But my masks are becoming too heavy for me. Their weight is crushing me. Behind them is buried a child who is screaming to get out, a frightened little girl who yearns to be enveloped in the warm arms of a loving parent.

As a child, every time I reached out I was met with cries of "Don't do that!" or "Bad girl!" Any attempt to grow by exploring was squelched with "Stay away from there!" and "You can't do that!" When I tried to learn through discovery I was stifled with "Don't touch!" and "Stop being so sneaky!" I was supposed to sit still, keep quiet and do as I was told. The message I got was "Be perfect."

It's no wonder I created a cache full of masks. I wanted to please, so I did as I was told. I kept quiet, I stayed away, I didn't touch. I began to curb my natural instincts, to withdraw my impulsive curiosity and to dampen my creative expression. If I displayed emotion or attempted to explore, I was only reprimanded — so why bother?

I stoically donned a mask of strength and stability. Gather 'round, feast your eyes on this remarkable sight: a woman as strong as granite.

That mask became so customary that it seemed like a part of me. It was almost impossible to peel it off. I lost my sense of identity and my ability to recognize my true feelings. Was my mask on or was it off? I could no longer tell. I hardly even knew, by then, that it was a mask.

Unable to elicit any sign from my parents — and later from my husband — that I was a worthy person, I sought solace in excess food. It took the place of a loving mother, an approving father, a doting husband. It became my indestructible fortress. But rather than just ward off the enemy, it became a prison: no one could get in and I could not get out.

With the help of Overeaters Anonymous I am finally venturing out of my lifelong dungeon and, one by one, I am slowly and painfully peeling away my masks. I am showing you, my OA family, the other side of me that has lain hidden in the deep, dark shadows of my being for so long. With your help I am discovering who I am and what I feel. I am learning to know myself, express myself, be myself. I am finding the acceptance, comfort and love I never got from my parents, my husband — or my food.

As I strip away all those old masks, the real me is emerging — curious, creative, expressive. Only this time, instead of feeling stifled and squelched, I am being encouraged and nurtured and loved. The more I reveal the real me, the more accepted I feel. And the more accepted I feel, the less I need those old masks.

How good it feels to put my face to the wind, bare and vulnerable and free!

November 1980

My Night in Jail

DOGMATIC. That word applied to me in every aspect of my life. I was unchanging and impossible.

Things were about as bad as they could get. I weighed close to 300 pounds. I was unemployed and broke. At twenty-four I was a failure, still being supported by a pair of loving parents who had reached the end of a seemingly endless rope.

They had tried everything to help me lose weight: diet clubs, doctors (some famous, some not), therapy, clinics, everything. After twenty years of failed efforts, I figure, the amount of money spent to help me lose weight could have put someone through a private college, with plenty left over.

But there I was, far from home and in jail! I used to think I was a cut above alcoholics. A lush could go to jail for drunken driving or public intoxication; but what reason could there be for *me* to be there?

I found out.

The police came to my door with two bad check warrants. The first, for a check written to my landlord, was due to a mistake on his part and the charges were dropped. The second warrant was for a check to the supermarket and . . . Well, I had needed to binge.

I don't even remember what I bought. It was just another one of the thousands of binges I had over the twenty-five years of my lifetime.

I could not bring myself to call my parents. By the time I finally contacted someone it was too late to get a money order delivered. Western Union closes early in small Southern college towns.

So I spent a hellish night in a cell block which I shared with five other women: a prostitute, a child beater, a thief and two drug addicts. They wanted to know why I was there. What was my crime? Robbery? Murder?

Now I can say Yes to both: I robbed the store of the merchandise I "needed," and I was murdering myself with food.

The next day I called my parents. They got me a lawyer and I was released from jail. All charges were dropped and my record was cleared.

That was fifteen months ago.

I had been attending OA meetings for eight months with little or no success. Although I had the desire to stop overeating compulsively, I still wanted someone else to do it for me.

Six weeks after my night in jail I was given the opportunity to go on an OA retreat. There I began abstinence.

Since that awful night more than a year ago, things have turned around radically. I moved, found myself a wonderful job and lost 90 pounds.

But all these blessings which I have received since attaining a lasting abstinence are not half as important as this one: I am happy. And, one day at a time, I have made a new friend: me.

I am still dogmatic in many ways, but I'm changing. And although change may be scary, it's far less frightening than staying where I was.

January 1981

Thinking of You

FOOD OBSESSED MY SOUL. I felt beaten, shattered, helpless, crying every morning, pacing the floor every night not knowing how to stop. At night I made promises to myself which I meant with all my heart but the next morning I could not keep them.

I lived through the hell of diet pills, booze, stomach relaxers, tranquilizers, hypnotism, acupuncture and self-induced vomiting. I was unable to break the pattern of eating and making myself throw up. One night I turned blue from food stuck in my throat.

When I came into Overeaters Anonymous six years ago I was so nervous and afraid I heard only one thing at my first meeting: "How many here have the desire to stop eating compulsively?" Then and there I knew I was not some freak who couldn't pull herself away from the table or eat only half. My problem had a name: compulsive overeating.

I asked whether anyone would sponsor me and a wonderful woman said she would if I wanted her to. I looked her over and said to myself,

"Well, she's not so slim but she is 50 pounds lighter than she was and she's on her way down."

I called her the next day and this beautiful woman said five words to me: "I'll be thinking of you." It was the first time in forty-five years that I felt someone cared for me!

I called her morning, noon and night. I called her when I saw someone eating an ice cream cone because if I saw, I wanted — and I got. All day long I called and I called again before going to bed. And every time I called my sponsor told me, "You don't have to eat."

I withdrew from sugar, flour, alcohol and diet pills all at the same time. And I didn't overeat, one day at a time. Whenever I thought about food I said the Lord's Prayer; and believe me, I was saying it almost every waking moment. I didn't know what else to do.

At night I sat in the bathtub sipping diet soda and smoking cigarettes to keep myself out of the kitchen. (Since then my cigarette obsession has been lifted through this program and the grace of God.)

After the first week I knew something had happened to me. Never in my life had I not overeaten for a whole week. Even when I was on diet pills I overate.

I believe today that my God lovingly scooped me up and placed me in OA, protecting and guiding me every moment. I am finally growing up and learning how to live. It has not been easy but God's grace is always there just for the asking. Instant help is available if I open myself up and accept my Higher Power's gifts.

Trusting, believing and expecting have given me the most beautiful freedom I have ever known — freedom to laugh and cry and love; freedom to live; freedom to be me. What a joy!

September 1981

Forever Friends

WHEN I ARRIVED in Overeaters Anonymous eight months ago I weighed 610 pounds. For the first two or three months I never really abstained but as of today I weigh 540 pounds. I have made it this far thanks to my "forever friends," and I know they'll be with me all the way.

I am a twenty-one-year-old male, the oldest (and biggest) of five children. I have been on every diet plan I ever heard about — and I mean every one. I've been to my family doctor, to a psychologist who specializes in weight reduction, to clinics where they use shots and pills and to the major weight reduction club. I've tried all these things and none of them worked at all, ever. Until I came to OA my compulsion ruined my diets and my life. I stole money, shoplifted and lied to get food.

I had an A average and made Phi Theta Kappa during my first year at a local college. Early in my second year I won an important calendar contest that is the key to a future in commercial art. I felt great about winning the grand prize of one hundred dollars, having my calendar framed and seeing it printed on the cover of a magazine; but I hated appearing at a banquet in my honor. Everyone was dressed up, some in tuxedos. I was wearing the only clothes I had that fit: jeans and an old shirt and sweater. It was a freezing cold January night but I couldn't fit into my coat, and I had to take a bus because I couldn't get into our family car.

At the pre-dinner gathering my weight was the topic of conversation, and all eyes were glued on me as I ate my meal. After dinner I had to go up in front of two thousand people to accept my award. I was terrified. When it was all over I was offered a ride home but, afraid I wouldn't fit, I said I already had one.

It was almost eleven o'clock and the buses had stopped running. For almost two hours I stood in zero degree temperature with no coat, hat or gloves, trying to find a way home. I had called a taxi from a nearby pay phone but when it arrived I couldn't get in. I tried another company and a cab finally came but I couldn't get into that one either. I made one last call. This time I managed to squeeze into the front seat. When we got to my house I couldn't get out. The driver had to apply all his strength to pull me out.

The next day I had the flu and that was the beginning of the worst year of my life. I rarely went to school. Instead, I stayed home and ate to the point where I should be dead today. It was unreal. As soon as everyone left I began eating. For six hours a day, five days a week I ate, using a salad bowl as a plate and an iced-tea pitcher as a cup. I consumed so much I had to eat in a prone position because I was too full to sit or stand.

I flunked out of college. I was never there, so how could I pass? I did not go out of the house except to pretend I was leaving, then I hid behind a bush about a block away. As soon as everyone was gone I returned home and began eating.

I tried the big diet club again; and I quit again.

Then I heard about OA on a radio talk show. From that moment on, life has been different. The people, the atmosphere and the suggestions for dealing with my problem are all different from anything I've ever known. The people here really care about each other and the program has one thing that no diet or weight-loss plan has, and that is God. I thought I didn't need God to diet. Now, each and every day I admit I am powerless over food and that my life is unmanageable. I reaffirm my belief that God can restore me to sanity and I turn my will and my life over to God's loving care. I have never felt better in my whole life.

Another thing this program has done for me is to get my mind off food except at mealtimes. When I feel hungry, angry or sad I get my mind on God, often using prayer or music to help.

For the first time in years I can fit into a car and get in and out without much hassle. I don't have a job earning money yet but I do have important goals toward which I'm working. I get bored sometimes but, with my OA friends and my family pulling for me, I can handle it.

My friends in OA are all dear to me, but there is one who is special. She and I are about the same age and we really understand each other. When I'm with her or talking to her on the phone I am so uplifted I feel I could fly. I love her, I really do. Because of her I am emotionally stronger.

The contrast between where I was and where I am now is unbelievable. I have come from the hopelessness of yesterday to these new days of sparkle and shine. And it's all because of the OA people I know and read about, God watching over me and a special friend who is helping me to reach my goal weight.

God love you all, my forever friends!

October 1981

Just Like Everyone Else

IDENTIFY, don't compare," they were always telling me at my AA meetings. But how could I identify in OA? There I was at my first meeting, and I felt like a tiny boat in an immense sea of women. I stood out not because I weighed 300 pounds but because I was the only man among nearly a hundred women. Back in 1975, men were almost unheard of at OA meetings in my area.

Women told of gaining weight after pregnancy. How could I identify with that? "That time of the month" for me only conjured up thoughts of mortgage payments being due. And what was a size 18 to me when I was having trouble closing my 46-inch waist pants?

One night I walked into a meeting late to behold a woman displaying the scar from her Caesarean section. Worse than that, the women at a step meeting told me I had to leave because they felt uncomfortable sharing in front of a man. *They* felt uncomfortable?

I began traveling out of my area to meet other OA men, however few. I looked for all-men's meetings but I soon realized that that kind of group suffered from the same limitations as did the all-women's meetings. The topic at the men's gatherings invariably turned to sex, which was one area in which I had more problems than I could handle. I didn't want to deal with it, so I began to stay away.

After losing 100 pounds I felt as if the body I had always compared to a '46 Chevy had been transformed into a brand new Corvette — sleek, powerful, sexy. Even though I was married, I wanted to take an extended test drive to see just what this new car could do. I shifted the gears and floored the gas pedal, but I couldn't seem to release the emergency brake. I was afraid. Girls had rejected me during my teen years because I was fat. Now that I was thin, would women still rebuff me? If so, what would be my excuse?

Women accepted and liked me, however, and I got over that fear; but my life was as unmanageable as when I was fat. I was thin, but I was still crazy. I discovered that, in my insanity, I really didn't want women to like me after all. So, to make myself as unattractive as possible, I put on weight. Obviously, I was not well.

The Big Book told me that no human power could relieve my obsession but that God could if God were sought. Finally, I reached my rock bottom. I was sick of being sick. I was willing to go to any lengths to get well.

As the fog in my brain slowly lifted I began to appreciate the program. My sponsor helped me work the steps — all of them — and I asked God to manage my life.

At long last, I began to identify more in meetings — with women as well as with men. The seed planted at my first meeting broke through the hard surface and I could share my pain and joy without feeling apologetic for being a man in a woman's world. I saw now that our problems are really the same: we are all compulsive overeaters, powerless over food. That is the bottom line.

Today my life is good. It is enjoyable and full of promise. As I look back at my early days in OA, I can laugh at myself; but I don't ever want to forget the pain and suffering and tears that led me to accept what I am: a compulsive overeater who needs the twelve-step program of recovery, just like everyone else in OA. I thank God daily for this program, for my sobriety and for my abstinence.

February 1982

A Disease of Isolation

BSTINENCE from compulsive overeating is the single most important thing in my life. Without it, I do not enjoy other people, places or things. At 237 pounds and abstinent I felt good about myself. I could see the good within me. At 138 pounds and not abstinent, I saw only a fat person who had no right to her own opinions.

Before OA, I believed thin people were right and fat people were wrong. Needing to feel accepted to stay alive, I presented myself as a doormat; but I became livid when anyone stepped on me. Self-condemnation made me see condemnation in the eyes of those who meant the most to me. What put me in that frame of mind? My inability to stop overeating.

Night after night I went to bed crying, "Tomorrow I won't do it anymore." Mornings, I woke up determined to control my uncontrollable craving. And each day, glutted with a heavy meal, I sat in front of the television, tears running down my face, simultaneously wanting to stay in my chair and get up and look for something to eat that would finally fill me up.

I decided death was preferable to my living hell. I quit trying to stop overeating. I'd had three phlebitis attacks, and now I invited a fourth.

I did not believe in God. How could I? God had not ordered my life the way I wanted. As a little girl I prayed to be like my thin sister, but it never happened. I asked to be loved, but I felt unlovable, and my wonderful, vital, generous mother died. I asked for a husband and children, but I was left single and childless. I had opportunities to marry, but those sweet men failed to arrive on white horses wearing Prince Charming suits.

"If you existed," I screamed at the God in whom I did not believe, "you would do something. Help me!"

As my disease progressed, I felt increasingly worthless. My saintly love for humanity turned into insane jealousy or intense hatred. My pent-up rage was unleashed on all who were brave enough to come near me.

In my growing isolation, I thought my condition was unique. I believed I was the only one who cried while eating, the only one who always felt

202

stuffed but never full, the only one who bolted my food because I was terrified someone would catch me eating.

I was lucky. At my first OA meeting the speaker told "my" story, even using words and phrases I thought I had originated. When I heard her describe my agony, and saw her serenity and happiness, I felt the return of an old emotion: hope. It seemed God was saying, "You asked for it. Here it is."

"My God," I gasped, "you *are* there!" Panic set in. I had been kicking my Higher Power in the teeth for years and now God was holding out a hand to me. I was terrified.

That night I asked the speaker to be my sponsor. When I disclosed my feelings about being so different, she told me, "If we don't stop feeling unique, we won't get well."

I went home and I didn't eat. I went to bed. I had nightmares. God had offered me a chance and I didn't think I could accept it. How could I stay abstinent the rest of my life when I couldn't stop eating for even one hour?

I called my sponsor, who told me, "Abstain for as many minutes as you can, and before you eat, call me. You only have to abstain today. Don't think of tomorrow. Don't even worry about the next hour. Just don't eat for as long as you can, then call me. I'll be here all day."

I wasn't alone! I gave her my food plan for the day and she gave me a job to do: Read the "Just for Today" card.

That day, seven years ago, I walked outside to the crisp air, brilliant sunshine and to a one minute at a time, one hour at a time, one day at a time miracle: abstinence. Since then there have been many miracles for me in this program, but that was the beginning of the greatest miracle of all.

June 1982

First Summer

HAT I HAVE EXPERIENCED in Overeaters Anonymous is more than a wonder to me; it is a miracle.

Less than a year ago, I had no friends and no contacts except for my son. Only rarely did I go out. My phone never rang, my curtains remained closed, and if anyone came to the door I kept silent until the intruder went away. I shopped at night so I would not be seen. I felt so alone I wished only to die. Twice I ended up in the hospital after attempting suicide. I spent a month in a mental hospital, where I was told I would have to go to a state institution if I did not improve, and I went through three years of psychotherapy.

Only when I came to OA did I find myself — and my freedom. I began to make friends and feel at home in a group of people who shared my sorrows and joys. Gradually, I became able to trust. As I opened my heart to a new life, I threw open the windows of my house and let in the bright sunlight. One day I left my door open and, instead of fear, tears of joy touched my cheek.

What a surprise it was when the phone calls began coming. I answered, and I was able to give back the love, understanding and friendship that were being given to me. At first I could not fathom why people were calling me for help, but they told me I had what they wanted. So I listened, and as I listened, I prayed.

I began to use the phone myself, calling my sponsors and other OA friends when I was hurting, when I wanted to share some happy event or when I just felt like saying hello. This from someone who wished to be invisible!

Now I am out of the house more than I am in it, basking in the bright sunshine — and getting whistled at. I smile, and there is laughter deep in my heart because it feels so good to be noticed and not to be afraid to go outside.

As I joyfully live each day I am seeing the promises come true. God is indeed doing for me what I could not do for myself. My abstinence is supremely important to me, for without it I would not be where I am now. I have lost more than 100 pounds, but my weight loss is just a bonus. This program has given me an opportunity to pick up and start over, a second chance to live.

This is my first OA summer and it has been very special for me. I rarely noticed all the living things around me before, but now I look around and see the green grass, the flowers, the trees, the sun, the clear blue sky, the singing birds. And I see the people. I look into their faces and give my smile to those who have none.

It is so good to be alive, to be aware. Sometimes I pinch myself to make sure I'm really awake.

When I open my eyes each morning, I ask my Higher Power to take my hand and be my partner for this day. Part of my prayer is, "Bring someone into my life whom I can love, encourage and help," for when I do that my problems seem small and the day is great. Then I thank God for my life and for the new day.

I am so glad I have a Higher Power and a family in OA and that, thanks to their help and support, I have myself. With each passing day, each new experience, I am getting to know myself better. I feel that I, too, am more than a wonder; I am a continuing miracle with whom God and OA are not yet finished.

August 1982

Feeling the Feelings

HERE I SIT, feeling high, and the first thing my mind goes to is food — out of habit, an oldtimer once said at a meeting. Happy or sad, in love or forlorn, with people or alone, our minds turn to food, just out of habit.

Food is not the problem; it's the feelings that used to make me compulsively overeat. I've got to get out of the food thoughts and into the feelings.

Before OA I didn't know how to handle those feelings so I tried to find comfort in food. When I came into the program eight months ago I weighed 240 pounds. (I'm five foot ten and twenty-two years old.) After four months I was down to 175, where I am presently maintaining.

Losing weight was the easy part. Now the question is what to do with all those feelings since I'm no longer compulsively overeating to cover them. My meals are not a problem; it's the in-between times, when my feelings — good, bad, happy or sad — take over that I have to catch myself. I have to remind myself that, today, I'm not running away; I'm opening myself up — to the feelings, to other people, to life.

Overeaters Anonymous has given me some powerful tools to help me do this, and my Higher Power supplies me with the strength and willingness to use them. I go to meetings so I can talk out my feelings, listen to others express theirs, and receive the love, understanding and contact for which I really hunger.

When things get rough, I make telephone calls to give me a lift and to share what I'm going through. I have a sponsor who's been abstaining a long time. He tells me over and over that working the program makes it possible to go through anything without overeating. He keeps reminding me, "You're not the only one who's been through this; it will pass." I trust him and talk with him about my personal problems and, sure enough, the bad times do pass.

I give service so I can get out of myself and stop thinking of just me all the time. When I get depressed, helping a newcomer makes my own problems seem less important.

There are also times when I go to the Big Book, the Twelve and Twelve and other AA and OA literature to help me get through one day at a time. And I try to work on the twelve steps a little every day. I rely on the steps to get rid of the fears and resentments that made me overeat in the past and to help me feel close to my Higher Power.

This is how I live through a day's feelings without overeating. At first, when people asked me how I manage to abstain, I said I didn't know. Then my sponsor gave me this insight: "You abstained the first day you came into OA, and continue to abstain, because you were tired of what you'd been doing out there."

It's true. I was so sick of being alone and destroying myself that when I came to my first meeting I had the willingness to do anything to feel better.

Eight months later, I'm learning to do things that before were fantasies. Now they're coming to life; they're realities. My excess weight is off and I look good. I have thousands of friends — OA people everywhere. All I have to do is pick up the phone, say my first name and that I'm in Overeaters Anonymous, and I have a friend who understands.

Thank God I'm here.

August 1982

Goodbye Off-Broadway, Hello World

KEEP THEM LAUGHING and they won't see how fat and ugly you are" was the motto I lived by.

I developed my act as a young teen, used it all through high school, then continued giving my sensational performance "off Broadway" for ten more years. I had it down pat and knew all my lines by heart. Quick with cute comebacks, always making people laugh, I was sought after to keep house parties from becoming dull, family get-togethers from getting too serious and club meetings from accomplishing too much business.

Always outgoing and the life of the party, even when there was no party, I came to think of myself as the Great Pretender. I had people (those who didn't live with me) believing I was easygoing and bubbly all the time and that nothing ever really bothered me. I was constantly told I should be on the stage. (What time does the next one leave? Ha, ha!)

My terrific reputation followed me everywhere but home, where there was painfully little laughter. After four children and ten years of living hell, the final curtain came down on my marriage. At that point my zaniness bloomed into full-fledged insanity. Go, go, go! Run, run, run! Do, do, do! Laugh, laugh, laugh!

My life was out of control and my eating with it. My weight went up and down the scale like a finger exercise: up to 200, down to 160; up to 220, down to 190; up to 248, down to 220. Always looking for that easier, softer way, I was willing to do almost anything to get the fat off. I tried diet pills, vomiting, fad diets, exercise salons, weight reducing clubs, diet clinics, mouth wiring and three gastric bypasses.

Seven months ago I came to OA. I have lost 55 pounds, but the biggest change — a miracle, to me — is that I am not performing as much as I used to. I have come to like myself and am better able to let go of that scared, insecure, unloved child who sought constant reassurance by making people laugh. Instead, I am increasingly letting God run the show. I occasionally catch myself falling into the old entertainment act, but I am quick to recognize it, take myself off the stage and come back to reality.

I thank the OA twelve-step program, my sponsor and especially my Higher Power for helping me put the Great Pretender into retirement. Hello, world; here is the real me!

September 1982

The "Macho" Hangup

SURGERY, divorce, custody battle, lawsuit, tax problems, job change, injury, car breakdown and hypertension — all within four months — plunged me into anxiety and depression. My treatment for the pain was food. It became the only comfort in my life.

But eating only added extreme overweight to my list of problems, deepening my depression and further raising my blood pressure.

Then a friend suggested OA. Having spent four years in Al-Anon, I knew the program would work; but I was reluctant to attend a meeting. Let's face it: overweight is not a very "macho" problem, and my male ego rebelled at admitting my weakness in front of a group composed mainly of women.

Fortunately, pain prevailed over pride and I started attending meetings, working the steps and eating according to a food plan. I expected weight loss, and I got it. I also got some unexpected benefits. Abstinence from unhealthful eating sharpened the mental skills I thought I had lost, and lessened my depression. I gained enough energy to begin an exercise program that contributed to the restoration of my health. I was able to face additional setbacks and problems with a more positive attitude, and I did not sink into despair.

As I became healthier physically and emotionally, my spiritual life grew stronger. I began to see my troubles — and their resolution — as evidence of God's love for me. I was able at last to grasp the simple truth that my happiness lies in doing God's will, not mine. Reliance on my own intelligence and willpower brought me only grief and sorrow.

I no longer ask for what I think I need. I have been so wrong, so often. The more I pray for God to send me what I need — not what I think I need — the happier I get.

Today I have greater physical health, emotional strength, mental power and spiritual peace than I have had in twenty years. The lesson was hard, but it was worthwhile. I doubt that I will ever be so slow to learn again.

December 1982

Three Words

HEN I CAME INTO Overeaters Anonymous it was to help a friend I'd met at a behavior modification, calorie-counting self-help group at college. Both of us were obese. She had heard that lasting weight loss was to be had by following the OA program, but she did not want to go alone, so I agreed to go with her. I did not have a problem myself, mind you. I was returning at an alarming rate to my top weight of 400 pounds; but I did not have a problem.

I went, I listened, and I heard two important ideas: (1) Keep coming back — it works; and (2) A Power greater than ourselves can restore us to sanity.

Sanity. That's what I wanted. I knew everyone else in the room was crazy, and I of course was not; but I sure could use some sanity in my life. I decided to give OA six to eight weeks and see what happened.

My Higher Power was a vending machine. Every night I ate fifteen to twenty assorted snacks, then puked my guts out. That's when I learned how to be humble and ask for help. I used just three words: "Oh, God, please . . ." I couldn't say anything more because I didn't know what to ask for. I really didn't have to. God knew.

By using this spiritual program of recovery, I have been able to forgive myself for many things, some of which are crimes. I have been abstinent for more than a year and my weight is approaching goal — a feat I've never achieved as an adult.

Thanks to OA, I am a happy and functioning human being who faces each new day optimistically, one day at a time.

May 1983

A Good Age

I AM SIXTY-NINE years young. At age sixty-three I started an OA group without ever having attended a meeting. Since no one else in the group had been to a meeting either, my mistakes went unnoticed and we all learned a lot.

Before OA, I was totally wrapped up in being a wife, raising children and being a grandmother and great-grandmother. I buried my longings for a career in food. But I was a widow when I found OA, so the path was open to finding *me*. As I learned to face my restlessness without overeating, my aspirations came to the surface. The doors opened, and with my newfound energy I dared to go through.

I went back to college and, because of my experience in dealing with the loss of my husband, as well as my compassionate nature, I was offered a job at a local mortuary. I am now a para-professional in grief counseling, a career position. My OA life has expanded my insight and sensitivity, greatly enhancing my ability to help people who are grieving.

The changes in my life were so drastic that I could hardly believe them. I anticipated each day with excitement and, after a while, I began to give myself credit for all that happened. I thought I was in control. I never stopped going to meetings or OA functions. Oh, no! I was no dropout, leaving only to come back seeking a new start. Besides, my ego told me I was an inspiration to others who were still suffering. I hid my shortcomings in my enthusiasm for OA, showing my "before" pictures to newcomers and anyone who was interested.

Before OA, I was a size 22½. I lost weight rapidly at first and ended up a 14½. I was feeling so good, so free, that I began to take things for granted. I stopped losing at a weight that was still unhealthy for me.

Recently I underwent major surgery and later learned that my blood pressure had gone way out of control. Well aware that overweight is danger-ous to such a condition, I realized that my complacency had caught up with me.

I'm grateful I have this program to help me live in the answer, not in the problem. I have a physical, emotional and spiritual disease, and I know what the solutions are: abstinence, prayer and meditation, living the twelve steps and giving my life to my Higher Power.

I'm not young anymore, but any age is a good age because it's where you are. Each twenty-four hours is vital and precious when I totally turn over my life and my will to a Power that has more wisdom than I can ever hope to have.

I don't know how I got where I am, or where I'm going; but my Higher Power does. So I'll trust God to guide me, and pray for the good sense to listen.

June 1983

Open Arms

THERE IS ONLY one photograph of me I really like. It shows a tow-headed urchin, grinning hugely, with her arms spread wide, greeting everyone. I was five years old.

My childhood was not unhappy. I grew up in a small midwestern community with a dog, a horse, summer camps, bicycles, an apple tree and family vacations that were half adventure, half whiz-bang good times. I had three sisters much older than I, one who taught me to ski, one who took me camping and a third who teased me incessantly. My mother tells me, "You were an exuberant child. You could do anything, and you wanted to do everything."

Eventually my sisters went away to college and I, about twelve years old, was left at home with a dad burdened by increasing responsibilities and a mom dealing with the empty-nest syndrome. I hit a slump. I withdrew into myself, buried myself in books and became a model student: quiet, diligent, straight A's, every teacher's dream.

I became obsessed with making every aspect of myself perfect. Perfect grades, perfect wardrobe, perfect runner, perfect daughter, perfect figure. Somehow, perfect was never enough, though, so I was always looking for some way to make it still better.

One day, when I was thirteen or fourteen, my best friend told me how her sister lost weight: "After she has a big meal, she makes herself throw up. Isn't that gross?"

Gross, yes, I thought, but intriguing. I tried it. Unpleasant as it was, it felt good to relieve that uncomfortably full feeling.

At first I told myself it would only be after big meals: Thanksgiving dinner, the football potluck, an eating session with my best friend. Then it became almost every Saturday night, because Saturday night without a date is a good time to eat and forget your problems. Then it became Friday and Saturday nights because, well, I never had dates on Friday either and I didn't like going to football games with a bunch of girls who were phony and boy-crazy. By the time I graduated from high school,

I was vomiting at least once every night.

In college I was even more socially dried up. I got straight A's, worked two part-time jobs and found a way to graduate within three years. I constantly berated myself for not also being a champion runner, a dancer, a flute player, a faithful piano player, a better daughter and a popular friend. Two or three times each night I gorged myself, alone in my room, with food I stole from roommates or the dorm cafeteria. I started each day with the same goal: lose 10 pounds, stop throwing up and become perfect in all the aforementioned ways.

I began having stomach problems and severe constipation. About this time, the college newspaper was filled with articles about binging and vomiting, and I found out I was not alone. I went to see a counselor who convinced me to tell my boyfriend, my sisters and parents. I did, in an agonizing and gut-wrenching confession. Then the counselor sent me to a psychiatrist who put me through elaborate testing and prescribed an anti-depressant.

The prescription helped. Too tired in the evening to do anything but sleep, I started to feel the joy of a clean system. I gained confidence, decided to marry my college boyfriend, and lost 15 pounds. However, about two weeks after I went off the anti-depressant, I plunged into a depression far worse than any I had known. I quit my job prematurely and I got divorced after six months of marriage. I floundered emotionally.

Now, about this time in most people's stories, they will tell you they found OA. Not me. During the next two years things picked up steadily, and I did a lot of growing on my own before I walked into my first meeting. I got my career organized and I worked on my self-esteem. A new job, a new relationship and a new lifestyle all helped me draw away from the need to constantly binge and vomit. I was happier than I had been in a long time. Still, I couldn't entirely shake the binge-vomit compulsion.

I was looking for something, so I went to a counselor, who suggested OA. I had been dying for someone to show me what I needed to do. I had figured out many things about why I had the disease but I still didn't know how to deal with it. The tools and steps of OA showed me how to change the behavior that was making my life unmanageable. I have been abstinent for nearly five months now, one day at a time.

Sure, there is a long way to go; but the relief and joy I feel at having my binging and vomiting behind me are worth everything. Although it takes a great deal of work, I feel I am returning to that joyous, open-arms state captured so well in that photograph taken twenty years ago. I feel the love of someone special, the support of many good friends, the acceptance of family, and my own strength and courage. And it's wonderful!

July 1983

A Teen in OA

I THINK I WAS FOURTEEN when I hit bottom, but it's not too clear because at the time I felt my entire life had been a bottom. I couldn't handle anything, so I retreated into a world of insanity. All I wanted was either for Prince Charming to come and take me away from it all, or to be placed somewhere under in-patient care.

Desperately, I tried to convince my mother that I was crazy and that I needed help; but at the same time I resented any attempt she made to help me. Being so deep in my own sickness, I could not see that Mom, too, needed help.

She soon found it in Overeaters Anonymous. The change that came over her seemed unearthly. The first thing I noticed was that one day in the grocery store I couldn't talk her into buying pastries from the bakery department. I called her a Goody Two-Shoes. It upset me to think I was being left behind to be miserable by myself.

Two weeks later I went to my first OA meeting. The people really cared and the program sounded pretty good, except for that part about rigorous honesty. I remember popping my empty diet soda can during meetings, and when I realized I was doing it, I would turn red and begin biting my fingernails. For everything I did I prepared a defense, figuring people would ask me why I did the weird things I did. If someone had asked about the can-popping, I would have said, "It comes naturally. My family's high-strung." But no one ever asked. They just loved and accepted me.

Four months into meetings I was still eating everything I could while Mom was out of the house. I couldn't stand the thought of her seeing my failure. She had experienced "automatic" abstinence, and there I was, just hanging around not doing anything. Still, I knew OA was the place for me, and that if I quit I would go back into that dark cell of my own making.

While I was at a retreat one weekend, my parents made a decision to move. When they broke the news, it hit me that I would have to leave

215

behind all the opportunity for recovery that had been available to me. I was furious with myself for having assumed I could loaf around and expect to start working my program "tomorrow."

When we moved, there were no meetings except for one that was fifty miles away. Mom and I made that long trip once a week, until our car broke down. But that didn't upset me. I knew we'd be out of that awful place within a few weeks.

Well, here we are, more than a year later, still in the same place! We went back to our old home town a few months ago, and the loveliest woman came and did an OA service workshop. Hearing her speak about the different problems she'd had giving service helped us to walk through our insecurities and start a meeting.

We sat there Thursday after Thursday seeing people drift in and out, until finally two women came and stayed. Within a short time, these wonderful newcomers had organized a second meeting.

I haven't mentioned a Higher Power so far because, until two months ago, when my abstinence began, I wasn't able to rely on my Higher Power for anything. It's still hard for me to let go, and to keep letting go.

Recently, I reached a place in program where I thought I was doing just great. I took back control of everything but my food — and I fell on my face. It hurt so bad to make those mistakes; but I've picked myself up and dusted myself off. I am trying to let go, just for today.

July 1983

A Different Summer

 UMMER VACATION has always been something I dreaded, like the measles. While most kids were counting the days until school would be out, I complained about how miserable the summer would be. To me, summer meant loneliness, self-pity and loads of guilt from continuous, uncontrollable binging. Thanks to OA, though, this summer is pleasantly different.

I am nineteen years old and an abstaining compulsive overeater. As an only child with two working parents, I spent quite a bit of time by myself, especially during the summer. I never made many friends, which further contributed to my misery.

I spent every day alone in the house, never going outside to enjoy the sunshine or the beauty of my surroundings. Blind to all of God's gifts, I never saw beauty in anything, only ugliness.

Every day I slept late, often past noon, to escape from worry, fear and boredom. Most of the time I never even got dressed until four o'clock, unless I went to the store for more food. I usually stayed in bed all afternoon watching soap operas, eating, feeling sorry for myself and sinking deeper into depression. I was miserable because I ate so much, and I ate so much because I was miserable.

Every summer got worse.

Then I found OA, and the program has literally been a lifesaver. I did more growing up in the past few months than in the entire eighteen years before.

With the help of my OA friends and my Higher Power, I lost between 60 and 80 pounds. This alone has changed my summer in countless ways. No longer ashamed to put on my bathing suit, I now enjoy swimming and soaking up the sun. I also love to water ski, and it sure is easier without that extra weight.

I cannot even begin to describe the recovery I have experienced emotionally. My self-esteem is slowly building up, and I have more friends and a brighter outlook on life. I am rarely inside the house on a beautiful day. I go outdoors and thoroughly enjoy the lovely sights and sounds. The beauty has always been there, but for the first time in my life I appreciate it. I am also managing to accept myself as I am — an imperfect human being who is capable of fantastic growth. Hope is present in my life now.

Most remarkable of all is my spiritual growth, and it is this that has enabled me to experience all the other changes. Relying on a Higher Power is a new experience for me.

Now I have a strong belief in a Higher Power and I often wonder how I survived without it. I see evidence of God's existence every minute of every day. I pray each morning for strength, and by turning over my will and my life, my food obsession has been lifted. One day at a time, I have been given the strength to accept God's will, no matter what it is.

I could never have made this progress alone. I am grateful for OA as a whole, and for each of its individual members. This summer, through OA, I have made the first real friends I ever had. My parents still work, but I am never alone anymore. My OA friends are just a phone call away, and my Higher Power is just a prayer away.

I hate to think of the eighteen summers I wasted — all the pretty flowers I refused to see, all the sunshine I refused to feel, all the birds I refused to hear, all the love I refused to experience. I guess it took suffering through those years to get me ready for this beautiful program.

Thanks, OA, for letting me have a more terrific summer than I ever believed possible!

July 1983

A Real Man

I MUST HAVE LOST something somewhere along the way since finding the program. I read publications with real stories in them — the Big Book, *Overeaters Anonymous,* Lifeline and Grapevine — and I feel compassion and love, and sometimes I even cry. I sit in my OA meeting and shed real tears when I hear people say they have finally found something to believe in, or that after years of loneliness they now have friends in OA. Somehow, I must have lost my manhood.

I remember my father saying, "Real men don't cry," and how I longed to become a real man. So I did not cry. I remember my mother and father working all day, then coming home and fighting with each other. But I did not cry. I remember feeling lonely because no one would talk to me or listen to me. But I did not cry. I remember my older brother sexually abusing me when I was young, and wishing I had resisted him even though he was bigger and offered me the acceptance I longed for. But I did not cry. I also remember stealing sweets from the corner store and the good feeling when I ate them.

I had no friends. I would not allow anyone to enter my shell. They might find out how lonely I was. They might discover how much fear and guilt I had that I might be a homosexual. As long as I kept these secrets, I could show everyone what a real man I was.

I did not cry when I married a woman who did not love me. I did not cry when she took a boyfriend and brought him into our house. I thought I was living in the sexual revolution. I did not cry when my oldest boy kept running away from home; I just didn't understand why he did it. I did not cry when my other children, out of fear, would not look at me and avoided all contact with me. I was a real man. I could only take love. I did not know how to give it.

I have been in Overeaters Anonymous just six months, and I have learned to cry — not to gain advantage over my wife and children, as I sometimes did, but because I have discovered God.

God walked beside me when I was running from myself, and God lifted a huge burden off my back when I asked to be relieved of my problems. All I did was take care of today. By providing evidence for the authorities that I am being helped and that I am helping myself and my children, God has kept me out of prison — and will continue to do so, I trust, as long as I keep growing.

God brought beginners to me when I needed them, and showed me how to twelfth-step and how to build a group. God gave me the sponsors I needed when I needed them: a tough one who opened my eyes to my other problem, alcoholism, and an easy one who did nothing except wait for me to get off my rear and go to work on my program.

But the greatest thing God did for me was to let me cry. When my youngest son looked up at me and laughed while we were swimming, I cried. When my other children turn to me and show they love me too, I cry. And I cry when my wife looks at me with a smile that shows she forgives me for what I was.

I must not be much of a man anymore, because I love to hug and get warm fuzzies. I want to talk and let you have part of me. I want to be able to cry and to accept tears from you whenever we meet. I want to look at myself and think about how beautiful we are.

I thank God for showing me OA. I don't have to *act* like a real man anymore. I'll just be me.

July 1983

Another Season

YOU COULD CALL IT a midlife crisis.

A few months ago I realized I would soon be having a birthday and the age I would be turning was not pleasant to contemplate. Suddenly — and it felt like overnight — I was feeling different about certain aspects of my life that had not been a problem before.

The husband to whom I had been dedicated for more than half my life began to get on my nerves and to look just plain bland. The children in whom I had taken such delight seemed to be tying me down and demanding more than I was willing to give. The home I had so lovingly tended became a burden, and I felt that if I had to clean one more toilet, I would flush myself down with the Vanish. My hobbies no longer held my interest. And I was looking longingly at food.

One morning I went back to bed because I did not want to face the day. The doors were locked, the phone was off the hook and I didn't want to think about *anything*. At ten thirty I got up and ate lunch. That sounds like the me of years ago, not the me of today.

Another development was extremely disturbing for a woman who has always been as faithful to her husband as I have been. I began looking at other men — something I never did before. I dreamed of leaving everything behind and having a mad fling with the man of my dreams. He would, of course, be perfect and exciting, and life would be wonderful.

It seemed that the God to whom I had grown so close had moved. Of course, it wasn't because I didn't want to pray, meditate or even think about God; or was it? I began to feel helpless, lost and miserable.

Today, however, I am secure in the knowledge that I am not alone in this season of my life, just as I was not alone with my disease of compulsive overeating.

Remembering what saved my sanity and my life when I came to OA, I decided to turn in that direction now. First is my abstinence. At a recent marathon, I heard someone say, "The good sometimes gets in the way of the best." I didn't understand it then, but today it makes sense.

My abstinence has been good, but by no means the best it could be. Getting food back into perspective — facing my feelings rather than covering them up with excess food — is the best abstinence I can have. It may be painful, but it's the only way I will get to the other side of my problem with my sanity, dignity and self-worth intact.

I have learned to share with others at meetings, on the phone and in any way I can. I am willing to learn how to take as well as give, to accept the love and experience others offer. I am willing to slow down and reserve some time for myself. Most of all, I am willing to depend on God. I know God loves me and wants me to have the best possible life.

I have taken my beloved Big Book down from the shelf. It was a comfort and an inspiration to me before, and it is again.

Thanks to this program, I have a way to make it through this season of my life and whatever others lie ahead. I thank God for this wonderful Fellowship and for each person who touches my life. I would hate to go through life without them.

August 1983

Conquering Depression

I FIRST THOUGHT of suicide at the age of thirteen. I forget the specific reason; I only know I envied the dead their peace. My excuse for not ending my life was that I would miss the next Disney episode on TV.

For the ensuing twenty years I lived within a cycle ranging from OK-ness to the deepest pits, including one serious suicide attempt during my freshman year at college. I was in and out of psychotherapy for most of those twenty years and, for the last six years, I have been in treatment continuously. Therapy was based on the assumption that my moods reflected cyclic disturbances in brain chemistry. I responded well to antidepressants, but they made it nearly impossible to stay awake.

One factor contributing to my problem was my inability to connect with people — to love and be loved. I had the illusion that I should be totally self-sufficient. There were times, though, when my needs overwhelmed my determination and I would curl up on the couch and scream my agony into a pillow. When the tears stopped, I always returned to my comforter, food.

Reading the Big Book was a revelation. Over the years I used food in druglike ways — as a stimulant, a tranquilizer and an antidepressant — without being conscious of it. Even though I hated my excess weight, I used the excuse that I needed some sort of pleasure in my life since no one, least of all myself, cared what happened to me.

Sixteen months after coming to OA I despaired of ever achieving abstinence. Several times I was on the verge of dropping out, only to have one of my new friends tell me exactly the right thing to keep my hope alive. Even if I wasn't abstaining, they cared about me. This was my first experience of acceptance and unconditional love. I had difficulty believing in this miracle at first, but I kept coming back to renew the contact. I quickly learned that hugging felt good and that it was not necessarily a sexual invitation. I even learned not to be threatened by another man's hug.

Seven months ago, I finally took steps two and three, and I've been abstinent, except for two minor slips, ever since. With my newfound faith in the program, I can draw strength from many sources never available to me before.

Two months into my current abstinence, I had another depressive episode. No longer using food as a means of dodging my emotions meant I had to live with them. This time, though, I could make choices. First, the Serenity Prayer had shown me that, if indeed my mood was outside my control, I was only frustrating myself if I tried to fight it. What I could control was my behavior in reaction to it. I could extend my depression indefinitely by eating over it, or I could ride it out. This was the beginning of true wisdom for me. Second, I could remember that nothing in life lasts forever, that "this too will pass." The old hopeless belief that I would feel this way forever was part of the illness, and was in direct opposition to experience.

That was five months ago. A depression that might have lasted for months was over in less than two weeks. Since then I've had occasions when my energy was low and my sleep disturbed, but I haven't experienced that crushing hopelessness characteristic of my old depressions.

One of the biggest changes in my attitude occurred just recently. I used to give OA credit for "turning me into" a loving, lovable man after being difficult to get along with all my life. Now, I give OA credit only for enabling me to free the loving, lovable man I'd buried under a hundred pounds of misery. I am discovering the joys of loving and being loved. In several close relationships with women, I am finding that love without sex can be rewarding too.

My therapist and I can't figure out whether the changes in my attitudes have affected my chemistry or whether the chemistry was never that important. At this point, I really don't need to know. With continued self-understanding, abstinence and progress in the twelve steps, I have reason to hope I will never go through that awful depressive cycle again.

September 1983

Another Kind of Darkness

RELAPSE — a word that made me shudder in dread; an experience I prayed would never be part of my OA story. I wanted to be able to point proudly to the fact that I was progressing toward spiritual recovery without interruption.

Naturally, the kind of relapse most visible in OA is that in which the individual returns to compulsive overeating. Not me, I swore.

As it happens, my relapse did not take me on a foray into compulsive overeating, but on an emotional journey through superiority feelings, loneliness, unrealistic expectations, self-deception, anger, complacency and, finally, a cold, paralyzing fear. It was a darkness which I did not share. No one asked about the inner me, and I didn't offer the information. After all, I wasn't overeating and I still had my physical recovery.

Then one of the people I sponsor lovingly educated me to the fact that overeating is the last symptom of relapse. Relapse, I was told, is a process which sometimes begins long before the actual return to food. Relapse begins in the heart and in the head. Overeating is only the final symptom of the collapse of good feelings and, ultimately, of hope. Thank God this woman loved me enough to look beyond the facade, take a risk and give me the insight I needed to make a crucial decision: For today, I choose to live fully in the recovery.

I am fascinated by the variety of ways my Higher Power uses to get my attention. In the past, it was my fat. Only when I was physically uncomfortable and sick would I stop overeating and begin to listen. Now, H.P. captures my attention through my emotions.

Hopefully, I will focus my powers of concentration on God — the source of my recovery — and remember the pain I felt when I focused only on me. As someone so aptly said, "It was not that I thought badly of myself, but that I thought only of myself." My emotional relapse was the result of self-will run riot.

I am not immune to relapse in any area of my recovery. My character defects did not leave me the moment I began to abstain and lose weight.

As a matter of fact, they never "left" me. I must constantly make the choice to live beyond them and without them.

Now that my story includes emotional relapse, I have attained a deeper level of compassion and understanding, a heightened sensitivity toward members who remain at their normal weight yet lack that spark of joy which marks spiritual recovery.

My emotional relapse has taught me some valuable lessons. The disease of compulsive overeating is perhaps even more cunning, baffling and powerful than we know. Any unwillingness on my part to work a total program opens the door to relapse. After having been there, I choose to keep that door firmly closed.

September 1983

Hills and Valleys

RECENTLY, after almost two years in program, I fell, inexplicably, into a depression. I felt so non-contributive that I avoided meetings and found every excuse not to be around people.

Unmotivated and feeling let down both at home and at work, I wondered whether I was having a nervous breakdown. I wasn't able to tell anyone, and I even left a couple of meetings and cried — not because the people weren't wonderful but because I felt so rotten inside. I had the awful fear that if I laid my problem on the group or an individual member, I would spread the depression. The result was, I simply could not express my feelings to anyone, not even the people I know love and care for me.

For the past few days I have been reading OA literature — all I could get my hands on — and this has guided me back to sanity. God does speak to us, if we listen. In each piece I read, I found something I could pull out and hang onto.

I have come to understand that hanging on is the important thing; we fail only when we stop trying. For each of us, there are hills to scale and valleys to pass through in this program, and in life. But we are not alone. H.P. can and will handle all problems, and show us what we need.

After making a mess of things, I've decided to let go and let God clear it all up. And God is doing it — beautifully.

September 1983

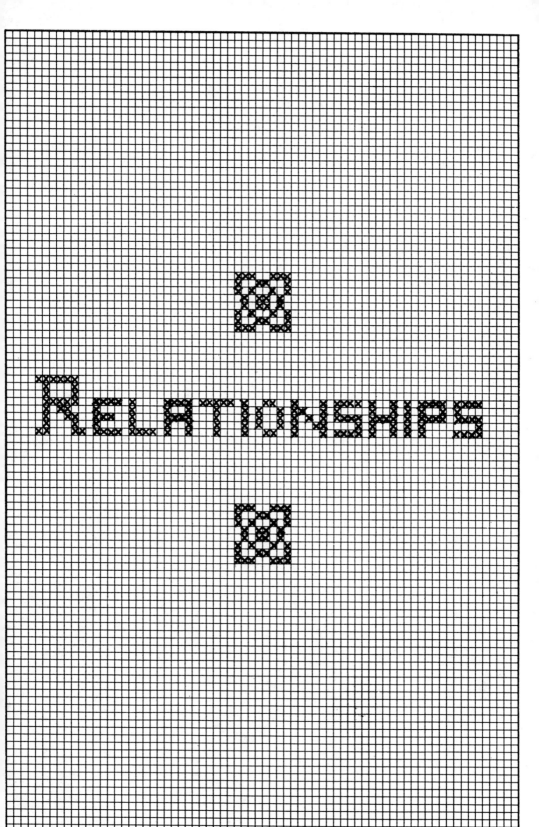

Relationships

Goodbye, Super Mother

EVEN BEFORE my children were born, I loved them. They fulfilled a deep maternal longing in me. I wanted to do everything for them, give them everything. I planned to teach and train them so wisely that they would have the perfect start in life.

As my children grew, there was only one thing I could be proud of: my accomplishments as a mother. I pictured myself as Super Mother.

Their father was an unhappy person, hardly able to deal with himself, much less his family. Yet I was sure Super Mother could compensate; I would give them so much love and guidance they could not fail to be Super Children.

Recently I found a fragment of an old diary. On every page I had written of desserts made, favorite foods prepared for my children. Even if it had occurred to me that I was expressing love through food, I would have seen nothing wrong with it. I cooked all these good things, therefore I was a good mother — a Super Mother.

I took part in all my children's activities. Who would be room mother? Who wanted to work at the school carnival; collect for the rummage sale; be den mother? Who else but Super Mother?

Self-sacrifice became my identifying characteristic. The children came first — and last, too. Mother might lack shoes, but the youngsters were decently dressed. Mother might be sick and, in time, recover without benefit of medical intercession, but a child with a fever was properly attended.

Mother had longed to play an instrument, ergo her children must have lessons. Many a cold winter morning before dawn found her folding newspapers or helping deliver them. She might lose a night's sleep, but her offspring's term papers were typed and turned in on time.

It never occurred to me that I was trying to live my life through my children. Is it possible to be so blind as to think that one parent can fill every need, every void, be all things and all people to a child? I did that, and I did it without the slightest suspicion that it might not be

231

right for them. They must have seen that all I had, all I hoped was bound up in them. Yet, I did not conceive of this as a heavy responsibility to place on children, an encumbrance that would harm them.

When I pictured their future, the view was bright and promising. It would be a time when all my "sacrifices" would be justified by my children's success. I saw myself in that great day as the Queen Bee, surrounded by adoring children and grandchildren.

Meanwhile, in the present, I gave them little to be proud of. They had to introduce me to their friends, a grotesquely obese mother carrying a terrible load of unhappiness. How could they be proud? True, their friends came to like me when they knew me; but I wonder how many times my children had to brace themselves for the first shock?

I tried to give them everything, but I could not give them a mother with self-worth and self-confidence. They saw me as a fellow victim of their father's unreasonable rages, his open abuse. We could not protect one another.

As the children grew up and reflected the sickness of their parents, my bright hopes went down to defeat. My children were not successful or happy people. In their problems, I saw my own failure. All of my "sacrifices" were in vain, and my life was hopeless.

At this point, I came to OA. A more depressing example of despair and self-hate is hard to imagine. One OA friend has told me that her unspoken judgment was, "Here's one who won't be around long." Another says she felt that I had sunk to such depths it didn't seem possible for anyone to climb out.

But there are miracles in OA. My new life began with that first meeting. I am now a healthy seven-year-old and still growing.

Many things changed as I changed. My children have worked through and fought clear of many problems with a new steadiness and sense of self-worth.

And where is Super Mother?

I have laid aside that title along with my fantasies of perfect self-sacrifice. OA has taught me that I do not have to be God anymore. What a relief!

OA has taught me that I have a right to be here. I am a person. I do not have to validate my worth through my children. They are people, too, and their choices are their own.

I have learned that my needs are important, that it is not wrong to love myself, to do things just because I enjoy them. I have a right to live. Does this seem childishly simple? It was news to me.

Now, I can be honest with my family. There were chapters in my life that I had hidden from them, but all is open now. Since I don't have to be a tower of strength, or that parental paragon, Super Mother, I can be myself — an imperfect human. My children know and love a real woman now. They are free to put their arms around me and say, "I love you, Mom." Some people may take this for granted. But my children never did that before. Could it be that they were afraid I would return their embrace with a stranglehold?

I used to feel that the one thing I did not want was for my children to feel duty bound to "poor Mother." But my sponsor pointed out that it was exactly what I was setting myself up for.

I am not sitting at home now, waiting for their visits and whining that they neglect me. I did not ask for shawl and slippers for Mother's Day. I hinted that I could use a book of road maps! I have had some complaints that, "You're never home; we have to make an appointment to see you." But it is said with a new respect. And when we are together, I know that they are there out of love and not duty to "poor Mother."

For years I had no life or identity of my own; all that is changed now. One thing led to another. I lost my weight and became active. The excess of maternal affection found outlets in sponsoring and sharing. I released my clutch on my now-grown children and ventured into new experiences, new fields. I learned to drive a car and found a new independence. A small talent that I had neglected for years led me to a fascinating new line of work.

I have more to discuss with my children than my latest aches and pains. Since I have let go some narrow and unrealistic old ideas, they feel free to talk honestly and openly with me, not censoring their words for me. My children are now my dear friends.

It seems to me that many mothers are placed in a picture frame. Loved and idealized, they are not treated as real people by their grown children. It is a sad reflection on our society that so many men and women grow sentimental on Mother's Day and neglect her the rest of the time.

As for me, I don't want to be in a picture frame. I'm alive, I'm real. I'm human. And my children know it.

We've said goodbye forever to Super Mother.

May 1978

I Came in out of the Rain

W HEN MY GROUP made the decision to have Big Book study on Tuesday evenings, I had been in Overeaters Anonymous more than a year. During that time, I learned that dieting in OA is exactly like dieting anywhere else: it doesn't work.

So, when we started on the Big Book, I had to confess that I had not read it. Oh, I would open it occasionally and take a quick peek, then snap it shut again.

How could I, a middle-aged grandmother who had been raised in a strictly teetotal family, relate to any of the alcoholic stories in the Big Book, I asked myself.

One evening, a young woman who was leading the meeting chose to review the story, "Stars Don't Fall," which appears on page 400 of the Big Book. I immediately identified with the author of this story. I had been married to a wealthy man. We lived in a beautiful, custom-built thirteen-room house, and I possessed anything and everything I had ever wanted — everything except happiness. My husband became obsessed with money and things, and I wasn't too far behind.

Soon, a much younger woman came along and my husband divorced me. I had joined the "five-o club," so he was through with grandma.

I was devastated. I thought I would die. But I figured I wasn't going to be that lucky. Besides, I still had a daughter to finish raising. Being a single parent isn't easy, but my daughter has been a comfort and a joy to me. There have been times when I felt like an old mother hen trying to raise a baby duck, but no matter.

Our family was torn to shreds. I turned to food to shield me from the agonizing pain. I mean, I went after sweets like Dracula after blood.

I tried several diets for brief periods without lasting success. I would jokingly comment, "I'm never going to eat rump roast again." This corn-fed midwesterner even began using chopsticks, hoping they would make me tired of trying to eat. But I proved an adroit pupil and ate better than ever.

234

Since my discovery of the Big Book, I have plunged into the program in earnest. I particularly enjoy my daily meditation. I truly believe my Higher Power guided me to this community for the purpose of finding OA friends as well as myself, and for rediscovering God.

I no longer live in the plush house that took extra help to keep up. My present home is about one-third the size of the former one. I don't fret about whether or not it looks like something out of the pages of the latest home decorating magazine.

For those who have had the rug pulled out from under them, it's just as that Big Book story says: "stars don't fall." I know that a cloud may cover them up now and then. But I have faith that my program will keep me steered in the right direction. As I grow older, I will not grow bitter but instead become a nicer, more mellow person as well as a slim and trim one. I feel I am on the right path now instead of on the path of destruction.

Even though I have to consciously re-program myself to accept as natural and healthy an average weight loss of only one pound a month; and despite the fact that my program has been a little shaggy, with detours and wrong turns, I know that I am coming out of the maze and heading right on target.

All the members of my group have become very dear to me. I have shared my feelings freely with them during meetings, yet I still have my own little island of privacy, as I would guess everyone does. No one imposes their ideas on others at these group meetings. We simply take what we need and allow others to do the same.

Currently, I am venturing forth on my moral inventory. I am ready and willing; spelling things out on paper is good therapy, I'm learning, as I keep dragging out more.

I have come in out of the rain, and OA is my shelter!

July 1979

Love, Marriage and Recovery

IT'S TIME WE CAME OUT of the closet and began talking about the massive upheavals in marriage and family relationships caused not only by compulsive overeating but also by the recovery from it.

Often, just when we're beginning to feel good about ourselves, when a glimmer of self-respect has returned, our spouses begin exerting subtle sabotage. This may range anywhere from a vaguely dissatisfied attitude which pulls our old "It's all my fault" strings, to an out-and-out threat to leave if we don't quit going to so many meetings.

This is not at all unusual. Changing the balance of power, the roles, the way we deal with each other is always unsettling to a relationship, particularly to the partner who is watching rather than doing much growing.

Healthy people don't marry sick people. If we look around, we'll probably find ourselves surrounded with emotionally unstable companions. Often, whether they too have self destructive compulsions or not, they suffer from the same deep lack of self-esteem which characterizes our disease. Were they not so afflicted, they would not have chosen relationships with people who dislike themselves.

Harsh as these statements are, I have found only a few exceptions. People have told me that they are afraid to "get with the program too much" because they see marriages breaking up all around them and they don't want it to happen to them. Having had this experience — and the good luck to work through it with my husband — I offer this account of our search for personal growth in the hope that it will help someone.

Years ago, when my husband and I began to turn our lives around, we made a pact. Part of it was unspoken, part carefully negotiated. Essentially, it was to stick together through our personal changes; to allow each of us to do whatever we needed to do to grow up and not to take any behavior personally; not to expect one partner to meet more than 35% of the other's needs, especially emotional needs; if necessary, to separate only after extensive marriage counseling. It was understood that each of us was responsible for telling the other what we wanted so that constant analysis of the other's feelings was not necessary. This, however, did not mean that either of us was obligated to perform as requested.

We both shed occasional tears over the distance between us as we went about setting up other people as part of our support systems. But the freedom created by that distance gave us more energy to change ourselves because we worried less about the other person and the marriage. Between the two of us and our individual growing, we were able to take better care of the children than ever before, and with a continually improving quality.

Instinctively, we had realized that, since we were not emotionally fit to establish a primary relationship, we might as well stay in familiar surroundings until we could see who each of us would turn out to be.

The next year was murderous. There was considerable fear, anxiety and pain. Hurt feelings and jealousy of each other's friends constantly arose. Gradually, however, we learned to deal with these feelings and they were put behind us. We began to experience a new personal freedom. No longer tiptoeing carefully around each other to avoid mistakes and therefore rejection, we found that we could accept a few errors in judgment, both our own and the other person's. As each of us improved, so did our ability to handle relationships. Our friendship grew right along with our respect for each other.

After several years, we both began to choose to put more into the marriage, not because we thought we should or because we were afraid not to, but because we just wanted to. When we began all this, I wouldn't have given a nickel for our chances of staying together. Now, it looks as though we will continue to be a partnership. Although we find that we do indeed love each other, the new solidity of our marriage is based primarily on the values and interests we share.

Where's the romance, you ask. There isn't any. Long ago, I recognized romance for the artificial high it is — just another sensation we misuse. Excitement does come and go, but I don't look for it or find disappointment creeping in when it doesn't happen. In other words, it isn't an addiction anymore. Besides, if I'm working the program, I already love everyone unconditionally anyway, so I must find other criteria for choosing a person to live with. Forming a primary relationship out of love alone would be like buying a house because it has a roof.

I'm glad we stayed together until we could make a reasonable decision. I believe I would feel that way even if we were now deciding to split up, because now I have confidence in the choices I make. Had I left when I was so sick, I would always have wondered if my perceptions had been accurate. Of course, a cooperating partner makes it much easier, though I have friends who stuck it out when they were the only ones growing and changing. They merely made that same pact with themselves and detached from the uncooperative partner's fears and threats, reassuring him that they were not ready to fly the coop. In some cases, the partner was forced to reevaluate his own life; in others, he merely sank into sullen acceptance. I know of no case where the spouse left the changing overeater, although some overeaters grew past their husbands or wives and eventually decided to leave. They, too, are glad they stayed until their emotions were stable.

Thus, the fear that the program will break up a marriage is probably unrealistic in most cases, because it appears that it is the recovering overeater, not the spouse, who is the initiator in such events. In other words, we recovering compulsive overeaters are usually in control of the marriage's survival or demise.

The bonus for my husband and me has been that each of us has developed a marvelous support system made up of several main people and numerous other friends. If he is busy or harassed and I need someone to listen to me, I can find a friendly ear without any trouble or resentment at all. If I'm away at an OA function for the weekend and he wants to go to a movie or out to dinner, he has many people he can call to do so, rather than moping around the house. It has meant less time for each other, of course, because one does not just use friends while the partner is out of town or busy and then dump them when the wife or husband returns. We both invest time in maintaining our friendships because we feel they have added a dimension to our lives that has enriched our partnership immeasurably.

This new freedom, given by the program, allowed us to support each other in our growing, saved the relationship and, finally, gave us steady love which now spells deep satisfaction to us both. No longer two sick people locked together through fear, we now have a wonderful new lifestyle filled with loving friends, meaningful work and a wealth of relationships, including our primary relationship which often, but not always, comes first.

Postscript: After reading this, my husband looked me in the eye and said, "Considering all the fine people we each love, I think the fact that we still choose each other is *very* romantic!"

September 1979

The Willingness To Be Sane

MY HUSBAND will never know how much he helped me to grow by losing his temper. The irony is that he always used his anger to control me. I hate arguments and I would do almost anything to keep peace, even if it meant giving in when I was right.

That was the sick game we played for years. I understand my husband and I do not judge him or love him any less, but the fact is I am through playing that game. It has been one of my defects of character, and what is happening in this area of my life demonstrates the soundness of the OA suggestion that when you ask God to remove your defects, you'd better be ready!

Looking back, I can see that playing the game was a way for me to shirk my responsibilities. I could always say, "Jack won't allow me to do that." Or, never really sure if what I was doing was right, I let Jack tell me because heaven forbid that I should make a mistake.

I started going to night school and I was doing well until Jack began to complain about my being gone two nights a week. I wasn't spending enough time with him and the children, and anyway, I didn't need a diploma at my age.

It's true that he supported the family well enough so that I didn't need to work, and that was enough to make me give up. I thought, he is right; I have no business going to school.

I do not judge my husband for this. On the contrary, I accept the responsibility for allowing it to happen. Now that I am involved with saving my life through OA, he is trying to use the same tactics and I feel sorry for him because they are not going to work this time.

I feel very serene about my decision not to play the game anymore. I know it will be hard for me to stand by my decision, but there is only one way for me to go: forward.

When I try to explain it to Jack, he cannot or will not understand what I mean. I don't expect people who are not in the program to know how I feel, but I believe it is my obligation to express my feelings as well and as considerately as I can and then leave others' reactions to them. The way for me to show that I really mean business is to just keep on keeping on, with joy and serenity and a smiling face.

Good things are happening for me, and it is exciting — and scary. It is a feeling I have never had before. It's so free. I don't have to try to manipulate my family by catering to them, by giving them all my time and my entire life so they will like me and want to do things my way in order for us to get along. I don't need that anymore. I like myself — at least, more than I did — and if my family can like and accept me as I really am, that is an extra; but it is no longer essential for me. Now that God is removing this defect, too, I am free of another burden. And I know that as the burdens roll off, the weight will roll off and I can become the person God wants me to be, one day at a time.

Like many men and some women, my husband can only see the physical side of a man-woman relationship, and he feels threatened if I am friends with another man. Perhaps if I were not in the program and our situations were reversed, I would feel the same way. But I will not put a limit on my friendships. My husband's jealousy, which extends to women as well as men, and to anything that takes my time, is his problem, not mine. He will have to grow up or be miserable. Much as I would like to ease his pain and have peace in our lives, I do not have the power to do it. I only have the power to ease the pain in me by working the steps, staying close to the people in the program and turning my life over to the care of God as I understand God.

I can honestly say that right now I am so happy and so in love with life that the turmoil I encounter on the outside is causing only a little ripple inside. Before the program, it would have been a tidal wave threatening to engulf and destroy me. Thank God, I have choices today: I have abstinence, I have serenity, I have friends who understand me and like me. I don't have to be alone. I don't have to be unhappy. I don't have to overeat. I don't have to fight with myself. I don't have to have anyone's approval but my own.

That is why I say that my husband's temper tantrums helped me. They helped me to see things as they really are and to accept what I cannot change. All this sounds so positive, and that is how I feel right now. But I know there will be times when I will want to give up, when I will feel that I am making a mistake.

But I have turned my life over to the care of God and I am putting my faith in God's power and God's love. The only thing *I* have to do today is to stay abstinent, and that is in God's hands too, unless I take it back. So really, the only thing I have to do is trust in God's love and in God's power.

Who would have thought that by looking in the mirror and asking God to remove my defects I would feel so strong through my weakness? Who would have thought that by simply accepting myself and my defects that I could be so happy? Who would have thought that I would feel so free? Not I. I would never have believed it. This program has taught me to expect miracles. It has taught me to *accept* miracles.

The program has given me the ability to accept people as they are without thinking I have to change them or save them in any way. I am free to love them just as they are. It is easy enough to do this with people in the program because we share so much. It is harder with the people in my life who are not in the program and who are trying their best to send me back to all those "fat" attitudes. But today, I *do* love and accept them, though I am not doing it on my own. "On my own" would mean condemning them and judging them and trying to get them to love me. I see this more plainly today than I ever have.

I am turning loose many old ideas, slowly but surely, and it feels good after I work through the pain. It is like having a tooth pulled: it hurts, but it feels so much better afterward. I am letting go of people, especially my children. They have lives of their own to do with as they wish, not as I would have them do. I'll just lay the triple "L" on the people in my life: *love, listen, let go.*

Surrender. There is such power in that! We are not perfect; wouldn't it be boring if we were? What would there be to look forward to each day? As long as we are on earth, we will always be able to grow and get better, but we each have to decide for ourselves if we want to grow or if we want to hang off the branches of life like the gray moss that hangs on the trees in the south.

I don't want to be old gray moss, dead and ugly, useless. I want to be like a beautiful flower opening up to enjoy the glories of God. One day at a time, slowly, serenely, gratefully enjoying all of God's creatures and everything that happens to come my way.

I am willing to become better; I am willing to have God remove my defects. I accept the fact that I will never be perfect, that the people around me will never be perfect. I am willing to let them live their own lives, and I am willing to live through my insanity to reach sanity. I am willing to live through my weakness to reach my strength. I am willing to show gratitude to God by accepting myself today, just as I am, right where I am, expecting a miracle. Knowing that the miracle has already begun.

In the words of the poet Kahlil Gibran, "I wake at dawn with a winged heart and give thanks for another day of loving."

October 1979

OA Mother

THERE I WAS, going to many meetings a week, involved heavily in OA service work and dashing in and out of the house waving to my kids as if they were mere acquaintances.

Could they throw some fish fillets in the microwave? I just had to get to the steering committee meeting; the group was having problems. I ignored their grumbles as the door slammed behind me.

I also blocked out my son's plaintive, "Mom, do you have a meeting tonight?" Every time he asked it (and he asked it every day), I felt a sudden flash of anger.

"Stop keeping track of me," I thought. "Why do you always say that?" I salved my guilt with reminders that I was "usually home after school, wasn't I?" Could I help it if the phone kept ringing while he tried to tell me about his day?

Another good defense was telling myself that it was also up to their father to spend some time with them. "He's worse than I am," I huffed. "He's always late for dinner and he yells at them when he gets here. They get more from me than they do from him. I'm doing the best I can; I only have two years of abstinence and I've got to take care of myself."

An alternative to anger was calm rationality. "This is a selfish program, and I'm improving all the time. No good can come from masochistic flagellation; guilt is self-defeating. I'm not the greatest mother in the world, but I'm *so* much better than I used to be. If I don't take care of myself the way I have to right now, there won't be anything left for the kids anyway. I'm doing what I have to do."

And so, what with ignoring, blocking, defensiveness and rationalization, I continued to have very little time for those two beings who had been with me since the beginning of the long decline into the illness. Through constant emotional battering ("What's the *matter* with you; you know better than that"; "I've had it!" "I *told* you what would happen if you did this again. You're grounded for a week!"), floods of being bought off with sweets and apologies and total inconsistency in their days, they had accompanied this very sick person through life. Once again, they rolled with the punches.

One day I was forced into some evaluative writing and a very gentle poke at the status quo emerged. I decided to try to spend more time with them. I thought that regular dinners together would be nice. It took me two months to actually implement the idea, and then it didn't last very long. But the seed had sprouted. Something shifted inside me. Like a mountain brook going underground to seek a new course after an earthquake, a major attitude adjustment was secretly taking place.

One day I realized that I wanted intensely to be more of a family person. The words of the old AA speaker who had ranted about how the program was supposed to return us to society, not set us apart from it, came back to me and were finally absorbable.

Everywhere I looked, I found evidence that this was the intent of the twelve steps. We are to be productive, contributing members of our families and our communities. I hadn't been ready to hear it, so I had never noticed all the references to this idea in OA and AA literature, and in the words of speakers with a lot of sobriety behind them.

Putting these discoveries into practice hasn't happened overnight; I'm still working on it. I'd like to report, though, the joy I feel at the *desire* to be a parent after all those years of believing I should never have had children because I was such a terrible mother and was damaging them, followed by the first years in OA, learning not to feel guilty about them but still avoiding the responsibility of meeting their emotional needs.

I am amazed at how well they have come through. Their early years were so tumultuous that any flak they threw up themselves was hardly noticeable amidst the turmoil caused by the adults around them. They never had a chance to try *not* to rock the boat. As things became calmer, a few of their own behavior problems emerged and were slowly worked out. They continue to grow along with me, and I really appreciate how charming and loving they manage to be much of the time. Further, I am thrilled that their sibling squabbles, which used to raise an instant battle cry in my heart, are now often just an annoyance.

So this year, I connive to get everyone together for dinner because I long to have time with them all, not because I feel it's the thing to do. Wanting this family contact is such a treasure that it brings tears to my eyes to write about it. I could never have forced it. No amount of "shoulding" myself could have made me really love them or given me the discipline to plan a way to have quality time with them.

I wish I knew exactly what process has caused all this to happen so I could pass on the secret, but I'm completely mystified. I doubt very much that it was anything I did at all. I abstained from practicing the illness, stayed positive as much as I could and tried to live the steps to the best of my ability — an ability that kept improving. Time carried me forward until my progress finally became evident, even to me.

Two summers ago I was taken to task about my traveling time away from home. It took a week of talking it out for the defensiveness to subside. Today, such a dressing down would raise no hackles. I really *feel* like a good mother. It's just one more unexpected gift this marvelous program has given me!

June 1980

The Courage To Be Free

IF I KNEW NOTHING else when I came into Overeaters Anonymous two years ago at more than 180 pounds, I knew I had a weight problem. I did not have to reach 200 to be convinced because I had already been there. I was always gaining, losing and gaining back.

I was totally miserable and unmanageable. Soap operas and food — that was all I lived for. I would put my children to bed for lengthy naps so my eating would be undisturbed. My house was a mess, though I will say the children were always clean. I took pride in them, but I resented their presence and the life I was locked into by my own choice.

Upon coming into the program I found abstinence right away, and I have maintained it to this day. From the start God has been with me, helping me accept my powerlessness over food.

A loving sponsor gently fed me program and, very gradually, I came to believe that I was a person — a good and loving one. With the help of my sponsor, other OA friends, the program and my Higher Power, I have maintained my weight at 105 pounds for more than a year and a half. Never before in my entire life did I maintain a weight loss.

To do this I had to become honest with myself. Those first months were not easy emotionally. In fact, it is not easy today either, because I do not want to deal with my problems or with myself. That is why I ate and ate.

Through reflection, I became aware of feelings I had long suppressed and was afraid to act on for fear of rejection by others. I came to realize that I was different, that I was living a lifestyle that was not right for me. No wonder I resented my children: I should never have had them. But I did, and I was responsible for them to a large degree.

After much pain, thought and therapy, I separated from my family. I gave my husband — a very good human being — temporary custody of our two young boys. Yes, I love them. I am finding out how much I love them. One day I might even want them with me again.

But for today I have to build a new life for myself. Through a friend in the program I was able to gain employment and get on my feet. I get by. There is enough money for rent, food, a little entertainment when I have the boys and some to carry around for an emergency.

And that is all I need for today. Material things are nice, but not all that necessary when what you need is freedom. For today I live the way I believe I was meant to live.

A new life — that is what I have. I have been called selfish, self-centered, uncaring and abnormal. But that's all right because in my heart I feel OK. Most of all, I feel free. I am not living in quiet desperation and bewilderment today.

Yes, there is guilt where my children are concerned. They are too young to understand. There are lonely moments when it hurts and I cry, wondering whether what I have done is right.

For today, it is right. I truly believe in a Higher Power, and that my family and I are being taken care of. I do what I can for them and I do what I can for myself.

I do not want to go back to the food. For today I am willing to do anything that will keep me from that destruction.

I thank OA and its program with all my heart. I give this Fellowship whatever I can and I do whatever I am capable of in terms of service because, if I don't, I will not keep what I have.

I was able to come to terms with myself only through the help and support of OA and my friends who did not abandon me because of who or what I am.

Thank you all for helping me find the courage to be free and for giving me a new life.

January 1981

Working with Others

LIFE IS GOING TO BE fantastic now," I said to myself.

By the grace of God and this program I had lost 100 pounds and was thinner than I had ever been. More than that, my bad temper — and the need to pick fights — had been lifted. The first few years of my marriage were rough, and I set out to make my amends. I was beginning to like myself so much that I could even believe my wife really loved me.

When the disease blows like a hurricane, it is difficult to have a positive sense of one's sexuality. With recovery, I began to experience a new sense of self-worth, along with an improved body image. We talked about having children, and we even chose names. Yes, my wife and I were on easy street, I felt.

Then one night I discovered that she was seeing another man. All I could think was, "How could she do that? I'm thin!"

It was strange that my temper did not flare up. I told her I realized what a poor husband I had been in the past, and what a royal pain in the neck to live with. Hearing this, my wife began to cry. She asked me to forgive her. I did — something I could not have done before this program.

When I learned that my wife had resumed the relationship with the other man, it was more of a shock than the first time. I couldn't believe it. This had never happened when I weighed 250 pounds. Now, she was telling me she no longer wanted to live with me.

All my old tapes began playing at full volume: "You see, you thought you could recover and be a good person. You thought you were sexy, a good husband, and spiritual. You fat fool. You have always been a repulsive failure. You have always been a dishonest person. Of course she is leaving you. If you were her you would do the same thing. Who are you to believe that some power is going to restore you to sanity? You have always been a worthless hunk of junk, and OA doesn't change the bottom line."

Soon the tapes went into the usual finish: "What's the use? I tried the best I could to work all three sides of this program, and I've failed. It's only a matter of time before I gain all the weight back and more, so why not start binging now? It doesn't make a damn bit of difference."

But then the strangest thing happened. A man called and said he was hurting and needed this program. He didn't want a woman sponsor. Would I help him?

I wanted to say, "Look, I'm just about ready to kill myself, so maybe I'm not your best choice."

But what came out was, "Sure, when can we meet?"

God knew what I needed.

We started talking about the disease, and we shared for many hours. Then a miracle happened. In working with this newcomer and sharing my program I was, as the Big Book promises, "amazingly lifted up and set on [my] feet. It is a design for living that works in rough going." My new friend needed help and I was able to give it. In this way I was pulled outside myself, and I knew that life was going to be fine — even if it was not going all my way.

The Big Book touches on just such a situation: "Let no alcoholic say he cannot recover unless he has his family back. This just isn't so. In some cases the wife will never come back. . . . Remind the prospect that his recovery is not dependent upon people. It is dependent upon his relationship with God."

Whenever the old tapes start to play, I have found that working with others is a sure way to get back on the road to sanity. I had always thought a divorce would be the end of the world. Thanks to this Fellowship, it has been a new beginning.

February 1981

An OA Fairy Tale

ONCE UPON A TIME, not so long ago, there was a young woman who was convinced she was a bad person and that people did not like her. The truth was that, being unable to control her world or herself — especially her urge to overeat — she did not like herself.

One day she read about an odd assortment of people who called themselves Overeaters Anonymous. They would not allow their pictures or full names to appear in the paper. She did not understand this; if they had such a great way of losing weight and gaining emotional strength, why not let the whole world know the secret of their success?

The woman was very skeptical. She had spent thousands of dollars and tried uncounted reducing methods to become thin (so that everyone would love her and she would love herself). This OA thing was probably like all the rest, she figured, but she might as well give it a try.

Wonder of wonders, the people in OA did not ask for money or insist on weighing her. They didn't measure her hips and they didn't push a diet in front of her. They only told her to keep her mind open, to try to be willing to learn and above all to be honest with herself.

This sounded simple enough but it turned out to be quite difficult. She tried being honest and it scared her. But she worked on keeping her mind open to the ideas she heard and she kept listening to the twelve steps and twelve traditions.

Soon, to her amazement, it all began to make sense. Little by little, she even gained a concept of a Higher Power that was totally different from any she had ever had.

The people in the program, and one man in particular, became very important to her. Because the man had been in OA a long time she thought he must be very wise. (And he was.) When he offered her his friendship she accepted, not realizing that she was still clinging to some of her old ideas. One of these was the notion that love between a man and a woman was always expressed sexually.

Her friend's understanding of love in the program, however, was much clearer than hers. It did not include sex. This puzzled her although as time passed her love and respect for him grew stronger, as did her physical attraction to him.

Thanks to the man's kindness and intelligence, as well as his practice of the principles of the program, the woman was encouraged to examine her true feelings and to accept them. After many hours of talking with the man and with her sponsor, she began to realize that love for a man does not necessarily involve a sexual relationship. She came to understand that she was free to love the man and all the other people in the program without feeling guilty and without being afraid that they would expect more from her than she was able to give.

Just as this man loved her but chose not to get involved sexually, so she could love other men without feeling obligated to fulfill their sexual expectations. She began to perceive that when a man in the program said he loved her, she did not need to leap to the conclusion that he was propositioning her; and she could likewise tell men she loved them without having erotic intentions.

The man had showed his friend that he loved her as an OA member, as a human being, as a woman. That was such a strange experience for her and her feelings were so new that it took her quite some time to assimilate everything. As she grew in the program she began to see that she was worthy of being loved, by herself and by others.

By attending meetings and continuing to read the OA and AA books and pamphlets, the young woman is learning more about herself all the time. She still has a long way to go in her recovery, but she has a program that helps her live and grow one day at a time. Out of this strange, painful and beautiful experience has come unconditional acceptance of herself and other people.

All this is so wondrous to her that it seems like a fairy tale come true.

The End.

Or is it The Beginning?

March 1981

Higher Power, It's All Yours

RECENTLY I'VE BEEN having a daily encounter with two familiar emotions: anger and resentment. They come up whenever I try to control my mate: what and when he smokes, what and when he drinks. In brief, his life.

Me, a controller, a manipulator?

Yes, me.

The pain that acting out my rage causes me, him and our relationship has finally made me willing to consider the possibility that I might need to give these reactions over to my Higher Power.

Believe me, I have tried to control my feelings — to keep them inside, to pretend they will go away. But trying to control emotional binges reminds me of the futile years I spent trying to control eating binges.

I have tried being calm and rational, dealing with each situation by using psychological insights. But plucking at a source of irritation with analytical tweezers is like trying to be calm and rational about my overeating by counting calories in those desperate days before OA.

No matter how hard I try not to, I still become judgmental, critical and condemning whenever my husband behaves in a way I don't approve. Then I become defensive and self-righteous, and since I no longer repress my anger with food I start arguing.

Afterward, of course, I feel guilty and remorseful. I make my apologies and tenth-step amends but I feel bad about myself, which I suspect is what I was aiming for in the first place. I still tend to sabotage feeling good about myself, though I must also say that I am getting better.

Which brings me to the twelve steps. Am I willing to give up the pain of controlling my partner? Am I willing to give up my rageful reactions, scornful looks and disapproving comments, no matter how justified I think I am? Am I willing to admit that I am powerless over him as well as over my own emotional tornadoes? Am I willing to admit that my life is unmanageable when I react in this way?

Yes! I am tired of fighting. I am weary of analyzing the relationship and each interaction. I turn to my Higher Power for the serenity, courage and acceptance I need to let go of my control and let God take over, to live my own life and let my husband live his.

I am not making this decision for his sake. I am doing it for me because my sanity depends on it.

The Big Book of Alcoholics Anonymous is right. Truly, this anger and resentment — my dramatic rages and emotional wringers — are luxuries I cannot afford if I want to live in a state of wholeness.

So, Higher Power, it's all yours.

Thank God I only have to do it one day at a time. In fact, I don't have to do it at all. The steps promise me, and my experience in the program assures me, that God will do for me what I cannot do alone. I don't have to understand it. Trying to understand only locks me up inside my head. I don't even have to believe it.

I simply know it.

April 1981

Objection Overruled

ANGER, DESPAIR, fear and a sense of impending disaster filled me as I walked through the door of my first OA meeting.

There were more than seventy people there and I remember little of what was said. I suppose something found its way into my head because I kept going to meetings.

Slowly I began making eye contact with people and even found the courage to respond when one of them spoke to me. I will always feel a special love for that person, the first to reach out to me in friendship. Soon I felt warmed by an abundance of unconditional love from many beautiful people.

I tried to resist the program but some spark deep inside refused to die. I came to believe there was hope for me and my assorted problems. I played around with the twelve steps for a long time until I finally realized they were the only way out of my bottomless pit. At that point I began to take them seriously.

Now I am confronted with the need to make another decision. My family objects to my spending so much time on the program and tells me I am foolish to expect any change in myself. My meetings are ridiculed as "fat shows," my newfound friends are given labels I resent and I am derided for associating with the people who have given me so much love.

What shall I do? Give in to the demands of my family and abandon the only hope I have? Or will I have the strength to insist that OA is my only chance for a sane life?

I wonder whether seeing me change and grow in self-respect has threatened my family in some way. I long to assure them that as I learn to love me I won't stop loving them, that my love for them is even stronger now. I wish I could make them understand that I cannot give up this program.

Viewing the situation realistically, I suspect I will never convince them of my need to live the OA program. None of them is or ever has been overweight so they cannot fully understand my problem. They have other difficulties, of course, and I try to be tolerant; but as time passes I see that the person I love the most will probably never be tolerant of my problems. How can I learn to live with this intolerance of anything less than perfection?

I turn this question over to my Higher Power every day. Day by day, step by step is my only hope for a solution. I cannot allow the past to pull me down now. I must go forward and live each day to its fullest, reaching out for the happiness I deserve.

Come what may I cannot — I will not — allow myself to be pulled away from OA. I am discovering that I have a strength that seems impossible. Imagine me standing up and telling my family that I will continue with OA no matter what they say or do.

I can be self-reliant now. And it is all thanks to this program and the wonderful people in it.

May 1981

Afraid No More

AFTER BEING IN OA a little more than a year, I went home to visit my parents. They hadn't seen me in all that time, and I felt quite anxious as I set off. This was the family I had allowed to manipulate me all my life. At thirty-six, I was still letting them put me in the role of a child. Their hold on me was so strong I was afraid even God and OA couldn't lift that burden from me.

My parents met me at the airport and greeted me warmly. They saw a new me, for I had lost 95 pounds. They knew about my being in OA but the change took them by surprise. The compliments soon subsided, however, and within two hours my parents were their old manipulating selves again, scolding me for not spending more time with the family and for not doing what they thought I should do. It was obvious they wanted control, but they weren't getting it.

I had indeed changed. Within the new body was a new person. At first I just listened, silently repeating the first three steps and the Serenity Prayer. Then, when my parents started to demand answers, I obliged them. I began by telling them that my life is my own and that I try to do what God wants me to do.

During my two weeks with the family, I learned nine things about myself, all of them having to do with emotional and spiritual recovery.

1. I learned that I could love, really love, unconditionally and that I was willing to go that extra mile. I couldn't do that before OA. I only loved people who loved me in return. With unconditional love I don't feel cheated or shortchanged if I am not loved back. I just love; and that is freedom.

2. I learned I am free to be me. I don't have to be someone I'm not just to be accepted. My family can accept me or reject me, but I am still me, and to be me is all right.

3. I learned I can be everything God meant me to be, and that means nothing less than the best. I recently discovered the prayer, "Show me what you had in mind when you made me." OA has taught me to make that request every day, then to live that way.

4. I learned that I can rejoice, reverse and relax — my formula for turning things over to God — in all circumstances. No matter how bad the situation may be, I rejoice that I am just where I'm supposed to be; I reverse my worry and seek God's will for my life; and I relax in the knowledge that God's love wants the best for me and that God's power will make it available. I couldn't do that before OA either.

5. I learned that ideas foreign to my program will enter my head from time to time, but I do not have to lose my serenity over them. Instead, I can recognize them for what they are and let go of them. Before OA I couldn't deal with threatening thoughts, so I stayed in turmoil all the time.

6. I learned that I am responsible only for myself, that I cannot control others. My mother is a beautiful person but she worries about everything and everyone. I saw how greatly my own attitudes had changed. Whenever my mother expressed her worries about matters that were strictly the concern of one or another of my brothers and sisters, I replied gently, "That's their problem, not ours." At first my mother thought I had become insensitive, but on my last day there, her eyes sparkling with understanding, she presented me with a new T-shirt. On the front it says, "It's their problem" and on the back, "It's not my problem." She got the message!

7. I learned that I could make decisions and stick to them. All too frequently no one could decide what to do next, so everyone sat around and did nothing. On a couple of excursions I announced that, as the driver, I would start the car and leave at such and such a time, regardless of who was or was not ready. At the specified time I pulled out of the driveway, and everyone who went had a great time.

8. I learned that sometimes it's OK not to make decisions. On one occasion the family was squabbling and asked me to settle the dispute. I

kept myself out of the argument by saying it didn't matter to me, and I let them resolve that one on their own.

9. I learned I didn't have to defend myself or argue. A year ago I would have lashed out at anyone who offended me and regretted it later. This time I sat outside in the moonlight watching the stars and mentally reciting the first three steps — and it wasn't hard to keep my mouth shut. I couldn't have done *that* before OA!

All these things I learned while I was home a few months ago. What the sum total means to me is that recovery is freedom. Freedom is not stopping something, giving it up, quitting, swearing off. Freedom is beginning, expanding, awakening, growing, learning, becoming and being aware.

I went home afraid that what I had learned in OA would not stick and that I would come back worse than ever. I returned from my trip afraid no more.

March 1982

Twelve Hugs To Grow On

I HAVE FOUR BEAUTIFUL, healthy children — three girls and a boy. I love them dearly, but until I came to Overeaters Anonymous I could not touch them. I was afraid. I felt unworthy of being a mother.

At meetings I asked people if there was hope for me because I so yearned to hug my youngsters. The answer I got was that I could change.

Over a four-year period I learned to hug and touch — and love — my fellow OA members. I became known as the lady who always hugged.

Each time I shared about not being able to touch or hug my children, people came up to me afterward with suggestions such as: "Go up to their room when they're asleep and kiss them."

While I was trying to follow these suggestions — without success — a lot was happening to me on the inside. I was learning to risk rejection in the security of the OA meeting rooms. I thank all those who, by responding to me with acceptance rather than turning away as I expected, gave me the courage to start reaching out to my children.

It was not easy. One day I stood in front of my thirteen-year-old daughter, feeling the old fear but knowing the time had come to put it aside.

Today I touch and hug all four of my children. They are wonderful kids who freely express their love for me and their father as well as their grandparents. I can't help thinking that, during their early years when I was too frightened to put my arms around them, I must have done something right in spite of my fear and inadequacy.

Had I known when I came to OA that I had all that growing up to do, I'm not sure I would have stayed. But losing weight started me on the road to recovery and, with help and love, I'm getting better.

At our house these days we have a hugging formula we like: four hugs to kick the blues, six to maintain wellbeing and twelve to grow on.

My wish for each of you is to give — and get — all the hugs you need today. I know I will.

April 1982

It's Catching

So MANY TIMES since coming to OA, I have been told by the older
generation of our Fellowship how fortunate it is for my children that I
found the program while they were still youngsters. Events have proved
the soundness of this observation. Over the years, my two boys have given
me countless reasons to thank God for the program and for my seven
years of recovery in OA.

The latest incident took place yesterday afternoon. Arriving home from
work, I was greeted at the door with a bear hug and a resounding kiss
from my nine-year-old son. Could he talk to me, he asked, adding that
it was OK if I needed to rest a little first.

Together we went into my husband's and my bedroom, which doubles
as a "talking room." With each of us propped up on one elbow, facing
each other, we began our conversation. Danny told me he had come to
a decision: he wanted to quit football. He'd spent the entire day thinking
over all the pros and cons, which he then proceeded to itemize. First
came his schoolwork; it was most important, he assured me, to maintain
his A average. Next was saxophone practice, which took an hour a day
and which he wanted to do "a whole lot," since he'd waited a year for
the opportunity. Football, he explained thoughtfully, required so much
extra time — two and a half hours of practice a day — that he felt he
wasn't able to do his best with either homework or sax.

As I listened attentively to Danny's childishly expressed yet amazingly
well-reasoned explanations, I felt my heart turn over with mingled love,
pride and gratitude. I could see from his expression and the lump in his
throat that his decision to give up football had not been easy. Yet he
had considered his dilemma objectively, put his priorities in order and
became willing to give up whatever threw the whole off balance.

Later in the afternoon, I went with him to return his football gear.
As I waited, I heard him tell the coach why he was quitting. The coach
shook Danny's hand, ruffled his hair and told him he admired him for
coming to such a sensible decision.

Today, as I reflect on my son's resolution of his problem, I am more grateful than ever that I have been able to apply the principles of this program at home as well as outside. I am thankful that I have been given the understanding that "I may be the only Big Book someone will ever read."

My program has had a wonderful effect on my children. It has given them a mother who can listen, who can allow her children to make their own decisions and mistakes and to learn from them. It has given me patience and a deeper love. I have often shared my emotions with my two boys: the fears, the "sillies" of life, always wondering if it was "right," even though it felt right. Today I know it *is* right. My sons know that Mom is human and real, and this allows them the freedom to be human and real, too.

The final grace note of this unforgettable episode was my son's sincere, "Thanks for listening, Mom. It's always easy to talk to you."

Thank you, God, and thank you, OA.

January 1983

Nice Guy

AS I APPROACH my fourth year in OA, I am only now beginning to realize the tremendous change that has taken place in me. When I walked through those doors, carrying 85 more pounds than I do today, my life was set. Spiritually, I knew what I believed. I was a respected member of my church and community.

My only problem was I ate too much. Most folks were willing to overlook that, however, because I was such a nice guy. Everybody liked me — everybody, that is, except me. I was a fairly gentle man and I never forced my will on others. But I sure did a lot of pushing when it came to myself.

You see, I had learned over many years to appear to be something I wasn't. I had taken my resentments and anxieties and painted a veneer of peace and good will over them. I masked my real feelings with a good theology and practiced plenty of perseverance. I thought that when you got to the end of your rope you just tied a knot and hung on. I didn't realize that people at the end of their rope often hang themselves. And I didn't know I could just let go.

My marriage was a challenge. For three years before I came to OA, my wife suffered from neurological ailments and was confined to a wheel-chair most of the time. This was a source of great pain for me, although secretly I reveled in being a martyr. In my church I was applauded for hanging in there and — what else? — for being such a nice guy. We were determined to persevere. We were also desperately unhappy. My wife tried suicide twice.

After about three years of program, I began to see some things. I learned that "compulsive" means "doing something you don't want to do." I had done that for years. I had learned to live up to outer standards and expectations with a complete denial of my inner self. OA taught me that God lives inside me, not out there. If I wanted to hear, I had to listen and let go my heavy ego control.

After going to fifteen doctors and three psychiatrists, I began going to God as I understood God to find the answer for me and my wife. I

259

finally realized that, having married for the wrong reasons, we were thoroughly miserable together and we were just manifesting our unhappiness differently: she with her neurological symptoms and I with my eating. We separated one year ago and eventually divorced. Within three weeks of our separation, my wife got up out of her wheelchair and has not needed it since. The housekeeper who cared for our children left, and the kids have their mother back. This is a true miracle, but not at all what I had expected.

Today, I am happier than ever before. Through the steps, and with lots of OA support, I have let go much of my anger. My ex-wife and I are still friends and joint custodians of our children. My goals and standards are no longer set in cement. With each decision I ask myself, "Is this what I really believe — and want?" More and more, the answers come.

I once clung to the myth that if something doesn't fit, you can make it fit. I am much more gentle with myself now. Letting go is easier and better.

March 1983

The Message Is Love

I STARTED OUT carrying the message by giving advice and fixing. (Do you realize how difficult it is to escape those nasty habits?) It's amusing that our program of ego reduction has forced me into more and more talk about self in order to avoid advising. Of course, it's possible to give advice just in the tone of voice: "Well, in *my* experience . . ."

After a few months of sponsoring, I stopped feeling terrible when someone ate again. I became self-righteous about those who were ready and those who weren't desperate enough yet. Much of the self-righteousness left me as the years passed and I saw the fluctuations in abstinence and maintenance so common to most of us, myself included.

About a year ago, I finally gave up fixing people. I know perfectly well that we're supposed to be responsible only for our own actions, not the results, but somehow I had never extended that to read: "I'm responsible for sponsoring you, not for how you turn out." Whenever I'm feeling pressure within myself to fix someone, I find that the relationship has taken on parent/child overtones.

It's easy to spot: if I'm struggling to find just the right thing to say instead of simply listening; if I realize I'm upset or judgmental when I hang up the phone, I know I've fallen back into the Great Fixer role.

I now believe that beginning abstainers and people in their first three steps need lots of attention. With my working schedule, I don't try to sponsor more than two on a daily basis, and I encourage them to begin building more relationships by calling other OAs too. Of course, former sponsorees who have become friends call from time to time to discuss whatever step they're on. It's one of the joys of my life that by the time a person is living in the maintenance steps, it is impossible to tell which of us is the sponsor.

That is what I really believe makes effective sponsoring: a two-way relationship in which trust is built. Sometimes, when I had one of those strong-willed newcomers to sponsor (I always seem to get the type of person I used to be!), I feared they would push right in and take over all my time. I have grown so much by dealing with this and letting them in anyway!

More than anything — more than saying the right thing, more than nudging them through the steps and not letting them settle for a food sponsor, more even than attention — my reason for being, my purpose and justification as a sponsor is to love. As I grow, so does my ability to embrace the common humanness in us all. It's a most wonderful experience to leave behind patronizing earth-mothering and love another as an equal. I've discovered that if I can really love a sponsoree, almost everything I say is right, no matter how fumble-tongued I might be that day. All they hear is the approval, the unconditional acceptance of what they *are*. I admit that I don't always leave it to them to disapprove of what they *do!*

I'm confident that love will heal the fear which is at the bottom of all our negatives. If I am to lead by example, then the best way I can show those I sponsor how to be mended inside is to let them see me loving everyone, including myself. My own health depends on it. This is the greatest lesson I've learned from Overeaters Anonymous: The message I must carry is love.

March 1983

To Be a Channel

H OW DO I BEGIN? By saying thank you, sponsor. For being there when I need you. For sharing. For being honest. For making me see reality. When I have a bad day and start to slide, you always manage to pull me back. You keep "progress, not perfection" in front of me at all times, reminding me that I have hundreds of reasons to be grateful, few for feeling sorry for myself.

In OA for two years, I had been treading water and barely keeping my head up. I knew what I needed to do, but I wasn't willing to walk that walk. I watched you grow and change, I saw God working in your life, and I desperately wanted what you have.

I came to you and you shared. At first you scared me, always telling me to get on my knees and ask God, always reminding me to let go, to detach yet still love. It all seemed so awesome, I couldn't grasp it. But I took the action anyway. Daily, I did a little more on steps four and five, writing and giving it to you. Slowly, my confidence grew.

Then my big fears started surfacing: fear of financial stress, fear of sex, fear that when I removed all the masks I would find a void. Sometimes I got mad. I'd stomp around mumbling that I wasn't going to do it; but self-preservation always won out and, my self-righteousness out of the way, I could function again.

The most helpful thing you've shared with me is your God. Mine had some pretty rough edges, but as I grow, so does my concept of H.P.

People are noticing a change in me. Even my husband has commented on my new attitude; but he's hesitant, and he has every right to be. Two weeks of nice person doesn't wipe out seven years of hell.

But I keep growing and changing, and when I'm done there won't be a void. There will be a loving person — loving because I want and need to love. My fear of rejection won't be as great because I am learning to love expecting nothing in return.

I can feel the difference both within and without. Internally, the roots of happiness are spreading, bringing forth satisfaction, love and tolerance.

On the outside, my clothes are looser and my face shines. Now that I love all of God's creation, I care more about myself inside and out.

I am learning to ask for God's will in my life. If I'm baffled, I relax and ask for guidance. It always comes — sometimes not as quickly as I would like, but I am aware that I am also learning patience. I am slowly finding out what the Big Book means when it says God wants us to be happy, joyous and free. I'm happy I'm a compulsive overeater; I'm joyous God showed me the way to OA; and I'm free because God has removed the bondage of compulsive overeating. What more could I ask?

People are calling *me* now, and I'm discovering what it's like to be a sponsor. It is enlightening to see both sides. Now I know how you must feel when I call you in despair and want an answer. I'm learning to say a quick prayer for guidance, then I hear myself giving, not advice or solutions, but a loving, attentive response. I'm grateful it's not just me sponsoring those people. Alone, I would be terrified to answer the phone, but with God working through me, things work out OK. Now I know what it means to be a channel.

The Big Book discusses only one type of sponsor, a spiritual one — a person who shows how the steps work and how God works in her life. You certainly fill that bill. You always highlight, lovingly, that I have a choice about how I do things and about whether I will stagnate or grow.

"You don't have problems; you have opportunities for growth," you are fond of saying. The first time I heard that, I wanted to hit you. But you are right. It *is* my choice. Thanks to your loving prodding, today I am willing to grow.

You are vital to my program, dear sponsor. Daily, I thank God for the gift of you. I love you.

March 1983

What Is a Sponsor?

A FRIEND, a role model, a source of information in my recovery process — a sponsor is all these things and often more. A sponsor is someone who is first of all willing to seek recovery for herself and then to help me find my own way — not by possessing all the answers but by accepting me as I am. The definition that stays in my mind is: a sponsor is one who guides by example, not someone who just points the way.

I was insulted some six years ago when a member of my family suggested I meet a friend who had lost more than 140 pounds in an organization called Overeaters Anonymous. I certainly didn't overeat, at least not in front of anyone. I had a weight problem, but I could stop eating anytime I wanted to, lose the weight and be forever thin. Such rationalizing had brought me to a top weight of 314 pounds and kept me in that neighborhood for about seven years.

The pain and humiliation of extreme obesity are almost impossible to describe; still, I did not for one minute consider going to OA until several months later when, during a CPR course, I realized I was a far better candidate for resuscitation than the dummy.

I contacted the woman who had lost 140 pounds and we made plans to attend a meeting together. She became my sponsor, a truly exceptional one, and a most special friend. She never discouraged me, never told me I was setting myself up for a binge. She just said, over and over, "If I can do it, you can do it. I'm nobody special." Then she would add, "The fact is, we're *both* special."

My excess weight was almost exactly the same as my sponsor's, which gave us a tremendous rapport. You just have to have been up in that bracket to understand the degradation of being stuck in a tub, theater seat, rocking chair or restaurant booth.

The example my sponsor set was one of a continuing losing abstinence and recovery via the twelve steps, one day at a time. She came into program about eight months before me, and she saved me from many a "skinned knee." For the first time, I was willing to let another's experience guide me; she was living the program and sharing it, and it was working!

Several times, problems that formerly would have been good for a 30-or 40-pound weight gain held no threat because she assured me my feelings were normal, that others felt the same way in the face of life's challenges.

The first person I sponsored left the Fellowship, and I was crushed. Why did she leave? What did I do wrong? My sponsor quickly assured me we all have the same decision to make: to recover or not. I cannot abstain for anyone but myself. "The first thing you do," she told me, "is don't eat. If you eat over a problem, then you've got two problems." That is still my philosophy.

Even though my sponsor and I did not follow the same losing abstinence, when I began to sponsor I refused to work with anyone who did not choose the same abstinence I had, whose weight was not close to my top weight and who was not a newcomer. Needless to say, I was very rigid and fearful. By the grace of God, my abstinence began on Day One, but after almost a year I worried about how long it would continue. What does one do on Day 366? The answer became clear when that day arrived. You do the same thing that made it work on Day One and Day 365: you abstain, you turn your life over to the care of God and you live your life *today.*

To recover, my sponsor told me, I needed to understand that a food plan is a means to an end, not the destination. A losing abstinence helps heal the physical illness and the twelve steps enable me to live my life to good purpose without the need — and for the most part, without the desire — for excess food.

I have mellowed greatly in almost six years. I still feel led to sponsor people who share my hope and need for recovery. I suspect it's out of a need to remember where I came from; a desperate newcomer jogs my memory.

I love to see people develop their spirituality and cultivate a set of principles to live by. It is exciting to watch recovery as it happens, to see the physical, emotional and spiritual thirds come into balance to form a whole person.

I do not sponsor a large number of people, usually no more than two or three. My program of recovery teaches me to let go, to allow others to assume responsibility. I am responsible for continuing my own recovery, which is all I have to share. And the beat goes on.

March 1983

How Miracles Happen

WHEN I FIRST walked into OA about a year ago, the rage that tormented me for twenty-nine years was readily apparent to the small group assembled in that quiet parish-house room. Not until six months later did those people dare disclose their initial impressions of me.

"This one will never make it," one member admits thinking. Another told me, "I was afraid to speak to you for fear you'd bite my head off."

During my first six months in OA I merely played with the program. I was too stubborn to give it my full concentration and effort. Four months passed before I became willing to take a sponsor. The members of my group told me to pray to my concept of God and I would be directed to the sponsor who was right for me. My prayers were stumbling and I had just a mustard seed of faith, but my Higher Power brought me to the one woman who could guide me. Only to her would I listen because we were as alike as the proverbial peas in a pod.

The sponsor to whom God directed me worked with me unceasingly to melt my stubbornness and get through my rage and arrogance. She understood because she felt the same way before she found the program four and a half years earlier. We compared notes on when the rage started but we couldn't pin it down. It began too early in life. It was just a part of us, something we lived with day after day. But it made life miserable.

When I was finally able to accept the fact that I am also an alcoholic, I reached a turning point. I knew then that the concept of God I brought into the program could not carry me through to the new life promised in the Big Book.

"Fire that God and find a new one," my sponsor suggested. "Write a list of qualities your dearest friend would have, then create your Higher Power from that list."

After two weeks of intensely self-destructive behavior, during which I seriously contemplated suicide, I relented. My sponsor drove me to a forest and sent me off by myself to "Try it and keep trying it till it works." It was either that or she would have to pull away from me. She couldn't bear to watch me complete the job of destroying myself.

I walked into the woods with a heart that weighed three tons. At first I could only whisper my anger and frustration at God, fearing that the distant personage I envisioned would strike me dead. Then I raised my voice and shook my fists at the sky, screaming, "If there really is a God, let me know who you are and show me how to approach you!"

Tears began pouring down my cheeks, and I felt a ray of sunlight on my face. Peace and serenity — the kind promised in the Big Book, and which I thought would never be mine — flooded me. I sat at the base of a pine tree and poured my heart out to this new God who had stirred in the depths of my soul when I finally hit bottom and asked for help with no dealing or bargaining.

My sponsor began crying as soon as she caught sight of me walking toward her. Neither of us spoke; we just hugged. Without actually seeing, I could feel the changes that were evident to my sponsor. The harsh lines of my face were gone and my body's angry stance had relaxed. The light of peace, contentment and love shone from my eyes.

That breakdown of the barriers allowed rapid growth to begin. In the six months that followed I lost 51 pounds, opened up and allowed myself to have honest friendships and took a job, abandoning the safety of welfare. I went into therapy to learn to manage my life better (never losing sight of my real manager), and I developed a more loving and accepting relationship with my young daughter.

The rage that burned unabated within me all those years is gone. That alone is miracle enough. With all the other changes in my life and personality, I can only conclude that God deals exclusively with miracles and sends volumes of them through sponsors in the twelve-step program.

March 1983

Program Mother

IF ONLY I HAD a chance to go back and do it right!" As often as I have entertained this wistful thought, I never imagined it would one day become a dream fulfilled.

Much of the pursuit of my disease took place during the years when my two sons were growing up. Many times I insisted they eat with me so I wouldn't feel guilty. I pushed them to the point where I made them cry, and they would beg, "But, Mama, I don't want it."

Even now, the hot, bitter tears well up when I remember how I abused these young spirits.

Sometime during the process of recovering in Overeaters Anonymous, I knew I had changed greatly; that, given the opportunity, I would be a far different mother than I had been.

Almost two years ago, God blessed me with the gift of a six-year-old child, a little girl. She came to us neglected and abused, in great need. In giving me the responsibility of caring for this child, God has helped me become aware of my own healing.

Food is no longer a medium of exchange in my home. Kim is neither rewarded nor punished with food. I have long since given up membership in the "clean plate club." The child I care for today eats to nourish her body, not to fill *my* void. I serve her food on a small plate: she is a child. I don't need to feed myself through her.

When she first came to us, Kim was unable to eat more than a few bites without becoming full, or even ill. I encouraged her to eat because her body needed it. It took about six weeks for her to get used to eating a full meal and to confine her eating to just three meals a day. I explained that her tummy needed the rest; it didn't need to be fed all the time. She quickly latched on to the principles of proper nutrition and soon began to say how much better her "motor" (brain) was running.

I don't keep junk food around. Kim's snacks are healthful, natural foods such as nuts, fruits, raisins and cheese. When she came to us, Kim was on several medications for nerves, stomach upsets and other ailments.

She has not needed any of these medicines for almost two years.

An interesting and unexpected sign of my healing came one morning at the breakfast table. Kim had seen a person without arms and asked, "How does she eat?"

I explained that the woman had learned to use her feet to do many of the things people do with their hands and arms. She could even change a baby's diaper and pin it with her toes, I told her.

"I bet I could eat with my toes," Kim said.

"Fine, why don't you try?"

Thrilled, she pulled off her slipper and proceeded to try to eat her cereal with a spoon between her toes. She spilled some, but finally managed to eat several bites.

I shall never forget the look on her face. Tears flowed down my cheeks as I silently thanked God for that special moment, that I had not let it slip away unused.

I have changed. My sons would probably have been punished had they dared to eat with their toes, and I certainly would not have encouraged them to try.

For several days after this incident, I heard Kim tell her friends about the experience and what a hard time people without arms have in learning to use their feet.

At the age of eight, both my sons were greatly overweight. After almost two years in my home, my eight-year-old blessing called Kim is a normal, active, healthy size. I know I will not open the closet door one day and find her sitting there crying because she is fat, as I once found my oldest son.

The greatest single amends I can make to my family is to maintain a continuing abstinence and to stay in the process of recovery. I cannot undo the harm done, and there are times when the memory haunts me. But I know that, by the grace of God, today I am different.

April 1983

My Father, My Friend

I HAVE NO MEMORY of ever doing anything with my father when I was growing up. I used to watch him as he napped on the couch or as we sat at the dinner table. There was no laughter or sign of affection. If my brother and I got the giggles, we had to leave the table.

I often saw my father talking to people and I wished he could talk to me like that. Many times I helped him with his work around the house and yard just so I could be around him, be his friend. It never worked out. I always thought I had failed him and felt guilty about it.

Once, when I was about fifteen, my dad caught me driving his pickup. He and my mother had gone out for the evening and, as I'd often done before, I piled in my neighborhood friends and went for a ride. Dad always left his keys in the ignition, unaware that I had taught myself the rudiments of driving. Anyway, when I brought the pickup back, there was my father's car in our driveway. He was standing on the porch, waiting. He didn't say much. Just, "Don't ever get in that truck again."

As I grew past adolescence, I still felt I was a disappointment to my dad; so I began living up to the image I thought he had of me. It was as though, if I couldn't please him, couldn't be the son he wanted, I was going to show him how bad I really was.

I was a grown man, convalescing in a hospital in Japan, when I got the only letter my father ever sent me. I cried like a baby. He actually wrote it himself, and signed it. For me.

When I married and had children of my own, I became a compulsive father whose only identity was my children. I stayed in a terrible marriage just to be with my kids, anesthetizing my pain with anything I could put into my body.

Then, at the age of thirty-nine, finally divorced, I married again. The day before the wedding, my bride-to-be asked me if I loved her. I told her I was very fond of her. That was as honest as I could be. I had long felt that I would never be able to love or be loved by anyone.

But I trusted this woman, and I knew she cared for me deeply. She had favorite colors and songs, and her special song for us was "The Impossible Dream." The day of our wedding, as I stood at the altar, I looked around and wondered what I was doing there. Then the doors opened and my bride started to walk down the aisle to the strains of "The Impossible Dream." At that instant, I fell in love for the first time in my life.

Looking back, I believe that God as I understand God today, figured out the way to get my attention was to send me a woman who was a compulsive overeater. In October 1971, at age 41, I went to great lengths to find out what was wrong with my wife: I attended this strange meeting called Overeaters Anonymous. I was willing to do anything to help fix her.

In the course of attending meetings for a month, I heard, out of the mouths of OA members, almost every one of my deepest, most terrifying secrets. For the first time, I felt I belonged to a family. On November 1, 1971, I raised my hand as a compulsive overeater.

When I was abstinent in the program for about two years, my wife and I attended the funeral of a close friend of my father's. Dad was crying and, in compassion, I put my arm around his shoulders. Suddenly, I felt a suffocating pain in my throat and in my heart. I wanted to love this man so badly, I couldn't breathe.

A few days later, I said to my wife, "I wish my father could love me." Then I proceeded to point out how impossible it was, my father being the cold person he was.

My wife said, "You're the one with the program. Why don't you make the first move. You know, 'action'."

It took me several months to get up the courage to take that action. Then one day, it was time. My father walked into our house and I went over and hugged him. I didn't know if he was going to push me away, throw up or ask me what I wanted. He did nothing. He was too shocked to know what to do. But he didn't push me away.

That was the beginning. Every time I saw my father after that, I hugged him. Soon I was hugging and kissing him hello and goodbye. And Dad responded. Instead of just waiting for me to approach, he would walk toward me, not only to receive my embrace, but to hug and kiss me in return.

We began to spend time together. I talked to him about my feelings. Can you imagine? He was really interested. He told me about things he did when he was a boy and how he felt as he was growing up. I soon began to understand that my father was just like me — a frightened child inside.

At my fiftieth birthday party, my father waited until the house quieted down and then, with tears in his eyes, he said, "I love you. I don't understand what's happened, but I'm very proud of the person you have become."

He died just two months later, while he was fishing. My first thought was, "It's not fair; I've just found my friend." And then, "But I've had these wonderful years."

Everyone who knew how deeply I loved my father expected me to fall apart with grief. Even I began to think something was wrong with me because I was so calm. Then I understood why I felt at peace. My dad has not died. His physical presence is gone, and I miss that. But he is very much alive inside me, and nothing can take his memory from me.

At my father's funeral, I was able to say a final goodbye: "Thank you, Dad, for being my friend."

I've been abstaining in OA for more than eleven years. Probably the greatest gift the people of OA have given me is the ability to love and be loved — and not to be afraid to say, "I love you."

June 1983

A Year of Surrender

IT WAS a living nightmare, the old life. I was a military spouse, living on a military base in assigned government housing. I was working part time, studying for the bar exam and isolating at home, usually in the kitchen. I went out only to shop at the PX or the commissary. Then I'd come home and binge, standing at the kitchen sink, staring out the window at the Golden Gate Bridge. My mind fogged up and my feelings anesthetized, I'd then lie down and fall asleep to escape from the reality of what I'd just done to myself.

A nightmare? Worse. It was slow suicide.

I hated myself. I felt absolutely worthless. Although I had graduated from law school, I failed the bar exam on my first few attempts. No wonder: I spent far more time binging and planning the next binge than I did studying. And I spent far more time sitting at my desk, worrying about how I would get all that stuff into my head, than I did trying to absorb the material.

My wife, a military nurse, was supporting me. She was out there in the world, being successful. I had provided her with some semblance of comfort and security earlier in our relationship, but when she did the same for me, I couldn't accept it. I felt worthless, resentful, unmanly and very sorry for myself. Needless to say, our marriage wasn't doing too well.

I had come to OA two years earlier, during my junior year of law school. I was not interested, really; just sort of curious. I'd met a woman who paid some attention to me and I accepted her invitation to a meeting.

I thought you OAs were really sick. "There but for the grace of God . . ." said my pride. I just had a little problem with food and weight. I knew that from my three hitches in a diet club.

My denial of the disease almost killed me. Today I realize how much time I spent in life-diminishing behavior. There I was, in one of the most exciting cities in the world, wasting day after day binging my brains out.

Somehow, though, I began to grasp the program. I applied its principles in preparing for the bar exam, and I passed. I got a responsible job that paid me a decent starting salary. But I continued to eat, and to hide from my feelings.

It finally happened, after two more years. My wife had had enough. She turned to another man, and I hit bottom. For the first time, I was ready to admit that my life was unmanageable. I had already admitted I was a compulsive overeater, but the second half of step one had been a sticking point.

When I found out about "the other man" I felt absolutely crazy. My worst fears had come true, and I had helped them do so. My own compulsive desires had led me into the world of massage parlors, where someone I didn't know and who wouldn't reject me would meet some of my needs. As long as I didn't actually make love to or get involved with another woman, I rationalized elaborately, I was not really being unfaithful to my wife.

That night I ended up at a meeting. There was an empty chair to my left, and in the seat next to it sat an older man in a jogging suit, with silver hair and warm blue eyes that reflected the pain of years past. I looked him in the eye, feeling overwhelmed and desperate. "Can I talk to you?" I asked.

Today, I call that man my sponsor. I love the guy. He was there for me every single day for the first two months, through my separation from my wife and through a move when my office was relocated. A few weeks ago, my sponsor gave me a candle to commemorate a year of surrender and recovery in this beautiful Fellowship and this inspired way of life. My sponsor and I sponsor each other today.

My marriage ended in divorce, but I have grown immeasurably. I made amends to my ex-wife and then let go the past. Now I try to live a day at a time.

Some people hit bottom just before or shortly after finding OA. For me, it took four and a half years of meetings. Some of us are just slower than others, I guess. But there was one suggestion I acted on that finally allowed recovery to take root: I kept coming back.

August 1983

A God Job

I'M GOING THROUGH a divorce, abstinently. It was one of the hardest decisions I've ever come to, and it has taken a tremendous amount of courage.

I was a fat housewife and mother who hated being where she was. I felt unnecessary, as if anyone could do what I was doing. My job description was: eating, washing dishes, clothes and floors, and screaming at the kids. I thought I was stuck. Miserable and desperate, I prayed, "God, change me into the person you want me to be." That prayer took courage.

Immediately after that, I found OA. Even the first meeting created a change in me. I saw hope for the first time.

"God," I pleaded next, "guide me in choosing a sponsor," and I was led to a beautiful and wise woman who became my closest friend. More changes followed as I reached out and, in reluctant but trusting love, touched another person with my innermost feelings.

When I first identified what I felt, my greatest fear was of divorce. Somehow, I knew deep inside what was coming. For months, I was terrified; but I couldn't stop changing.

I also feared taking an inventory. Unleashing all that internal turmoil seemed more than I could bear. But I knew it had to be done, so I kept praying, "God, change me."

I wrote my inventory and gave it away. Then the changes came — in floods. I became aware of my talents and abilities as well as my defects, and I saw few of the limitations that used to discourage me. I grew. Gradually, God gave me the courage to change from an obese, self-hating housewife into a beautiful, confident career woman with a vision; to get out of a depressing environment and move into the unrestricted unknown; to build a new life. Two years ago I could not have faced the trauma of divorce because of my low self-esteem. Today, after working daily with two sponsors for a long time, I can face whatever comes.

Sadly, the hardest part of changing has been the judgmental attitude of some of my fellow OAs, who perhaps feel threatened by my changes. Even within the safe walls of OA, where change is encouraged, we occasionally pull each other down with our restricting fears. When one member risks change, it offers hope to the others, but some will invariably feel threatened by it. Fortunately, I kept searching for my own validation, and I found it.

Unless we face and walk through our fears, they keep us bound. Only by daring to change can we eliminate the fears that held us captive in the past. Change is risky and it takes courage, but it is absolutely necessary to our recovery. It's a God job — and we're worth it.

October 1983

The Bondage of Self

FTER FIVE YEARS in this beloved program, and many changes physically, mentally and spiritually, it is more evident than ever that "self" is my biggest problem. Not food. I study the Big Book a great deal, and in the last few months the word "self" has jumped out at me more and more. "Self-will run riot," "self-centeredness," "selfishness," "our problems are of our own making," and so on. All these manifestations of self-obsession block me off from God, the one source of help for all my problems.

One of the areas in my life where self gets in the way is sex. I did not handle my sexuality well as a teenager, or even as a young adult. I had little confidence in myself and my appearance. My body image was so poor, even when I was thin and had a knockout figure, that eventually my body always caught up with my fat head.

Showers after PE were horrible, and I hated wearing gym clothes in front of boys. Dating and having boys try to get close was excruciatingly painful, and I avoided it. I must add that I was not grossly obese at that time, just plump.

I married someone who loved me, needed me, thought I was beautiful and sexy and that I'd be a good mother. He had no idea what he was getting himself into when he picked me as his sex partner. I hated sex because my figure was never good enough or sexy enough. If the poor man had waited until I thought my body was perfect, he would still be waiting.

Worst of all were those times when I was actually fatter, or felt fatter. Then my disinterest in sex was total. As much as my husband loved me — and he loved me a great deal to put up with that mentality — I do not think our marriage would have lasted if OA had not intervened.

I was taking a mental inventory one day during my walk, when it occurred to me that my body was not the real problem in our sex life. The real problem was my selfishness, my self-centeredness, my always thinking about myself and my body. It was suddenly clear to me that the act of sex is when two people are the closest, most intimate and most vulnerable. It is the time when one gives to the other person one's whole self.

It is impossible to overstate how greatly this attitude change has helped me. I am more giving and less selfish in my sex life, no matter what I think my body looks like.

I must also be completely honest and tell you I am not yet perfect in this area. But it feels good to be aware of the actual problem and to know that I have a way to work myself out of it.

December 1983

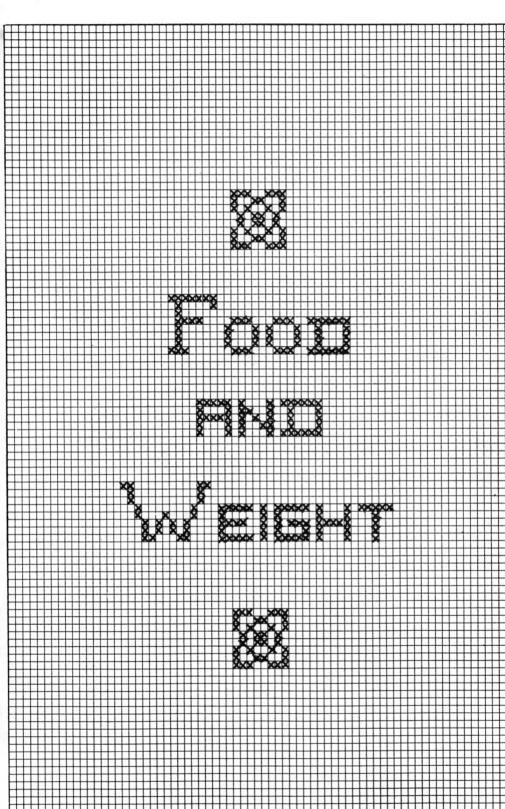

FOOD AND WEIGHT

Confessions of a Former Fat Man

SOMETIMES I wake up in the middle of the night with the gnawing fear that I have gained 50 pounds or even more. I can usually calm myself immediately, but occasionally I must get out of bed and stare at my naked body in the mirror to reassure myself that my apprehension is absurd. When I shop for clothing, I find myself taking items at least three sizes too large. I can never believe that I will get into my correct size. My closets are packed with clothing as much as eight sizes too big which I cannot bear to rid myself of; this despite the fact that I pride myself on my charity and generosity.

On boarding a fairly crowded bus or subway car, my first inclination is to stand rather than squeeze and push into a single available seat. I still must consciously adjust the way I sit down on a hard surface, because if I forget I often sit with such impact that I bruise myself.

The cause of all of this seemingly aberrant behavior is a rapid and huge weight loss: 90 pounds in seven months. I had been fat from the age of seven, except for a few brief periods after rigorous dieting.

I was the victim of the human yo-yo syndrome. I never really came to grips with my compulsive overeating or my need to wrap myself in a cocoon of fat. After a minor illness was unduly complicated by obesity, I decided to rid myself of the life-threatening weight. I joined an OA group and began the process of dealing with myself. I am still making progress. The weight is off and I am emerging as a person I can like and respect. I am not brainwashed, nor do I wish to cast aside all of the "old me," much of which was good and I think interesting.

Unfortunately, too little seems to be known about compulsive behavior of any kind and especially overeating. Our society places a premium on svelteness for aesthetic as well as for health reasons, and yet encourages eating. Our lives revolve around refrains such as, "Let's get together for lunch"; "You are invited to dinner"; "The affair will have a nine-course sit-down meal"; "Get your cold beer, candy, ice cream." Few are sympathetic to the real emotional pain of the fat person and even fewer to the psychological trauma of the formerly fat.

I am a fat man in a thin body and will probably always be so — if with God's help I can keep my compulsion under control. The number of difficulties is enormous. I must, for example, deal with my sexuality in a new and different way. When I was unattractive, I had to pursue and convince people through force of personality that I was a person of worth. I bewailed my fate, but now I sometimes long for the luxury of choosing whom to pursue. I am twenty-nine but have very little experience as the object of pursuit. It is not easy to handle.

I love the feeling of being able to do what I want, of being attractive, of feeling physically alive and alert. Now that I have been seen and complimented by people who knew me before, I no longer have the psychic gratification of being reminded by others that I have succeeded. I am passing in the thin world, and few know or care that I had a fat past. It is marvelous but it is difficult, so bear with me.

May/June 1975

The Real Magic

I HAVE ALWAYS spent a lot of time imagining what it would be like when I lost my weight. For, of course, the weight was all that was wrong with me and the very next diet was going to make everything all right.

I go back a long time, and my overeating probably started at my first feeding. I think I must have tried four out of every five diets I ever came across, matched torment for torment by some wonders of my own invention. There were the orange diet, the chew every bite until your teeth fall out or you erode your upper lip, whichever comes first diet; and the starve five days and binge two, among those I remember well.

Anyway, it was always that new diet that was going to do it, and the hottest-off-the-press self-help book that would complete the cure. I searched my psyche, contemplated my navel, explored offbeat religions, anything and everything except the one thing that finally worked.

OA abstinence is different. When I started to get some of the fat off my body, I began to realize how much mental fat I had accumulated. Fat that clouded my thinking. Fat that got between me and reality so I never saw things the way they really were. I saw them as I hoped they were or soon would be.

I am sure that many of my fears and fantasies were tied up with my conceptions — or misconceptions — of my sexuality. I had the fat girl's dream: if I weren't so fat, men would be after me in swarms. It was an awful letdown to discover that losing weight didn't change a thing. They still didn't pay any attention to me. So, in part at least, my weight was protecting me against something that wasn't going to happen anyhow. One more old idea out the window.

Facing the world and coping without the heavy artillery of food and fat is scary. There are no two ways about that. I can't hide anymore. I can't use my fat as an excuse to get out of something I don't want to do. When I was at my heaviest, certain things were not expected of me; today, I receive no such exemptions.

Just getting up in the morning and contemplating the tasks of the day is a real test for me. It leaves me feeling naked and vulnerable. But fears and anxieties are more or less a part of the human condition. Why should I expect to be excused?

Nobody told me this program was going to be easy. My wonderful sponsors all stressed this: the program is possible, not easy. It is possible for a fear-ridden scared rabbit like me to dare to be different. I can quit believing that someone or something is going to take care of me and make it all better. I can begin to believe in the real magic of OA: that by holding on to the hands held out to me, working the steps to the best of my ability and going along in faith one day at a time, I can become the person I want to be.

August 1978

Starting Thin

AS INCREASING NUMBERS of OAs come to believe that weight is not our problem, many are beginning to understand the special meaning this has for people who do not come in fat.

On the night of my first meeting, I was underweight by medical standards. I joined OA because I had been on a five-day binge, and I did not have the courage to keep up the masquerade any longer.

There were several times in my life when I was fat, but what is much more important for me to tell you about is my attitude toward being thin.

When I was thirteen years old, I found myself the center of attention after losing ten pounds. Until this time, I had always been on the outside of the "in" crowd. I became obsessed with my new identity.

But it was a shaky existence. I felt certain that my peers would not give me a second thought if I couldn't keep on impressing them with a new weight loss or new diet information. I went to great lengths to maintain an image of undeterred willpower and boasted of every pound lost, every dieting triumph. What I did not tell anyone was that every morning I had lonely, desperate binges over the anxiety of facing a new day.

I let my bathroom scale measure my self-worth. The numbers would move up or down a few pounds, but my feelings about myself would swing from the highest peak to the lowest valley. My eating patterns were as erratic as my self-image: it was either feast or famine.

I will be forever thankful that the people at my first OA meeting understood how much I needed them. If they had only seen my weight, I would not have asked for help. I would have left with my major defense against rejection intact: my feelings of superiority toward those who showed their fat.

OA works for me because I am a compulsive overeater. No one had to rewrite the twelve steps for me because I am thin. Abstinence is the same for me at goal weight as it is for the overweight newcomer. It means that I eat only what is on my food plan.

When I joined, I had what many newcomers want: thinness. But that is *all* I had. I have used OA to gain. I will continue to gain for the rest of my life if I work the steps and traditions and use the tools to keep building an identity for myself that is measured by love and not by pounds.

March 1979

Speaking of Numbers

HEN PEOPLE in OA say that weight loss is not the most important benefit of program, I believe them. But, since my weight loss was directly responsible for saving my life, I do sort of tend to see it as a benefit.

On September 20, 1978 I weighed six hundred pounds. The following Valentine's Day — February 14, 1979 — I was down to 341 pounds, a loss of 259 pounds. This happened through the following: reading *Lifeline* magazines, my Big Book and the letters I receive from my OA correspondents in Canada.

I am in a nursing home and unable to attend OA meetings. I have plenty of chances to cheat on the diet my doctor has me on, but I don't want to. I have learned a lot since my first time in OA when I lost 175 pounds in a year and figured I knew how to handle the food. I didn't. I almost lost my family and my life.

When I was placed in the nursing home, my doctor gave me only one to two months to live. I have learned, and accepted, that there are certain foods I can't eat, ever. I've also learned that I can live without them, just for today.

My family and I are getting closer every day. I still have a long way to go before I reach maintenance weight, but I only have 77 pounds to lose before I can go home.

I sincerely hope my recovery story helps someone, somewhere not to have to go through the hell and the pain I have.

May 1979

An Article in the Paper

HEN THE NURSE called me, I got up and walked slowly into the doctor's office. I felt sullen and remote.

The doctor looked up. "Please sit down," he said. His expression was stern. What he was about to say was not going to be pleasant.

"This is very serious and I want you to listen carefully," he began. My eyes drifted to my lap. My shoulders hunched forward with the tension I felt in my stomach.

"Your situation is grave and your life expectancy is limited. You've been here many times and I have continually warned you that this diagnosis was inevitable unless you changed. You have chosen to ignore my warning. I told you this could happen!"

His voice trailed off, and my thoughts took over. He was right; he had warned me. Why hadn't I listened? I had tried. God knows how I had tried. But I had failed. I had a problem and I couldn't conquer it. But why hadn't *he* listened? Couldn't he sense my pain, my fear? Why did I always feel as if it was sinful to be fat? Why? Because he had said that *I* held the key to my recovery. How I hated him! His voice was pressing in on me, louder and louder. I had to listen.

"You will not live to see thirty," he said. "Your heart is working much too hard and your body is deteriorating fast. You have signs of crippling arthritis, high blood pressure, severe spinal problems, blood sugar problems and more. *Your obesity is killing you!*"

My heart skipped a beat. He had said I would die, and worse than that, from obesity. God, how I hated that word. It puzzled me that my mind was on that word — obesity — and not the fact that I was going to die. The years of pain surrounding that one word. Perhaps dying was better than living with the pain of trying again and again.

I recalled the conversation we had had a year ago. "You are a lucky young lady to have a problem you can control. You could have cancer or be blind or deaf, or have a limb missing. All *you* have to do to save your life is limit your food intake." It had sounded so simple.

286

The sound of my own voice startled me. "Couldn't you perform surgery?"

"There are no known surgical procedures that have proven successful without drastic side effects. I would not perform any of them on you."

Tears flooded my eyes and spilled onto my massive bosom. I dropped slowly to my knees. "Dear God, oh please, dear God, if You're there, tell me what to do! How can I stop? How can I deal with it? Please teach me what I must know. The pain — oh, God, the pain is killing me. Take this problem from me. No one can help me, not even the doctors."

I felt an arm around my shoulder and warm breath on my face. I opened my eyes to see the doctor kneeling beside me, misty tears in his eyes. In a soft voice he said, "I will pray for you." He gently helped me up and saw me to the door in silence.

I started for my car. The air was cold and the snow softly drifted onto my cheeks. I felt physically drained but, somehow, spiritually renewed.

As I drove through the city streets, my eyes fell on the brown, bare-looking trees. The lightly falling snow seemed to fade into nowhere. There were still piles of dirty snow jutting against the landscape. Where was the sunshine and laughter; the promise of good things? Where had they gone? Weren't we supposed to grow up, get married, have children and live happily ever after? It seemed ironic that I had everything people said "should" make me happy. A nice home, a nice husband, nice kids and enough money to live comfortably. So why did this thing called "fat" surround my body? Its very presence seemed to take away the right to enjoy all the things that "should" make me happy.

I pulled into my driveway, hardly aware that I was home. On my way into the house, I picked up the newspaper that was jammed into the screen door. I sighed deeply and glanced at my watch. What a day! Thank God, I had a little time before the kids came flying in from school. I settled into my easy chair and glanced at the newspaper with little real interest. The headline of an article at the bottom of the page caught my eye:

"Compulsive Overeating Treated as a Disease. Group Offers Hope."

I couldn't believe it. *That* article in *that* day's paper. Was this what I had prayed for?

The story explained that the group, called Overeaters Anonymous, was a support group for weight loss; a non-profit organization — no dues, no fees, no scales. No requirements to join except the desire to stop eating compulsively. They have something called "the twelve steps." The group believes that compulsive overeating is a disease. They do not believe that overeaters are just weak-willed people or people lacking strong character. There are meetings all over the city at various times. All I had to do was call the OA number and find out where and when I could attend a meeting.

Tears glistened on my face as a peace settled upon me. I felt greater hope than I had dared to dream of.

I went to my first meeting and it changed my life. I found that I have an illness only one symptom of which is compulsive overeating. My sickness was spiritual and emotional as well as physical. Amid the plausible descriptions, one stunning reality: the OA program is modeled after the Alcoholics Anonymous program, and *there are hundreds of thousands of recovering alcoholics.*

As the months passed, my prayer in the doctor's office was answered. It wasn't one of those instant miracles you hear about, but rather a gradual learning and growth process. OA showed me how to change my life. I had to learn to live one day at a time. Even with the fat on my body, I had to learn to like myself, today, the way I am. I had to evaluate openly and honestly what I imagine I am and what I know I am.

The group is supportive and together we discover what those twelve steps are and how to apply them to our compulsion and other areas of life. I learned how to stop blaming others for my fat and my failures. I learned to "let go" of the past — the pain and the disappointments — and live for today. I learned to identify my attributes and my good qualities as well as my shortcomings.

I learned that in all the world there is only one person I can change, and that person is me. I have to leave the rest of the world to a power greater than myself and learn that this power could and would free me from eating binges. The spiritual guidance I received through OA allowed me to choose my own Higher Power, whether that be another person, the group or God as I understand God. The important thing is that there is "someone or something" other than myself I can rely on.

I have found a group of people so loving and caring that their concern for me has overwhelmed me with joy. Their hope, strength and experience have saved my life. I have lost 70 pounds of excess weight and regained my self-worth.

I am a recovering compulsive overeater; I will not die at age thirty.

October 1979

Mellowing in the Program

I N OUR LITERATURE, Overeaters Anonymous is described as not concerned with diets, weight, calories or the medical aspect of obesity — only the feelings that lie behind our compulsive overeating. Yet, a recent national magazine article about OA made frequent reference to a "food sponsor."

In the course of thirteen years in the Fellowship (maintaining a 125-pound weight loss for more than eleven years), I have never heard anyone deny that our program is the selfsame one that is found in the Big Book of Alcoholics Anonymous. To turn ourselves around and be free of our obsessions, we are told, we need only the willingness to follow these simple directions. Taking it upon ourselves to add or subtract is an act of self-will.

Food plans and food sponsoring are a matter of individual choice; they are not the program. A major problem with making food plans appear to be a part of the program is the guilt produced by any deviation from the prescribed plan. Many food sponsors whose advocacy of a food plan is on a par with their advocacy of the steps have admitted carrying a great burden of guilt when they eat differently from the way they insist their "food babies" eat. And, of course, the "babies" suffer the same guilt.

Just as each OA group is autonomous, each member is free to choose a daily food ration that will, hopefully, produce a sane and reasonable weight loss. What works for each of us with regard to food arrangements is a tool that frees us to work the program; it is *not* the program.

The first step informs me of my powerlessness over food. For me to try to control what I eat for twenty-one days is to contradict the concept of powerlessness. Twenty-one days — or thirty or a hundred — may be a successful tool for you, but it is not for me, and for this reason it is important that when I carry the message, I state only the principles of the program.

I love all my OA family, and I want to attract more members to this great Fellowship. That is why I try always to remind myself as well as others to stick to the principles of the program when sharing how it works.

Keeping it simple is often difficult for us complicated people, but it works.

The group conscience of my home meeting is: "We don't talk of individual food plans; we are here to learn how the program works."

It's great to have tools for a program of recovery that rewards us with sanity. But let's not mistake the tools for the program. Let's help each other find what works best for us and move on toward growth, recovery and a Fellowship blessed with the wisdom and mellowness of maturity.

October 1979

The Promise

MY "WEIGHT PROBLEM" became apparent in childhood, though no one seemed to think I ate too much. I was just "heavy."

I had few friends, and the one place I felt comfortable in was our church. Everyone needs to feel comfortable at least part of the time, so I spent a lot of time in church. By the time I was sixteen years old, I was the pastor of a small church.

After a good deal of education and experience, I was ordained. The day of my ordination I was asked by the bishop, "Will you recommend fasting or abstinence, both by precept and example?"

I answered that I would, though I did not really know what I was promising, and no one could explain it to me.

Many years went by, years during which I continued to overeat. I was able to do my work, but every doctor I saw told me I had to lose weight. None of them could ever tell me how.

In the course of my ministry, I encountered Alcoholics Anonymous and became active in it as an outsider (I do not drink). I always admired the AA program and the kind of help it gave people. Once in a while, I wondered who was going to help me.

Then I heard about Overeaters Anonymous. One might expect to hear that I rushed to get there. I did not. I kept looking in the paper to see if the announcement was still there. In the back of my mind was the notion that if they ever stopped meeting I could tell people that I had been planning to go but since the meeting was discontinued, it was *their* fault I was still fat!

But they never did stop meeting. The notice was there in the paper every week.

Then, early in October 1977, a funny thing happened. I became aware that I was going to an OA meeting. So help me, that is what happened. I did not make a decision to go. It was as if the decision had been made and revealed to me. After several days of eating that was completely out of control, I showed up at the meeting place. I really didn't want to go. But there I was.

And what a day it was! I will never forget it.

There was that whole AA program that I knew so well and thought was great for other people. And there, too, was the long forgotten word from my ordination: *abstinence.* That was the secret key that made the twelve-step program apply to my problem.

In the two years since that great day, I have been on abstinence. It is not perfect, but it works for me — one day at a time.

I have lost 50 pounds. My blood pressure, which used to be controlled by medication, is now OK. I have not taken a pill for more than a year.

I am a far better minister and an immeasurably nicer and happier person. I am finally, after all these years, keeping the promise I made on the day of my ordination.

My deep thanks to Overeaters Anonymous, to all my fellow members and to that Higher Power who answered my prayers by sending me to that first meeting.

February 1980

Keep Loving Me

STARVATION is a self-imposed prison — emotionally, physically and spiritually. When I put up walls and isolate myself from God and loved ones, I stop growing. I refuse food, both literal and figurative.

That is anorexia, for me.

As a compulsive overeater, I controlled my weight problem through diet and exercise. I could take a food plan and follow it rigidly. I wanted approval badly, and I thought a thin body would get it for me.

After many years of diets and binges, I finally reached normal weight in OA and began maintenance for the first time in my life. With a good deal of fear, I started work on the steps. At first, fear of facing the world without food to soothe the emotional pain kept me hiding in my home. Later, fear of going back to work and becoming independent without the periodic oblivion of binging drove me to the edge of anorexia and depression.

I took the fourth step and turned it over to my sponsor. But I was still fearful, still refusing to see my good qualities. I also denied myself the experiences and people I needed in order to grow. I did not allow myself to enjoy food, people or anything else about my life. I even denied myself sunshine, air, rest and play.

My work and my rigid food plan had become a prison. I ate diet foods in limited quantities and with little variety. If I was physically hungry, I still would not eat. As I dipped below normal weight, my bones and veins appeared. Physically, I felt drained of energy. My emotions ran wild. At that point, I panicked and began counseling.

For a time I did not feel like eating, but kept following a food plan with my sponsor. I had a deep-seated belief that I should not enjoy food, though I wanted to be alone at meals so I could relax and concentrate on eating. I used food, caffeine, gum, diet drinks, exercise, reading and lots of fantasy for support instead of people. I lived with unfulfilled dreams and ideas. I was proud to show friends my thin body because I felt it was proof of my success. But inwardly I was starving and unhappy. I did not like the way I looked or felt.

With an abundance of false energy created partly by caffeine, I became hyperactive. Busy and successful on the surface, I refused to acknowledge the physical and mental fatigue I actually felt. I also denied my emotions, especially anger and fear. I felt apart and isolated even from OA friends and family in my new thin body. I was like an autistic child, locked in a peculiar antisocial behavior and beyond reach, even by loved ones.

It is said that unless anorexics can remember the horror of their starvation, they will not get well. But I believe that most anorexics can be helped if they are willing to accept love.

In my recovery I have had to let go my ideas about many things: food plans, self-image, love, friendship, what I need to live. I have had to try new ideas, new food plans, new ways of giving and receiving love. Sometimes it meant pain and even binging to find what I needed. I have had to trust.

I am getting better now because I remember the pain of my self-imposed starvation. I hurt and I grieve for myself. I am beginning to care for and love my new body, not at a fashionable weight, but at a comfortable weight. I am caring for my healing mind and spirit.

Through my struggles you keep loving me — as I was and as I grow and change. You keep reaching out to me when I cannot reach out to you. I am glad to say you have touched me.

Thank you, OA friends, for my life.

April 1980

Bypass and Back

THE DOCTORS told me there might be complications but I didn't listen. I heard only what I wanted to hear: weight loss.

I had once weighed 325 pounds, then reduced to 145. Despite diet clubs, medication, spas, psychiatry, fasting and drastic diets, my weight soared back up to 300.

My constant hope was that someone would come up with a fast and easy way to lose weight. When I heard about the intestinal bypass procedure I thought I had found the answer to my problem. So I had the operation.

That was about ten years ago.

Jejunoileal bypass is a surgical procedure that alters the body's ability to absorb nutrients by sending food directly from the stomach to the large intestine, bypassing the small intestine (the chief site of absorption of digested nutrients). The food is barely digested — which causes serious problems.

Diarrhea was my most immediate trouble right after the operation. I was running to the bathroom twenty to forty times a day.

Although I was consuming five or six thousand calories a day, my weight fell to 155 pounds. My body did not absorb the calories from all that food — but neither did it absorb the vital nutrients.

I ate constantly in a vain effort to feed not only my compulsion but my starving body.

Despite the nutritional supplements I was taking, I developed severe deficiencies which resulted in pellagra, a condition caused by a lack of the B vitamin, niacin; and acute calcium depletion, a medical emergency which required intravenous injections of calcium. In addition, I suffered liver malfunction and an intolerance to dairy products. All this was accompanied by extreme fatigue, nervousness, grotesque swelling of my feet, arthritis, hair loss, loosening of my teeth and rectal problems that required five operations.

My mental processes had slowed down and I had all but ceased to function as a human being. All I could do was eat, go to the bathroom and watch TV.

Had enough?

I hadn't.

I fought having the bypass reversed; I still had my compulsive gluttony to cater to.

Wanting desperately to believe that some undiscovered disease was causing all the trouble, I finally checked into a well-known medical clinic. Surely they would tell me I had cancer, or perhaps multiple sclerosis. I wanted to hear anything but the truth.

After extensive medical tests, the doctors had one answer: my difficulties were all complications of the bypass. I was starving myself to death while eating continuously.

I knew I couldn't go on much longer. I gave in and had the bypass reversal.

Before the surgery could be done, however, I had to receive hyperalimentation — intravenous feeding of proteins and other vital nutrients — to ensure that I would survive the operation and that my body would heal. I spent one month in the hospital for hyperalimentation and surgery. For three weeks of this time I was not permitted to eat or even to drink liquids.

On November 1, 1979 I weighed 124 pounds. The doctors gave me an ideal goal weight of 135 and told me to go home and eat normally.

"After all you've been through," said my husband, "you'll never overeat again. Surely you've learned your lesson!"

He was so pleased with my restored health that he bought me a new car. I rewarded myself with an outrageously expensive evening gown. I was never going to gain weight again. How could I?

By Christmas I weighed 140.

"I'm OK," I consoled myself. "Everyone gains weight over the holidays."

By February 1, I was 185 pounds — and badly frightened.

When I heard about OA, I went to my first meeting expecting to learn a bunch of new diet tricks to take away my 50 extra pounds.

What a surprise! I learned, instead, that I had to face my problem honestly. Obesity was not my problem. My problem was *me*.

Thanks to OA, now I know that the answer to compulsive overeating lies not in diets or willpower or magic operations, but in a Power greater than myself. All I had to do was let it happen — and I still do.

July 1980

Abstinence Is Guilt-Free Eating

TRULY BELIEVE that if you are in the right spiritual condition you can eat any food. By depending on a Higher Power and turning your will and life over to that Power, you are liberated from the need to compulsively overeat. So it follows that when you are in touch with your Higher Power — really one with whatever God is for you — food has no power over you.

I've heard many long-term abstainers say this, and I believe it, too — for them. I hope one day I can reach that place. But the truth is that today I cannot eat one cookie without finishing the entire package.

Sometimes I start to believe that I can handle certain foods in certain instances. For example, if dessert is included with my dinner at a restaurant, why can't I eat it? After all, I would be served only one portion — no temptation to "sliver, slice, slab, slob" an entire cake. I could enjoy a normal portion with a cup of tea, then go right home and go to bed. Just today, can't that one dessert be part of my abstinence? I wouldn't be binging.

But if I'm honest with myself, I can't rationalize that dessert into my abstinence. Why? Because I would feel guilty. And I believe that abstinence is guilt-free eating. So, for me, eating that dessert would not be abstaining.

Let's say that I did manage to eat it and stop at just one. That might be even more dangerous than if it had led to a binge. Because I might start to think, "Hey, that's pretty good! You ate sugar and you didn't binge. Maybe you're not really a compulsive overeater. Maybe you're cured!"

I must remember this. When I hear oldtimers with years of abstinence say that no particular food has any power over them anymore, my hat is off to them. More (higher) power to them! But I'm not in that place. Although I've made great strides, I'm still working on my character defects; I'm still learning to turn things over.

I've learned never to say "never" in this program. Maybe one day I can reach that place. I have great hopes because I see how far I've come.

296

I have maintained my weight loss for fifteen months and I am happier, more serene and just a nicer person to be with. The program is working.

I have to resist the temptation to compare my program to anyone else's program. I only lose when I do that. There will always be someone with more abstinence, more weight loss, more spirituality. All I can do is grow at the rate God wills for me.

September 1980

The Invisible Fat Man

IT HAPPENED to me again one day last week. I suddenly, inexplicably, felt fat. I mean, I felt that the image staring back at me out of the mirror was a mistake or a joke.

Often in OA we hear that we are going to discover a slim person living inside our fat body. And, sure enough, after two and a half years in this program, I am maintaining a normal weight and have been doing so for more than twenty months.

But there are times when I feel like a fat man wearing a skinny suit. At these times I find myself adopting mannerisms and attitudes from my past obese life.

I look in the mirror and I see the small person looking back; but somehow I feel he is only temporary. That's my fear: that someday I'll gain back all the weight. I've done that before.

I have lost all my excess weight more than once before discovering Overeaters Anonymous. At the time I came to my first meeting, I prided myself on the willpower I possessed. I had lost 50 pounds or more on at least two occasions and lesser amounts innumerable times. Each time, as soon as I reached my goal, I would start the climb again. I don't recall maintaining a steady weight for a single month before coming to OA. I was always either on the way up or on the way down.

Now I'm maintaining and have been doing so for nearly two years, but the old fear is still there anytime I start to take my program for granted.

First I begin to act like my old, heavier self. When I came to OA, I sported a 41-inch waistline and nearly 200 pounds on a five-foot, two-inch frame. I kidded myself that all that bulk was muscle. I used my size as a battering ram. I didn't open doors with my hands and arms by pushing; I would just get the weight in motion and ram through a door — or straight-arm it, then lean and let the weight force it open. I did that in chores, too. My wife would want a piece of furniture moved and I could just kind of lean into it and it would go wherever it was pointed.

There are other mannerisms I affect from time to time: I'll pass a mirror and suddenly I find myself sucking in my gut and throwing out my chest. Now I don't have a gut that needs to be sucked in. I'm a small man at just under 130 pounds, and I have a 29-inch waist. But the fat man in me reacts instinctively when he's in control.

Because I am a compulsive overeater, I must realize that there will always be that fat man in me ready to come out again whenever I'm ready to turn my will and my life over to him instead of to my God.

He's insidious and can make me miserable even when I'm eating normally. Sometimes he whispers, "It's only a matter of time until you go hog-wild and start eating like you used to." Or, "You can't keep this up forever, you know."

Then my program tells me, "Maybe not, but you can do it just for today."

And I tell that to the fat man.

October 1980

Distinctly OA

I DON'T CARE how much I substitute the words food and compulsive overeating for alcohol and alcoholism, it's different being a compulsive overeater.

It's that last abstinent bite that gets me. Sometimes I'm not even hungry, but I eat because it's mealtime (and because I love to eat). When I come to that final mouthful, I feel ravenous! Often my portions look gigantic and I fantasize being unable to finish, but when it's all gone I feel as if I could go on eating forever.

Sometimes I get to the end of my allotted food and I am so turned on that I feel as if I'll go into orbit. (Thanks to this program and the grace of God, I don't — one meal at a time.)

And you should see me shopping for my lovely food. (Or maybe you shouldn't. You'd probably find me hilarious — or pathetic, depending on where *you're* at.) Broccoli or peas? Peas, I decide, and scoop them into a plastic bag. On second thought, those stringbeans look beautiful. Dump out the peas, grab a few handfuls of beans. God, that okra is tempting. I haven't had it in ages. Another quick exchange. Maybe I should splurge on artichokes instead. . . .

Finally, I'm so mixed up I feel like walking out. If I can't have it all, I don't want any.

"Keep it simple, silly," I tell myself. "Take broccoli. It's the cheapest. It's the easiest. And you love it."

I won't go into such dramatic detail about my tizzies over muenster or cheddar, apples or melon — or about my shenanigans to ensure that I get the biggest eggs. (I switch them around a bit, getting the best of several boxes.)

Et cetera.

Sometimes I feel guilty about all this. "The obsession hasn't been lifted," I cry in dismay, and I despair of ever qualifying for the ranks of the spiritually fit. When in such a morass, I remember how it was when I was compulsively overeating and suddenly this behavior seems mild by comparison.

I also remind myself that whatever it is I'm doing has allowed me to be abstinent in OA for six years, maintaining a 60-pound weight loss.

"Thank God I'm using all that energy constructively now," I think.

In the back of my mind, though, I am convinced that other OAs would be utterly horrified and would disqualify me as a true-blue-and-recovering member of our Fellowship.

At times I just plain accept myself. I'm grateful that I care about myself enough to give myself the best. Remembering my tendency to feel more comfortable with deprivation and suffering, I endorse myself for allowing myself the pleasure of my wonderful food. And if the obsession has not been completely annihilated, so what? My pretending it's gone when it isn't will not help me one bit. On the contrary, recognizing what I'm still capable of doing with food enables me to choose not to act on the obsession but to continue taking the options OA offers me instead.

In fairness, the craziness I have described (if it *is* craziness) is not a permanent state. When the food tizzies hit, I remind myself that they come and go, that they won't last forever — and they never do. When I am free of the obsession I remind myself that this freedom also comes and goes, that I shouldn't be surprised if it doesn't last forever — and it never does.

Most of the time I'm somewhere in between these two extremes. And that's what is important for me to recognize and accept so I can just live with it and quit fighting it. If I think of myself as either totally food-crazy or totally food-free, I'm passing unfair judgment on myself on the one hand and placing unrealistic expectations on myself on the other.

The point I'm trying to make is that compulsive overeating is different from alcoholism. And we all know why: we *have* to eat. We handle dynamite three times a day.

AAs don't have to take just three moderate drinks a day, nor do they have to choose between a daquiri and a whiskey sour, or decide whether it will be Red Label or Black.

I used to envy alcoholics because they could totally abstain from alcohol and be done with it.

I envy them no more. Thanks to Overeaters Anonymous, I now enjoy my food to the hilt. Abstinence has given me back the pleasure of eating. And, occasional tizzies notwithstanding, I love every abstinent bite — especially the last!

January 1981

To All of You, My Thanks

I WAS A SKINNY KID and a trim teenager. I never gave my weight a thought until I gained 60 pounds during my first pregnancy. I truly believed I had to eat for two!

After my second child was born I realized I was in deep trouble. Not only was I stuck with two babies but I was fat and miserable as well. My husband is extremely handsome and I began to feel overwhelmingly insecure.

By the time my third baby came along the battle was on. I could not stop eating. I even devoured the baby's puddings. I was convinced I was a bad person and cried continually, hating myself for having no willpower.

I began driving 120 miles a week to get shots and pills from a well-known diet doctor. At last I became thin. I was the life of the party — and sicker than ever.

When I discovered I was pregnant again I went off the diet pills, but our beautiful daughter was born with birth defects. She is fine today, by the grace of God, but after her birth I set out on a ten-year guilt trip. The agony we went through as a family is indescribable. I resorted to shots and pills again and I became withdrawn, angry, jealous and terrified. I began hallucinating, and my husband gave me a choice: the pills or him. I chose him.

My mental anguish while "coming down" off the pills was devastating. What had only been paranoid tendencies now became full-fledged paranoia. And the pounds piled on.

When my husband threatened to leave and take the children with him, I frantically tried to be the wife and mother I thought I ought to be. To avoid getting fat, I now turned to alcohol. By drinking instead of eating, I stayed thin for a couple of years and managed to do all the things expected of a good wife and mother. I now had an alcohol problem, but I knew I could regain control whenever I wanted to. And I did. I quit drinking and resumed eating.

This time I hit 280 pounds. What hurt most was that my children were ashamed of me. I tried to compensate by becoming Supermom — fat but jolly. I was the den mother, the short-order cook, the driver to everywhere and anywhere and the always-available school volunteer. I did anything no one else would do, and I did it with a smile to show how happy I was.

I went to weight clinics. I underwent hypnosis. I contemplated suicide. I prayed to wake up thin. Instead, I woke up every morning fatter than the day before.

At 340 pounds I went into shock from high blood pressure and was hospitalized. I lost 30 pounds, then ate myself right up to 350. I was hospitalized again, this time for gallbladder trouble. I was such a high risk that the doctors would not operate or prescribe painkillers. I was certain I would die.

Released from the hospital, I went to an OA meeting and cried through the entire proceedings. When I was called on to share, I literally begged for help.

There were many thin people at the meeting and when I heard them say, "It works!" I believed them. They were my proof and I took their suggestions. I went to meetings, read the Big Book and the OA literature and began working the steps to the best of my ability. One day at a time, I stayed away from excess food.

In eight months I lost 170 pounds. My blood pressure is normal, I am free of all medication and I have no physical problems whatsoever. I am not only back among the living, but my life is better than I ever imagined it could be. To give you an example of what I mean: I love wearing jeans and sweaters again, like everybody else, but it's an even bigger kick to be different if I feel like it: to wear a hat when no one else is wearing one and feel it's OK! And what a miracle it is to look in the mirror and love me, to look at others and love them and to hug people any time I want to!

I'm not afraid anymore. I can laugh and I can cry. I can console others and I can forgive and be tolerant of mistakes. I have faith, hope and joy — and I try to give it all away wherever I go.

I attend many meetings, participating and speaking whenever I am asked. My program is the most important thing in my life. Slowly, one step at a time, it enables me to make the absolute best of what God has already made.

I have never met a person in this Fellowship who has not given me something, and to all of you go my thanks and my love.

To those not yet in this program: If I can do it, so can you, one day at a time.

February 1981

Good Health, Good Abstinence

THIS IS MY THIRD time around in OA. Each time I lost my abstinence it was for the same reason: I was trying to adhere to a food plan that was not suitable for my physiological needs. When I follow "gray sheet," which is the only plan recommended by OA groups in my area, my menstrual cycle stops — a phenomenon which many other young women on that plan also experience.

It was extremely frustrating for me to live with the notion that the only food plan that could keep me abstinent might also seriously damage my health. At twenty-four, it did not seem normal to miss my menstrual cycle for three to six months consecutively, especially after having been regular all my life.

I remained convinced, however, that sticking to my food plan was better than the binging and starving insanity I had been living through. I gave it another try. When my period stopped again, my abstinence became shaky.

My sponsor continually reminded me that a binge would only make me feel worse and that once I lost my abstinence I might not get it back. I became angry and started to question OA; but I continued to work the program, and I held on for dear life.

I felt uneasy about my physical condition. My body began to swell. There was a slight chance that I might be pregnant, but I had no regular period to give me a clue. Physically, I was extremely uncomfortable. Emotionally, I was climbing the walls. Spiritually, I kept searching for some kind of balance. Although I continued using the tools of the program, it became harder and harder to hold on to my abstinence.

Then, just in time, I heard a longtime abstainer describe my food plan in a way I had never heard before. (She did it at my regular meeting, and I later learned that some people were annoyed. But it was exactly what I needed to hear.)

"This food plan is just a guide to help us learn to live abstinently," she explained. "It was not devised by a doctor or a dietitian but by four

303

women in a living room.

"If one plan doesn't work for you," she continued, "try another. Stick with the program and use the tools and you will be successful. Too many of us are stuck on the food level, but a food plan is just one of the many tools in our kit.

"Our main goal is to abstain from compulsive overeating by eating well-balanced, moderate meals. Ours is a twelve-step program of recovery, not a diet club. There should not be so much emphasis on or dependence upon any one food plan."

After the meeting I chose a different food plan, which I have been following since then. Happily, on the day before a scheduled doctor's appointment, my menstrual cycle began. I feel much better now, and much more relaxed about my program.

I really love OA. It has helped me in so many ways. When my abstinence is strong I feel as though I can do anything, and my self-confidence reaches a high that makes me wonder how I ever lived without it.

I give service as the program chairperson, I follow the steps and I have become friendly with other OAs.

I am learning to avoid slippery places and situations. An unsuitable food plan is an obstacle to abstinence for me because it is not adequate for my physical needs.

OAs with similar problems might consider trying the suggestion I followed: change your food plan and continue to work the program and to use the tools.

Although many come to our Fellowship for a food plan, the great majority find that our program has far more to offer. I am grateful to all the people who helped me through this difficult time, especially the woman who showed me that I need not be afraid to change food plans, and my sponsor, who kept me going by talking with me three times a day.

Finally, I am thankful that I learned that abstinence — not adherence to a particular way of eating — is the goal.

February 1981

If I Never Lose Another Pound

ADMITTEDLY, at 260 pounds I am still obese. But I'm 50 pounds lighter than I was when I "became willing" in OA almost a year ago — so it was hard to take when a doctor recently suggested that I have a bypass operation.

After several months of ignoring a physical problem that was getting worse, I finally began to care enough about myself to go for treatment. On one of my visits, the association doctor who was substituting for my regular physician — without bothering to ask questions — reacted to my weight as if I were a weak-willed glutton and recommended the by-pass.

All my old feelings of worthlessness surged up and, goaded by self-doubt, guilt and hostility, I lashed out at the man.

I thought that would end any possibility of seeing him again, but my Higher Power had something else in store. I had been scheduled to have minor surgery done by my own doctor. When I entered the operating room, however, there was my newfound adversary waiting to perform the procedure.

To say I was startled would be putting it mildly. I was instantly filled with hatred and resentment, which mounted as he muttered a few more crude remarks about my size.

When the simple operation was over (he had done an excellent job), I continued to hold onto my anger and to entertain familiar thoughts of defiance.

"I'll show him!" I vowed. "I'll eat until I weigh 350 pounds. No one can say those things to me. I won't lose weight for *him!*"

Thank God for the wonderful people in my OA group. When I shared that story I was lovingly encouraged to let go of the episode, to turn it over. I had been so full of hostility I hadn't even thought of doing that.

As we said the Lord's Prayer at the end of the meeting, the words "Forgive us our trespasses as we forgive those who trespass against us" hit home. I knew at that moment that I could "let go and let God."

My thinking was greatly changed that day. I know that my OA sisters and brothers love me no matter what I weigh, and that they will continue to love me even if I never lose another pound. (And that, paradoxically, is precisely what enables me to go on losing weight.)

To my surprise, I felt compassion even for that poor doctor, who might never know such acceptance.

One day at a time, I am learning to practice these principles in all my affairs. I am so glad to be able to let go the hostility that was leading me to a binge and self-destruction.

April 1981

Nine-Month Miracle

BEFORE COMING to Overeaters Anonymous I had been informed that I might never have children because of the toll continuous eating and dieting had taken on my body. My physical condition was moot, however, since the man to whom I was married didn't want children.

When, a little more than seven years ago, I joined OA, made the program a part of my life and became abstinent, I realized that some changes had to be made. One of them was a divorce.

Free to make my own decisions, I began to think seriously about adopting a child on my own, but I was reminded that "easy does it" and I waited.

Then the first miracle happened: I met a man in the program and I discovered that I had at last been given the ability to love. Ironically, he wasn't sure he wanted children. We decided we would marry and if it was God's will for us to have children we would.

A year after we were married I became pregnant. To my surprise, my husband was as excited as I was. It was a joyous time for us, as well as a time of adjustment. As always, the program helped. I took a copy of my food plan to my doctor and, using that and the physician's recommended eating regimen for expectant mothers, we worked out an acceptable compromise. It was a gift to be able to value my own needs enough to assert myself. Before OA I would have felt too worthless and fearful to do so.

As it turned out, I was troubled with nausea much of the time and I could no longer eat the foods I had been eating. I often called my sponsor in the middle of a meal to commit myself to a change.

The OA program helped in other ways. During the early stages of labor I took on the twelfth-step job of returning telephone calls made to our intergroup office. This absorbing activity enabled me to keep my mind off myself and the time passed quickly.

All told, I gained a moderate amount of weight with the pregnancy and I lost it all before I left the hospital. More meaningful to me than the weight, however, was the fact that I had been both abstinent and sane throughout the entire nine months. Needless to say, our baby boy was a great joy to me and to his father.

The whole experience had been so special for us that we decided to have another child right away. With the second pregnancy I followed the same food plan but the nausea was worse. Toward the end I began to run into problems because I was not gaining as much weight as my doctor thought advisable, and I had to go to the hospital on a weekly basis for tests.

I couldn't ask for a better excuse to deviate from my plan of eating and I was tempted. But I concluded that I was doing the best I could and I turned it over to my Higher Power. That was a time when faith had to replace fear and again the program gave me what I needed. When our little girl was born she weighed 7 pounds, 8 ounces, and as before I lost all the weight I had gained.

This time I spent the early stages of labor answering OA correspondence and writing a report for the World Service Office. Toward the end of my labor I told the nurse I simply could not go on. Her reply was that I only had to get through one contraction at a time, which reminded me so much of the program, I had to laugh.

In recounting the story of my two pregnancies I have come to realize that there are many miracles for which I am grateful. Before OA I could not possibly have gone through these experiences with so much serenity — and without resorting to compulsive overeating.

There are three basic suggestions I can share with anyone who is concerned about maintaining abstinence and peace of mind in pregnancy: (1) Discuss your food plan with your doctor and be willing to adopt a medically sound eating plan; (2) work the twelve-step program each day to the best of your ability; and (3) leave the rest to your Higher Power.

As you can see, there is nothing exclusive about these suggestions. They constitute what to most recovering compulsive overeaters is the OA way of life.

July 1981

Secret Formula

WHEN I CAME INTO OA four years ago I wanted what you people had — but not at the expense of giving up what *I* had.

What I had was my own secret formula for keeping my weight down while eating uncontrollably. I discovered my "diet trick" when I was fifteen and forcing myself to vomit after binging soon became a ritual. At first, vomiting helped me lose weight but it quickly backfired. I started to eat twice what I would normally eat, then three or four times as much. Losing weight was no longer the issue; I was lucky to be maintaining. Everything was food, from morning till night. I lived to eat.

My life between the ages of fifteen and twenty-one is a blur. I got married, had a beautiful baby boy, went to college for a license in nursing, switched careers and am presently employed at a job I will probably keep for a long time. But I do not remember consciously choosing to do any of these things.

I came into this program desperate, lonely and afraid. I was afraid of myself and of the terrible thing inside me. How could I do this to myself over and over again? I turned away from people for fear they would find out. I became resentful and jealous of their successes, then blamed myself even more.

Finally, I let go. I decided to take the steps, walk with God and be guided by a sponsor to work the program as it is written.

Miracles have happened. I stopped overeating and started living. For fifteen months I have abstained from both compulsions one day at a time. My Higher Power woke me up after a long sleep and said, "Come with me and I'll show you how to be happy, feel loved and never be alone again."

For the gift of life as it was meant to be, instead of the desperate existence through which I was drifting, I am grateful to this program and to all of you.

December 1981

It's a Girl!

HIS IS THE STORY of an OA baby — a real one. After being abstinent in the Fellowship for nine years, I have a six-month-old daughter. What I experienced to reach this point all but made me despair that my husband and I would ever become parents.

For four years I knew the pain and frustration of infertility. The patience to wait for what comes so easily to others takes great inner strength. Only the twelve steps kept me relatively sane. Again and again I prayed for knowledge of God's will.

To add to the emotional turmoil and depression, I found myself gaining weight even though I was abstinent. I later learned it was a side effect of the medication I had been taking, which had affected my thyroid.

Finally, I became pregnant. Now, a whole new set of problems presented itself. What does one do when she has just upchucked her dinner and there are still twelve hours till breakfast? What if diet soda must go because of its salt content? How does one alleviate nausea when the doctor says to eat crackers and one does not eat crackers?

I talked about my food plan with my husband, who is also in program. I made new commitments and followed them. I added certain foods and took away others. I constantly asked God for help, knowing that the Power that brought me the miracle of pregnancy would also carry me through.

Staying abstinent, I gained 37 pounds. That terrified me. Going to the doctor and watching the scale go up was always disconcerting, and it reminded me of all those years when doctors scolded me for being obese.

"How did I ever gain so much?" I couldn't help asking when my 6-pound, 8-ounce baby was born. I continued to abstain, but as long as that excess weight hung on I kept imploring God for help. By the time my daughter was five months old, my weight was back to normal.

During those five months I often asked myself whether I was eating too much. The answer was always No. The next step was to ask for the patience and willingness to believe that whatever my body did was God's business, not mine. Every time I heard of someone leaving the hospital in her regular clothes I questioned myself again.

I was thrown into another dilemma when I read that a nursing mother must eat 1000 additional calories a day, whereas I was eating just enough to maintain my 110 pounds. Still, I was abstinent.

When our daughter was born, the nurses commented that she was unusually alert. That alertness has continued and I cannot help but believe it is because I treated my body so well, both before and during pregnancy.

My husband and I are somewhat concerned that, as the child of two compulsive overeaters, our daughter may have inherited a tendency toward obesity. But we are confident that, just as the program has enabled us to face life head on, so it will help us give our daughter the tools that will make it unnecessary for her to abuse food or any other substance.

February 1982

Squooshy-Soft and Lovable

W HEN I WAS AT my top weight I got on the scale every morning, looked at the number and groaned, "I hate myself at this weight." Then I hoisted myself into the bathtub, which is directly across from a full-length mirror. As I climbed out and saw my reflection, I again told myself how ugly I looked and how I detested being heavy. Eventually, my morning commentary was shortened from "I hate myself at this weight" to just plain "I hate myself."

During the past eighteen months in OA I've been decreasing in size and growing in self-acceptance. Through much hard work with two dedicated sponsors, my self-image has improved immensely. Although I've shrunk from a size 20 to a size 10, I'm still me. I had to learn to accept myself as a person in the process of changing — not quite finished, but well on my way.

Today I get on the scale and I am delighted. No, I'm not at my goal yet, but that is not important. I know it will happen. I climb out of the bathtub, look in the mirror and see me — a thin, beautiful person. Not Racquel Welch, to be sure, but *me* — five-foot-four, 140 pounds, with baggy skin, sagging breasts and a squooshy-soft stomach. And I love it!

I look at myself, giggle with delight, give myself a hug and thank God for my abstinence, my sponsors and the fellowship of this program.

May 1982

Leave the Numbers to H.P.

I LEFT AN OA MEETING feeling charged and elated from the evening's sharing and drove out to the university to jog. Upon entering the locker room, I did just what I had told myself I wasn't going to do: I stepped onto the scale.

I hadn't lost as much weight as I thought I had. In an instant, all the peace and serenity I had gained at the meeting slipped away.

Reluctantly, I put on my sneakers and went out to the track. As I jogged around and around, I reflected on what had just happened. I had allowed the numbers on a machine to change the way I felt about myself, to drain my self-esteem and the security of my program.

Had I not had nearly two months of back-to-back abstinence? (The most I'd ever had since coming into the program more than a year and a half ago.) Had I not been staying in touch with a sponsor and with other members of the program on a daily basis? Had I not been working the twelve steps and maintaining contact with a Higher Power?

The answer to all these questions was Yes. I had been working my program more rigorously than ever before, with absolutely fantastic results. Why, then, should a scale affect my serenity?

It did not take me long to bounce back, but that experience drove home the truth of something I once heard at a meeting: "My weight is God's business, not mine."

July 1982

Program Baby

"ONE DAY AT A TIME" and "Let go and let God" are two slogans that helped me through a wonderful but frightening phase of my life. At age twenty-nine, maintaining my normal weight at last, I became pregnant with our fourth child — my first OA baby.

Fear was my worst enemy. With each of my previous pregnancies I gained 25 to 50 pounds, and always retained some of the excess weight after delivery. Following my third child's birth I stayed at 150 pounds. Being only 5'1" tall, my weight caused me so much anguish I was driven to OA, where I became abstinent and lost the weight. Now, with my fourth pregnancy, I quite naturally dreaded getting fat again.

Several months into the pregnancy and abstinent, I gained weight slowly. A number of people commented that I didn't seem to be gaining enough and that I would harm both myself and the baby. By discussing this with my doctor, my husband and my OA friends, then taking my doctor's advice and putting the matter in God's hands, I got through.

When I entered the hospital to have the baby I weighed 17 pounds more than before pregnancy. All went well and we were presented with a beautiful, 7-pound, 13-ounce girl, perfectly normal in every way. When I left the hospital the following day I had lost all but one pound of the extra weight, and within five weeks I was wearing my regular clothes — an outward sign that the program is working in my life.

Our new daughter seems to be the brightest and most alert of all our children. I wouldn't be surprised if this is because the program enabled me to take such good care of myself both before and during my pregnancy. By taking those nine months one day at a time, following my doctor's advice and completely entrusting myself to God, this ended up being the happiest and sanest childbirth experience I have ever had.

July 1982

In Praise of Being Thin

THINNESS HAS BEEN given a bad name by many of us in program. If anyone had asked me what I wanted most when I came to Overeaters Anonymous seven and a half years ago, I would have answered without hesitation: to be thin. But soon I began saying that being thin is not really important, that working the steps is where it's at. Today I know I could not have taken the first three steps honestly while I was still overeating, and that steps four through twelve are impossible for one who is not abstinent.

Two years ago, quite miraculously, I became willing to let go of the problem and live in the solution — to think of myself as a healthy person in body, mind and spirit. Every day I took step three, making a conscious decision to eat only what I needed for a healthy body. Trusting that my Higher Power could do for me what I could not do for myself, I turned everything over to God. And I got thin. Wonder of wonders, I discovered that thin is not the enemy I thought it was. I'll even go so far as to say I would take thin-and-crazy over fat-and-crazy any day. Fat is a problem in itself and it creates additional problems.

I realize now that when I insisted that thin was not important I was justifying my unwillingness to be disciplined and vulnerable. I was resisting the program's suggestions to take life on by opening myself up to the joy and pain; by going ahead and doing what needed to be done.

When I became aware that my self-loathing came partly from loathing the fat, I changed my mind about which came first, the physical or the spiritual. I began having moderate, well-balanced meals, became abstinent and then dug in to work the steps and practice the principles.

I like being thin. Thin is not a destination but a vehicle. Thin says I think I'm OK, that I value myself and will not punish or "reward" myself with anything harmful. Thin is a willingness to turn from hurting myself. Thin, for me, is no longer a goal of perfection but a comfortable weight within a range that makes me look normal to myself and others.

The real test for me has been looking at myself in the mirror with

acceptance and kindness. Always a yo-yo, I never gave myself a chance
to get used to the new image and embrace it as mine. Now I value seeing
myself as I truly am.

When I was overeating, I never felt I had the rewards of the program.
The rewards came as I became abstinent and began to work the program.
The greatest reward is that I have self-respect rather than self-contempt.
I like myself today.

The only way I can maintain my new body and attitude is by being
honest with myself, living the steps and staying in contact with my Higher
Power. I cannot store up program. It has to be lived every day.

Being thin, for me, goes along with being spiritually OK. This is a
spiritual program. Thin is just a beginning.

August 1982

The Biggest One at the Meeting

I GREW UP in a family that encouraged us to fill our plates and come
back for more, which wasn't hard for me to do. I first became aware of
my problem with weight and compulsive overeating when I was sixteen.
In high school, I occasionally tried to lose weight by skipping meals until
I got so weak and shaky I couldn't keep going. Then my mother would
urge me to eat, and of course I obliged by eating too much. In college I
had my own room in the dormitory and it became even easier to eat
whenever I wanted to.

At nineteen I was married, still just a size sixteen. But, being a good
cook who loved to experiment with new dishes, I put on weight fast.
After five children my health began to deteriorate, and through the years
I had four operations. Each time, I was able to lose the weight required
for surgery, but when I recovered I became even heavier than before.

For thirty-three years of marriage I tried diet pills, liquid protein and
fad diets, but the same vicious cycle of weight loss and gain repeated
itself over and over again.

Then last summer I learned that an Overeaters Anonymous group was being formed here in town. My daughter was helping to get it started. She tried hard to get me to join, but I gave her every excuse in the book, even though I was terribly depressed and unhappy with myself. She talked to me about OA every chance she got and shared how much it was helping her and how happy she was. Finally, eight months ago, I agreed to go to a meeting. I had suffered as much pain as I could stand.

My main excuse for not going sooner was that, with 200 pounds to lose, I was afraid I would be the biggest one there. And I was! But the OA members did not stare at me as I feared they would and as people on the street do. Instead, they accepted me just as I was. I found love and encouragement and the help I have needed for years — a Higher Power of my understanding.

When I began abstaining from compulsive overeating I also began abstaining from the pain pills I was taking too often. I have gotten rid of 44 pounds so far and my health improves with each pound lost. My doctor is one hundred percent behind the OA program, and when I step on the scale the nurse is almost as happy as I am.

I am no longer a semi-invalid. I don't need pain relievers, and I am far more active than I was. I am learning to deal with all the anger I stored up throughout my lifetime of compulsive overeating.

Now, thanks to God and Overeaters Anonymous, I wake up each morning ready to reach out to life instead of hiding from it as I did for so many years.

August 1982

"For You and Countless Others"

SOMETHING I CAN only describe as a profound spiritual experience happened to me several months ago. After losing and gaining weight in Overeaters Anonymous for two years, I realized on a gut level that I cannot control my food. I abandoned the struggle and gave my food problem to God, who just took it away.

I feel as if a giant burden has been lifted from my shoulders. A tremendous sense of release and total wellness has swept over me. I don't have to try to diet or stay on a food plan anymore; I can't. I'm not worrying about food today; I don't have to. When it's time to eat, I ask God to help me make wise choices and to give me the strength to stop when I've had enough. I don't have to spend unnecessary time planning and worrying.

An alcoholic can have perfect abstinence from alcohol but I cannot have perfect abstinence from compulsive overeating. I no longer want it to be perfect. Any way I do it is fine. I don't care what I ate for lunch or what I will eat for dinner, as long as each meal is healthful, tasty and moderate.

No food was ever good enough or plentiful enough for me, but today I am not obsessed with food. It no longer has to be the most or the best. My apple doesn't have to be the largest one in the store.

I'm so grateful to God, I want to shout my thanks from the rooftops. I feel like a toy soldier standing before my creator: "Reporting for duty, God. Tell me what you want me to do and I'll do it!" The third-step prayer reads, in part, "Take away my difficulties, that victory over them may bear witness to those I would help of Thy Power, Thy Love, and Thy Way of Life" (*Alcoholics Anonymous,* p. 63). This is happening for me. God is taking away my difficulties: my food compulsion, my anxiety, my worry, my depression, my immaturity, my unwillingness and inability to face life.

I don't know why this has happened for me. I know we can't earn God's grace; we have it automatically, just because we're human. But I

316

have been working the program to the best of my ability: going to meetings, taking the steps and adhering to the traditions, as well as sponsoring and giving service. And I continue to see a therapist. Most important, I've been willing to work on building a relationship with my Higher Power.

My program is far from perfect. The most entrenched of my character defects sometimes seem to ooze from every pore. All I can do is pray to God to remove them.

I don't know what tomorrow will bring. I could go berserk and binge. This disease is everything it's been made out to be, and I hope I never underestimate its force; but for today I am free as never before. Since turning over my food to God, I have been eating sanely, just the way I always dreamed of doing but could never do.

I have escaped from my prison of compulsive overeating and I am building a new life based on freedom from bondage. This is indeed a miracle. It has happened for countless others, so why not for me? And if it can happen for me, it can happen for you.

August 1982

Vomiting: A Deadly Magic

I HAVE NO "fat pictures" to pass around at meetings, nor can I report any significant weight loss. I can, however, tell of bizarre eating binges — of stuffing my emotions down my throat by eating so much I could hardly breathe.

So why was I not fat? Because I was a vomiter. I controlled my weight for fifteen years by vomiting and taking diet pills.

When I was seventeen, a friend lost weight with diet pills and I decided to do the same. I lost so much, I became too weak to participate in sports. I resumed "normal" eating and, you guessed it, I gained weight. Then, during my first year of college, I learned about vomiting. It was disgusting, but it was also "magic." I could have my cake and eat it too! I binged and vomited once or twice a week throughout my college years.

When I married and became pregnant, I stopped vomiting for the baby's sake, then started again after I gave birth. I thought I would outgrow the habit, but by the time I was thirty, I was vomiting four or five times a week. When I read a magazine article about binging and vomiting, I knew I wasn't the only one who did it. I felt my disease would kill me, so I cut the article out and put it with my personal belongings so when I died my family would know what I had gone through to be thin.

I tried to stop many times. I had my ears stapled, and once I put cleaning fluid on my hands to keep them out of my mouth. Nothing helped. By now, gorging and vomiting had become a daily routine, one that was controlling me. The physical consequences were frightening. I was bleeding from the esophagus, I had scar tissue in my throat and I had to have my teeth recapped three times in ten years. I was often hoarse and there were cracks in the corners of my mouth. I had stopped menstruating.

I hit rock bottom about a year ago. I fled to my mother's, two hundred miles away, desperate for help. But I couldn't tell anyone my secret. Even there, I binged and vomited after everyone had gone to bed, then cried all night. The next day, as the family admired my mother's first great-grandchild, I found myself thinking, "I won't even live to see my children grow up." I cried when I left my mother's because I thought I'd never see her again.

My husband was at work when I got home, but he had left a message for me on the refrigerator door. It was a magazine article about a model who had died from binging and fasting. I knew then that my husband was aware of what I was doing and that he cared about me.

The next morning I called Overeaters Anonymous. (I had tucked the number in my billfold long before.) At my first meeting, I tried not to pay attention to such comments as "You must be an oldtimer" or "How much weight did you lose?" I knew that on the inside I was just like the others. Feeling a little out of place, I didn't speak to anyone; but one person made me feel I had come home. Knowing I was a newcomer, she hugged me and welcomed me but said nothing about my weight. That convinced me OA was the place for me.

I made a commitment not to binge and vomit anymore, and I kept it. Food to me meant fat and I didn't know how I would handle that. My sponsor asked one thing of me: to call her before I threw up. Wow! That really got to me. Whenever I wanted to vomit after dinner, I thought, "I can't call and tell her that."

For the first month my objective was simply to refrain from vomiting and not gain weight. Was I surprised when I actually lost a couple of pounds!

By the grace of God and this program, I have been abstinent for almost a year. Every morning I thank God for the many miracles in my life. Not only has the compulsion to binge and vomit been taken away, but my fifteen-year obsession with diet pills has been removed. When I told my mother about my problem and what OA is doing for me, she broke down and cried. "Thank God, they're saving my daughter," she said.

It's true. OA is saving me. I'm not cured but, one day at a time, I am recovering. Thank you, OA, for giving me life.

November 1982

Abstinence: A Living Process

LONG-TERM ABSTINENCE. I've got it. Ten plus years. I love it. But what is it and what does it mean? Is it strict adherence to a food plan? Is it abstaining from compulsive overeating? Is it an attitude, a fullness from within? Is it God in my life?

For my first eight and a half years in Overeaters Anonymous, abstinence was an elusive bubble: just when I thought I had it, it would burst. I spent all those years trying to be perfect and have perfect gray sheet abstinence. It was disaster. For me, "perfect gray sheet abstinence" was another club with which to beat myself. Each time I fell short of the mark I would resort to binging, which resulted in more weight gain and "pitiful and incomprehensible demoralization."

Notwithstanding the binge-producing effects of gray sheet, I knew that breads, sweets and certain other foods stimulated my appetite to the point where there was no power to resist. This was hard to accept. But I just kept on keeping on, working with program people, committing myself each day to a sponsor, writing inventories, expressing feelings, going to meetings, being active in the Fellowship. I was sure the answers were in the twelve steps. And they are.

Nineteen years later, abstinence has come to mean much more than merely abstaining from compulsive overeating, although I believe that must be the primary goal. The discipline of strict adherence to a food plan got me to be honest with myself, to stop rationalizing. Perhaps that is why I kept running from strict food plan adherence: it was too dangerous to face myself head-on. But eventually strict adherence became a way of life that lasted at least two and a half years of my current ten and a half years of abstinence.

Then one day I understood that living life to the fullest did not mean having a piece of paper run my life. Our program promises that we will be restored to sanity and returned to society. Was I truly returned to sanity and society when I was afraid to go into an Italian restaurant, or to be near cookies?

320

Somehow, the fear dissipated as love entered my being. People often ask, "How did it happen? What was the turning point?" I always say, "I wish I could bottle it, or tell you in twenty-five words or less how it happened." The fact is it happened in stages, over a long period of time — not through memorizing words, taking notes, writing assignments or theorizing, but by *doing*.

I believe that the value of adhering to a food plan in the beginning cannot be overestimated. But it is a temporary solution to a permanent problem. For long-term abstinence — and recovery — the only answer is the twelve steps. The most a food plan can do is lead us to the permanent solution of the design for living found in the steps. Practice of the twelve-step program has lifted many obsessions from me in addition to the food. No food plan can do that.

Abstinence continues to be a living, changing, growing process for me, constantly refining what I eat and adapting my food to my lifestyle. It still amazes me that the simplest foods often satisfy more than the grand volume I once ate.

I am not what I eat. What I eat is what I eat. Who I am is who I am. Eating has no power to make me feel bad. Sometimes I eat too much, trying to see what I can get away with. Sometimes I eat too little, and tend to starve my body. My body lets me know. We're friends, my body and I. The abuse and self-hatred of binge behavior are history for me. I think of this as sobriety, or wellness.

There are so many gifts in the program, not the least of which is loving ourselves, knowing there is a Power greater than ourselves that loves us unconditionally, and discovering that abstinence leads the way to recovery, sobriety and wholeness of body, mind and spirit.

There is a growing "knowingness" inside me today. A fullness. A sureness. I need to nurture this feeling and learn to live successfully with the power God gives me. It isn't easy, when my natural tendencies are to tear myself down and destroy the good I have found. But I'm learning, and I'm willing to go to any length to continue in this beautiful twelve-step process.

November 1982

In a Word, "Freedom"

RECENTLY at a meeting a member earnestly wanted a definition of abstinence. She felt we were confusing and losing newcomers because there were so many opinions.

This led me to do some thinking about how my own ideas have changed over the years. Eleven years ago, when I came into OA, there was no need to ask for a definition of abstinence. We ate what was listed on the gray sheet and if there was the slightest deviation, the guilt was overpowering. Gray sheet offered even less variety in those days than it did when it was finally taken out of print. But with such a strict food plan and no choice, I did not have to ask what abstinence was. Believe me, I knew. I did not have to take any responsibility for myself.

There is a description of abstinence in the OA Brown Book (pages 117 and 118) that fits my present thinking: "I believe abstinence can be anything we want it to be, as long as we are honest with ourselves."

I used to sponsor "string bean strict." So did everyone I knew. I'd been using the bathroom scales as God for years. Then that food plan became God to me. And I did lose weight. So did the others. It took a long time, but I came to realize that when I am busy talking about food to those I sponsor and at meetings, I am avoiding talking and thinking about what is really my problem. It is a way of being evasive about working the steps. We were all doing that. Oh, we gave the steps lip-service.

Then I saw dear friends who were thin but still suffering from the same old character defects. It was so easy to see theirs. I looked at myself and thought, "Is this all there is?" I continued to be passive, sometimes passively manipulative, though I didn't know it. I did know I was searching for something more and that I didn't want to quit eating compulsively. I actually wanted to fill my lack with food, but didn't dare — and didn't dare say so. Being thin hadn't done much for me. I'd been thin on many diets before OA.

I used to wish I had enough money to go to a fat farm on a regular basis to keep the weight down. Now I'm glad I never had that much money. I would probably still never have hit bottom and discovered this serene, honest way of life. I've changed from inside out and I am more content than I ever knew was possible.

When I started paying more attention to the steps, I was far more successful, both in my own recovery and as a sponsor. Of course, there are those who don't want to work the steps and prefer to find sponsors who sponsor only food problems. It takes what it takes to learn that the compulsion to overeat dies in direct proportion to the spiritual and emotional recovery found in the steps.

Now when I sponsor, the ones being sponsored are asked to define abstinence as they want to and to decide what they are going to adopt as their food plan. If they choose to write it down and/or call it to me, that's fine. But it is their decision, not mine. I am no longer God, nor is food. We don't talk much about what we are eating. Talking about food keeps us from finding out about ourselves.

I do strongly urge those I sponsor to read the Twelve and Twelve, the AA Big Book, our Brown Book, Lifeline and the OA pamphlets. They read and I read the same thing. We discuss it on the phone and in person, paragraph by paragraph. We write about pertinent parts. We lead meetings on those topics that leap out at us with a need for further input. We share and love and care about one another, not about food. We do lose weight, but it doesn't compare with the burdens of the soul we've dropped.

I thank the beautiful young woman who requested a definition of abstinence. In a word, mine is "freedom."

November 1982

I Threw Out the Food Plans

BSTINENCE is something I struggled with for years until I finally accepted my condition, admitted my powerlessness over food and began working and living the twelve-step program.

Eight years ago there were two suggested food plans in OA. I chose one that I felt was best for me and began to follow it "perfectly." That food plan was my program; I was not using the steps and knew little about abstinence as a tool for sober thinking. I judged people according to the way they ate. It was OK if you followed one of the two suggested plans or your doctor's plan, as long as you did it perfectly. If you did something else, you were doing it wrong. I was frequently among those who, in my judgment, were doing it wrong.

My early tussles with food plans were a growing experience through which I had to walk. Today my beliefs about abstinence are altogether different.

Recently I had the opportunity to share my experience in following a medical diet. A fellow member was struggling with her sponsor's opposition to any food plan other than the rigid, disciplined one she herself followed. The sponsor even questioned the food plan her sponsoree's doctor was recommending.

That really hit home. About three years ago I had to switch to a doctor's diet temporarily. When I went on the plan, however, I didn't know whether or not it would be permanent. Through talks with my sponsor and others in the program I was able to accept that, for today, I had to follow the medical plan or continue to be in physical pain. It wasn't easy; the change from my former food plan was drastic. Fortunately, I had two years of abstinence and was able to apply the principles of the program to my problem. Since that time I have developed a food allergy which caused another change, but this time acceptance came more easily.

Today I believe abstinence is not a particular food plan but a tool I use to achieve my goal of sobriety. When I was rigidly following a food plan and not working the steps, I did not have peace in my life. Food was still my god. It was only when I worked the twelve steps and applied them in all aspects of my life that I achieved the serenity and peace that had long been my goals.

I had to throw out the food plans. I worked at not compulsively overeating and eliminated foods that gave me problems. Today I am grateful that I was able to learn that there is no right or wrong way; I just had to find out what worked for me and do it.

November 1982

Ten-Pound Chubbies

IF IT SOUNDS AS IF I'm begging, I am. If it sounds as if I'm desperate, I am.

Rock bottom? Yes, I think I've hit it. Some days I cry over my obsession with food and the battle between staying away from it and admitting defeat one more time.

Are you ready to reach out your heart and hand to help me? Then let me give you the clincher: I don't have 150 pounds to lose, or 100; not even 50. I'm 10 pounds overweight.

When I came to Overeaters Anonymous a year ago I was 20 pounds above my goal weight, and that is the most I've ever weighed. Now I'm halfway to goal but still desperate. I can't work the steps without you, and I need you to take me seriously.

I have the disease of compulsive overeating. This means I have an obsession with food — an obsession that controls my life in more ways than I ever realized. It controls my ups and downs, my actions and reactions, my thoughts and feelings. It turns me into a person I don't want to be.

At times I have felt almost apologetic for not having extreme symptoms. I don't need to apologize anymore, just as I would not apologize for anything else that is a part of me. To be sure, it's a part of me I hope to change, but whether I succeed or not, I have stopped apologizing for being me.

I came to OA because I believed I *needed* junk food between meals, and that scared me. Thanks to God and OA, I have learned the difference between "need" and "want." I still want those snacks sometimes, but I no longer believe I need them. That's a start; but I still have a long way to go and I can't go on alone. What I need now is your help and understanding.

I need you to help me stay sane. Don't think I'm strong; I'm weak. Don't think I've arrived; I'm not even sure where I'm going yet. If I break abstinence, don't say it's OK because it doesn't show. Look closer.

I'm begging, not only for myself but also for all the other "ten-pound chubbies" who find their way home to OA. Believe us. Help us. We need you!

December 1982

After the Frost

WHEN I CAME INTO Overeaters Anonymous seven years ago, the emphasis in my area was strictly on gray sheet. I believed that if I broke out of the confines of that plan in even the smallest way, such as eating an apple when that was not an "allowable" fruit, I was breaking my abstinence and failing to adhere to my program. Many people came and went because they could not comply with such rigidity.

I have grown and changed since then and, after struggling with my weight and with life, I have come to believe differently. I lost my excess weight and regained it several times over. Each time I came back more convinced that the only answer for me is in OA, and that my problem is not a fat-skinny problem but a living problem. The real issue is not how much I weigh or whether I follow a food plan but whether I am living by God's will rather than my own.

If we would all live and let live, no one would feel threatened that their freedom of choice will be taken away. God alone knows what is right for each individual. No one can take from me the freedom to allow my Higher Power to show me what is best for me.

I am abstinent, by the grace of God, though I have not lost all my excess weight. The most important question to me now, however, is not "How much do I weigh?" but "Am I doing God's will?" If I am truly surrendered, not just on my lips but in my heart, the weight will disappear as naturally as frost on a warm and sunlit winter morning.

February 1983

Weight Control: The Delusion That Never Dies

I WAS IN PAIN and tears when I made that preliminary phone call to OA two and a half years ago. Just off a diet, I weighed 118 pounds, but I was binging my way right back up the scale again.

During my first month in the program, I binged sporadically, then became abstinent. After three days of easy abstinence, however, I had a terrible white-knuckle day — and so it went for fifteen months: a couple of easy days followed by a white-knuckle day. I continued to take diet pills, which had become a psychological crutch. They never relieved the craving, but I was addicted to them.

Those white-knuckle days were the worst days of my life. They made me insane. They were indescribably painful. I was terrified of the first compulsive bite. I was in agony because the craving was unrelenting. Eating only made it worse, so I underate, and I ate no refined sugar, white flour or "binge foods." I was nervous, irritable and filled with terror and rage. I rarely had any peace. My food plan was so rigid I was bored to death with it. My weight dropped to 107 pounds. I went to meetings every day, but I was miserable.

One day, after fifteen months of this kind of abstinence, I felt defenseless against that first compulsive bite. I binged all day, and every third day or so for the next nine months. I tried every trick in the book, every coping mechanism I used in the past to get back control. I took diet pills for another six months, until I realized the futility of that and gave up. I tried dieting, weighing and measuring my food, counting calories, fasting. Nothing worked.

I used every OA tool and I begged God to remove the compulsion. Instead, I was stripped of any control I ever had over food. The weight came back — 18 pounds. For nine months I was in pain and tears and despair until I accepted my powerlessness, gave up my fear of food and surrendered to God. I accepted the binging, the weight gain, the possibility that my goal weight was not the same as God's. I accepted the fact that I might go back up to my top weight of 175 pounds — or beyond. I became willing to be fat if that was what it took to restore me to sanity, but I believed God did not want me to stay fat and that any extra weight I gained would come off in God's time and in God's way.

I surrendered all control of my food and weight. I became willing to endure whatever pain I had to go through to recover from this disease. I trusted God to handle it in whatever way God saw fit. I didn't like it, but I had to accept it because I literally had no choice.

Nine months later, the binging episodes began to slacken off and my weight started to stabilize. I saw that God was doing for me what I could never do for myself: enabling me to eat sanely. The futility of food plans and other controls was never more apparent.

Today my eating is pretty normal and my weight is fairly stable. This is not to say that the craving never returns; it does, and if God does not remove it, I give in to it. I cannot white-knuckle it anymore. But the binges are nowhere near as bad or as frequent as they used to be.

Through prayer, I am slowly developing a trust in God. But I have a long way to go. I still test God with the scale and the tape measure, and I still feel uneasy about this disease. But the terror and despair are almost gone. Gone, too, is the guilt when I do overeat. How can I feel guilty about something over which my Higher Power has complete control? I have given God control of when and how much I eat. I don't remember when I made this surrender but it was gradual.

I thank God for the serenity and peace of mind that come my way. I have no inkling of what will happen tomorrow, but that is God's business. My business is to continue to work the twelve-step program to the best of my ability, one day at a time.

April 1983

Neither Full Nor Hungry

I F FOOD WERE something from which I could totally abstain, there would be nothing at all to say about how, when, where or whether to eat it.

The complexities of keeping body and soul together probably vary with individual perceptions, but I'm fairly certain that, for compulsive overeaters, it's never simple.

In years past, hunger to me meant not feeling full — or, more bluntly, not feeling absolutely stuffed. Consequently, whenever I felt less than full, I thought I was hungry and I ate. But I can be not-full and not-hungry at the same time. My awareness of this distinction led me to redefine hunger and marked real growth for me.

From the emotional neutrality of abstinence, I have observed that hunger pangs usually hit when I am upset or angry, or just lonely or tired. I've been hungry right after a satisfying meal. If I examine my feelings instead of going to the refrigerator, I often find that I'm fretting over something that happened or worrying about something that might happen. With this awareness, the sensation of hunger usually leaves.

Recalling the taste of certain foods can also trigger the phony notion that I'm hungry. Every time I gave in and ate that fondly-remembered food, however, I found it didn't taste nearly as good as I expected. So now I remind myself that the memory is better than the reality, and my desire to eat diminishes.

In helping me to distinguish between actual and false hunger, OA has encouraged me to get in touch with my feelings and to deal with them on middle ground. I am erasing the memory tapes of food. I know now that, as a compulsive overeater, much of my hunger is in my head, and food will not satisfy it.

I believe that giving me these new perspectives is my Higher Power's way of removing my compulsion to overeat.

April 1983

Dinner in Italy

I'M ON A TRAIN headed for Rome after visiting relatives overnight. So far, this trip to Italy has been a thrilling example of how beautifully my Higher Power works in my life.

I had never been away from home for more than ten days, and I'd never been to a country where English is not spoken. Before beginning my vacation, I had fears about food, about my inability to make calls and about not getting to meetings. I discussed these anxieties with OA friends. They reminded me to take it one day at a time and assured me that my Higher Power, who had already given me three years of abstinence, would be with me at all times and in all places.

One of my food fears was realized while visiting my relatives last night. They served a huge Italian meal, loaded with things I don't eat. I prayed for God to help me and the message I got was: "It's OK to eat some of those things. Don't be so crazy over food that you make dinner a difficult situation for all."

I thought there would be only one course, but it turned out to be a four-course feast. God protected me through the entire meal, giving me a strong sense of what to eat and how much. The dinner was wonderful, and I was able to relax and thoroughly enjoy my relatives.

That evening, it came to me that the second step says a Power greater than ourselves can *restore us to sanity*. To me, this means not acting "special" when it's clear that God is freeing me from obsession.

I am not saying I have license to eat whatever I want, whenever I want it, or that I can eat all of those foods at home. The OA program is practiced one day at a time.

What this experience tells me is that, if I ask for help, God will take care of me in any situation. Last night, God did just that.

May 1983

330

Small Joys

FORTY-THREE YEARS of self-destruction have ended. My life is so good today that I awake each morning with eager expectancy. Depression and paralyzing anxiety have left me. In their place is a growing maturity, marked by feelings of tolerance, kindness and love.

There was never enough food to fill the aching hole in my gut. Deprived of love and proper nutrition in early childhood, I somehow became set on a lifelong course of self-hatred. My twenties and thirties were spent on my back, pathologically depressed. Food became my drug and lover and friend. The isolation was terrible. No one dared reach past the fortress of my 425-pound body to touch me. It was my protection and my agony: the pain of carrying that load was almost unbearable.

I walked into Overeaters Anonymous afraid to live and afraid to die. My sponsor said, "Keep coming back; I love you."

I cried, my shell of pain cracking.

Three months of withdrawal from excess food followed, characterized by anxiety and the shakes. At first I had trouble staying awake through meetings, I was so fatigued from dragging around such a heavy body. But each meeting and each hug brought me a little further along.

Change has come gradually during the past nine months. One hundred and thirty pounds lighter and more than halfway to my goal, I am grateful to be alive. Sharing God's love through sponsoring is adding years to my life. And I have the healthiest dependency possible: on God.

The age of miracles is not past. Today, feeling serene and confident, I donned an attractive outfit and went out into the world to savor the small joys of living: window shopping, sitting at a coffee shop counter, crossing my legs, fitting comfortably in a theater seat, wearing panty hose and stylish shoes. These are all so dear to me, and so new.

As wonderful as they are, I know that the peace I feel does not come from these things. It is within.

May 1983

Body Talk

I STARTED IN OA a few years ago and right away I lost a large amount of weight. Time after time people asked me how I was slimming down, and I always replied with a brief description of the OA program and my personal abstinence.

"Do you exercise?" people invariably asked, and each time I told then i insistently, "You don't have to exercise to lose weight." With my thin body, I was perfect proof.

About a year and a half ago I injured my back. Six weeks ago I landed in the hospital with a herniated disc, and I have been confined to bed ever since. As I lie here, I suspect that, after my great weight loss, my sagging muscles made me ripe for injury.

Right now I would do anything to have toned up my body as I lost weight. Other factors were also involved in my injury, I imagine, but now I realize that we abstain for health reasons, as well as to be relieved of our food obsession. And exercise is another way to improve health. I have read that exercise reduces the likelihood of heart attacks, strokes and various diseases; many experts claim it reduces appetite; and there's even evidence that it contributes to good mental health.

I hope that abstaining OAs who think exercise is not really important will reconsider. Part of taking care of ourselves is taking care of our bodies — not only through proper eating but also by flexing our muscles. Many of us say we're too tired, but people who exercise regularly report that they actually feel more energetic. Anyone intimidated by the thought of exercise might feel comforted to know that even walking is highly beneficial. Also, there is a variety of gentle approaches, such as yoga, for those who don't relish strenuous movement.

I will recover. I might have surgery, and it may take a while but, with the help of God, my trouble will pass. Through all this, I've learned an important lesson about taking better care of my body.

August 1983

Under the Knife

HOW MANY TIMES has each of us searched for the easy way out of our sickness?

One of my quests for an easy way out began three years ago in Gitmo Bay, Cuba, where I desperately tried to convince the Navy doctors that I was a prime candidate for gastric stapling. It didn't take much convincing because the doctors were as confused as I was. We were all looking for the easy way out — I, for the solution to my compulsive overeating and weight problem; the doctors, for a way to rid themselves of something they didn't understand.

After a week of paperwork and phone calls, I was on a plane headed for Bethesda Naval Hospital.

On arriving in the States, I called my family and told them the news. Both my sisters lovingly offered to come to Maryland to be with me, but I asked them not to. However, while my mouth was saying "I don't want you to go to the expense; I got myself into this and I have to get myself out," my heart was crying "Please help me! Please love me!" Today I can see that part of my sickness was my inability to reach out for help, which in turn stemmed from the low opinion I had of myself: I wasn't worth the time, expense and trouble it would take for my sisters to come and be with me.

I went into surgery weighing 337 pounds. I was cut from breastbone to bellybutton, and after the stapling was done I spent twenty-four hours in intensive care. A suction tube went up my nose and into my stomach and remained there for five days, during which I was allowed nothing by mouth, not even water. I went through thirty-five bottles of that stuff they hang from poles. My arms and hands looked like pin cushions and "Ouch, it hurts" hardly seems strong enough to describe the pain. After three weeks in the hospital, I was given instructions that would permit the operation to work, and I flew back to Cuba.

It would be nice to say that going under the knife did turn out to be the easy way out, but it didn't. When I returned for a physical eighteen months later, it seemed the ultimate irony that I weighed exactly 337 pounds.

That was the end of my search for the easy way out. Insane as it is to think of surgery as "easy," it was really an extreme example of everything else I tried: it dealt only with the physical part of me, not with my problem. There may be some for whom this operation has worked, and if it solved their problem, I'm happy for them. But it didn't work for me, except to propel me toward a different way — a way that does work.

Writing about my experience brings tears as well as smiles. The tears are tears of growth in Overeaters Anonymous. OA has given me new vision and I can now see the sadness of putting my life on the line to deal with my problem. The smiles, too, are smiles of OA growth. I know now that help is there for me, that I don't require knives, pills or other drastic measures.

I've been abstaining for two months and I've given away 29 pounds. I can't say it has been easy. I was reborn in OA and I am growing and learning, just as I did as an infant. When I fall down, I pick myself up and start where I left off. I am a slow learner, but the falls are not as frequent as they used to be.

With the help of my Higher Power, I try to work the program every minute of every day. When I can do this, I'm OK. The list of what OA has given me could go on and on, but most important, I think, is the ability to look in the mirror and like the person looking back at me.

September 1983

Snack Attack

I HAD WAITED too late to prepare supper. As I began throwing things into a pan, my glance fell on a bag of snacks on the counter. Instantly I decided to have a handful to take the edge off my appetite.

Just as suddenly, I thought, No, I don't want to do that. So I prayed to my Higher Power to remove the obsession.

My next impulse was to go ahead and have some anyway. As I was reaching out, a voice rang in my head,

"Give me a chance!"

I was so astonished, I laughed out loud. When I returned to my work after the momentary distraction, all desire for a snack was gone. I couldn't even pick at the food I was preparing.

Reflecting on this, I see two essentials for recovery at work. First, I need to affirm to myself that I don't *want* to carry out the act; that it is unacceptable to me. Second, I must admit my own powerlessness and ask for help. If there is a third, it is to let it happen, to "Give God a chance."

September 1983

In the Family Way

IN MY EIGHT YEARS of abstinence, OA and my Higher Power have helped me cope successfully with many challenging situations including, most recently, pregnancy, childbirth and caring for an infant. To come through abstinent, sane, serene and joyful has taken the application of my program on many levels, much trial and error and a well-developed sense of humor.

The most obvious effect of pregnancy is physical. Having to gain weight, I wondered whether I would feel fat again; whether I would become used to the extra food and be unable to cut back later. I was afraid of gaining too much weight or not enough; of having morning sickness or unavoidable food cravings. None of these fears and negative projections materialized. I had no appreciable morning sickness, and my flexible eating plan amply accommodated any food cravings or aversions I experienced. I felt, not fat, but glorious and beautiful in pregnancy.

At first I tried to deal with the weight and the food fears by control, which included weighing myself twice a week. When I gained four pounds in three days with sane eating, I realized that wasn't the solution. I surrendered my will, life and food once again to God, praying to make right choices and weighing myself only at my checkups. OA phone calls helped me deal with the confusion over my new way of eating until I became comfortable with it.

In spite of my fears, I did very well physically, gaining a total of 24 pounds and staying remarkably healthy. And, with trust in my instincts (also known as God's guidance) and support from OA and the La Leche League, I have adjusted to nursing maintenance. Six weeks after my son's birth, I was back to my pre-pregnant weight.

Emotionally and spiritually, the teachings of the program sustained me throughout my pregnancy, and they continue to do so. Living one day at a time is invaluable in pregnancy. In my final months, I had several bouts of panic, dreading labor and doubting my ability to face it. Sometimes reminding myself that I wasn't in labor that day and that God would give me the strength to handle it was enough to end the panic. Other times I had to use different tools, sharing my fears with someone or at worst riding out the attack.

During labor, my focus shifted to the moment. We were taught in my childbirth preparation class to take labor "one contraction at a time." It was comforting to hear this familiar phrase and to discover that, as always, it worked. Experiencing labor in this way enabled me to be relatively comfortable throughout a ten-hour labor and to have a drug- and anxiety-free delivery.

The end of pregnancy has brought new and different challenges. My son often cries with hunger just as I sit down to my meals, leaving me the choice of waiting to eat a cold meal later or to try to feed him and eat simultaneously. I learned to nurse while I eat, a solution many nursing mothers use.

Quite normally, I have felt anger at my son when he is cranky and demanding and also at my husband when he fails to meet my new expectations. Accepting these feelings, doing inventory, sharing with my sponsor, communicating with my husband and learning how to nurture myself so I don't feel like a victim, all help me deal with the anger when it strikes. And my faith in my relationship with my husband helps me maintain my perspective and enables me to give us both a little more room to adjust to the new demands that are making our marriage stronger, if different.

At first, being cooped up in the house with a newborn left me lonely and frighteningly food-obsessed. As the baby grew, I began to resume old activities, taking him along. Now we go many places together, including OA meetings, where we both find a warm welcome.

Tiredness is the classic bane of the new parent. During my son's early weeks, I was awakened every two hours. These sleepless nights are sometimes accompanied by exhausting, fussy times during the day. I've had to learn the hard way to give in and nap when my son does, putting first things first and eliminating nonessential tasks.

I have had to become more flexible in my OA activities and disciplines. Some days I get to read my morning books, others I don't. Prayers may be on the run or in the shower. I am not able to give service at my meeting, since I can't guarantee weekly attendance. I can take phone calls only sporadically, when the baby is quiet and I'm not trying to catch up on much-needed sleep. Within these bounds, I do what I can.

Giving up some of my former pleasures, such as movies or coffee after the meeting, can bring on anger and self-pity. Again, it is the steps and tools of the program — phone calls, inventory, prayers, meetings and sponsorship — that bail me out.

Once these negatives are handled, I'm left with what the program promises: gratitude and the joy of living. When I play with my son, watch him smile and feel him cuddled trustingly in my arms, I feel an incredible awe and a love that is beyond anything I have ever known. I look forward happily to the many days I will share with this new person and trust that, with the continued help of God and OA, they will be filled with growth, joy and goodness.

December 1983

Give Me Thin Serenity

WHEN I CAME to Overeaters Anonymous two years ago, I was told that the program was designed for compulsive overeaters who believe they must find a way to arrest their illness in order to live. The people at the meeting were sure that inside each fat person's body is a thin person capable of getting out with the aid of this program.

I saw a ray of hope for the first time. If Ann, Betty, Bill and John could lose large amounts of weight and keep it off, why not me? Maybe, just maybe, "once a fat person, always a fat person" was a lie.

There are many twelve-step Fellowships, but I chose OA because I need a support group to help me overcome my food obsession. You go to AA to arrest the disease of alcoholism, not to learn how to live with the consequences of drinking. You go to GA to arrest the compulsion to gamble, not to learn how to recoup the rent and grocery money. And you go to OA to arrest the compulsion to overeat, not to learn to like being fat for the rest of your life.

Please don't tell me that food is not my problem. Certainly, it is not my only problem, but I must admit I'm a compulsive overeater before I can admit other character defects.

Abstinence for me is like sobriety for the member of AA. It must be the most important thing in my life. Without it, all my defects reappear. I go back into isolation and self-hate, and I lose my desire to live a happy life, or even to live.

Although abstinence is the same for everyone in that we all abstain from compulsive overeating, each person chooses an individually appropriate eating plan. If a certain food causes problems, I avoid it. If a physical condition requires adding or omitting specific foods, I do it with the support of my group and my sponsor.

I attend OA meetings to get what I need, which is not always what I want. What I need is to learn to live without excess food from those who have done it before me. I wouldn't think of going to a church whose congregation speaks in tongues and telling them I don't feel it's right and would they please refrain from doing it. No more would I go to an OA group whose members recommend certain ways of eating or working the program and tell them I want what they have, yet try to convince them to change.

Respect for individual differences has led to different concepts, but we are all united in a common purpose: to stop the progression of our illness. To do that, I, like most OAs, had to address the food obsession first. Only then did I care enough to want to face the other problems. I needed to get rid of my excess weight before I could see that the fat was only the outer manifestation of a deeper disorder.

I cannot be fat and serene, and I don't want to be. Thin by itself is not necessarily well, but OA is teaching me how to be both thin and serene.

December 1983

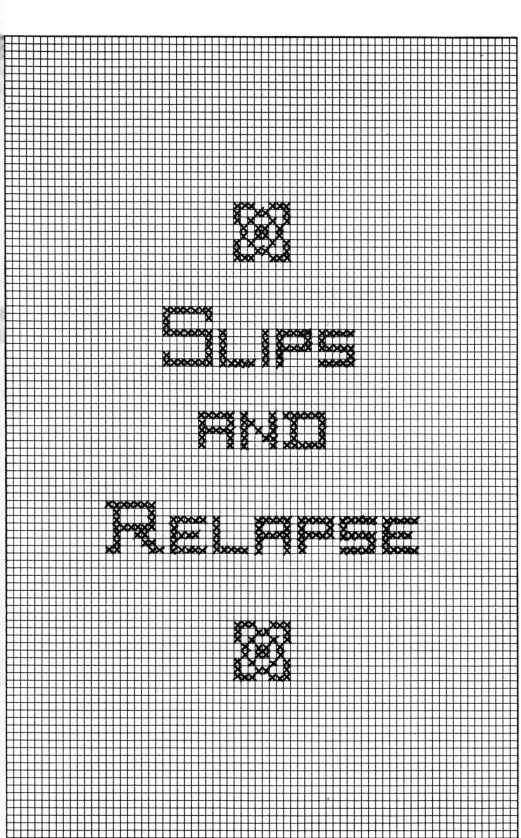

Slips
and
Relapse

Death of an OA Superstar

WHEN I WAS GROWING UP I felt like a stupid dummy. I never felt a part of anything, I never belonged. I was never popular. My "wall" was to be a clown. I was always on the outside of life looking in.

I first came to Overeaters Anonymous at nineteen. I went to one meeting, listened, identified, but wasn't ready. I weighed 172 pounds. A few years later I came back weighing 200 pounds. I stayed two months, lost 60 pounds and left. I wanted only to be thin; and that's all I was.

At twenty-nine I returned. I now weighed 243 pounds and this re-entry set the stage for the birth of a superstar. I believed then, as I do now, that this program could save me. It did! But I didn't appreciate what was given to me so freely. And I threw it away.

I was on gray sheet for three years. It took two years to lose my excess weight: 110 pounds. I was down to 133 pounds. I did everything I was asked to do. I never turned down any service. For the first time in my life, I was a part of something. I put away chairs, greeted people at the door, talked with newcomers, helped clean the kitchen, pitched when I was called on, led meetings and spoke when I was asked, no matter how far I had to travel.

I was offered a job as secretary at the local OA central service office and I worked there for almost three years. I became known throughout OA. I spoke at meetings up and down the state. I was flown all over the country by local intergroups to lead retreats and speak at conventions. I also spoke at colleges and universities. OAs were always coming up to me with someone in tow, saying, "This is the one I was telling you about."

I was everything I had always dreamed of being. Popular, thin, well-dressed, admired. I was somebody. Everybody knew me. I always looked great at meetings. Gave wonderful, positive, dynamic pitches. My hair and makeup were always perfect. I went to meetings to show off a new outfit, to see who was there, to chat. I was involved in everything: marathons, convention committees, retreats. I spoke each year at the World Service Convention. OAs from all over the country knew me by name.

People came to me for answers. Ask her, she'll know. And I did. I had all the answers. I had a host of babies, all sharp, all popular, all in the so-called "clique." If a baby of mine slipped more than three times, I dropped her. I did not waste my time. When people thanked me after I spoke, I said, "You're welcome," as if I had done *them* a favor.

After a time, I no longer traveled just to be a leader. I wouldn't waste my time unless I was the main speaker. Then I wouldn't waste my time at all. I was too busy.

When did my life begin falling apart? I really don't know. All I do know is that I became too good, too important, too whatever. I stopped greeting at the door, talking with newcomers, helping in the kitchen, picking up coffee cups. It was all beneath me. I looked down on people who were having trouble. They had a choice. If they chose to eat, it was their problem. I would say, "Show me someone who isn't on gray sheet and I'll show you a drunk!" Gray sheet was the only way; *my* way was the only way.

People in OA are quick to put someone who is pretty, thin and popular on a pedestal, especially if she's lost 110 pounds. And I let them put me up there.

After maintaining on gray sheet for a year, I took my third-year candle and began maintenance eating. I ate whatever I wanted, provided the food was on my maintenance sheet and I stayed within 10 pounds of goal weight.

I no longer went to seven meetings a week. I cut down to one or two, depending on TV and my social life. I no longer made phone calls. I no longer gave service. I dropped my babies. I was too busy, I told them. When I realized I was having trouble, there was no one I could turn to. I didn't want anyone to know. God, a pedestal is a lonely place to be! The only reason I am alive and abstinent today is the love, the caring and the patience of some of the people in OA who would not stop calling, would not let me go.

I tried to come back. I pitched, I talked on a one-to-one basis. I put my hand up as a newcomer. I got a sponsor. But deep down I really didn't believe I had broken my abstinence. After all, I never ate refined sugar or refined carbohydrates. (Today I know it doesn't matter what you binge on.) My new sponsor talked to me for hours, but I didn't believe her, not deep down.

I was going downhill fast. I resented going to meetings; they bored me. Talking to newcomers — yuch! In all this insanity I decided the only solution would be to eat refined sugar and refined carbohydrates. Funny how logical it all seemed. My binges became more and more frequent. I gained 30 pounds. I could no longer wear my pretty clothes. I didn't care about doing my hair or putting on makeup. I kept my phone off the hook most of the time.

When the phone was on the hook, however, it rang with OA love. People kept calling and coming over. My sponsor reacted to my binging with love and patience, never with reproach. God only knows where I'd be if she had said, "Three slips and forget it; I won't waste my time," as I had done.

I know today that there is no such thing as perfect abstinence. I am a human being. I love the freedom my sponsor has with food. She eats three meals a day with nothing in between. Some days it's a losing abstinence, some days not. She reviews her food each night and looks for patterns. One pattern I found was that each of my binges started with a weighed and measured amount of popcorn. Today I'm not eating popcorn.

Today I work the steps, greet newcomers and talk with them. I do whatever I am asked to do. Oh yes, I sit and listen at meetings — the entire meeting, not just half. When someone thanks me for speaking or giving some service, I say, "Thank *you!*" and I mean it. When I am not doing all this, I am not working a program of life, and the only choice I have is to eat.

At our last retreat we sang a song called, "You've Got a Friend." It goes something like this: "If clouds are cloudy, just reach out and call, and I'll come running, I'll be there, you've got a friend."

That's this program: so deep, so loving, so *God.* I couldn't reach out, I couldn't call; but mentally I was screaming for help, and OA heard me and came running.

I share this with all the OA superstars who insist on having things done their way, who are not willing to put away chairs, clean up, take calls at night, talk to newcomers or merely lead a meeting; people who are working on committees, retreats, marathons, conventions for ego and not for the service or for the good of Overeaters Anonymous.

Beware, friends. This is a program of humility. The chiefs fall. Only the Indians make it.

January/February 1976

Beating the Fat

I BECAME a compulsive overeater at an age when many children frighten the wits out of their parents by refusing to eat. I was four.

My family had problems I could not handle. I turned to food. When I became fat, they rejected me. They were all thin people and they could not understand. They tried to help, but they only hurt me more and my problem grew worse.

All through my school years and adulthood — until I was thirty-eight and found OA — I felt rejected because of my weight. I stored up a lot of anger, and a conviction that I had a right to it.

In Overeaters Anonymous, I was not rejected. On the contrary, I found so much gratuitous, unquestioning love it did not seem real. I could not respond to it. For every caring word or act, I retaliated with scorn.

But I stayed. I had found the perfect target for my anger: sitting ducks whose reaction to my disdain was a kind of affectionate, knowing tolerance instead of the rejection I knew I deserved.

I started running to meetings every night; I had nothing else to do anyway. Through a nonstop round of meetings, working fulltime and dieting, I lost ninety pounds in six months. No thanks to the program. I had not followed it, so I certainly could not attribute my weight loss to that.

Suddenly, I was Queen of the May. I began attracting attention from many different directions, something I had never experienced in my entire life. I was on a "high" and rising like a hot air balloon on an ego and pride trip that put an even greater distance between me and reality than had my compulsion.

I decided not to go to meetings anymore. It was not OA that had given me what I wanted. God may have had some hand in it, I conceded, but I really didn't need God anymore, either.

It was not easy, pulling away from OA, with all those daft people saying, "We love you; you're OK." But I did it. I was free to lose the rest of my weight as I pleased.

I quickly took advantage of my newfound "freedom" and "pleasure." In no time at all, my life was revolving around two major activities: compulsive overeating and frantic efforts to lose the weight that accumulated inexorably day by day. There was no way to keep ahead of the fat. I panicked. I went to diet clubs and doctors. I tried everything I could afford.

Within a year I had all my weight back and not a trace of that splendid new world I had created.

One day I broke down and just sat and cried. Strange therapy, crying! It can reduce, temporarily, the most painful swellings of pride and ego; and if one acts quickly, without stopping to think about it, there can be lasting relief.

I called an OA member I trusted and said, "Please help me. I need someone."

This man, God bless him, responded with the magic words — incredibly powerful words of OA love and acceptance. I actually felt the lifting of that crushing load of despair. In that moment was born a feeling that I was *really* worth something: not me minus ninety pounds or plus two hundred, but me as a person, as I am inside.

That day, my eating began to improve. Five days later, I went to a meeting. I saw new faces and old, and I saw immense growth and progress. Like a sponge, I absorbed all the love that was there, that had always been there. And I loved in return. For the first time, I felt a great, almost uncontainable love for every one of those OAs.

I moved through that meeting as though in a dream: I was *living* all the clichés I once scorned. Words like *willingness* and *openmindedness* came to life: I got a sponsor; I began abstinence. I was *home*.

Ready at last to accept the program on its own terms, not mine, I knew that all I had to do was be willing to make an honest effort. I had already taken the initial step that made all this possible: I had surrendered.

Of all the unfailingly beautiful experiences stemming from that meeting, three stand apart in the magnitude of their effect on my life. They are: the discovery of my ability to love — I mean gut level feel it, and not just another word; the joy of abstinence; and being allowed to be myself and be loved for it.

Before I could let myself have all these things, I had to reach not one rock bottom, but two. Believe me, the second is worse than the first.

I do not know if there are any more bottoms to be endured. I only know that all the blessings I have received are still intact. They create ongoing changes for the better, and the benefits spread in geometrical progression.

I know that some compulsive overeaters hit bottom many times and still make it. If they are anything like me, they return because the pain is finally too much, and because there is nowhere else to go.

May 1978

Main Event

ARLY IN THE PROGRAM I tried several suggestions I had picked up at meetings, and they seemed to work. After a time, I got brave and began to go a little deeper into the literature.

I was home alone one day, sitting in a comfortable chair reading a book I had borrowed from the group, when suddenly I started fighting with myself. I didn't want to read any more because I didn't want to learn any more. I threw the book down. At the same moment, I decided I wasn't going to any more meetings. I didn't have to go, and nobody could make me go.

I fantasized going back once more to thank everyone for all their sharing and to let them know, as a courtesy, that I wouldn't be back. (After all, they had told me I had a choice; I didn't have to do anything I didn't want to do.)

I sat there imagining just how my last meeting would go. When it came my turn, I would give my prepared goodbye speech and certain people would say kind things to me.

After rehearsing the scene thoroughly in my mind, I had a terrific idea: I would eat. Nobody else was home, and I had been "good" long enough. I'd had several months of abstinence; I deserved a little treat. Besides, no one would know.

I thought it would be pleasant to lie down while I planned my binge for the afternoon. It had been a long time and I wanted it to be special. As I lay there mapping out the details, something began butting into my thoughts. Vague images flitted through my mind, and I found myself unwillingly turning my attention to them. As soon as I did this, the images crystallized, assuming a recognizable form. They were the OA slogans I had so cleverly learned when I first started the program.

It had seemed a good idea to develop a "first aid kit" so that wherever I was I would have resources to fall back on in the absence of a sponsor. I didn't want to become too dependent on my sponsor; sponsors are just folks, too — they sleep, they go out and they have a life apart from their

OA babies.

So, I memorized all kinds of good things: "Let the feeling pass"; "Handle the situation, don't let the situation handle you"; "Easy does it"; and so on.

One by one, these phrases started coming at me from all directions. I had the eerie feeling that I was no longer alone. I wrapped myself up in a blanket and started to cry. My mind kept jumping from negative to positive:

"I'm going to quit this stupid program."

Easy does it.

"I'm not going back; I don't have to."

Let go and let God.

I couldn't understand why I was crying. Was it anger, fear, frustration or what?

The battle went on for about an hour, but it seemed much longer. I felt so miserable and confused, I couldn't have said for certain whether I would ever get up off the bed, let alone determine which direction I would take.

At last, my crying subsided, and as it did, so did the inner struggle. I know now that this was the turning point for me in the program. The realization hit me that something was changing: the part of me who wanted to love herself was emerging, telling me there was help if I reached out for it; that I was not alone; that those OA "strangers" really cared about me and always welcomed me back, no matter what I said at previous meetings. They did not judge or criticize.

They had suggested that I weigh once a month; I weighed once a day. They said, the sooner you get a sponsor the better; I waited awhile just to show them I wasn't that weak. They encouraged me to take phone numbers and call people; not me. They didn't know — nor would I admit — how scared I was. They suggested I talk to my Higher Power; but why should I? H.P. hadn't done anything I had asked before.

Slogans, tools, suggestions — one by one, I pounded and stomped them, testing for weak spots. I couldn't find any. Suddenly, I saw clearly that it was *my* arguments and defenses which didn't hold up, which were irrational. It was at this point that I was finally able to comprehend the value of keeping an open mind and being honest with the program.

I did go back to the meeting, but it was not for a farewell visit. My life has changed completely as a result of my efforts to follow the suggestions of the program. The beauty and serenity that blossom in my life today took root on that day I fought so hard — the day I could no longer deny the presence of a Higher Power.

April 1979

Getting Out of the Food

TODAY, after nearly two years in the purgatory of relapse, I realized that I am not alone.

I was driving home from the dentist's, thinking about having to call my sponsor as soon as I got home. I was afraid I would slip back into my habitual negativity, fear — and binging.

Remembering the morass I had so recently staggered out of, I wondered what was sustaining me. Why was I abstaining now, at this hectic time in my life, when I had been totally incapable of returning to abstinence for so long? For two years, I had explained this inability by rationalizing that my life was too unhappy, too unstructured to maintain abstinence. Yet I knew that the weight gain and periodic binging only increased my anxiety and loss of control.

Like so many, I came to OA because I was desperate. At meetings, the fear and anger expressed by some members frightened me. But I continued to attend because I was even more frightened by my sense of isolation. I was unable to tell anyone how I felt. Truth had become an enemy to be avoided. My self-image veered between extremes. On the one hand I was sure I was still attractive though overweight; on the other, I was equally certain I was an irreparably dissipated has-been.

My relationships were almost as volatile. For some time, I had played the role of the good natured fat friend, while inwardly I raged at those close to me who did not appreciate what a special person I was. When I needed a sponsor, I chose the youngest and prettiest one in the group. Thinking about it now, I realize that I must have believed she would guarantee my victory over obesity and middle age.

I lost 50 pounds in six months. Once again I had the problem licked. I would never overeat again. The compliments, the positive feelings I derived from being a "success" were too important to toss away. I wasn't overly concerned about the steps, though I did take an inventory.

Through the program, I was able to change my concept of a cruel, scorekeeping God. But I didn't call too often on my new and kinder

Higher Power because I felt God had better things to do than care if I was eating or not, particularly when I was handling matters so well myself.

I was impatient with members who cried and whined about their loss of abstinence, and those who gained weight frightened me. I wanted no part of failure. I could hardly have guessed how soon it was to be mine.

Having lost weight and regained enough of my former appearance to give me confidence, I decided to quit school where I had been taking a few enjoyable classes, and go back to work. It was a scary change. I was not accustomed to the pressure of having to be somewhere every day, having to learn and prove myself not out of choice but necessity. My old need to be perfect resurfaced, causing tremendous anxiety.

I began having a diet snack in the late afternoon to "tide me over" and help alleviate my fatigue. This was the straw that started crumbling my abstinence. Unable to cope with the guilt produced by the snacking, and unable to stop, I soon began having medium-size binges.

My feelings now were those of the typical "slipper" described in our beautiful new OA pamphlet, "Welcome Back." I believed that one bite warranted a binge. Just as I once saw myself in extreme terms, with no middle ground, I thought there was only one way to abstain: by following the rigid food plan on which I had previously lost weight.

For the next two years, I tried to abstain in this way, and being unable to, I despaired of ever abstaining again. Any other plan, no matter how earnestly I tried it or for how long, left me with the guilty feeling that I was not doing it.

Living in an area that predominantly adhered to a rigid food plan, I was afraid to ask for help in abstaining any other way.

Once again, I was desperate. I began to pray for a Higher Power somewhere out there who could care for me. My weight gain had given me the priceless gift of humility. I was more than willing to let — no, beg — God to manage my life.

With this willingness, I began abstaining again. It is a moderate meal abstinence which I am able to live with. And I am losing weight.

Having been obsessed with fear all my life, I am so grateful for the help that now comes when I'm frightened. I finally understand that I never have to rely solely on my own power again. I never have to feel alone again.

I'm beginning to know and accept myself and my limitations. I know now what is sustaining me, and I hope I never forget.

But if I should forget; if I should move away even for a little while, I now have two things I never had before: freedom from a rigid way of eating, and the sure knowledge that help is always within reach.

July 1979

Anatomy of a Slip

HOW HONEST AM I with myself? Learning to live the OA way is leading me to examine this question in depth.

I have been involved in Al-Anon for several years, but facing up to my disease of compulsive overeating six months ago brought me to a deeper level of acceptance and self-honesty than I had before.

To illustrate my dishonesty: At a meeting recently I described how the compulsion to overeat had that day "hit me so strongly, fiercely and suddenly" that I had a slip.

At the time, I couldn't see how dishonest that statement was. As I spoke, I felt almost self-righteous and quite full of self-pity. Poor old me, I just couldn't take it when the compulsion hit. I saw other members nodding sympathetically and felt even more smug.

Next day, reading the "Twenty-Four Hour Book," I came upon the following:

"Nobody entirely escapes temptation. You must expect it and be ready for it when it comes. None of us is entirely safe. . . . You must be able to recognize temptation when it comes. The first step towards conquering temptation is to see it clearly as temptation and not to harbor it in your mind. Disassociate yourself from it, put it out of your mind as soon as it appears. Do not think of excuses for yielding to it. Turn at once to the Higher Power for help."

I saw clearly my lack of honesty. My slip had not been "strong, fierce and sudden." It had been quite premeditated. I had not recognized temptation and had let food thoughts stay in my mind.

So, it's back to the first step, and more soul-searching with the fourth. I realize now that as a compulsive overeater I have always been dishonest with myself about my motives.

With the help of our program, I am growing slowly into a more honest person — and a far freer and happier one.

March 1980

Someone Cares

URING MY FOURTH YEAR in Overeaters Anonymous I began to feel settled in. I started to consider myself an oldtimer.

With three years of abstinence I no longer suffered from the stomach trouble that had plagued me for many years. My hypoglycemia was under control. In addition, thanks mainly to the elimination of refined sugars and starches from my food plan, I no longer cried at the slightest provocation and I wasn't the emotional wreck I had once been. I used to be terribly embarrassed by the constant trembling of my hands, but that stopped, too.

My relationships with other people improved greatly. I learned not to carry the burdens of others; I found that I could help by listening and then allowing them to grow by dealing with their own problems and making their own decisions.

The program had become a way of life for me. I thought I had most of the answers and that everything was well under control. Little did I realize how complacent I was becoming.

I began fooling around with my food plan: eating a little more here, adding higher carbohydrates there. The more I seemed to get away with it, the more I added.

My clothes began getting tight and pretty soon there were garments I could no longer squeeze into. I was horrified when my dungarees didn't fit and I had to buy a new pair — three sizes larger.

I yearned to ask for help but my pride got in the way. I was an oldtimer: I was supposed to be an example to newcomers that the compulsion to overeat leaves us after a period of time.

Only one member of our group had been in OA longer than I; the rest, less than a year. I couldn't ask *them* for help! And I didn't want to admit defeat. Besides, I rationalized, I didn't want to let the newer members down.

So I kept letting myself down instead. My emotional symptoms were flaring up again and the extra weight was becoming more and more obvious, though no one mentioned it.

I felt sick about what was happening to me. I longed to call a certain woman who had been in the program for several months and was progressing beautifully, but I kept putting it off. She was at a meeting I attended one evening, but I didn't say a word to her.

The next morning my telephone rang. It was the woman with whom I wanted to speak!

She was worried that something might be wrong and wondered how I was doing. I quickly told her everything.

Resolutely but lovingly, she came back with just what I needed to hear: I would have to get back on my food plan and follow the program. She encouraged me to read my literature first thing in the morning and she repeated the very suggestions I had made to her when she entered OA. As I sat there listening, I got all choked up. Someone knew what hell I was going through. Someone really wanted to help me. Someone cared!

I felt that my Higher Power had directed her to call me and to find the right words to say. She was right on target when she remarked, "Accept your weight. Go out and buy some new clothes. I know you can afford them . . ."

I didn't hear the rest. This was exactly what I was fighting! Yes, I could afford them; but, dammit, I didn't want to admit defeat. Not larger sizes!

But my friend's voice was firm and reassuring. I listened.

Today, I am following my food plan again, reading my literature and practicing the steps. I was able to accept reality and buy larger clothes — without guilt or self-hate, but with faith that one day at a time their use will be temporary.

I am grateful to my Higher Power who knows exactly what I need and sends it precisely when I am ready for it.

And I am grateful to the woman who called and was up-front with me. I was falling and she grabbed me by the scruff of the neck and helped me get up.

Thank God, someone cares.

September 1980

Sponsorship: A New Way of Life

I DID NOT WANT a sponsor. I didn't need one. I came from AA to OA: I knew all about it. In fact, I was doing it — abstaining, maintaining a 30-pound weight loss. I came to meetings to straighten *you* out!

That was my attitude five years ago when I came to Overeaters Anonymous, and it stayed that way for a year and a half. I had what I have since come to know as "white knuckle" abstinence. Motivated by vanity and stubbornness, I managed to scrape along hour by hour. I was angry, nasty, still obsessed with food and self. And even though I condescended to grace the OA meetings one night a week, I had no idea what you were talking about.

The thing that finally deflated my fat ego was a slow, insidious adding of food: a teaspoon of this, a dash of that. Mind you, I was measuring — and that, I rationalized, made it all right. It wasn't until this error in judgment began to show on the scale — 2 pounds, 5 pounds — that I realized what was happening. And I thank God that I did keep coming back to meetings, so I could realize that I had been on a diet and an ego trip. Then and only then did I really come to desire abstinence for its own sake, and peace of mind through sharing.

So I got a sponsor. I didn't like it at first. I balked. I beat around the bush. She pinned me down: "What vegetable? How much?" She dared to ask *me* these kinds of questions. I slowly began to get used to it. Then it became such a blessing and a relief. Little by little I began to share my daily ups and downs as well. I let her get to know me. I began to change my attitude, to soften, to love myself.

Today, I believe that sponsorship, like abstinence, is more than a "tool." It is a new way of life. Over the years my sponsor has become the closest of friends, even closer than kin. She literally knows me inside and out. She knows when I'm under stress and when life is a breeze. She knows what precautions I need in order to abstain in all situations.

Recently I was under a great deal of pressure and wound up having dinner out at 10:00 P.M. I called my sponsor before I went out. She said,

"You have a disease that tells you to starve yourself now and make up for it later."

Yes, of course. I had forgotten that completely. That is exactly how my head works on its own. And I had been in such a turmoil that I might have blown it if I hadn't made that call!

Being a sponsor is just as important to me as having one, but I couldn't be one until I had one. Up until that point, when I had tried to sponsor, I just couldn't handle it. I let my ego try to run the whole show. I handed out advice and got upset when my baby had a slip because that was such a poor reflection on me.

Today, I am grateful that I've learned to have some compassion for others who suffer from this compulsion to overeat. A new person who is really trying is a breath of fresh air in my life. With each person I sponsor I grow, I learn. So many times I felt impatient, or too busy or that there were too many at once. Sometimes I listen with half an ear, or I'm not listening at all. Sometimes my "tough love" is too tender, or not really loving. But turning to my Higher Power, I ask that I may "carry the message" and I trust. I have learned to let go of judgment and praise. I find I'm most helpful when I do less.

But most of all, through sponsorship I have let go of that clutchiness I had about my abstinence. Today I know it is a gift to share and that multiplies as it is shared. It shows itself in graceful and beautiful forms: the gleaming eyes, the hearty laugh, the open arms, the growing love and deepening commitment to this way of life.

"Sponsorship" is a wonderful answer to the question so often heard: What do you do when you stop overeating?

September 1980

Just One of the Faces

MUCH OF MY FIRST five years in Overeaters Anonymous was spent on a good diet and an inflated ego. I spoke at meetings, led retreats, had spiritual experiences and boasted of friends in high places. I was a "big shot."

What I did not have was the plain, simple humility described in the Big Book. I played games with myself and others, hurting and being hurt, lying and being lied to. Worst of all, I lost faith in God — the one thing that could save me from my own insanity.

I "did my thing" until I fell flat on my face. Now I am willing to be just one of the faces in the rooms where we meet, just another OA member. I must stop compulsively overeating to stay alive.

I overate as far back as I can remember, drank since age thirteen and was a narcotics addict during my teens.

Today, two stickers taken from prescription drug containers are pasted on the cover of my Big Book: "Do not drink alcoholic beverages when taking this medication" and "Use only as directed."

My compulsive overeating fits right in there. I refuse to dig my grave with my teeth any longer. For today I am not punishing myself, making myself ugly and unattractive or beating my head against a wall with compulsive overeating.

Abstinence, for me, can be defined simply as refraining from compulsive overeating one day at a time. Anything in excess of three moderate meals is an anesthetic for me. I have no problem in defining excess: I know when I'm killing myself through eating.

I have read the Big Book, listened to tapes and gone on retreats, but I believe that only God can give me a program of recovery — something that perhaps I've never really had. I must pick up that kit of tools and work them toward my goal of serenity and peace. I need to totally restructure my thoughts and actions, unquestioningly praying for knowledge of God's will for me and the power to carry it out.

I don't mean to sound like a religious fanatic. I am not one. But I hope I am on the road to spiritual fitness, to that "entire psychic change" spoken of in the Big Book.

Morbidly obese, overweight, fat, thin or underweight — I don't care. All I want is sanity: good, orderly direction in my life. I cry out for release from my old ways, for inner wings to carry me where I will discover the honesty and love I need to attain my desired goal — not in weight, but in mind.

The answers are all in the Big Book, the Twelve and Twelve and the literature of our program. If I follow these guides I will be free.

To those I have hurt and to whom I cannot make direct amends: I am sorry. Please forgive my insanity. It has taken me a long time to forgive myself.

To those I have helped along the way by extending my hand and heart: Please extend your hands and hearts, for I need them now in my struggle.

To those I do not know: Please pray for me as I pray for you. I love you. You are my sisters and brothers. I suffer with you in your pain and I rejoice with you in your happiness.

You and God have given me back myself. You have given me a second chance.

Thank you.

October 1980

Color Me Grateful

DON'T KNOW WHY I did it. I mean, I had made the decision a thousand times before: I would go on a diet and lose all the weight and be beautiful and happy. But usually I hardly finished breakfast before I was eating again.

Once I overate, the day was lost. I never made it a whole day on a diet. When you have more than 80 pounds to lose and it can't be done in one day, why bother? That's what I told myself.

Yet I wanted to be thin more than anything. I hated myself and the way I looked. I felt I was beneath everyone, that I could never have self-respect and the things that come with it: friends, a worthwhile job, a man who loved me. Those were for the pretty, thin women.

Why it was different this time I don't know. I just knew I was willing. I stopped consuming the enormous quantities of junk to which I was accustomed and instead I ate three simple meals a day.

It has been a long journey since that day almost two years ago. Six weeks and 30 pounds into the diet I began attending OA meetings. I didn't think it would do much for me but I liked the group's support and encouragement. I was grateful to have friends with whom to share my excitement and fears as a thin, attractive me began to emerge.

I did not understand the spiritual side of the program nor did I want it. I was doing well without it, and so much the better. I am still amazed at how little I chose to hear those first few months. I made only one commitment, but it was a crucial one: I would not leave OA, no matter what.

It was not that I disagreed with the program. It was just that I thought I was handling things pretty well on my own. I was not at all sure of this Higher Power or God business and I was not convinced that my life was unmanageable. The food, I conceded, was out of my control; but the rest of my life I could handle just fine, thank you.

And I did. With food fixes eliminated and thin for the first time in my life, I decided that drugs might fill some of the gaps. After all, I rationalized, they aren't fattening. Drugs had always been a minor part of my life but now I adopted a lifestyle in which they were the main activity. I began sleeping with men to get cocaine or because I was angry with someone or because I was stoned and I didn't have the self-worth to say No. Within six months I had gone from being so ugly that men went out of their way to point out how bad I looked to being so attractive that I had my pick of men, including some who had rejected me when I was fat.

I was maintaining my weight loss. But since I was not doing it through the program, which would have taught me to live by faith, I lived by fear. I was terrified of getting fat again so I either ate nothing at all or I made myself throw up whatever food I ate. At 100 pounds I was not exactly attractive; but I thought if I lost another 5 pounds I would be happy.

Through all this I kept coming back to OA every week, although I never told anyone what I was doing to lose weight. In spite of myself, I knew the answers were at those meetings.

I was aware that I had to make some changes. But I was afraid. If I turned my will and my life over to God, how did I know I'd be taken care of? By doing it my way, I reasoned, at least I wouldn't get fat. I could not imagine eating without throwing up. I had no energy at all, except for the highs I found through drugs. I didn't know if or when or how this hell would end.

Then someone new started coming to the meetings I attended. Bob had been a sober member of Alcoholics Anonymous for four years and he was the first person I encountered who lived the kind of life I wanted for myself. I had been afraid that if I turned my will and my life over to God I couldn't be myself anymore, that I would have to forfeit my familiar emotions. I thought I would have to live a pure, nunlike life and that I wouldn't be allowed my beliefs and feelings because they would conflict with how I "should" feel.

Through my new friend I learned that my feelings and beliefs are OK. God created all of me, including my thoughts and emotions. I am not a bad person because I become angry or because I want to eat or use drugs. I am powerless over my feelings but I am responsible for my actions. Instead of acting on my emotions I can turn to a Power greater than myself.

It was through trusting Bob that I began first to trust and accept myself and then to feel God's acceptance of me. At that point I began to build a relationship with God. I came to see that when I lose the feeling of closeness to my Higher Power, it is because *I* am moving away; God is always there.

None of this came easy. I had one out-of-town weekend of total insanity during which I abused every substance I could get my hands on. Filled with fear, I couldn't sleep. I was sure I had left God back home. I hung on till 7:00 A.M., then called Bob. He talked me through the rest of the weekend, which proved to be a turning point for me. By the time I got home I knew the value of the steps, especially step three. I began serious housecleaning and, with Bob's encouragement, I told my home group about my behavior, including the vomiting. It was humiliating, but I knew I could either have my pride or I could get well. I could not have both.

With God's help I have maintained a normal weight — 115 pounds — for nearly a year. I eat three healthful meals a day with nothing in between and I no longer need to starve or throw up.

At age twenty-three I know that I have seriously abused myself. But today I can only be grateful that I no longer need the food, the drugs, the sex or the excitement I used to crave. I have found the peace of mind that comes with self-respect and with depending on God as I understand and trust God.

Most of all, I am grateful that I kept coming back, no matter what. It works.

August 1981

Translation

COMING INTO OVEREATERS Anonymous from AA, the most difficult thing for me was translation. Having accepted the twelve steps of recovery as a way of life, I arrived in OA expecting to "get it" with the same ease as I had "gotten" AA. The obsession to drink and use drugs had been immediately removed for me. When it came to my overeating, however, I was an unwilling unbeliever. But I kept coming back.

Putting down everything and everyone, I compared OA's wordy formats and endless readings, the long meetings and somber faces with the happy, joyous AA meetings. I kept coming back. Got a sponsor, called her, worked the steps grumbling all the way. This won't work for me, I thought. I must be one of those poor souls who are constitutionally incapable.

Recently I suffered an emotional setback following the illness and death of a loved one. Along with the sadness and pain, I was left feeling bewildered, angry and lonely, wondering what was happening to me.

I had no answers until it came to me that I had learned one lesson in Alcoholics Anonymous: Don't drink and go to meetings, no matter what.

Finally, today, I "got it." Don't eat and go to meetings, and things will get better.

It translates.

September 1981

Home Again

I T COULD NEVER happen to me. Why, I had been in OA for three years, lost more than 100 pounds and gone from size 50 pants to size 38. I laughed at the "retreads" who came back to OA after leaving. *I* would never be like that.

I wanted to attend Bible study on Wednesday nights, which was when my OA meeting was held. What to do?

"I can handle my food," I assured myself, and I dropped out of OA.

I started eating sugar again. The old thinking came creeping back: "One won't hurt," "I'll do better tomorrow" and my favorite, "The dryer is shrinking my clothes."

I was putting on weight but I didn't call my OA friends. I didn't open the Big Book, I didn't look at Lifeline. I didn't even want to read my Bible and I didn't feel comfortable talking about my overeating with church members.

So I ate still more. My size 40s were getting tight. Darn dryers! I let out another notch in my belt.

"Maybe I'd better go back to OA," I finally conceded. I called a member and learned that the meeting had been changed to Thursday night. When I returned to my group I felt the same love and caring as before. I knew I was right where I belonged.

I am a compulsive overeater and I will be one as long as I am in this mortal body. I need other compulsive overeaters with whom to share, to laugh and to cry. I still have great difficulty turning my life over to my Higher Power. Sometimes all I can do is keep coming back.

But I'm home again. Thank God for OA.

December 1981

Come Back, We Need You

A WOMAN WHO had dropped out of the program got a call from a member of the OA group she used to attend. They had the following conversation:

First OA: I've really missed you at meetings. How are you?

Second OA: Terrible. I can't stop eating, and I've gained a lot of weight.

First OA: Why don't you come back? I'd love to see you at the meeting tonight.

Second OA: I can't. How can I go to meetings when it's not working? I can't relate to those abstainers.

First OA: You don't have to be abstinent to go to meetings and be with other compulsive overeaters. The only requirement for membership is a desire to stop eating compulsively.

Second OA: I want to get abstinent, but I can't.

First OA: Getting abstinent after a lifetime or even a short time of compulsive overeating can be a slow process. It involves getting in touch with your Higher Power, working the program and becoming willing to have the compulsion lifted.

Second OA: I *am* willing, but I can't do it. I can't stop eating.

First OA: Of course you can't — not by yourself. That's the point of step one. Remember? We are powerless over food.

Second OA: Another thing bothering me is that I feel like a failure at meetings. I don't have anything valuable to share.

First OA: Other compulsive overeaters need you as much as you need them. Abstainers need to hear your story. We may be taking our abstinence for granted, or we may even be on the verge of breaking it. Eating can sure look like a great way out of a problem sometimes. Maybe you can tell us a thing or two we've forgotten about that.

Besides, every compulsive overeater has a right to sit around the OA table. Talking about your feelings will help *you* — and that's what matters.

Second OA: I'm so tired and impatient. And people at meetings don't seem accepting and understanding. It seems to me they look at me and think, "Why can't you get with it?"

First OA: When we're so down on ourselves, the tendency is to think other people are too. But the truth is, we OAs love each other for going through what all of us have gone through. And we're all there because we have the desire to stop. Remember, *that's* what is required, not success.

Second OA: I've got the desire, all right, but how do I stop?

First OA: Come to meetings, for a start, and use the tools and practice the steps in whatever way you can. There are certain things you *can* do, just for today.

Second OA: How can I go back to meetings looking the way I do, and after all the crazy things I've said and the way I've treated my friends?

First OA: No one is keeping score. You're always welcome in OA, no matter what. It's like home — always there for you regardless of what you said or did, how long you've been away or how far you've wandered. You can never be a "former member" of your family, can you? Well, you can't be an ex-OA member either.

Second OA: Maybe I'll give it another try.

First OA: I hope you do. You'll be welcomed with open arms, just like the first time. You'll see.

Second OA: I think I *will* give it a try. Know anyone who needs a lift to the meeting tonight?

February 1982

Psst . . . Wanna Be Thin and Sane?

WHEN I CAME INTO OA six years ago I was a dumpy 225-pound housewife with three children and a husband who didn't bother to come home at night. He always referred to me as "Mom" or "your mother." No one seemed to know my name, or maybe they had forgotten it.

On my part, I overate, overslept, neglected my children and left wet laundry to mildew in the washing machine. I was scared to death someone would find me out and lock me up. Only when I came close to being discovered did I temporarily shape up, lose weight, clean house and act as if I knew what I was doing. But the truth is I didn't have the foggiest notion of what I was doing on this earth, and I really didn't want to know. I just wanted everybody to go away and leave me alone.

Anyone coming to my door sent me running to the bathroom with a child under my arm, hoping the intruder didn't hear me. My little boy never could figure out why we stood in the shower without turning on the water.

I would face death rather than allow anyone to see me in a muu-muu that should have been washed a week ago and with a mess of hair that hadn't been combed for three or four days. I had great difficulty keeping track of time. One day was as bad as another and they all just kind of blurred together.

One day I gave my oldest son the impossible task of fastening the back laces of my girdle so I could pay my respects at a funeral. I was screaming, he was crying and I ended up staying home, putting the children to bed and taking my comfort in food.

My mouth hurt from chewing through the late show and my lips bled from too much salt, but good old Vaseline got me through another salty bag of insanity. I ached from lying down so much and I had no strength to stand very long. I prayed to God that I wanted to change, only to awake with crumbs on my pillow — evidence that I had eaten during the night without even remembering.

What happened to change me is that I entered a roomful of people who said they were recovering compulsive overeaters and hugged one another even though they weren't related. Feeling somewhat like a spy about to discover a secret, I watched and listened. In no time at all they were freely blabbing their "secret" to me: Abstain from compulsive overeating, follow the twelve steps and you too can be thin and sane.

Eight months later, 100 pounds slimmer, I was on my way. I no longer shoved dirty dishes into the oven when someone dropped by. I was newly divorced. I was driving my own car for the first time in my life. Sailing along with my head high and my stomach in, I was ready to live, to love and to be loved. I married a wonderfully caring man who knew my name.

After maintaining my weight loss for three and a half years I stopped going to meetings — and started gaining weight. It didn't take me long to regain 40 pounds, and to realize I needed to get back to that roomful of people.

I have returned to meetings and I'm going on my third week of abstinence. OA was there for me before, it's there for me now and it always will be there for me — and for all of us.

February 1982

The Two-Year Itch

AFTER TWO YEARS in OA, I began having a love affair with food.

Nine months into the program, I reached my goal weight and felt terrific. I was fond of saying that I was eating less and enjoying it more. I had become very innovative with food and I sought out recipes mainly for their taste and appetite appeal.

Throughout the next year I became increasingly adept at glorifying food. Boldly, I introduced some high carbohydrate foods into my menus. Slowly but surely, I drifted blindly into the trap that caused me so much grief in the past. The insane old thinking made me believe my thin body could handle foods that my fat body could not.

Inevitably, a few pounds came back. Not enough to worry about. I could lose them anytime. Several more appeared, and before I knew it I had gained nearly 10 pounds. I was scared. How could it be? I was still eating only three meals a day with nothing in between.

It's funny how honesty will catch us unawares. One day, while sharing at a meeting, I heard myself saying that, although faithfully adhering to three meals a day, I was making some pretty stupid choices. Suddenly the truth hit me: I was eating for all the wrong reasons. I had crossed over an invisible line. Instead of enjoying food as just food, I was substituting food for companionship, creativity, love, God, whatever.

Fortunately, my two years in OA had impressed on me the importance of taking personal inventory. The God of my understanding gave me the insight I needed and the ability and courage to correct a dangerous situation. Today, whenever I find myself excessively absorbed in food, I immediately ask, "Am I enjoying my food as food, or am I seeking gratification of longings that food cannot satisfy?"

My love affair is back where it belongs: with the OA program, OA people and especially with my God, whose love, intervention and gentle guidance have made OA such a fulfilling and vital part of my life.

July 1982

How To Get Over a Slip, Fast

THANK GOD I have a program this morning. Last night, after several months of abstinence, I played out an old pattern — the nighttime refrigerator raid.

Before becoming abstinent in Overeaters Anonymous, I awakened every night between midnight and 3:00 A.M. and, driven by some nameless fear, headed for the kitchen and ate until I felt sufficiently narcotized to go back to bed. In the morning, I hated to return to consciousness. When I did, I felt heavy, dull and hopeless.

Knowing how it feels to wake up abstinent, energetic and in contact with my Higher Power, I recognize that I am sick this morning. Physically, I feel hung over and bloated. My mental processes are sluggish and I'm plagued by my old enemies, guilt, self-doubt and despair. I'm having trouble tuning in to my Higher Power. (These days I know the broadcast from H.P. is loud and clear; it's my receiver that goes on the blink.)

This morning my program brought me downstairs to the literature. For many months my habit has been to read Lifeline and other OA literature in the early morning before eating. I still awaken with an urgent need for nourishment, but I know now that reading and prayer nourish me in ways no food ever could.

My program allows me to turn away from the old, destructive thoughts that threatened to flood my mind just minutes ago: "I've really blown it" . . . "I'm a hopeless pig" . . . "I knew I couldn't maintain for long." These thoughts no longer hold up against the ammunition I've stockpiled in OA: "progress, not perfection," "turn it over," "just for today," "God grant me serenity . . ."

My program allows me to begin right now to let go of my binge. It enables me to reflect on how I set myself up during the past few weeks, accumulating tiredness, worrying over an unamended wrong, isolating myself in subtle ways. My program lets me see the decisions I made that cut me off from available support: "I can't call anyone at 2:30 in the morning." (Not true.) "I can't wake up my wife." (Wrong again. My

369

wife is in OA *and* she loves me. She would have been there for me if I had asked her for help. She would have hugged me and stayed with me until the frightened little boy inside me fell asleep.)

My program allows me to feel the fear and sadness and to shed some tears as I write these words. It allows me to feel gratitude for a wonderful woman who loves me even when I cannot love myself.

My program allows me to hear a bird singing in *this* instant and to realize that yesterday is gone, today is new, and I can live in recovery this twenty-four hours. It allows me to be grateful for a substantial weight loss and to realize I don't have to give up my solid maintenance because of one slip. The program has taught me to write as a way of letting go, and putting these words on paper has been a healing process for me.

I'm off to my Saturday morning meeting, grateful for our program and even grateful for my slip, which brought me back to step one — where I need to be today.

August 1982

The Slip Syndrome

AFTER BEING IN OA five years, maintaining a 50-pound weight loss the entire time, I began easing into what I now call the slip syndrome.

It began innocuously enough: a little extra food at supper "to get me through the night," a snack at four o'clock in the afternoon "to calm me down so I can finish my work." No outright binging, mind you; just a little extra food here and there.

All the time I was turning to a little more food to get me through, I kept reassuring myself that my program was good and my thinking was sane. Sure, I ate a little too much at meals and sometimes in between; but then, I reasoned, no one has perfect abstinence.

After two months, I weighed myself. I had gained 6 pounds. This, coupled with the fact that I was sick and tired of feeling too full, drove me back to a willingness to abstain from slips.

To my consternation, refraining from those slips caused full-blown withdrawal symptoms, both physical and mental. I realized I had been turning to that extra bit of food to help me cope instead of dealing directly with my everyday problems, tensions and joys.

At that point, I knew I'd never make it unless I applied the steps. I began with the most obvious, step one. For a few weeks I felt like a newcomer again. I wanted my extra food back. But as the steps began to unfold, I discovered that I had been using five rationalizations for overeating, none of which could stand up under honest examination.

"I'm hungry" is my first justification for eating extra; but the honest reality is that I am not physically hungry. I am emotionally and spiritually hungry, and there isn't enough food in the world to fill those needs.

"I must have something to eat" follows next, but thanks to my Higher Power and the twelve steps, I no longer have to act on the compulsion to overeat. I can choose to accept the gift of abstinence, no matter how hopeless and desperate I feel. And my feelings are just that — feelings, not facts.

"I'll just have one piece and then I'll stop" is my third self-deception.

This is my oldest tape and my biggest dishonesty. I never eat just one. Once I choose to eat compulsively, I am powerless to stop by my own willpower.

"Something to eat will calm me down and I'll feel better" is another teaser. As far as I can remember, something to eat has never made me calmer, nor has it made a situation better. I usually end up feeling bloated, stuffed and tormented by my old insane thinking. I certainly don't feel better.

"I can handle not eating" is my ultimate delusion. The truth is that trying not to overeat by using willpower is like trying to stay on a diet, and I have never been successful with diets.

That's why I need OA. When I see through my insanity and ask my Higher Power for the willingness to abstain, work the steps and use the tools, *the compulsion passes.* This is the bottom line. The program does work, if I am willing.

So, with step work, meetings, and calls to my sponsor, the food called a little less insistently and I began having flashes of sane thinking. I again had the choice to say No to compulsive overeating. While living in the slip syndrome I didn't feel I had that choice. Now I have a healthy fear of slips because I know the insanity that comes with practicing my disease, even on that level.

For today, I choose to abstain from slips. Thank God for this program and for my restored sanity!

November 1982

A Journey, Not a Destination

WHAT DOES a longtime OA do when food plans no longer work? She turns to the program.

"You can't work the program until you're abstinent," I was told. But I had to use the program to get abstinent, not the other way around.

I had always abstained by going on a diet, and I managed to maintain my weight for a whole year. Then I decided to take my "comfort" one night, fully expecting to start over the next day. It was six months before I even wanted to stop, nine more before I finally *could* stop. My clothes got tight, then no longer fit. In spite of my humiliation, I kept coming back because I heard of someone else who did.

During the year I was maintaining, I worked only enough program to get by. I concentrated on abstaining by controlling my food and by compulsively drinking diet soda and chewing sugarless gum.

I had not had a sponsor for more than a year when one day I found one. This woman had had a spiritual awakening and was truly restored to sanity. I knew it immediately because she changed so suddenly. She agreed to sponsor me and though I was still struggling, binging on and off, she suggested I make the amends I'd been putting off for years.

I binged some more, then finally became willing. I no longer cared about my pride or my reputation or any of the things I feared losing. I made my list and began to write my letters. I wrote, binged, mailed, binged and so on. During this time my compulsion sometimes went away, but whenever it came back, I ate. I had lost the ability to resist. It's true that I couldn't work the greatest program when "drunk" on food, but I was powerless to abstain. If the best I could do was a half-drunk program, that was OK. All I needed was willingness and it would get better.

Finally, I admitted that I can't control food and I became willing for there to be a God who could do it for me. I don't know whether there is such a God, but I am willing to act as if there is because I have the example of my sponsor and other abstaining OAs and AAs.

After six years of searching, I am finally free. I am neither on a diet nor on a food plan. I am on the program. Progress has been slow. Spiritually, I am just an infant. Sometimes I white-knuckle it, but that is only when I'm trying to avoid the growing pains. When I mess up it is no longer a cause for guilt; it is a signal that my spiritual condition is a bit rundown.

Now that I'm following program, I am able to do what I could never do before. I put my energy into working the program, not into dieting or avoiding food. When I do overeat I go right to the steps, starting all over again. Sometimes the compulsion goes away quickly; sometimes it hangs around and I get discouraged. But I keep trying, and I keep making steady progress.

I am trying to face life. God will take care of my food and my weight. I no longer know what my goal weight is. If I stay sane I will reach a proper weight for my body. I now believe that, for me, a food plan is a way to control food — and I am powerless to do that. There is something wrong with a diet of cottage cheese, salad and not much else. When I ate that way I was replacing the obsession for eating with an obsession for dieting.

My recovery is a journey, not a destination. I'll be traveling this path with my Higher Power and my OA companions for the rest of my life, one day at a time.

November 1982

After Relapse

I THOUGHT it would never happen, but it did. As painful as a return to the illness is — and I have been through a terrible time — it is not the end of the world. Being able to reach out for help is one redeeming feature of the nightmare. I am seeking recovery again, but the path I am on is somewhat different than the one I took before.

I was an OA fanatic, and I finally suffered OA burnout. My frenzy of activity could not last because it kept me from the real source of healing: that quiet center within.

During my relapse, I wrote on steps one through three, took additional inventories, made amends once again and meditated longer. Then I realized that I need to *renew* the steps in my life rather than just redo them. What I want from inventory is to see where I've blocked myself off from God, not to repeat that I stole a plum when I was thirteen.

I need to talk to God in plain English, then shut up and listen. When I do, I hear that my Higher Power loves me. This amazes me because for several months I've hated myself: the 20 pounds, the return to old ways I thought I'd never see, the shame. It is that self-hatred, of course, that fuels and perpetuates the binging.

"Easy does it" has become more than a cliché for me. A return to frenzied OA activity is not the way to love, respect and take care of myself. I need do only one thing: bring my life into harmony with what I perceive God's will to be. That may involve anything from making a commitment to abstinence to taking a shower in the morning; from attending meetings to being diligent at work.

At the same time, I must realize — and accept — that I cannot be perfect. Expecting perfection is central to my problem. Believing others have achieved this is a tremendous disservice to them, just as their seeing me as superhuman was to me. What they did not see was that my squeaky-clean abstinence for all those years was absurd: I was so addicted to "three meals a day with nothing in between" that if dinner was delayed I'd shake for two hours rather than eat an apple. What my OA friends and I failed to perceive was that I was practicing recovery in only the compulsive overeating half of my disease. The other component of this affliction, for me and probably for most of us, is the obsession to be thin. When I was manifesting this part of the illness, people applauded, called me up and invited me to speak at marathons.

If I am to be well and whole and happy, I must put God's will first: the size of my body has to be up to God. Please understand that I do not consider this an excuse for "fat serenity." My Higher Power does not will me to abuse food. I just need to be aware that my craving for thinness can be as intense and destructive as any hot fudge hankerings.

I cannot recover in a world of extremes. I cannot settle for swinging between being obsessed with eating and with not eating. I cannot accept everything I hear at meetings, nor can I reject everything said there. I cannot avoid OA because I'm ashamed of my weight gain, and neither can I spend every evening with OA people because I'm afraid of everybody else.

There is a balance to be found in every twenty-four hours. It's mine when I slow down and take it easy. The results are up to God.

February 1983

Tired

FOR A LONG TIME, I was tired. All the time. I yawned a lot. Some nights I couldn't bring myself to fix dinner, and the thought of doing just one more thing made me want to scream. Finally, I got tired of being tired and called the doctor, hoping I could go in that day. I had to wait two days, and I ended up staying home sleeping and resting.

The doctor took four vials of blood and ran twenty tests. As I awaited the results, diagnoses of anemia, hypoglycemia, diabetes and leukemia ran through my head. I begged God to do something. I prayed the Serenity Prayer and the third step prayer, and declared I'd go to any length to remedy the problem.

The test results were all perfectly normal. "You probably picked up a virus," the doctor said. "Call me if you don't feel well in a week."

A week later, I still felt tired. My boss commented that she was concerned about me and wanted my "old ebullient self" back. I called the doctor, listed my symptoms, made another appointment and underwent more tests. On my way back to work I stopped for lunch. Soon afterward, I suffered what seemed to be a sugar reaction, even though I had eaten a regular abstinence meal. Convinced I had hypoglycemia, I began having cheese and fruit as a between-meal snack.

In a few days I called for the results of the second series of tests. Everything was normal!

"But I still feel tired!" I moaned. Afraid of further reactions to food, my primary concern now was for my abstinence, my serenity and my sanity. I told the doctor I couldn't trust anything I ate anymore, and that I couldn't live like that.

"Either you have something exotic or you're depressed," the doctor said.

"But I have nothing to be depressed about!"

"Do you know what depression is?"

"Sure, when it's obvious."

"What about when it isn't?"

377

"I guess not."

"Tell you what. Make another appointment and we'll talk about it."

I made an appointment for two weeks later and vowed I'd get a book on hypoglycemia and follow the diet.

At lunch that day I talked to a friend. Yes, I was depressed. I felt overburdened, angry, jealous and judgmental, but I had pushed it all away. I shouldn't have those feelings after four years of program!

Yes, I should. I am human. Feelings mean I have to look at myself, change my attitude, accept the things I cannot change, work my program. But the disease of compulsive overeating really is cunning, baffling and powerful. It's also sneaky. Those feelings came upon me so quietly I didn't see them coming and, without a clue as to what was happening, I slipped into emotional relapse.

Looking back to the time when I began feeling tired, I remember having flashes of my husband's death and my own funeral. I remember feeling that I was waiting for the other shoe to drop, that all the good I was experiencing had to be paid for. I didn't see that it was enough to be abstaining and working the program.

The anger I had unwittingly buried alive brought me depression in the guise of fatigue. As a result of this discovery, I returned some extra work I had undertaken, explaining why I couldn't do it and apologizing for the inconvenience I had caused. It is humbling to admit I can't do everything, but I'm shucking the superwoman suit and reminding "the judge" that I'm not perfect.

The steps, taken in honesty and humility, turned out to be the cure for the disease I thought I had — not medicine or a diet. Today, I feel terrific. I am my "old ebullient self" again, learning from my mistakes and thankful to be abstinent. I'm glad I went through this.

February 1983

Back to Basics

BOUT A YEAR and a half ago I asked my Higher Power to take away my addiction to refined sugar and white flour. I was powerless over it and I didn't want to hurt under its lash any longer.

The merciless obsession was lifted and I had peace and serenity. In the months that followed, I faced almost unbearable emotional turmoil but, miraculously, I came through abstinently. Shortly after that I experienced a big ego trip, and that's when additional food started slipping in: extra salad, extra protein, extra vegetables. First I stopped losing, then I began to gain.

I was baffled. What was wrong with me? What was wrong with my program? I applied the steps and discovered many new truths about myself. I was growing in new areas, yet my overeating still progressed.

I was thoroughly confused. How could I feel so close to my Higher Power, how could I feel so good inside, how could I feel so happy about my new life, how could I feel so full of love — and still be overeating? Where was the hole in the way I was living my program?

Although my eating was out of control, I was still free of the obsession for sweets. I wondered at this until I realized that I had asked my Higher Power to take away my addiction to refined sugar and white flour. That's what I asked for, and that's what I got! I did not admit I was powerless over food. I did not ask that my food obsession be removed.

I realized that deep inside I had not admitted I am powerless over all food, be it sugar, pickles or lettuce. Deep inside I had not admitted I am a compulsive overeater. I was willing to let go the foods that hurt me physically, causing headaches and facial sores, but I was not willing to let go overeating. I thought that with refined sugar and white flour out of my life I could control my consumption of any kind of food.

Now I am back at step one. I am powerless over food — all food. I am a compulsive overeater.

February 1983

No Time Schedule

WHERE ELSE CAN YOU GO and be told, "Go at your own pace" and "Easy does it"? In OA we have no time schedule. You get your abstinence when you're ready; you take the steps when you're ready; you come to know your Higher Power when you're ready.

I am a slow learner in OA, so I am thankful there is no pressure. I was glad to hear one is considered a baby in the program for the first five years and that slow growth is good growth. I believe that. Like a baby, I have crawled, walked, stumbled, picked myself up and tried again. After seven years in program, I'm still here, learning and recovering one day at a time.

Always I have felt the support and love — truly unconditional love — of my OA friends. Unfailingly, I have heard what I needed to hear, starting with "Keep coming back." I believe this is the most important OA suggestion of all.

Recovery starts when we come to our first meeting. So what if we failed the first, second or twenty-second time? We are not on a time schedule. We will never graduate.

So keep coming back. It works.

May 1983

Did You Hear the One about Sloppy Abstinence?

AFTER TWO AND A HALF years, I realized something I never wanted to admit: I am powerless over food; not just junk food and "empty calories," but plain old food, period.

"There's no such thing as sloppy abstinence," I once heard a speaker say. "Either you are abstinent or you are not."

Those words, "sloppy abstinence," bugged me. I wrestled with them until I finally understood why they bothered me: I didn't want to admit to myself, let alone anyone else, that I was eating more food than I needed. I rationalized one immoderate meal after another, only to discover that this compulsive overeater doesn't need an excuse to turn to excess food.

Now that I'm able to be honest with myself, I can say with new conviction, "I am a compulsive overeater." I don't like it one bit, but I admit it. Kick and fuss as I might, I must be honest. I must surrender totally to the twelve steps, walking up and down them as diligently as I can, over and over again. I must make abstinence my first love, as it was when I started a few years ago. I must use all the tools. And I must seek my loving Higher Power's perfect will on a one-day-at-a-time basis.

Sloppy abstinence, as that speaker said, is a joke. The only problem is, it isn't funny. It hurts. Sloppy abstinence turned on old tapes and brought back stinking thinking, low self-esteem and feelings of hopelessness and despair. It made me let persons, places and things bother me as they once did. Sloppy abstinence also put some unwanted pounds on me.

My OA friends accepted me even though I was heavier and unhappy about myself. I loved and appreciated their acceptance, but I used it as permission to keep on eating excessively. Once I saw that, I was shaken back to reality. Abstinence to me now means freedom from eating excessively, regardless of the kind of food.

The way I am returning to sanity is by rediscovering the Big Book.

I've learned that the only way to get abstinent and live abstinently is to devote the same time and attention to my spiritual and emotional needs that I give to the physical. So every morning I turn over my life and my will, including my food, to God; then I make a commitment to abstinence to myself, to God and to another OA member. It works! My abstinence is once again a freedom.

Now that I'm able to be honest with myself, I am growing instead of stagnating. This old butterfly has found new strength in her wings and is soaring as God intended.

May 1983

The Willingness To Change

A WHILE BACK I led a meeting and, during my pitch, I mentioned that it has taken me more than four years to get any decent back-to-back abstinence, and that it took nine years for another woman I know. If you're still struggling, or if you are a perennial "slipper," I said, don't give up and don't leave. You're not bad if you binge. You are the victim of your cunning, baffling, powerful disease.

Keep coming to meetings, I urged; keep writing your inventory, even if you don't have the willingness to write until after you binge. Keep calling your sponsor, keep meditating, keep praying; and eventually you will acquire and maintain a sane abstinence. The Big Book says its main object is "to enable you to find a Power greater than yourself which will solve your problem." It does not say, This book is to be read and its suggestions followed only if you are abstaining. I could not stress enough, I told the group, that we are not bad trying to get good, but sick trying to get well.

Later that week, a woman who has abstained from day one told me that I was giving people license to go out and eat. Her accusation stuck in my mind and made me realize that one of the big obstacles to recovery for me has been the fact that, to many in OA, I am bad when I overeat.

What that experience made me see is that, if I am working my program, I need to show you love whether you are eating or not. That is what is meant by acceptance. If being thin, happy, joyous and free is not enough incentive to abstain, I don't believe my saying I love and accept you just the way you are is enough incentive to make you binge. Only through acceptance do people change. I certainly run the other way when people tell me they don't like the way I am and to "Change!" But when someone says, "You're fine the way you are," my defenses are down; my mind is open to self-analysis and I suddenly acquire the willingness to change.

That same day, a newcomer told me she was glad I had said what I did because she thought everyone else in the meeting was abstaining perfectly and she was the only one messing up; therefore, OA must not work for her. She said she was about to stop coming to meetings; because, you see, she has this funny disease called compulsive overeating and food has this incredible power over her.

Recovery is not an overnight job. It is slow. But it *is* — if we work for it. If we keep coming to meetings, keep working the steps to the best of our ability, keep accepting our disease without judging and hating ourselves, we will recover.

I know I'm not the only one taking time to get a healthy abstinence. Many of my friends, with four to six years of consistent program, still struggle with binging. For me, it has gotten better. It's still not perfect, but I've lost 35 pounds and kept them off. I hope to lose 10 more. Slowly. And lovingly.

If you are still struggling or binging off and on — or just plain binging all the time — don't give up. You are in the right place; we are concerned with eliminating the causes of our destructive behavior and that can be a long, involved process which has lasting results. You are not alone and you are not bad. The answer is this program. You may not achieve food perfection today. And maybe not even tomorrow. But eventually it becomes easier to abstain than it is to binge. Take it from one with four and a half years of recovery in OA and much struggle. Welcome to OA; welcome home.

July 1983

Facing Up to a Downer

A YEAR AGO I wasn't sure I would finish my freshman year of college. I thought more about suicide than finals. Binging off and on, I withdrew from my friends, gained weight and suffered horrible food hangovers. I could barely put together a paper, though even in the middle of my worst eating I somehow got my assignments in on time.

It all came to a head at the end of the term, when I got so sick and scared that I had to get away from school. Two days later I got on the bus and went home. I hadn't yet taken my finals; we had a week with no classes before exams began, and the thought of all that unstructured time terrified me. I would be free to eat constantly, going from cafeteria to cafeteria and spending all the money I had. I decided I would rather admit defeat than risk that, but I felt like a complete failure, and I hated myself and my life.

I had been in Overeaters Anonymous for more than three years, during which I had months of abstinence followed by periods of binging. Every time I got abstinent, I heard a nagging voice in the back of my head telling me I might not make it this time — and I never did. There was always some overwhelming problem that set me off, and I wasn't willing to see those times through to better days.

When I got home that week before finals, I found I had acquired new knowledge of my disease. I knew in my gut as well as in my head what compulsive overeating really is. I also knew there was nothing left except to try the twelve steps again, this time with new willingness.

I have a wise sponsor who doesn't spare me the truth, even when it is painful. She made no bones about the fact that I would have to grow up. No matter how brilliantly I had spoken at meetings in the past, no matter how much I had learned, I had to go back to step one and start again. She laughed at me a lot. We compulsive overeaters take ourselves so seriously. After I got over being furious at her for not sympathizing with my many problems, I realized that she was usually right in laughing.

"Don't eat; ask for help; go to meetings," my sponsor kept reminding me. The bottom line was, "Don't eat, no matter what." That meant I could scream, run, cry, throw tantrums — but I couldn't run to food anymore. An OA friend once told me she was glad she understood that our disease is not a matter of fat or thin; it is a matter of life or death. For the first time, I knew what she meant.

It has been more than a year now, and I have done plenty of screaming and crying, not to mention throwing an occasional tantrum. But that doesn't mean I spend all my time in pain. Most of the time I am content. I have faith in a Higher Power — a faith that works under all conditions. I have no doubt that this Higher Power will see me through the wildest of storms.

Now I'm facing another set of finals and, although I'm a little edgy, I am able to keep things in perspective. I know that in the long run, what matters is my sanity. No academic, social or emotional concern can become more important than my abstinence and my faith in God.

September 1983

At Last, Peace

I SPENT THREE YEARS searching for an easy answer to my disease. I looked for it in meetings, often traveling long distances from home; in sponsors, switching every few months; and in phone calls, frequently making three or four in rapid succession, but without listening.

I struggled to remain abstinent, and I constantly beat myself with negative thoughts and self-hate: "I've been in program so long, why can't I get it?" "When will I learn? I deserve to feel sick." "I must be one of those people who are constitutionally incapable."

I couldn't reconcile myself to who I was and where I was. I wanted to be in control of my recovery.

Recently, I began accepting myself exactly as I am, with my "sloppy" meals, my once-a-week binging and what I thought was the end of my recovery.

You know what happened? As soon as I accepted my sloppiness with food and my binging, I became abstinent. As soon as I accepted my weight, I lost the last five pounds and reached goal. As soon as I stopped frantically looking for the answer in a profusion of meetings, sponsors and phone calls, I found it right here inside me and in my Higher Power.

It took me three years to realize that if I let go and accept, I would begin my road to recovery.

My program is simple now. I take a daily inventory, I help other compulsive overeaters and I stay close to my Higher Power. For today, I am calm and at peace — and forever grateful.

September 1983

Anniversary Reflections

NEXT WEEK I will celebrate, with quiet gratitude, my eighth OA anniversary. As I reflect on my growth over the years, I am moved to share with you my progress in just one area: my understanding of abstinence. It has changed greatly over these eight years.

When I first came through the OA door, everything in my life was undisciplined. I was slovenly (hadn't showered in a week), and isolation had left me unable to look another person in the eye. Because extremes in behavior are characteristic of many compulsive overeaters, I believe there had to be, for me, a swing of the pendulum to a severe and rigidly disciplined kind of abstinence. My eating schedule was strict: I ate at a specific time of day. Every smidgen of food was weighed or measured and cleared with my sponsor. When in doubt, I left it out.

After seven months of bite-perfect abstinence, I slipped. For nearly a year and a half, I struggled desperately to regain what I'd lost. I never found that abstinence again. But what I did eventually discover was a new freedom. In my second year of program, it all kind of settled together and made sense. I stopped trying so hard to get abstinent, and just tried to not eat compulsively one day at a time, and to let my dear Friend and Traveling Companion show me what to do.

Almost six years of abstinence have unfolded for me. Today, I have quite a different sense of what abstinence is for me. I imagine a wild pony that runs free, kicking its hooves with joy and feeling the cool breezes ruffle its mane. It runs and frolics through the day. It has everything it needs for survival and growth: tender, sweet grass to graze on, cool mountain-stream water to drink and shade trees for respite from the hot sun. There are even hills and forests to explore. But far off in the distance, there is a boundary line beyond which the pony does not venture.

I used to spend a lot of time at the boundaries of my abstinence, testing it. Sadly, I crossed over and was hurt. But that eighteen months or so when I struggled to get back taught me a great deal, so I have no regrets. I learned to be aware of what and how I was eating. I learned that sugar

387

and starches are not crave producers in my body. What a disappointment that was! It had been so easy to believe that if I just omitted those two items I'd be abstinent. I am a compulsive overeater, and food in any and all forms is my addictive substance.

My understanding of abstinence today is based on the manner in which I react to food. Am I using food primarily to escape from life or as a process that nourishes my body? Through trial and error, I learned not to test my abstinence boundaries. It only means pain. So, for today, I again choose to live within the broad and beautiful boundaries of abstinence. It has everything I need. But most of all, it has freedom.

October 1983

"You're Going To Make It!"

ON AUGUST 23, 1976 the phone rang. A friend from my diet club was calling to tell me she had met someone who'd lost 135 pounds in a program called Overeaters Anonymous and she felt sure it was for us. There was a lot of "God" connected with the group, she warned me, and I told her I didn't care. I believed in God.

After we hung up I sat thinking about how God had worked in my life. At that point — 260 pounds, thirty-six years old, just three years into a happy second marriage and shrouded in a big, ugly purple caftan — I was willing to try anything to lose weight, even going to a God I feared (because of my sinful life).

At a time when my whole world had finally fallen into a reasonable, orderly, secure existence, I wanted to die. I had a handsome husband who loved me and two beautiful children, his daughter and my son. His family loved me and my family loved him. We had an attractive apartment, secure jobs and no money problems. Everyone was happy and they thought I was happy too.

I was miserable. For the better part of each day I walked around feeling offended by what people said or didn't say. I ate over everything, and every Monday I started a diet that failed by Tuesday. I had gained so much weight since I was married I couldn't believe my husband loved me. I thought he just said he did because he knew I wanted to hear it. His favorite line was, "The only one your weight bothers is you." Since I'd been fat all my life, I was bothered by it all my life. I had tried everything. One time I counted fifty-seven "vain attempts." Nothing helped me take it off and keep it off.

The date in my Big Book is August 24, 1976. That was my first OA meeting, where I heard words I'd never encountered in relation to my eating problem: abstinence, sponsor, Big Book and "one day at a time," to name a few. A woman talked about the changes in her life. She was raising several children, and her program was helping her do that better too. I asked her to be my sponsor. After three weeks of what I thought was impossible for me to do, I was still abstinent. A lovely blonde woman pointed to me and said, "You're going to make it!" Thank God I never forgot those words.

For the next five and a half years I played the old diet game, ignoring the steps and zeroing in on the food. Whether or not to eat was all I could deal with. But I kept coming back. Once in a while I even dusted off my Big Book and looked for my bolt of lightning within its covers. I kept hearing, "Our program is in the Big Book; the answers are there." But I thought making phone calls, setting up chairs, preparing coffee, praying and committing my food to someone was enough. I regained the 73 pounds I lost, then left OA for a year.

During that time one OA friend kept calling, reminding me I was still a compulsive overeater. Sometimes I hated him for it. Sometimes I even ate while talking to him. Once he told me he was going to ninety meetings in ninety days. I laughed and said I had better things to do with my summer. Finally, for the survival of his own growing program, he stopped calling. Then one day he called and asked whether I was interested in a small "R & R" (relapse and recovery) group he was starting. There would be sixteen weeks of meetings using the OA steps and tools. I said Yes.

For sixteen weeks I attended every meeting. I really tried, but I kept crying, "I can't." When we finished our meetings I had a beautiful new circle of friends and a shaky program.

Then one day in February I stood at the turning point. I came home from the office to find that our eight-month-old Great Dane had destroyed our living room. What was once the couch was now a frame. The arms were chewed, the cushions unzipped and emptied of their contents, and foam rubber and upholstery fabric were strewn across the carpet. To top it all off, the room was covered with feathers from a large throw pillow.

The weakness I felt was overwhelming. I sat down on the remains of the couch because I was afraid I would faint from the shock. My first thought was, "I need something to eat." I got up and headed for the kitchen, then stopped and sat back down. I said the first sincere prayer of my life. I asked God, simply, "What would a normal person do?"

Tears filled my eyes and rolled down my face. Thoughts rushed through my head and laughter followed. God had answered my prayer in an instant. I felt like a normal person, crying over the situation instead of eating. I called my friend, committed myself to ninety meetings in ninety days, and surrendered.

Thirteen pounds from goal weight, I am filled with gratitude for whatever made me keep coming back. I think that blonde woman was right: I'm going to make it.

October 1983

Never Give Up Hope

FOR THE FIRST TIME in my life, I didn't quit or give up on myself when I started regaining weight. My relapse began fifteen months ago, exactly one year after joining OA, and was highly visible within a couple of months. I continued attending meetings and giving service because I never gave up hope that to keep coming back was my *only* hope.

I was finally able to verbalize my pain and my fears and to share these feelings openly and honestly in meetings and on a one-to-one basis. Without exception, everyone in OA responded to me with love and compassion and understanding. I was not criticized or given unasked-for advice. I was assured that if I kept coming back, everything would work out and I would be OK. Well, I kept coming back because I believed them, and I never gave up hope.

I saw the program working all around me in my co-members' long-term maintenance of spiritual and emotional serenity, together with goal weight. Many of them had lost and gained while struggling with the program, and they went out of their way to share their experience.

And I kept coming back because there was no place left for me to go. OA was and is my final hope.

Because I kept coming back and listening with an open mind, my time finally came a couple of months ago, and I have had sane abstinence ever since. (I now refer to my initial ten months in OA as "stark-raving" abstinence.)

For many of us, the physical part of recovery comes last. There are some, too, who lose the weight first but who continue to flounder in spiritual darkness and emotional chaos. The important thing is to keep coming back and it will all come together when it's time.

There are those who say you must be abstinent to work the twelve steps, and those who believe you must work the twelve steps to become abstinent. Both schools of thought are right because they both work for some people. Whatever works for me is right for me.

December 1983

Humor

The Fantastic World
of the Formerly Fat

FOR THOSE OF US who have been plump, stout, outsize — all right, *fat* — there is a whole new world to explore. Sometimes ludicrous, sometimes frightening, but always exciting, each day is an adventure.

First comes the discovery that we no longer wear a badge of shame. At 250 pounds (down from 315) I met a dear little child who pointed a small finger at me and shrilled, "Hey, Mommy, see the fat lady!" To my own amazement my only reaction was the thought, "That's right, son, I'm fat. But you should have seen me a month ago. You missed it!"

My next surprise was the plug in the bathtub. You know, if you have ever been obese, that bathtubs are very badly designed. They are so narrow, and then that plug is way out of reach. You have to climb out of the tub first and then bend down to take the plug out. But came the day when I reached down, and there it was, right in front of my feet! Could it be that it was not the tub that had been non-functional?

At about this time I found that my blood pressure was normal for the first time in twenty years. My feet and ankles didn't swell anymore and I could stop taking diuretics and blood pressure pills.

People no longer turned to look at me on the street. Just to be inconspicuous was joy untold. I could pass for normal.

Next, I learned that seats in buses are meant for two. I knew because someone sat down beside me. And then one day, a friend let me get in the back seat of her car instead of steering me automatically to the front. I don't know when it happened exactly, but gradually I became aware that I was no longer dreading turnstiles in stores. I was sliding into restaurant booths with nonchalance. And I startled friends by crying out, "Look, look!" because I had crossed my knees.

Soon there came the joyous shock of finding myself stepping out briskly with a long, free stride I thought had vanished with my girlhood. Goodbye to the waddle, the shuffle, the puff!

Still the weight came off. My doctor displayed me with pride: See, ladies and gentlemen, it can be done. Long-time neighbors passed me without a sign of recognition. An old friend said, "Do you know why I always used to put my purse on the floor when you rode with me?" Of course I knew, but now her purse and mine were on the seat between us and we had room to spare.

The first time I actually bought a blouse in an ordinary store was a red-letter day. Extra-large, of course, but not from my old haunt, the fat boutique. Just a regular store, like other people.

As I lost weight, OA friends kept giving me clothes. My closet had three sections: a-little-too-small, wearable-now and getting-too-big. My racks had nearly as much turnover as a dress shop's with clothes moving in on one end and out the door on the other.

When I found that I wore a size twelve and that there were racks and racks of things I could wear in the stores, I really lost my cool. I had a choice! Was this too old? Was that too young? After having to wear grandma clothes for years, I didn't know what was suitable and what was not. How old was I, anyway?

I went through a typical Barbie-doll stage, dressing and undressing my new slim body. I gave away all my shoes because I couldn't keep them on. My thimble fell off my finger. It seemed strange that I lost weight even in my fingertips.

So many overwhelming changes were appearing, so many new possibilities presenting themselves, it is hardly strange that there were times when I got a bit carried away. I took up square dancing. I hiked with my grandchildren. I slid downhill in the snow on an inner tube. But then I tried a toboggan and came to grief with a severe laceration on my shin that required many stitches. I heard the doctor saying, "She's *how* old and she got hurt on a *what*?"

The topper came when I got "picked up." I mistook for one of my neighbors a man who offered me a ride, and he evidently mistook me for some young chick. Fortunately, I was able to dispel the illusion, and he dropped me off safely at my destination.

I had to realize, though, that the reason I was so unwary was that I was still carrying the image of myself at three hundred pounds, immured in my blubber tower, when that was not the reality. It was pointed out to me, "You are no longer a bystander; you are a participant."

So, world, here I am, a new-hatched player in the game of life. I am not too sure I know the rules or the score, but I have twelve steps and many new friends to guide me.

And I need not envy the young. It's even more exciting the second time around.

April 1978

Abstinence Makes the Heart
Grow Fonder

I KNEW I NEEDED HELP and I needed it bad, but I kept on gorging. Then one day while sitting at the kitchen table, listening to the gas in my stomach gurgle "My Heart Cries for You," it came to me: not the light but a big, fat massive heart attack.

Bonk! Over onto the table I flopped, right into the gorgeous gooey gob I was about to devour. Why hadn't I listened to my doctor? Why hadn't I listened to my husband? Why hadn't I listened to my dancing teacher in the third grade? Oh, woe is me!

"Wait, Lord! I'm not ready yet! Things are a mess here. Give me another chance. I can't leave like this — they'll find all my hidden goodies when they sort my clothes for the church! Oh, Lord, I promise I'll stick to my diet this time!"

I was spared. Boy, was I grateful! I stayed right on my diet. Lost weight real good. Had my husband give my dresses to the church (the Mary Magdalenes made curtains out of them for the young people's social club).

Then, slowly but surely, like two minutes after I got home from the hospital, I started restocking all my hiding places. I was stuffing a bag of cookies into a shoebox under the bed when I noticed a letter addressed to "The Most Important Person in My Life." How sweet. Tears filled my eyes. I opened the letter, prepared to discover more. It read:

Dear Person:

This is your heart speaking. If you don't shape up, I'm checking out — like for good. Ya got me? Swell! I can't take it! I'm going someplace where they have a union! And remember, Sweet Cakes, if I go, it's lights out.

Signed,

Barely Beating

P.S.: While you were stuffing that well in the front of your face, I was reading the classifieds. Something about Overeaters Anonymous. I jotted down the number: 778–5678. Call them. Now. Today. This minute. DO IT!

Trembling all over, I dialed the number, scribbled down the address and meeting place, and the next day my bulk was sitting in my first OA meeting. Remembering the letter, I listened very carefully to what was said.

Hey! They understand! They know how I feel! Abstinence? Oh yeah! I abstained one time. I was about to break a leg off the chair I was sitting in and inhale it, but I decided I didn't need all that roughage. That's abstinence, isn't it?

Oh, it's not? Well, what is it then? Three moderate meals a day with no snacks in between except coffee and diet drinks? You've got to be kidding! For the rest of my life? I know I can't do that!

I can? You know I can? Well, Know-It-All, just how do you know I can? Because others just like me have done it? They were compulsive overeaters too? They were? They really did it, huh? They did. You really think I can? You do. Right now? But what do I do with all that stuff I have stashed? Throw it away? Right! That's what I'll do. Throw it away.

But . . . but . . . but . . . OK, if it wasn't good for me, it's not good for anyone else either. Right? Right! I'll throw it away. How about if I come back next month. It'll be gone next month. You're right. Why wait. My heart's mad enough at me as it is. I owe it to the little ticker. We used to be pretty good buddies.

You say I don't have to do it alone? Friends will help me? Really? But I don't have any friends. I do now? Really? I can call anytime I get the urge? Gee! Tell me again. One day at a time, right? Right! Hey, heart, whaddaya think about that!

When I got home, I took a big garbage bag and went from room to room. It was like Halloween. Trick or treat, couch! Trick or treat, clothes hamper. Trick or treat, mop bucket. The witching hour was nigh. Could I really go through with it? Sure. They said I could. I believed them, too. And then I did it. I threw it all in the dumpster on Market Street. I was excited. I made the first step toward my recovery.

"How d'ya like that, heart!" I crossed my arm over my chest sort of like a pledge of allegiance. Yes, with help I can do it . . . and I will . . . and I did.

And now I know for sure that abstinence makes the heart grow fonder.

November 1979

Mirrors

I ACTUALLY HAD TO WEAR dark glasses in the house to screen out my reflection in the mirror. Dressed in solid dark colors, I would look into the full length mirror and there it was: a head walking around with no body at all.

I looked into the bathroom mirror; the head throbbed with anger. I looked into a hand mirror; my hand trembled with fear. I held up a narrow pocket mirror; that was better. I could see only my eyebrows, but even they needed plucking.

Then I came to OA and saw myself reflected in other people's eyes. Startled, I quickly dropped my gaze. I refused to look at a good reflection of myself.

"Wait till you see what I'm really like," I challenged my OA group. "You won't like me when you really know me."

"Try us," they said.

"I steal food from my children," I intoned.

"We strive for spiritual progress, not perfection," they answered and refused to call the police.

"I need to lose 60 pounds by tonight at the latest," I moaned urgently.

"One day at a time," they counseled patiently.

"I'm afraid to be thin," I protested. "I don't know what it's like."

"You're honest," they nodded.

"I'm not a spiritual person," I wailed.

"God doesn't make junk," they reminded me.

"I weigh myself standing backwards and my husband looks at the numbers," I blurted.

"You have a good sense of humor," they smiled.

"I crunch chicken bones — loudly," I admitted.

"You're allowed," they told me.

"I'm a walking 'Fragile — Handle with Care' package," I groaned.

"You express ideas well," they said lovingly.

"I'm keeping an open mind about a Higher Power," I stated nobly.

399

"You have clarity of mind," they encouraged.

I looked into the mirror of OA eyes and saw myself reflected. They liked me; so I began to like myself. They cared about me; so I began to care about myself. They respected me; so I began to respect myself. They had confidence in me; so I began to have confidence in myself.

I finally threw away my dark glasses. I mean, after all, I want you to see that terrific reflection of yourself in the mirror of my eyes.

October 1981

Have I Got an H.P. for You!

I DON'T HAVE one of those boring Higher Powers. When I close my eyes to do morning meditations, mine appears in many guises: sometimes as royalty or a rainbow; once as a teenage boy leaning against a fence.

"But you can't be a man!" I gasped when I saw him.

He grinned. "How else could I get your attention today?"

This morning my Higher Power appeared in a kitchen scene, a bustling bubba busy among steaming pots and pans.

"So what do you want?" she said, stirring the contents of one pot and sniffing another.

"I need your help," I began.

"Ask. You got." She lowered a flame.

"It's about the car . . ."

"Which car? The old one that's wrecked, or the new one you want?"

"Both. I don't know what to do, and I'm so broke . . . it's making me frantic."

"OK, stop worrying. I'll take care of it."

"And my job. My co-worker turned supervisor, and we don't get along so good . . ." Already I was beginning to talk like her.

"Don't worry, I'll take care of that too."

"And my weight . . ." I hesitated; she was pretty hefty herself. "I can't stand it. I want to fit into my clothes again; this damn 20 pounds."

"Please don't say 'damn'," she said absently. "How's the food?"

"Good," I said. "I feel free." Then I added, "I'm losing weight, but it's so slow. Sometimes I eat too big a lunch or too much at night."

"Well, don't worry; I'll take care of it. Just remind me in the mornings."

"And my sex life . . ." I muttered.

She laughed. "I know a nice boy. When you're ready, I'll send him along. Don't worry."

I hesitated. "My bills . . ."

"Can you pay them today?"

"Yes, but next month . . ."

"Just pay today's, and leave it to me," she ordered. "Don't worry."

"OK." Suddenly I got angry. "Look, you've taken care of the car, the job, my love life, the finances. What does that leave me? I'm beginning to feel like the hole in the donut."

She laughed, wiping her hands on a ragged dishtowel. "The hole in the donut; that's a good one. What do I leave you?" She pointed a sturdy finger at me.

"STOP WORRYING!"

July 1983

The Hole Truth

BEING OF CRAZED MIND and somewhat chubby body, I would like to share that there are various things I have never done.

I have never pushed my weighed and measured lettuce so far down into the measuring cup that the bottom of the cup broke. I absolutely have never licked my breakfast plate clean nor used my cantaloupe rind for typing paper. I have never written inventory in the washroom of the restaurant while on a date nor called my sponsor in the middle of the movie.

I have heard of people who, before weighing themselves, remove all clothing, jewelry, barrettes, rubber bands, bobby pins; make sure their hair is completely dry, nails are cut as short as possible, eyebrows are plucked, and go to the bathroom three times. Not me.

I always accept my body exactly as it is. I don't have three sizes of clothes hanging in my closet. I have never carried dietetic salad dressing in my purse only to find it all over my address book and lipstick case when I go to apply it to my salad.

I have never sat at my typewriter at work pretending to turn out a legal document when actually documenting my desperate hatred for my nagging boss. I have never refused my lunch partner one of my seven and a half slices of cucumber, nor have I ever thought about my meals at any time other than mealtime.

I love explaining to my hosts at a dinner party why I won't try the casserole they have slaved over for the last ten hours. I adore schlepping around a five gallon coffee pot, paper cups, thirty different flavors of herb tea, a box of artificial sweetener, paper towels and plastic spoons in the trunk of my car. Service is its own reward, you know! I didn't even mind when the decaffeinated coffee spilled and ran into the cracks in the upholstery; I'm just so grateful, every time I drive my car, that I can drink coffee and sleep at night as well.

It is always a pleasure running from the office to my car, going through red lights and getting tickets so I can open the six o'clock meeting.

I never find myself trying to sound nonchalant as I tell the waitress that we're "ready to order," hiding my desperation to be fed right away. I never overeat at family events and holidays. I have never lied about my weight on job applications or my driver's license. I am not the least bit jealous of Cheryl Tiegs.

Watching people eat when I am not eating doesn't bother me in the least. I never worry about losing the rest of my weight, and I certainly don't daydream about the clothes I will wear and the activities I will do "when I am thin."

I would never casually bring up my involvement in OA to an unsuspecting overweight friend, hoping he or she will pursue the matter. I have always loved muu-muu's, black stretchy pants and overalls.

And, most of all, I absolutely cannot stand the tremendous abundance of love I receive from my OA friends.

And that's the trrruuuththth!

August 1983

Service

and

O.A. History

An Outrageously Optimistic Prophecy

I T WAS CHILLY that long-ago night. We were one hour into the very first meeting of Overeaters Anonymous (January 19, 1960), when I turned to the only two other members of the Fellowship, Jo and Bernice, and said, "You know, someday this organization will be as big, or even bigger than Alcoholics Anonymous. It will be all around the world, you'll see!"

Well, it is now eighteen years since that cold midwinter night, and during the past six months I have had the opportunity to see for myself that the dream is fast becoming a reality.

First, I was a guest at a retreat in Portland, Oregon in mid-July. Then in September came a marathon a continent away in Buffalo, New York. Right after that, the Hicksville, Long Island group celebrated its tenth birthday, and a week later a number of New York groups held a retreat in the Catskill mountains.

I had quite forgotten how magnificent the autumn foliage is in the colder regions of the country. Reds, oranges, russets and golds formed a mosaic of color that was a tribute to the workings of nature. Those of us who live in Southern California are not accustomed to seasonal changes, and it was a treat to have my midwestern memories stirred.

While my impressions of these trips are still strong, I want to share them with you. I discovered that although all of OA uses the same twelve steps and twelve traditions, our methods of interpretation and application — especially of the "physical" aspects of the program — can be totally different from area to area, even from group to group. Some people proclaim that the entire OA program is a "must" and nothing is "suggested." Others have evolved an elaborate set of ceremonies and rituals to mark periods of abstinence, completion of certain assignments and the like. Still others are engaged in debate to prove that a certain eating plan is better or more effective than any other plan. I shared with my new friends the origins of some of their practices.

How well I remember when, and in what manner, the concept of "abstinence" first came into being. It was 1962, and the idea came from something

407

I had heard at an AA meeting. I suggested that abstinence for us compulsive overeaters might mean three moderate meals a day with nothing in between.

Then, a year later, Irene B. came along with *AA Today,* a book published on AA's twenty-fifth birthday. Based on Father Dowling's article in that book, she insisted that we should eat no refined carbohydrates and no food with more than ten percent natural carbohydrate. What a ruckus ensued! Irene printed up her own food plan, called the "gold sheet." Later, as the paper colors changed, "gold sheet" became "green sheet." Eventually, when the printer ran out of green paper, we needed some plans in a hurry and told him to use his available gray paper. You guessed it: we called it "gray sheet."

How did the concept of "twenty-one days" come to such estate, one of my listeners wanted to know. A logical question deserves a like answer: a certain book, it was discovered by one of our tireless early servants, suggested that it took twenty-one days to break a habit. So, we were off and running with another ritual. Some groups declared that you had to "make" twenty-one days even to be a member!

Convinced that we should have a Basic Four food plan to balance the low carbohydrate plan, we managed to get everyone to agree on the food lists for this new plan. We decided we'd better give our members some idea of how to apportion all these foods; otherwise, we feared, some people might eat everything in the morning and starve for the rest of the day. How we underestimated our fellow compulsive overeaters!

The decision to put salad at dinner instead of at lunch was made by two people. If we'd had more room on the sheet, we would have given more options.

Then came the matter of "sugar must be fifth or below." Maxine, when questioned, said she felt that since ingredients were listed in order of the amount present, if sugar were fifth or below there wouldn't be enough to set up a craving. It seemed logical enough to us, although we were just as willing to make it fourth, sixth or seventh.

Everywhere I went, all across the country, today's OA members were eager to hear about the Fellowship's beginnings. Many were astonished to learn the origins of these so-called physical elements of our program. Some people told me that they had felt that these humbly conceived and offered do's and don'ts had come down to present-day OA as though graven on stone, sort of like the Ten Commandments. It seemed incredible to them that the arbitrary decisions made by those early overeaters could have such tremendous and long-term impact.

As in matters dealing with personal honesty, however, I believe that this new understanding of the human fallibility of our dedicated OA servants, past and present, can only encourage greater reliance on the twelve-step program of recovery and the twelve traditions. This is where the real strength of OA lies, and it is what unites and sustains us through disagreements and trials.

Despite the differences and the disagreements, I discovered everywhere an overwhelming love and desire for unity among the OA people I met. Everyone, I found, wants to abstain from compulsive overeating; everyone wants to continue to reach for new levels of emotional and spiritual growth; and everyone wants and needs the love and understanding of those around us.

If we look at our common illness as the one great leveler for all of us, then we can begin to use both our differences and our similarities as forces for good. We can love and help one another; we can learn from one another; we can grow together.

To those OA members around the country whom I met and to all of you in other parts of the world whom I hope to meet one day, I send my everlasting gratitude and love. That outrageously optimistic half-dream, half-prophecy I made at the first OA meeting is coming true because of all of you: our dream is indeed becoming a reality.

January 1978

And OA Goes On

WE HAVE ALL heard of "survivors" — people who have taken everything life could hurl at them and come through with all flags flying. Recently it has been made clear to me that OA itself is a survivor.

I have been a member of Overeaters Anonymous for more than seventeen years, though I have been practicing the twelve steps of recovery only since January 1969 and I have been abstaining from compulsive overeating since October 1971. I am maintaining a weight loss of 60 pounds.

Many obsessions in addition to the food have been lifted from me: pills, cigarettes, coffee, tea, cola and emotionally induced illnesses (spastic colon, oversleeping, tiredness, palpitations, leg cramps).

I have seen people come and go — some fat, some thin, some with sure-fire answers for everyone and some who pleaded for the right to be wrong.

And OA goes on.

There has been the war of the "gray sheeters" vs. the "moderate meal-ers."

And OA goes on.

There was the formation of "Carboholics Anonymous" (which lasted nine months).

And OA goes on.

There were those who advocated eight glasses of water a day.

And OA goes on.

And remember those who fought for weighing and measuring, and those who fought against it?

And OA goes on.

There were those among my OA friends who believed that the steps weren't enough, that we had to advocate psychological therapy.

And OA goes on.

There were those who went about professing they were no longer compulsive overeaters.

And OA goes on.

Always, in every cycle of years, controversy in the Fellowship arises. Very often some of our number come under the spell of a few people who have strong personalities, who seem to "have it together," who advocate *the* answer or the one approach or the one way that will make one's life work. The overwhelming experience of many of us who have been around a while has been to wait and see and watch OA "take the best and leave the rest."

For sure, my experience has taught me to beware of what I term the "OA hawkers." OA hawkers are people who go about "selling" OA. They continually badger us with instructions on how to work the program, what to do, what to say, when to call, when to write, when to read, what to read, how to eat, how not to eat, which people to listen to, what meetings to attend. In short, they have instructions for us on everything.

I have learned that these people, in attempting to convince us, are really trying to convince themselves. They must keep advocating and selling because they can't live what they are promoting or preaching.

Ours is not a sales or promotional program. In the final analysis, it is the person we have grown to be and the life we are living that we share with our fellows. The sharing of our life process with one another is our strength — the cornerstone on which our Fellowship is founded. No sales pitch or preaching is necessary.

You can always spot OA hawkers: they take great care to denounce other approaches to the program and they give instructions on the *right* way to work the twelve steps (their way). The next time you hear people "hawking," ask yourself: Are they living what they are advocating? Are they sharing themselves and their program or are they merely instructing or preaching? And lastly ask yourself, Do these people have what I want or are they merely giving lip service to spiritual principles?

In my opinion, hawkers don't want to hurt OA. They only want to feed their egos by getting others to comform to their views and making themselves more important or authoritative.

What I know today is that I am a real person living a beautiful and productive life in a crazy mixed-up world. I have been given strength, security, love and perception through the twelve steps and the grace of God.

No hawker, no splinter group, no outside enterprise, no religious or psychological dogma can take that away from me today.

October 1980

A Power Greater Than Ourselves

MUCH TO OUR RELIEF, we discovered we did not need to consider another's conception of God."

These words from the Big Book ran through my mind as I looked around at the confused faces in the workshop on spirituality. I thought of them again later as some members of my home group expressed concern at the insistent implication of the leader that her Higher Power was the only true one.

The leader was a Born Again Christian, and while I do not in any way question her sincerity, I seriously question her motives in applying her principles to the OA program with such inflexibility. My heart ached for a young Jewish woman at the workshop, and I admired her courage in commenting that she had difficulty at every meeting when the Lord's Prayer was said.

Sometimes we forget that this is not a religious program, nor is it for Christians only. I am glad that in my home group the leader always remembers to say, "Will those who *wish to do so,* please join me in the Lord's Prayer." I hope that OAs who choose not to say the prayer are using this time to meditate or say a prayer to whatever Higher Power they have chosen.

Of course, a number of non-Christian OAs, including many of the Jewish faith, believe that just as one's concept of God may be whatever one chooses, so may one's concept of the Lord's Prayer. The Big Book tells us: "Do not let any prejudice you may have against spiritual terms deter you from honestly asking yourself what they mean to you."

Ours is a spiritual program, but it was never intended to be a religious program. It is a spiritual way of living — honest thinking, openmindedness, a willingness to try and a faith to accept. It means patience, tolerance and humility, and above all a belief that a Power greater than ourselves can help. I choose to call that Power God, but others do not have to agree with my concept.

The main thing is that if we want success in the program, we must be willing to believe in a Power greater than ourselves and to live by spiritual principles.

Willingness, honesty and openmindedness are the essentials of recovery. They are indispensable. God *as we understand God* comes to all who honestly seek a spiritual way of life.

November 1980

The People in the Book

I WISH I COULD SAY I was patient as I waited for someone to show up for the meeting. I wasn't. I resented it. I wish I could say I was tolerant when one member interrupted another to give advice during a meeting. I wasn't. I resented it. I wish I could say it helped me remember where I came from when a whole meeting was devoted to the disease rather than the recovery. It didn't. I resented it.

I resented everyone and everything they said and did. If only they had the special insights I had and were making the spiritual progress I had made, our meetings would be far better. If only I had started in an area where the program was strong, meetings were disciplined and members were abstinent, things would be different.

"I'll never go back!" I told my sponsor one day last summer. I had made a dramatic exit from a meeting full of cross talk, giggling and interruptions. Then I called her in tears.

"There's nothing wrong with a dramatic exit," she comforted me, "if you let them know why you left. You have to weigh your needs against your resentments. But don't think about it too much. By next week God will show you what to do."

The following week someone called to ask me for a ride, and there I was back at the meeting.

Gradually I began to see that being so judgmental did not have very much to do with "them" but had everything to do with me. I began praying for patience and tolerance. "Here comes the judge," I wrote in lipstick on my bathroom mirror; and in my bedroom I put up a poster with the third-step prayer printed on it to remind me to pray for relief from the bondage of self. I abstained from speaking at meetings because I could not open my mouth without self-will running riot, or without feeling resentful that no one praised me for the wisdom I had shared.

Then I surrendered and let God take over. My Higher Power began by showing me that other people felt just as I did about the undisciplined meetings and that together we could change. Then God filled that empty

413

meeting room with people and gave me a small amount of the patience and tolerance for which I had prayed.

I have often said that Overeaters Anonymous saved my life, but I usually thought of OA as something distant: speakers at conventions, people in the book, *Overeaters Anonymous,* thin members somewhere else. Then at a meeting one night I was hit right between the eyes with the words of the first tradition: "Our common welfare should come first; personal recovery depends upon OA unity."

That means *my* recovery depends on OA unity! All those people who are "undisciplined," "sick," and who sometimes don't show up for meetings are the very people who help me stay abstinent. They are OA. I owe my life to them. Without them I won't recover.

The words in the OA book have new meaning for me now: "Sometimes we fail to be all that we could be, and sometimes we aren't there to give you all you need from us. Accept our imperfections, too. Love and help us in return. That is what we are in OA — imperfect but progressing. Let us rejoice together in our recovery. . . ."

September 1981

Helping Old So-and-So

I'VE GONE TO MEETINGS in three states during the last four years, and in every city there are a few members who won't go to certain meetings because So-and-So might be there.

You all know who So-and-So is. She's the one who takes everybody else's inventory but still hasn't written her own. She's the one who insists on talking longer than anyone else, and what she always talks about is living with the problem instead of living in the solution. Her problems are worse than anyone else's and she's generally the first to complain that other people aren't holding up their end of things. So-and-So goes to many meetings and has many names. And I've finally figured out why she bugs me so much. It's because, more often than I'd like to admit, old So-and-So has turned out to be me.

But I didn't learn that until I got to be a sponsor. First I sponsored people pretty much like me, which is to say thirtyish, single, career-oriented. They called in their food, wrote inventories and came to be close friends. After a while it was a toss-up as to who was sponsoring whom. So far so good. Then I moved to a small town where there was only one OA meeting a week. Soon it became dominated by a young woman I'll call Willie who had all the qualities of the classic So-and-So plus a few she'd invented. She whined. She complained. She criticized. And wouldn't you know it? Before two weeks had passed, Willie asked me to be her sponsor. I tried to get out of it. I hemmed and hawed. Overnight, I thought up reasons why somebody else would be a better sponsor for Willie. But before I could speak to her, I found myself at a party talking the whole thing over with a man from AA.

"I prefer to sponsor people I'm not too crazy about," he said. "I learn more from them. Why spend all your time talking to carbon copies of yourself?" I had to think about that for a minute. I didn't really agree, but I decided to sponsor Willie to test this theory.

Two days later I told Willie that I would be her sponsor if she still hadn't found somebody "more suitable." Willie immediately burst into tears and then poured out her story. She had been turned down by five possible sponsors in the last month. "I know I'm obnoxious," she sobbed, "but I made up my mind that if you weren't willing to help me I was going to quit OA." Then she told me about a childhood of neglect and abuse that would have staggered Charles Dickens. I felt a pang of guilt about my own small-mindedness and sent up a silent prayer to have it removed.

It hasn't been easy being Willie's sponsor. She is less hostile at meetings, but her critical attitudes still push my buttons in private conversations. Nevertheless, I have to admit that Willie has taught me more about how to live the twelve steps than my sponsors did (my fault: I was too busy trying to impress them with my lightning progress). I now believe that Willie was put in my path by a Higher Power that knew she had some important lessons to teach me, not the least of which was the depth and variety of my own judgmental attitudes. I have come to see that whenever Willie gets to me, it's because she's mirroring some characteristic I thought I'd gotten rid of.

I also have to say that I've been a lot more honest with Willie than any other person I've sponsored or been sponsored by. Willie has a B.S. detector that can search out and destroy legions of subtle evasions and efforts to be "nice." Now I frankly let her know when I think she's doing something inappropriate such as interrupting at meetings, and I don't worry about whether or not she'll continue to like me. I can't think of another instance where that was the case. I've always wanted everyone to like me, whether it was parents, teachers, boyfriends or OA newcomers. In fact, it was especially important to my self-esteem to be liked by newcomers, which is why I chose to ignore the disagreeable ones who, I now see, were just hurting more than some of the rest of us. Willie has given me a new freedom in relationships that I am beginning to apply to other areas of my life.

Willie, not only have I come to like you — in many surprising ways — but I have come to love you, really love you, with all my heart. Thanks.

April 1982

Israeli OA, My Lucky Star

MY GRANDPARENTS started the first kibbutz, nestled in Israel's lush Jordan Valley. There I was born on the day my country received its independence: May 14, 1948.

I was totally loved and accepted in the kibbutz. Everyone knew me, and no one minded that I was fat. I felt thoroughly protected and cared for.

When I was twenty-one I married a very special man and moved to Tel-Aviv. There my war with myself began. Suddenly I was an unhappy, homesick housewife, 52 pounds overweight and constantly crying. I missed the kibbutz and I missed being with my friends at mealtimes in the big friendly dining room where there was always a "Good morning" and a "Good night" for everyone. I missed the grassy fields, the majestic mountains, the beautiful Jordan River. The city was strange and terrifying. I felt lonely and judged, as if I had lost my identity and become just a fat woman, known only as Ishai's wife.

I began grabbing every diet I could find, sometimes trying four different ones in the same day. None lasted more than half an hour, even with the aid of diet doctors and pills. By the time I turned thirty-one I had two children and I was 73 pounds overweight and terribly unhappy. I kept searching for home, for friends who love one another and share.

Always inquiring about diets, I finally heard about OA. At my first meeting I found a group of half a dozen women who spoke only English, a language I did not know well. But I knew I was home. These OAs were my kind of people. For the first time since leaving the kibbutz I felt loved just as I was — frightened, shy, crying, lonely, sad, fat. They did not judge me nor did they ask who I was, what my husband did or where I lived. I was what I was and it was OK.

I loved that meeting. I felt born anew. Like a baby, I began living just for today. I could be honest with those OA women. I could tell them I didn't like what had become of me, that I was addicted to thirty-seven pills a day, that I bought my friends, shopped compulsively and hated my life.

A visitor from the States brought a convention cassette titled "Miracles" and I heard my story. I was a miracle, too. I wanted to see more of them, so the following year I flew to Miami Beach for the 1980 Convention. I was amazed to discover that OA is much more than a few isolated groups of five or six women. I felt like Cinderella. I had spent ten years looking for what I had left behind in the kibbutz. But the new life I found in OA was far better than any story. It seemed that my world changed overnight.

I returned to Israel with a desire to start Hebrew meetings, to make OA in Israel a small part of the big, beautiful OA-USA. I knew little English, but I had a dictionary. I translated "Just for Today" into Hebrew and printed three hundred copies. Next, I translated the meeting format and some other basic literature. Our first meeting in Hebrew was strange and funny. My English-speaking OA friends said it would never work, and I sometimes wondered myself. Israelis are generally proud people who claim they do not need help, that they can do anything by themselves.

That was true, I mused, but I'm an Israeli and I'm proud too. I never asked for help until finally I was desperate enough for OA. So maybe there is someone else in this country who needs a little help and a lot of understanding and love.

Soon, magazine articles and newspaper stories appeared and my telephone rang all day long. One day I took seventy-two calls! It was hard, but I felt blessed to be able to share my hope and joy with others.

By early 1981, seven Hebrew-speaking groups were thriving. That year I attended the Seattle convention and sought out step sponsors. When I returned I started a Sunday evening step meeting. For five months, a large group of OAs read, wrote and shared, and now there are many Israeli step sponsors.

Today we have twenty-two meetings and more than three hundred members. I can find a meeting almost every day, anywhere I go — Tel-Aviv, Jerusalem, Haifa. Every month we have an all-day "convention," just like the marathons in the USA.

Like my grandparents, I have helped make a dream come true — a dream of people loving, caring and sharing. I am not alone anymore. Perhaps my Higher Power sent me from the kibbutz, from my home, from my beautiful valley to look for a wonderful new world and to learn that happiness is wherever I am — not in a certain place, but always with me.

By the way, I lost my excess weight in OA. But that is only "by the way."

I love the OA program more than anything. I will never run from myself again. My heart is full of joy. My lucky star is with me all the way.

June 1982

I Missed You

SOMETIMES I consider not attending my weekly OA meeting because I'm tired or busy. Other times I hesitate to go because I'm feeling guilty about something and I don't relish the honesty. Sometimes I almost stay home because I'm feeling down: "Nobody will miss me. They'll have a fine meeting without me."

But even if I think I don't need a meeting, I always go — unless it's absolutely impossible. Why? I am committed to my OA family and to my own recovery. I've learned that I mean something to others, that even by just being there I help other members. This has been proven to me, to my amazement and delight, on many occasions, and I always feel blessed that it should be so. But most of all I go just for me, for my own sanity. I depend on that meeting as a place where I can share my joys and sorrows, my triumphs and failures, and listen to others share theirs. And every time I go, however reluctantly, I'm glad I did.

During the past week I made many discoveries, felt much pain, reached glorious heights. I went to tonight's meeting, nervous about sharing my experiences, but comforted by the knowledge that my fellow members would understand. I went, hoping to be of help to someone else, in however small a way. I went in honor of my commitment to my OA family and to myself. I went, and no one was there!

I know there are times when we truly cannot get to a meeting, but please remember me next time you consider staying away. And remember yourself. You missed the joy and comfort and inspiration of that meeting as much as I did.

August 1982

Those Frustrating Newcomers

AN OA FRIEND recently shared with me his sense of frustration when he helps newcomers who are enthusiastic about the program in the beginning, then drift away.

I was one of those "frustrating newcomers." Six years ago I attended my first OA meeting while on a business trip in San Francisco. Because of my intense preoccupation with myself and my discomfort in those surroundings, I don't remember anything that was said during the meeting. But I do remember exactly what clothes my 220-pound body was wearing, and I remember the comment from the OA member who said I looked like a pretty much "together" lady. I had taken particular care to be sure my clothes, hair, jewelry, shoes, manicure and makeup were impeccable. If I could be perfect on the outside, no one would notice the excess weight or guess what a self-hating, self-pitying, self-righteous, miserable person was living on the inside.

The hugging, the laughter, the love and the caring which filled that room made me feel even more self-conscious and isolated, probably because I feared I could never have the real belonging and unconditional acceptance those people obviously had with one another and with a Higher Power.

That was my first OA meeting; and it was my last until four years later. During those four years I did more independent research on compulsive overeating. I had to learn firsthand that this is a progressive illness. I also needed to try a variety of easier, softer cures which always worked for a few weeks or months but never provided a realistic way of living through one day at a time, dealing with the things I needed to deal with. Those easier, softer ways always resulted in either an obsession with eating or an obsession with not eating. They never gave me a way to keep food, or myself, in perspective.

I have been back in OA for two years and now I too am hugging and laughing and loving and caring. I have been given the absolutely free gift of comfortable abstinence. I no longer try to convince myself, or anyone else, that I am perfect. I have been given the ability to accept myself exactly as I am. When I think, speak or act inappropriately, I admit it to God and to myself, I forgive myself, I make amends and I put it behind me and get on with the business of living.

In the past two years, in an effort to give back what I have so generously been given, I have been attending several meetings a week, giving service and doing my imperfect best to practice the principles of the program in all my affairs. OA has become such an essential part of my life and my way of thinking that it's difficult for me to imagine what it's like to live without a twelve-step program.

Although my first contact with OA did not result in an immediate desire for this way of life, I can now say that it is infinitely more wonderful than anything I could have put together for myself.

Based on my own experience, I have learned that if I do my best in working with newcomers and in sponsoring, I don't need to worry about the results. If some people choose not to come back at this time, I certainly have no reason to feel frustrated or that I've failed in some way. I only need to do the best I can under the circumstances, then leave the results to God.

December 1982

A Place for You

A WARM, COZY ROOM is waiting for you, and all who wish may enter. In it you will find everything you need.

The first object to catch your eye is a sturdy wooden clothes rack on which hangs, for all to see, hope. Take all you need, for there is a never-ending supply.

Next you will encounter an oak table on which are piled dreams of all shapes and sizes. Take as many as you wish, and stay around to watch many of them come true.

To the right stands an old-fashioned roll-top desk filled ever so carefully with love, which keeps the spirit of this room alive. Please take all you can hold, then take extra and share it with a friend who couldn't be here this time.

Next you will view a chest of pine, so full of understanding that it cannot hold anymore. Fill up on all you want.

Over there in the corner is a huge fireplace in which a roaring fire burns twenty-four hours a day, three hundred and sixty-five days a year. There you may deposit all the anger, fear, hate and pain with which you entered, and you will be free to enjoy all the other treasures this room has to offer.

Come to this room whenever you like, spend as much time here as you wish, use whatever you want from it. There is enough for everyone. Accept what is always being freely given by others who once came into this room as strangers themselves.

Come back whenever you want. We will be here when you return, waiting to give you more, and glad to see you again.

To find this special place, just look for a small sign that reads:

OA MEETING INSIDE
WELCOME!

January 1983

A Legacy of Caring

THE SUN WAS SHINING, the sky was blue, and the whole glorious summer lay ahead of me. It was in this mood of happy anticipation late last May that I received my surprise telephone call.

"Hi, Rozanne, this is Mary from Gamblers Anonymous. I just wanted to let you know that GA will be celebrating its twenty-fifth anniversary this July 3rd weekend at the Anaheim Marriott."

"Twenty-five years?" I was incredulous. "I can't believe it's almost a quarter of a century since I met those first GA members and got the idea for starting Overeaters Anonymous!"

But where was Jim W., the founder of GA? I had been searching for him for several years, but no one had known of his whereabouts.

"Jim is being brought down from a nursing home in Oxnard," Mary explained. "He has had several strokes and heart attacks. He can hardly see and uses a wheelchair, but he will be at the banquet."

My heart sang. My dear Jim, OA's first mentor and guardian angel — I would see him at last!

"Marvin," I ran to my husband. "Guess who just called!" I told him the story. "Will you come with me?"

"I wouldn't miss it," he grinned. "After all, I was in on the beginning of OA too."

Braving the holiday traffic, Marv and I arrived at the hotel for the GA celebration. And what a celebration it was!

Four hundred people from around the world came to mark the silver anniversary of their Fellowship's tentative beginnings. I met men and women from England, Ireland, Australia, Scotland, Canada and all over the United States. There was Ray M. with twenty-four and a half years' abstinence from gambling, Irving with twenty-three years, and several others among the original GA members.

As they reminisced, they spoke of the Paul Coates interview on his TV show, "Confidential File," in November 1958. That was my first contact with GA. My mind wandered back to that night nearly twenty-four years ago. I was watching television with my usual late-night binge. Fascinated by the interview, I felt that GA might be a solution for Marvin's compulsive gambler friend. I didn't know it would change my life as well.

Marv and I took his friend to a GA meeting, and it was on that wondrous night that I realized I was not alone with my terrible feelings of lying, cheating, stealing, anger, resentment and all the rest. But my compulsion and theirs were not the same, so I didn't return to their meetings.

A year later, fatter and more desperate, I went back to Gamblers Anonymous and asked their founder, Jim W., if he thought a program like theirs would work for people like me.

He smiled at me and replied, "I don't see why not. What can I do to help?" There it was — a hand outstretched to steady me as I stumbled along! It was my first experience with the twelfth step, the first time anyone had offered to help me with no thought of return. I went home and told Marvin, "I think I finally have a chance." That evening we found a name for the yet-unborn organization: Overeaters Anonymous.

All through OA's first years Jim helped us, guided us, trying to coax my self-willed zeal into more spiritual pathways. He was our first teacher, our first inspiration, and all of us in OA owe him an immeasurable debt of gratitude.

Just before the anniversary banquet started, I spent a few quiet, private moments with Jim in his hotel room. His mind was quite alert, though he had difficulty talking and seeing.

I held his hand and told him of OA's miraculous growth. "Do you remember that night I came to you, Jim? There was nothing, and now there are more than six thousand OA groups in thirty-three countries. Isn't that amazing?" His eyes glistened and he squeezed my hand in understanding.

I thought of all these things as I listened to the speakers at the banquet. Jim sat there looking so frail, yet so appreciative of the outpouring of love and gratitude. Toward the end, a plaque expressing the devotion of the GA members was presented to him.

The final tribute came in a quotation from a letter written to Jim in 1964. It was from Bill W., AA's co-founder, and it said in part, "When God can't come, he sends someone else."

God sent you to us, Jim. As we in Overeaters Anonymous celebrate our twenty-third anniversary this January 19th, we join in expressing gratitude to you for all your support, guidance and devotion during our birth and infancy. May you be with us at our own silver anniversary. We are a legacy of your sharing and caring — a magnificent example of Higher Power in action.

January 1983

Take What You Like

A FRIEND RECENTLY wrote to tell me she is disenchanted with OA and is thinking of leaving the program. I remember how desperate and hurt I felt when I saw our Fellowship the way she is seeing it. I am deeply grateful that I stayed to see my negative feelings change to positive ones.

In looking around to find the "perfect" sponsor, I discovered that no one person has a perfect program, or even a strong program, in all areas. Then I realized that instead of seeking one sponsor I could turn to several people, each with certain strengths such as serenity, abstinence, weight loss, or a particular step or tool. I began listening carefully when people pitched at meetings. When someone exhibited an attitude I admired, I called that person to talk about that aspect of program.

I learned about step three from Pat, abstinence from Nancy, serenity from Ann and honesty from Frank. When I ran into problems with which no one in my home group could help me, I began traveling to other meetings. There I met other OAs and found what I needed. The time I spent and the gas I used were more than reimbursed by the benefits I received. I also began writing to members whose names were on my region's correspondence list, and I have grown enormously thanks to what I learned from them. Each person I seek out helps me supplement my program in a different way, and from each one I take what I like and leave the rest.

Similarly, when someone interprets the slogans, steps, traditions, tools or literature in a way that seems negative to me (such as using "It's a selfish program" as an excuse to be inconsiderate of others) I reject that interpretation for myself. Of course, I have to be careful not to take other people's inventories just because I disagree with the choices *they* make.

I used to worry about groups that didn't send representatives to inter-group meetings, or didn't donate money or services. Then I began to apply tradition eleven in this area. OA is a program of attraction, not promotion. Those who are attracted to our intergroup will be there and I can learn from them. Those who are not attracted will not be there, and I really don't need them.

I also found myself stuck with more work than I cared to do. Then I realized I had a compulsion to accept any and every job for which no one else volunteered. Sometimes it was my way of controlling, of ensuring that the job would be done "right"; sometimes I did it so I would be liked. But always I did it with a lot of resentment because no one else was willing to help out. I learned the hard way that I need to give service, but my program suffers if I give more than is comfortable for me. Now I volunteer only for what I want to do and know I can do. I sit on my hands and lock my mouth when volunteers are requested for a job that would overextend my service commitment.

It took a long time and some hurt feelings for me to work this out, and I came dangerously close to leaving OA in the process. Through my multiple sponsors, I attained the insight I needed to come to terms with my negative attitudes. Now I see what a truly positive experience OA can be when I make choices that are positive for me, taking what I like and leaving the rest.

February 1983

Over the Coffee Cups

THREE OF US WHO have known each other for four years went for coffee after the meeting, and an unsettling conversation unfolded.

"Name one person in program who had trouble with abstinence in the beginning and is maintaining goal weight now," one of my companions challenged. "Or, someone who had abstinence, lost it and got it all together again."

"Are you serious?" The question took me by surprise. She was sitting with just such a person — me — and she knew it. How many times had she heard me qualify? It took me two years to lose the weight, two years to regain it and now, after another three years, I'm 20 pounds from goal.

I thought of all the other OAs I know who'd had similar problems and were now making good progress. Not wanting to break anyone's anonymity, I said, "You've heard plenty of OA stories and you know lots of people who struggled a long time before getting — and staying — abstinent. Some of us are slow learners."

She was not convinced. I got the feeling she was seeking support for the notion that if it doesn't come easily, it doesn't come at all, or it doesn't last. The implication was that no one had done what she had not yet been able to do.

"Look," I continued, "a lot of people go through a discouraging time before getting abstinent; and even some of those who abstained from the start have to struggle with food sometimes. That's the compulsion; that's our problem."

She gave me a "Yes, but . . ." Then, eyeing the third person at our table, she said, "Look at Gladys. It's been easy for her."

I stared in disbelief. "Do you think Gladys always has it easy just because she's been in program six years and never lost her abstinence?" I turned to Gladys, who happens to be my sponsor. "Talk to her, would you?"

"It's not always easy," Gladys said, "but when you don't eat and get through the hard days, it does make it easier to get through the next time. From all I've heard, I'm sure it's easier to maintain abstinence than it is to get it back."

"Well, I'm glad you feel you're like the rest of us," our friend snapped. She fell silent then, and left soon afterward.

I turned to Gladys. "Is she mad at us or what? She must be kidding. Abstinence is either easy or impossible to her. If it was easy, we'd all lose weight, give a farewell address and take up bowling instead of spending our time at meetings."

"She's not mad at us," Gladys said quietly. "She's mad at herself."

"I know," I agreed, "but how could she think it was easy for me? The second time around came hard. You know that. I thought I'd never get abstinent again. If it hadn't been for the ties I had, I'd have walked away."

"But you didn't."

"Thanks to you. You never stopped believing I could do it. You always told me I'd find God again, even though I thought God had left me."

I stopped, remembering how awful it had been. "All those times I called you and cried because I had eaten, but you always said, 'You're OK.' You never let me go."

"I would never have let you go, no matter how long it took."

"Thank God!"

We finished the last of our coffee and left, going our separate ways. I walked home slowly, enjoying the night air and thinking about the evening's discussion.

No, what I have did not come easily; but it was well worth what it took to get it.

May 1983

The Gray and the Orange

.**I**.N THE SUMMER OF 1974, I went to my first OA meeting. How well
I remember those days! There were only three meetings a week in the
whole area, and a small core of members went to all of them. I was the
only man.

Among the core group were several women on gray sheet who felt
they "had" the program. There were also a few renegades who were secretly
using the "orange sheet," a modified version of the gray sheet which allowed
more carbohydrates. At most meetings I attended, proponents of gray
sheet made pitches for it and also threw curve balls to the orange sheet
adherents. "I can only speak for myself," they would begin, "but . . ."
Then came the zinger.

I was an odd bird. I even ate bread.

After meetings, some of us would get together for coffee and invariably
someone would say, "I've been thinking about trying orange sheet. What
do you think?"

Eyes would dart around the table and finally another member would
respond, "I've been using it for six weeks now." The first person would
let out a sigh of relief as she confessed, "I'm on orange sheet, too, but
I'm afraid to tell my sponsor."

For six months, I went to as many meetings as I could and read everything I could get my hands on, only to be repeatedly rebuffed by the
women. I suspect it was because, as the only male, I represented an intru-
sion into their privacy; they probably felt they couldn't talk "women talk"
with me around. In addition, I followed a food plan neither the gray
nor the orange sheeters tolerated. Finally, I buckled under the ostracism
and left.

In 1980, I came back. There were more men now, but the biggest surprise
was that there were no gray sheets. Oldtimers had dogeared copies, rever-
ently taken from billfolds and displayed like some saint's relic. But OA
had outgrown the gray sheet. Now there were choices in food plans. Of
course, there were a few diehards who were willing to give xerox copies

of their gray sheet to people who declared themselves ready for the "real" OA program.

After a few months I could see a great deal of recovery. People still binged, but not as often as before. Some weren't losing weight, but they had stopped gaining. I went to a retreat where I found even more recovery. I was down to my goal weight by then, but I was still afraid to wear shorts in public. Here were people twice my size, and they were able to show their legs — cellulite and all. I was awed.

I also met people who had been set free of years of resentment, people who had never known how they felt and who had now reached the place where they could express anger, cry and laugh. Recovery surrounded me. OA had really changed.

But I soon discovered that, although the gray sheet debate had died out, the underlying mentality lived on. Now the advocates of "back-to-back abstinence" ruled the day. They celebrated anniversaries, talked about "winners" and pointed a finger at the rest of the Fellowship for "not recovering."

Now, in the old days, what gray sheet people did not tell was that they often couldn't keep up with the rigorous demands of their food plan. Sure enough, the back-to-backers follow the same pattern. I know, because I was one of them. I had celebrated two years of abstinence and was halfway to my third when I started taking a good look at my abstinence. I was not binging. I was not slipping. But I was padding my meals with rationalizations that showed up as a 17-pound weight gain over two years.

Slowly, I faced the truth. In the last year of my back-to-back abstinence, I had been withdrawing from the mainstream of the Fellowship. I went only to "strong" meetings. I associated only with "winners." I resented people without abstinence having the nerve to pitch, let alone lead meetings.

An open mind had brought me recovery and here I was, as closed-minded as ever. In 1974, closed-minded people put such pressure on me that I left; and now I was just as arrogant, self-righteous and overbearing as any of them!

I opened my mind and listened to the new renegades who talk about progressive recovery and progressive abstinence. Like these people, I had long ago quit binging. There was a time when I thought I would never be free of binges. Today, I am able to keep food in the house overnight. That is a miracle. My weight fluctuations are small, whereas they used to be tremendous. There has been undeniable progress in my relationship to food. But it's not perfect.

The change in my attitude toward myself is even more miraculous. Here I am, 17 pounds over my ideal weight, but I accept myself. I go to parties, protruding stomach and all. Before, I would cancel. Now, I look in the mirror and say, "You've got a gut; but you're cute anyway."

I returned to meetings that weren't "strong." I listened to members who weren't abstaining and I learned to accept progress without perfection. I learned to sponsor the "he'll never make it" types, to believe in the

Fellowship and *all* the people in it. I became honest about my abstinence and patient with myself and others. With time, the conviction grew within me that we — all of us — are indeed walking the high road of recovery.

I am no longer a back-to-backer. I was forced to lay down my rigid ideas about abstinence, about other members and about myself. Only after I let go those old ideas did I come to believe that a Power greater than ourselves is restoring us to sanity.

"My God," I thought, "how many of us have been abstinent all along without knowing it?"

August 1983

How To Be a Trusted Servant

THE OTHER DAY, after a morning meeting, I sat down to lunch with two people fairly new to program. During our conversation, I sensed the admiration they had for me, and I suddenly remembered what it was like when I came into OA.

I listened to every word the oldtimers said. They seemed so confident and important that I just knew these bigwigs had it all together. I put them up on pedestals, and if one of them approached me, or if I dared to ask a question and a conversation ensued, I was in awe for days.

Then, disillusionment struck. First one, then another fell off the pedestals on which I had placed them. They proved to be human, with faults and failings. They didn't have all the answers. They had trouble with food, too. They were not always as confident as they seemed. They made errors in judgment, broke anonymity and acted selfishly, among any number of shortcomings.

Now, as I talked with these two new people, I realized I was enjoying their reverential attitude; that I could easily like being a bigwig.

Then I recalled how my demigods had fallen from their pedestals, the pain they went through when they couldn't live up to others' expectations, their admission that a sense of self-importance had cut them off from the help of this Fellowship. I saw that I could easily set myself up for a similar fall.

I thought about our second tradition. I knew that, for my own survival, I had to stay off pedestals.

I explained to my companions that I do not have all the answers, that at times I am as afraid as they are, that I came into OA because I needed help and I'm still here for the same reason. I can't do it alone. True, I give more service now, but that's because I need to return a little of what has been given to me to continue my recovery — not because I want to be in charge. Don't give me that much importance, I told them; I can't handle it.

I came home with a prayer in my heart that I never forget my own words: May God remind me always that I am but a trusted servant, and give me the strength and wisdom to uphold that trust.

September 1983

Index